Ideas and Insights

Ideas and Insights

Language Arts in the Elementary School

Dorothy J. Watson, Editor
University of Missouri–Columbia

Ideas and Insights Editorial Board

Ralph Peterson
Arizona State University

Ruie Pritchard
University of North Carolina

Elizabeth M. Baker
Columbia, Missouri, Public Schools

National Council of Teachers of English
1111 Kenyon Road, Urbana, Illinois 61801

Dedication and Invitation: This book is dedicated to the teachers who lived the lessons, offered them to other teachers, and became greater teachers for having done so. It is also dedicated to teachers who are searching. We invite you to choose the best of our best to fit your own classrooms and, when you see gaps and thin spots, to weave them whole with your own knowledge, genius, and love.

Ideas and Insights Editorial Board: Ralph Peterson, Arizona State University; Ruie Pritchard, University of North Carolina; and Elizabeth M. Baker, Columbia, Missouri, Public Schools

NCTE Editorial Board: Candy Carter, Julie M. Jensen, Delores Lipscomb, John S. Mayher, Thomas Newkirk, John C. Maxwell, *ex officio,* Paul O'Dea, *ex officio*

Staff Editor: Jane M. Curran

Book Design: Tom Kovacs for TGK Design; cover illustration by Louise Krauss

NCTE Stock Number 22590

Library of Congress Cataloging-in-Publication Data

Ideas and insights.

  Bibliography: p.
  1. Language arts (Elementary)—United States.
2. Reading (Elementary)—United States—Language
experience approach. I. Watson, Dorothy J. (Dorothy
Jo), 1930-   . II. National Council of Teachers
of English.
LB1576.I33 1987   372.6   87-22110
ISBN 0-8141-2259-0

Contents

An Invitation

If you are a dreamer, come in.
. . . .
For we have some flax-golden tales to spin.
Come in!
> — Shel Silverstein, from "Invitation," in *Where the Sidewalk Ends* (Harper and Row, 1974)

The many authors and editors of this book invite you to come in and to consider our best teaching ideas — activities that have found success in classrooms across the United States, Canada, and Australia. We are keenly aware that most books that present ideas to teachers are often referred to as being "recipe books" or "old hat." We presume to suggest that our ideas are a different offering; that, to borrow from Silverstein, in the hands of "dreamers, wishers, liars, hope-ers, pray-ers, and magic bean buyers" — in other words, teachers — our suggestions can become "flax-golden tales" for you and your students.

It won't take long for readers of this book to discover that there are no skill, drill, and fill-in-the-blank exercises to be found on these pages, for this is not the way children learn to write, read, listen, and speak. What you will find, however, are activities that encourage language in its fullness, activities that are based on the whole language approach to learning.

In this approach, all the systems of language including semantics, grammar, letters, and sounds are integrated in teaching and learning situations rather than disintegrated and drilled on. Students are invited daily to read whole stories, poems, and books; to write self-generated stories, poems, and books; and to have conversations and conferences with peers, teachers, parents, senior citizens, and other interested and interesting people. Language is learned as children *use it* in reading, writing, listening, and speaking about science, math, and social studies, and as they transact with their world and the people in it. The artifacts of real language (complete texts and writing materials) and the circumstances of real thought (hypothesizing, risk taking, organizing, getting it wrong, getting it right, categorizing, summarizing, pondering, modifying, and a thousand other *-ing*s) take the place of pre-fabricated language arts programs that may not accommodate the different interests and talents of students. The whole language approach nourishes the development of each child's thoughts and language and gives consideration to each child's beliefs, lifestyles, values, and needs. Children of all cultures and subcultures have a place in the society of their classroom, and their contributions are celebrated.

Ideas and Insights

We selected a title indicating that these were not just random ideas to "spice up" a traditional language arts program. We wanted to emphasize that the suggestions offered here were firmly anchored in both practical theory and in theoretical practice. The activities not only needed a *Who* and *How* explanation, but they needed a rationale — a *Why* as well. Each activity is introduced with the teacher's special reasons for inviting children to spend their time, energy, and enthusiasm on it. We acknowledge that some *Why* sections could be longer and more in-depth, but we leave it to you to add your reasons for giving the activity a try.

To support the *Why* sections, we contacted three teachers who have given freely of their knowledge to other teachers throughout the world: Leland Jacobs, Kenneth Goodman, and Donald Graves. Leland Jacobs confirms what whole language teachers have suspected for a long time — literature is a way of knowing; and when it is given its rightful place in the language arts curriculum, there is an aesthetic awareness for children that is an experience of living. Kenneth Goodman tells of whole language teachers who have "detechnologized" reading instruction by bringing children and meaningful materials together, by helping students recognize their need for written language, and by supporting their efforts to make sense of and through print. Donald Graves brings a writing program to life for us. Through the work of a student and his teacher, research findings about writers and writing are revealed, supported, and clearly articulated.

Format of the Book

The book is organized into five parts. Part 1 concentrates on learning language by focusing on reading, supported by the other language arts. *Chapter 1: A World of Language in Use* presents activities that help children realize that the language surrounding them is theirs to enjoy, to explore, and to use — that, indeed, they already have a great deal of control over the language in their lives. *Chapter 2: Literature Points the Way* suggests activities in which literature and learners are brought together to establish a solid base for the language arts program. *Chapter 3: Making Sense by Reading* emphasizes reading, and thinking about the reading process, in activities that also involve writing, speaking, and listening.

Part 2 focuses attention on writing, supported by the other language arts. *Chapter 4: Writing for Self-Expression* presents activities that invite children to let their thoughts be known, to say, "This is me." *Chapter 5: Learning about Writing by Writing* gives suggestions for learning the conventions of written language while building students' confidence and fluency. *Chapter 6: Writing for an Audience* invites writers to write for real and imaginary audiences, and includes a section on messages, notes, and pen pals.

Part 3 addresses language across the curriculum. *Chapter 7: Reading, Writing, Listening, and Speaking across the Content Areas* presents activities that use the content areas as the grist for the language arts mill. It concludes with ideas that invite students to read, discuss, and write newspapers.

Part 4 focuses attention on students as resources and on parents. *Chapter 8: Kids Helping Kids: The Collaborative Effort* offers activities in which children enrich each other as partners, editors, teachers, and friends. *Chapter 9: Home Is Where the Start Is*

provides suggestions that bring the home and the classroom together.

Part 5 looks at the thorny problem of assessment. *Chapter 10: Valuing and Evaluating the Learners and Their Language* presents ideas, again based on the whole language approach, that help teachers assess children's developing strengths as language users.

The book concludes with a large bibliography of recommended books, including read-aloud books, wordless books, and books employing predictable language.

A Final Invitation

We hope these activities allow both students and teachers freedom and space, for this is what encourages marvelous things to happen. When teachers and children discard the up-tight, must-be-right model of literacy that fetters their eager zest for language; when they let go of nonproductive, time- and energy-draining strategies and activities; when they begin to take linguistic as well as teaching and learning risks; when they are encouraged to think; then they begin to pay attention to things that are important — learning something, teaching someone, doing their best.

In whole language classrooms students attend to their own behavior and attend to (care for) each other; they even act as models for each other. Modeling as the fashion model does it isn't what we are talking about. This special kind of modeling involves providing examples and demonstrating for each other (teacher for student, student for teacher, student for student). Modeling must involve believ-ability and authenticity — students must believe they can do, are wanted to do, and need to do various activities in settings that make sense to them. But even more important than modeling, the participants actively bring others into what they are doing — they invite. Modeling without follow-through (invitation, encouragement, and facilitation) is a hollow fashion parade that may enhance the teacher's ego, but it surely diminishes the students' self-esteem.

Once again we invite you to come in, to consider our suggestions for possible use in your own curriculum. We trust that our ideas will never be used as discrete activities; if they are, they could become anemic routines rather than the "flax-golden tales" we wanted to share with you.

Dorothy J. Watson

Introduction

Literature: Its Rightful Place in the Curriculum

Leland B. Jacobs, Professor Emeritus, Teachers College, Columbia University

From the beginnings of public education on this continent, literature has been considered important in the school experience of children. The reasons for literature in the curriculum have varied from era to era. At times the emphasis has been on fostering moral instruction, or indoctrinating for national pride, or as therapy, or as motivation for learning to read, or as aesthetic knowing. Whatever the reasons, the idea that literature has something of value to contribute to children's school experiences has persisted and seemingly will continue to be included in future curricula.

When one looks at the inclusion of literature in the curriculum today, there are pivotal bearings. In the first place, there can be no question about the quantity and quality of a literature for children. There are plenty of attractive publications, and there is a body of realistic, romantic, and fanciful writings that deserve to be called distinguished.

It is also to be noted that children's literature is receiving considerable scholarly attention. Teachers are being provided new insights and new approaches that affect what they select, present, and carry out as activities with children.

In many classrooms teachers are developing practices in line with current thought about what literature is and what it can mean for children. While it is frequently noted that children's creative endeavors are fostered by their reading and listening, the justifications that this is a way to develop lifetime reading habits and that this will provide a happy interlude in the school day, although important, are not pivotal. What is pivotal is that literature is a way to know. It is an aesthetic ordering of some components of existence. It is an exploration and an illumination of the human condition. Through literature, the child can, with aesthetic feeling, enter into quests, encounters, circumstances, happenings, longings, enterprises not possible in any other way, since what the reader or listener is experiencing is a metaphorically created reality. And this reality exists in words fitly spoken and in language patterns that are appropriate and appealing. The child listener or reader is receiving "news that remains news" about a created world that is but never was, a world that is made believable when the minds of a writer and of a child become partners in the exploration of the imaginable.

Beyond making literature available to children, the teacher needs to make decisions about activities related to a text — decisions that square with the theoretical bases espoused. The teacher, knowing that the children already have lived through the text, must propose activities that foster a critical consideration of that text, activities that teach children to review rather than to report what has been written. To review is to reconsider the selection, to respond out of one's own "selective attention" to what has been written, to view what one aesthetically knows in a new light. To report is primarily to restate in one's own words what has been heard or read. A reviewer is primarily a critic. A reporter is merely an informer.

To give children opportunities to be critical reviewers does not call for activities different from many already used: discussion, interpretive reading, dramatizations, for example. Intent is what differs. The activities selected call upon children to view a literary selection from a different stance, which requires a fresh consideration of what has been lived through in the listening or reading. Now judgment (insight, discernment, valuation) becomes strategic in the larger comprehension of the text. This means, at the children's level of development, they are assuming the role of critic.

When literature is presented as aesthetic knowing,

children are learning that it is an experience of living. When teachers encourage children to re-view what has been aesthetically enjoyed, they are avoiding the exploitation of literature to such extraneous ends as instruction in skills, motivation for various school subjects, personal character development, or the learning of facts and information. Instead, they are helping children recapture by appropriate means what was the import and impact of the original contact with the literature. They are helping children to be critics. And by so doing, they are giving literature its dignity, its rightful place in the language arts curriculum, so that it produces in young learners "an educated imagination" and provides, as Alfred North Whitehead wrote in *The Aims of Education,* the "activity of thought, receptivity to beauty, and humane feelings."

Teachers Detechnologizing Reading

Kenneth S. Goodman, University of Arizona, Tucson

The more we learn about language and language learning, the clearer it becomes that learning to read and write should be no harder than learning to talk or to understand aural language. People have the marvelous ability to develop the language resources they need to meet their communicative needs. They learn to speak the language(s) of their family and community at very early ages without any professional assistance.

Literacy comes later because the need for written language develops more slowly, even in highly literate cultures. But research among a wide range of children in a wide range of cultures shows that this development begins well before many children enter school. In some societies with heavy cultural stress on early literacy, many, perhaps most, children come to school already reading and writing.

The key to literacy development is the same as oral/aural development: it will be easy if the literacy is functional for the learners and if the written language they encounter is whole, real, relevant, and meaningful.

In the United States we developed a complex technology of reading instruction largely before we learned to understand the reading process as one of making sense of print and largely before we appreciated the importance of language being whole and functional for ease of learning. The technology in-

cludes graded basal readers, readability formulas, skill sequences, and abundant tests. The technology has so overwhelmed the teaching of reading in the United States (and in other countries to which we've exported it) that scores on tests and progress through basals became confused with reading itself.

For many years, responsible teachers have modified their use of basals when, in their professional judgment, they thought it would help their pupils. These teachers knew that what is important is how well children comprehend what they read even if they seem unable to handle the silly exercises. Now there are many highly informed teachers who feel confident in their knowledge of the reading process, of how children develop as readers, and of how teaching can support learning. They've come to understand that helping children become literate is a matter of supporting children's efforts to make sense of and through print. It involves bringing young readers in contact with a wide range of meaningful written materials, helping them recognize their own needs for written language, and then supporting their development. These teachers are setting aside the workbooks and skill drills. They're using as reading materials books, magazines, newspapers, street signs, cereal boxes, and anything else that is authentic and that catches the interest of their pupils. They're turning their classrooms into literate environments in which children are surrounded by meaningful written language.

These confident teachers are taking back control of their classrooms from the publishers and the testmakers. They're involving their pupils in authentic literacy events — occasions where written language is functional and necessary. The teachers know that three kinds of language learning take place at the same time: children learn language; they learn through language; and they learn about language. So reading is integrated in thematic units. There are no word lists or drills on isolated skills. Rather, there are strategy lessons in which the teachers focus students' attention on aspects of the real texts used in thematic units to support the comprehension strategies the children are developing.

Wordless picture books and predictable books replace the basals, with their artificial language and preprimer approach. Predictable books have strong structures, often involving repeated patterns, and are easy for beginners because they can quickly pick up the patterns and predict what's coming.

These hard-working teachers build classroom libraries of paperback books, which replace the graded readers. Instead, children choose their own reading materials based on their own tastes, interests, and abilities. Teachers concentrate their classroom efforts on linking children with books, thus helping them broaden their tastes and interests and increase their reading ability through reading.

The children help plan their own curriculum and work with the teacher in choosing topics for thematic units, building the classroom library, and maintaining the literate environment of the classroom. These are not classrooms in which pupils must be kept occupied with busy work while others are being instructed. All the learners are involved in productive learning because their activities are authentic and of their own choosing.

These teachers are expert kid-watchers. They don't need standardized tests from New Jersey, Iowa, or California to tell them how their students are progressing. They know because evaluation is continuous in their classrooms. It's part of every interaction between teacher and pupil. It happens during regular teacher-pupil reading conferences; it happens during small group activities; it happens when teachers are noting miscues as a child reads. Good kid-watchers know how to interpret what their kids are doing — or not doing; they know when to ask a question, when to offer a suggestion, when to give a pat on the back or a gentle push. They know which book to put in which child's hand — and just the right time to do it. And they know when it might be useful to bring a small group together for some special help.

One of the special bonuses such teachers produce is that their pupils not only know how to read but enjoy doing so. Because the students' reading is always authentic, there never is a question about its usefulness. The pupils develop favorite books, favorite authors, and a sense that reading is a pleasant way to spend some of their leisure time. Self-evaluation is ultimately the most useful kind of evaluation, and pupils who read authentic materials for their own purposes know when they are successful and when they are not. They know when they have understood and when they have not.

Today's good reading teachers have made the reading technology, with its tests, basals, and workbooks, completely obsolete. Some of the publishers are catching on to this and are offering programs with selections from fine children's literature that hasn't been tinkered with to suit a readability formula. They are including well-written expository materials on a wide range of topics. But the future of reading is in the hands of its teachers. They will make the difference between whether literacy is truly available to some or to all children.

Writing to Learn, Learning to Write

Donald H. Graves, University of New Hampshire, Durham

The text that follows describes Jason and his teacher, Leslie Funkhouser of the Mast Way School in Lee, New Hampshire. The parenthetical statements in italic refer to a related research finding pertaining to what is known about writers and writing.

Jason isn't sure how sea otters eat clams. "Do they get a rock from the bottom of the ocean, bring it up, then crack the clam, or do they crack the clam on the ocean bottom?" Jason is a second-grade perfectionist who wants the information in his report on endangered species to be accurate. Earlier he had held up publishing his piece on "Making a Puppet Booth" until he determined that the directions actually worked. When Jason composes, he reads, draws diagrams, writes, reads, touches up a drawing, and then writes again. *(The writing process is made up of many subprocesses that the child uses in recursive fashion: reading, drawing, spelling, speaking, listening, planning, organizing, and so on. In short, there is no set order to the writing process.)* At times Jason tries the effect of a sentence by reading it aloud to one or more of the eleven students in his classroom who are gathering information on endangered species for a science fair. The remaining eleven students are working on other projects.

Jason is in a classroom where the teacher follows the contours of a child's growth and applies the research about children's learning, language, and writing. His teacher, Leslie Funkhouser, reads, writes with the children, shows how she learns, and demonstrates an understanding of research principles. Even more than her understanding of research, Funkhouser demonstrates the function of writing.

Jason writes every day and chooses most of his topics. *(When writers write each day, they seldom struggle for topics; best of all, they think about their topics when they are not writing.)* Yesterday Jason's information went down quickly; today he composes slowly as he tries to use information and language with greater precision. *(The writing process is highly variable, flowing one day, thwarted the next, or even blocked for several days.)* He knows the other children in the room will respond to his information with both enjoyment and further questions. He is learning what writing is for: to make sense of the world and to enjoy new understandings of how the world is put together, as well as to share that information with other people. *(Writing is a social act; even writing only for ourselves helps us understand ourselves and others. Writing also creates a document that can be shared with an entire class or specific persons, and at other places and times.)*

Jason turns to contemplate his other publications: a story about a trip, his account of constructing a puppet booth, and an imaginative outer-space narrative. As he surveys his writings, he reexperiences his short history as a writer; he recalls the laughter of classmates who read about his wild creature from outer space and their enjoyment in reading about his trip at an afternoon library session. *(Every writer has a history; part of learning to write involves building up a notion of what makes up the history. Sadly, many children are not aware of their power as writers; in fact, they carry negative baggage that thwarts their attempts to write. Publications, collections in writing folders, and the responses of other children can make positive contributions to a child's sense of history.)*

Making meaning with language didn't begin yesterday for Jason. *(From birth, children act to make sense of their world; they draw, scribble, tell stories, read faces, and talk with friends; writing is one more opportunity to enjoy and make sense of the world.)* From birth, Jason has manipulated his universe to make sense of it. He explored the world with hand, mouth, and language. The world, in turn, acted on Jason, challenging him with language, objects, television, and the attentions of adults and other children. At home Jason is hardly systematic, yet he functions with high purpose as he chooses, experiments, discards, accepts, adapts, generalizes, tells stories, and recounts short narratives to explain his day, all in the space of a single hour. His school environment should maintain the same variety and challenge as his home.

Jason's actual history as a writer began at about the age of two and one-half when he randomly moved a crayon across a newspaper. Fascinated with the marks, he gradually increased his drawing/writing over the years until he could anticipate his intentions, moving from random marks to circular and angular figures, writing his name, and experimenting with sound-symbol combinations. He composed signs and directives for his parents (such as "Iwtstop" — "I want to stay up"), discovering, by the way his parents reacted, an authority in written words more powerful than in spoken words.

Although there are patterns to Jason's development as a writer that are similar to those of other children, these same patterns can never be predictable enough to be accommodated by instructional guides, workbooks, or textbooks. *(No textbook can anticipate where a child as writer may be on any given day. At best, they provide decontextualized exercises that have little to do with the real game — writing.)* Each day any piece that Jason composes produces its own unique demand for response.

Jason's teacher, Leslie Funkhouser, attempts to follow the contours of his development by providing a human and physical environment that reflects the nature of growth itself. She recognizes that Jason's growth comes through challenge as he tries to solve the problems encountered on the way to making sense of his world; in this instance the problem solving is accomplished through writing. *(Growth in writing comes through accepting and extending children's notions of what they mean when they write. Taking risks, solving problems, and making errors are synonymous with growth and learning.)*

Since writing is for the writer and the reader (or listener), Funkhouser works hard to build a society of children who know how to respond to each other. Her questions in response to their writing show this: "Do you think the other children will understand this? You'll need to help me with this one; I don't know why the space station was blown up. Where is the information here that will show the children why the space station was blown up?" *(Since writing is a social act, teachers work hard to develop a community of learners — including themselves — who share, accept, and challenge the meaning that others have created through writing.)*

Funkhouser works hard to have a highly predictable environment as a baseline against unpredictable challenges. The children help make the classroom predictable by handling most of the major chores: attendance, lunch counts, weather charts, book organization, escorting visitors, and so forth. Interviews of students in her room show that most of the children can articulate territorial guidelines for room use, books, supplies, and so forth, and demonstrate which children are the best consultants, which students are reading what books and how they are reading them, and what the reading and writing habits of the teacher are. Summaries of the interviews reveal a high range of choice (particularly of writing topics), which trade books were read (the major source of the students' reading), what is taboo, and which territories are negotiable. Structure, so necessary for successful scaffolding, is evident at every turn. *(Teachers who use scaffolding principles in teaching writing provide predictable classrooms, workable solutions, reversible roles, a language for learning, and a sense of play.)*

Children make choices at important junctures: writing topics, which children to work with, information to back up main points, organization, use of language, experiments with new words, when a trip to the library is needed for information, interpretations of texts (with supporting information), genre selection, and so forth. There are also areas in which the choice is strongly suggested, such as use of a new genre (fiction, informational writing, personal narrative, persuasion, a letter), helping other writers, and finding the best place in the room to work. But there are also strong directives in which children sometimes have no choice: helping another child write, listening to another child, finishing a piece, and shifting to a new topic. *(Teachers provide a wide band of choice for children through self-selected topics, different genres, use of language, interpretation. But choice is also surrounded with recommendations and some directives that involve no choice.)*

Funkhouser recognizes that her own way of learning affects the way children learn. She reads, shares her writing, and asks the children to help with room decisions and to solve problems with texts, topics, and group sharing. She demonstrates in her own teaching and writing that language is for oneself and for others. The excitement of learning to write occurs when she and the children take risks together; teaching writing then involves membership in a society of risk takers who know how to help each other write to learn. *(The teacher may be the most important learner in the classroom. How he or she consults with children, writes, reads, solves room problems, and enjoys learning new things about the world and about himself or herself has the greatest effect on the children's enjoyment of learning and literacy.)*

PART 1

If you dot know a
word, what is a thing to do

You thik to yourself
one possibility is to ask
a neigbbor like Kurt or
Shella if they are around me
Dot' just blab it aut please whisper!
You cowld Look at the pictures to help,
You could Look at the word If there are
no vowels its Probably an abbreviation.
You can also skip that word and you
could come back toit later If you dot'
know that word, just leave it and go no
to the rest of the story.
You could make a word up that makes sense
After you use all these strategies and when
You read You can maybe be a
teacher too.   Shanda

Chapter 1:
A World of Language in Use

The child's construction of reality is achieved largely through the medium of language. But to say this does not resolve the puzzle; if anything, it enhances it. It is not as if anyone teaches a child the mysteries of the social system — the social structure, systems of knowledge, systems of values and the like. Yet before he ever comes to school he has accumulated a vast store of information about these things; and he has done so not only without instruction but without those from whom he has learnt it being aware that they know themselves. And he has learnt it largely through language: through the small change of everyday speech, the casual linguistic interaction of the home, the street and the neighbourhood.

— M.A.K. Halliday, *Learning How to Mean: Explorations in the Development of Language* (Edward Arnold, 1975), 120

The activities in this chapter help children explore the functions and forms of language and encourage children's awareness of their own linguistic knowledge and abilities. This chapter will be particularly useful to teachers of insecure readers and writers, especially those who ask, "When will I read and write?"

Learning and Learning to Read and Write

Why

The more children develop accurate concepts about written language, the more effective they will be as language users. The activities described below will help students learn that the purpose of reading and writing is communication. This desire to communicate stimulates their learning to read and write, and it is by practicing these skills that they become more proficient. During the learning process students must take chances, take risks, make guesses, make predictions. As a result, they make mistakes, but they learn from making mistakes. It's important for

children to realize that just as they may misread a word or an idea, or may misspell or punctuate incorrectly as they write, other readers and writers may also be imperfect. Even books may contain poor writing, inaccuracies, or a viewpoint or perspective that differs from the reader's. Students should also realize that readers use many different kinds of clues (or cues) at the same time and make their own interpretations of a written piece.

Who

Middle and upper elementary students, especially nonproficient readers and writers

How

To get students thinking about how they learn, use the example of bicycle riding. Most students learned to ride on their own, with minimal assistance or interference from a parent, sibling, or friend; thus few recall being the student while someone else taught them to ride. If bicycle riding is not popular in your community, pick an activity in which almost all children participate, but one that they do not consider an "educational" experience.

Ask the class, "How did you learn to ride a bicycle?" Students respond to the question in brainstorming fashion. Don't comment as you record their answers, but ask questions that require further introspection. Allow students to share stories of their experiences, and then summarize their points on the board.

After the initial discussion, group the student responses into general categories for further discussion of "How we learn things." The responses generally fall into three broad categories:

1. Wanting to Learn

> "I just got on my bike and rode away."
>
> "I wanted to so much I just kept trying and trying."
>
> "My older brothers and sisters could all ride bikes."
>
> "I begged and begged for a bike for my birthday."

Ask how many students wanted to learn to ride a bike. Occasionally students will say they did not want to learn. They may have been pushed by a parent, in which case it was a much different experience. Ask these students to name an activity that they did want to learn and to explain which of the two activities they do better. If they wanted to learn to skate, for example, chances are they are better skaters than bike riders (which is the point of the activity).

2. Learning by Practicing

> "I rode every day."
>
> "I rode all the way around the block."
>
> "I used training wheels."
>
> "My mom [dad] held onto the back of the seat to help me balance."

Explain to students that they have to ride a lot to be good bike riders, but that they probably don't think of it as practicing — they think of it as bike riding. You might ask if any of the children practiced first by steering, then pedaling, then sitting on the seat, and so forth, to explain this point further.

3. Making Mistakes

> "I went six pedals and then fell."
>
> "I just got back up on the bike every time I fell."
>
> "When I first tried a wheelie, I kept flipping the bike over."

Ask how many children fell down when they were learning to ride. Also, ask what happened when they tried to ride one-handed or do a wheelie. Most students will agree that in learning to ride they will fall down, that mistakes occur whenever they learn something new. Some students may insist they have never fallen (these are not your risk takers). Suggest that all of us may be able to learn something new without making mistakes, but that we probably won't learn as fast or as well because learning requires that we take risks. Another good question to ask is whether bicycle racers ever fall.

Learning to Read and Write

Now tie the discussion to literacy learning, using examples from your classroom.

1. *Wanting to learn.* When students select their own books to read, they are reading about a topic that interests them. They should switch to a new book if they don't like the one they've selected. The same is true for writing. When they choose their own writing topics, they are writing about something that interests them.

2. *Learning by practicing.* Remind students that they practice by reading and writing what they want to read and write. Point out that the main difference between "good" and "not-so-good" readers and writers is that "good" readers and writers like to read and write, and do a lot of reading and writing. Repeat this several times so students realize that there is no magic or superintelligence required.

3. *Making mistakes.* It's important to stress that all language learners make mistakes and sometimes have difficulties. Ask the class if anyone ever makes mistakes when reading or writing. This may be a revelation to the less proficient readers. You may suggest that if they don't make mistakes when reading and writing, they aren't taking risks by tackling more challenging materials. Point out how accomplished readers and writers still make mistakes as they read and write.

What Else

This discussion may challenge the thinking of many students. They need not be convinced at first. Post a list of learning guidelines and refer back to it as students discuss reading and review their own progress. Discuss these points again as you review a journal, writing folder, or reading list.

Debra Goodman, Detroit Public Schools, Michigan

Language Detectives

Why

To awaken students' awareness and broaden their understanding of language in use

Who

Students in grades 3–6; with adaptation, other students

How

Introduce the activity by asking students the following questions about reading (or modify the activity to pertain to writing or speaking): "What is reading? When do you read? Why do you read?" Do not prompt student responses in any manner. The idea is that their initial concepts will be modified as they work through the activity.

Set up the activity as one in which students become detectives, super sleuths, spies. Distribute and discuss a grid-type worksheet containing places to enter information under the following category headings: *Time, Who was reading? What was being read? Why was it being read?* Give students the following directions: "You are about to become a Reading Detective, one who spies on friends, family, and perhaps even people you don't know to discover when, what, and why they are reading. Complete this chart (parents and friends may help you) and be prepared to discuss some of the information you discover." Explain to the students that they may record their data on the worksheet, giving examples for each category.

Give students a time limit (a case deadline); twenty-four hours is sufficient for collecting data. Discuss possible scenes or locations where data may be collected: school halls, offices, buses, homes, supermarkets, and so forth. Encourage students to be on the lookout constantly because people may be reading anyplace, anytime. After the time limit has lapsed, ask students to read aloud their findings. List the data in columns on the chalkboard, recording samples from as many students as possible.

Discuss again the original questions — when people read, who reads, why they read. List the purposes for reading on the board, categorizing them when possible (for leisure, for an occupation, for information, and so forth). Discuss again the basic question — what is reading? Then have students compare their ideas with the concepts they held (or the ones they could verbalize) at the beginning of the activity.

What Else

1. If the response was good, suggest that students become detectives in search of other information — this time writing or speaking data. Perhaps the class will want to divide up, with half the students spying on writers and half on speakers. Once the activity has been completed for one component of language (such as reading), students will be better prepared to answer questions about the other components; encourage them to find clues and facts to support their answers.
2. Students can analyze and write about their own reading habits. Then they share and compare what they discover with the findings of the other readers in the class.

Jane A. Disinger, Desert Winds Elementary School, Tucson, Arizona

What Have You Read (or Written) Today?

Why

To help students explore the functions and forms of written language

Who

Middle and upper elementary students

How

Begin the discussion by asking students, "What have you read today?" Children tend to name just books and reading done in school. Some may say, "Nothing." Encourage students to think about their activities during the day and to name all the types of reading they have done. Did they brush their teeth? Was there something to read on the tube of toothpaste? Did they read the front or back of the cereal box? Eventually students will begin to name many different kinds of print, and a list can be made on the board. This activity can be repeated at another time with students listing the types of writing they have done. These informal surveys can be followed by any of the following activities.

1. Initial activities to discover forms of writing and their functions:
    a. "What Did I Read?" list: Ask children to spend two days (a school day and a weekend day) writing down everything they read. Share the lists in a class discussion and ask the students to tell why they read each form of writing. Categorize the items on the board according to their functions.
    b. "What Did I Read?" center: This center consists of a bulletin board, a table or shelf with 3″ × 5″ cards and pencils, and perhaps a box of magazines, advertisement pages, and scissors to cut out print samples. Have students list on the cards the different things they read, and pin the cards to the bulletin board. Students can also add samples or draw pictures of what they read. Later, take the cards down and talk about the functions or purposes of the reading listed on each card. Come up with some general categories. Divide the bulletin board by written language functions (such as those listed below) and ask the children to categorize their cards and samples under each heading.
    c. "What Have You Read Today?" survey: Following the class discussion, develop a questionnaire asking people to describe the various kinds of reading and writing they do. Have students interview parents, other students, school staff, and others about what they read and write at home, at work, in a store, and so forth. Present the interviews in a class discussion or compile them in a book about reading. The interview information might also be compiled into general categories, such as those listed below.

2. Further activities to explore reading and writing functions:
    a. *Recreational:* Reading and writing for personal enjoyment.
        (1) Plan a literature, poetry, or creative writing unit in which students select their own reading materials.
        (2) Students interview people about their favorite books when they were children — parents, the principal, teachers, neighbors, other students.
        (3) Possible references for this activity are *Books I Read When I Was Young,* edited by Bernice Cullinan and M. Jerry Weiss, or *A Celebration of Teachers.*
    b. *Informational:* Reading to find things out, writing to inform.
        (1) Begin a unit that requires informational reading, such as one on signs and symbols.
        (2) Invite students to write how-to instructions for playing games — either made-up or actual games. Start the activity with a class discussion of the best strategies for playing Hangman, a language adventure in itself. Or read *The Shrinking of Treehorn* by Florence Perry Heide and ask students to invent a board game and to write out the instructions.
        (3) Have students investigate school reading materials, such as texts, handbooks, outside reading. Are they well written? Are they accurate? What is the best way to read them? What makes nonfiction easy or hard to read?
    c. *Occupational:* Reading and writing for jobs.
        (1) Students interview many types of workers (parents, school staff, neighbors, others) about the reading and writing required for their jobs.
        (2) Students investigate required reading and writing at school. What's the purpose of textbooks, tests, rule books, notes for home, and other sources of reading and writing?
    d. *Environmental:* Reading done just because the text is there.
        (1) Students make a scrapbook or collage of ads, schedules, instructions, labels, and so forth for classroom discussion.

(2) Plan a unit on advertisements. Students make scrapbooks that categorize different advertising ploys.

(3) Make available copies of *Penny Power,* a children's magazine produced by the editors of *Consumer Reports.*

Works Cited

A Celebration of Teachers. National Council of Teachers of English, 1986.

Cullinan, Bernice, and M. Jerry Weiss, eds. *Books I Read When I Was Young: The Favorite Books of Famous People.* Avon, 1980.

Debra Goodman, Detroit Public Schools, Michigan

An Environmental Print Walk

Why

Kristy recognizes the word *Sears* in a magazine advertisement. Danny reads the word *exit* as we walk down the hallway. Children are surrounded by meaningful print — in school, at home, and in the neighborhood. Their experiences with such print reinforces their belief in themselves as readers.

Who

Kindergartners, first graders, and other beginning readers

How

Have the class go for a walk through the school and read aloud the important signs that help students, teachers, or visitors: *Boys, Girls, Library, Quiet, Please, Principal's Office, Kindergarten, Cafeteria, Welcome to Boothbay Elementary School.*

Plan an outdoor environmental print walk where students read aloud such signs as *No Parking, Stop, School Crossing, Speed Limit: 15,* and *Entrance.*

What Else

My students and I read together all of the signs, advertisements, and instructions that I put around the room for them. They are encouraged to identify parts of the room for work and play (such as transforming a table into a restaurant), to label possessions, and to record information by labeling or listing. I write notes and messages to them; they write notes and messages to me and to each other. They advertise activities going on in our class to others in the school. They write rules, keep a planning calendar, and write their own notes to inform their parents of a class activity. Such writing means there is much to read.

By using environmental print in reading and writing, I am able to understand what children know about print and to build upon it. I can tap their knowledge about how written language "works" — the written language in which they have been immersed in their personal worlds. This includes the print on the milk carton, on a lunch box, or on a T-shirt; the signs marking local businesses or regulating traffic; and postcards, letters, and invitations from relatives and friends. Reading environmental print informs children of their world. Writing their own environmental print is a way of becoming a part of that world.

Susan Stires, Boothbay Region Elementary School, Boothbay Harbor, Maine

From Trash to Treasure

Why

1. To promote language awareness and appreciation
2. To demonstrate to students their reading abilities
3. To provide an opportunity for students to read, write, speak, and listen

Who

Preschool and early primary students who want to have fun with language

How

Bring out the classroom wastebasket and have students look through the trash for examples of written language. (You may need to add a few special objects earlier in the day, such as empty glue bottles, crayon boxes, crumpled notes, and so forth.)

Take the discovered words and place them in a special paper sack decorated with your name. Explain to students that for one week they are going to save words from the trash at home. Give everyone a sack and invite students to decorate their special trash sacks.

Send a letter home to parents explaining the

activity. Suggest that they help their children by saving junk mail and labels from food and household items. The child's sack can be placed in a special place, and parents and the child can put "language" samples in it. Explain this to students so that they won't continually be going through the garbage in search of words.

At the end of a week, ask students to bring their trash sacks to school. Give each student a large piece of paper; posterboard can be used, or staple two or three open newspaper pages together for support. Invite students to glue, tape, staple, or paste their trash words onto the paper. Parent helpers might be useful at this point.

Encourage students to take turns showing the class their artwork, reading the words they found, and sharing any interesting experiences they had when collecting their trash. Display the artwork, perhaps in the hall where other classes can view it.

What Else

Invite students to write about their experiences as "language" collectors. They may write individually or as a group, comparing the writing samples they found.

Susan M. Chevalier, University of Missouri–Columbia

The Literacy Olympics

Why

Examining the purposes for reading and writing can provide crucial insights for beginning readers and writers. Such purposes are integral to decisions concerning what we read and write, why we read and write, and how we do so. If, for instance, the washing machine breaks down, we will turn to the instruction sheet that came with the machine. We will skim through this document, passing over such items as "how to install the machine" or "how to care for the machine," and concentrate instead upon the section that explains how to search for faults and/or how to contact the service department. Similarly, children need to think about why people read and write and what they select to read and write. In this way students gain important insights into the functions and forms of written language.

Who

Middle and upper elementary students

How

Involve the children in a survey to establish what and why adults and other children read and write. To provide an incentive for children, hold a "Literacy Olympics" and award medals each day of the survey to the team that finds out the most interesting reason for reading and writing, the team that collects the greatest number of items, and the team that interviews the most people. The team winning the most daily medals might be announced at the end of the survey.

Prepare and duplicate a simple survey form for recording what and why people are reading and writing. Give each student several copies. Draw a copy of the survey form on the chalkboard and invite an adult to visit the classroom, bringing along samples of items that he or she has read and written within the last few days. Interview the person and fill out the survey form on the board as you obtain information.

Next give each child a survey form to complete with information about his or her recent reading and writing. Over the next few days ask the students to collect samples of the reading and writing that they do — television schedules, labels on clothing, books, magazines, newspapers, notes and letters, game cards, direct mail advertising, signs, cereal boxes, and so forth. Ask the children to discuss their surveys and the reading and writing samples in small groups and to add to their own forms if other children's responses help them remember other items of reading and writing.

Then have the students use other copies of the survey forms to interview family members, friends, school staff, and other children — anyone who will join in.

What Else

1. Each day invite the children to tell the class about the results of their surveys and to share the samples of reading and writing they have collected. The print samples can be sorted into categories. For instance, the children might separate *TV programs* from *cards,* and both of these from *advertisements; letters* would be a different category. The children could attach samples of each category to sheets of paper labeled

with an appropriate heading. They could then collate the sheets to form a book entitled What People Read and Write. Children will enjoy exploring this book and discussing the samples with their friends.
2. Develop class books with samples of the children's own writing collected during the school year. Original copies and photocopies of children's writing can provide interesting and meaningful reading for the class library.
3. Compile a class book entitled Our Favorite Books. It could include children's illustrations and written comments about favorite books, photocopied book covers, and examples of the range of reading you share with the children. For instance, if you have children assist in locating a telephone number in a directory, a photocopy of the directory page could be added to help children remember such an important use of a book. It is not necessary for children to be able to "read" every item in the class book; rather, the book serves to exemplify purposes for reading.

Judith Ann Smith, Brisbane College of Advanced Education, Mt. Gravatt, Queensland, Australia

When Will I Read?

Why

1. To convince beginning readers that they are already reading
2. To help students see that reading is important and enjoyable
3. To provide enjoyable reading and writing activities
4. To allow students room to explore print, to experiment, to make mistakes, and to develop concepts and generalizations that are a part of language learning

Who

Early primary students, especially those who do not think of themselves as readers

How

Read aloud *When Will I Read?* by Miriam Cohen. This book describes a whole language first-grade class in which Jim is grappling with the all-important question "When will I read?" Many aspects of reading are explored.

After reading the book, invite children to tell what kinds of things Jim read in the book and what kinds of things they can read. Encourage many children to participate and try to have them list a variety of reading activities.

During the discussion it is likely that one of the children will say, "But we can't read!" Children are often incredulous when adults suggest that they can read. Some laugh, some get angry, and others become nervous. At this time, introduce one of the two major activities described below. Follow this with a statement like, "What good readers you are. And you told me you couldn't read!"

Every few days, return to *When Will I Read?* and continue to discuss it and to relate it to unit activities and other language activities. Questions such as the following might be used to begin a discussion.

Why did Jim think he couldn't read?

How do you suppose Jim learned to read?

Who taught Jim to read?

Jim's classroom had some signs in it. What are some of the signs in our classroom? What do we need signs for?

Jim drew a picture and told a story. Why do we sometimes put pictures with stories? What are the pictures good for?

What are the stories good for?

The two major activities of this unit follow. Although they are described separately, they should take place concurrently.

1. Reading Print in Our Environment

Make a print collection by collecting signs, logos, and labels from magazines, newspapers, or the products themselves. For actual labels, include the whole box front, back, or top; for magazines, tear out the whole page on which there is an advertisement (an entire magazine is a little unwieldy for small children to look through). Look for advertising sections in newspapers, and also pull out baseball tables, front-page stories, weather maps, movie ads, comic strips, picture pages. Keep the print collection in a large cardboard box. (*I Read Signs, I Read Symbols,* and *I Walk and Read* by Tana Hoban can also be used with this unit.)

Tell the children that they are going to do some reading. Hold up a sign or label and ask who can read it. Ask the child who reads it correctly to point to where he or she is reading. Then ask the children if there is anything else they can read on the page. Continue the activity for a period of time, allowing other children to read aloud.

Some children will respond with the product name, such as *Jif,* while others will say the generic name, *peanut butter.* Most children will read and identify the large logo. Some children will read other aspects of the label, such as numbers or a word like *off;* others will point to the picture as identifying the message. If children spell out letters, ask them, "And what does it say?" to focus on the message.

Don't correct children's responses or allow children to correct each other. Focus on convincing children that they are able to interpret written language on their own. Let one child read each selection, and explain to the other children that each will have a turn: "We are all learning, and we each need our own chance to read." Keep the collection of labels handy so that the children can read labels to themselves later.

2. "I Can Read" Book

Help students prepare a class book. Each day, meet at a table with three or four students until all have had at least one turn. Each student has a large piece of paper, a pair of scissors, and access to paste or glue. You will need an empty book made from construction paper or other large sheets of paper, a felt-tip marker, and a pencil. In the middle of the table is a pile of printed samples from the print collection. Invite the children to find some things that they can read and paste onto their papers.

As students work individually on their own pages, ask them to choose one item to paste in the class book that you are assembling. Each child's page will list his or her name followed by the words *can read* and will include the child's printed selection pasted on the page. For the sake of variety, you may want to help the child make his or her selection. The class book might include logos, traffic signs, movie ads, weather maps, and other print samples.

Each child brings the completed large page to you to read. Write the date and what the child says near each print sample. These pages can be used on bulletin boards and later made into a large scrapbook.

What Else

1. At some point each day, read aloud the new additions to the class book. Ask each child to read his or her own page. The children learn as they hear each other read, and may categorize a reading based on another child's interpretation. A can of Crisco shortening, for example, may be labeled *grease* by the entire class. At other times, children will reinterpret a label or read other parts of the label.
2. This activity can provide insight into children and the progress they are making. The children's reading shows what they know about print. Do they know that the print carries the message? Are they able to gain meaning from a logo alone, without a picture of the product? Do they know what print is for? ("That's the news." "Those are people's names.") Can they assign a meaning to print? ("That tells how much it costs.") From time to time, ask students to reread their scrapbook pages; record and date their new responses. This will give a record of students' progress from September to June.
3. The "I Can Read" Book and scrapbook are of tremendous value in discussing children's progress in reading with their parents. Share the books with the parents, telling them what the children said while reading and what this indicates about their strengths as readers. *Reading Begins at Home* by Dorothy Butler and Marie Clay is a good reference book for parents.
4. Other class books might be built around the topics of signs found around school and photographed during a walk, T-shirt slogans, or children's drawings of print they see around them.

Work Cited

Butler, Dorothy, and Marie Clay. *Reading Begins at Home: Preparing Children for Reading Before They Go to School.* Heinemann, 1982.

Debra Goodman, Detroit Public Schools, Michigan

I Can Read Nursery Rhymes

Why

To integrate language and art activities through the use of the highly predictable, rhyming, and rhythmic language patterns of nursery rhymes

Who

Kindergartners

How

Assemble the following materials: a collection of nursery rhymes, chart paper containing outlines of nursery rhyme characters and appropriate backgrounds, blank chart paper, felt-tip pens, and such collage materials as tissue paper, crepe paper, vinyl and fabric scraps, buttons, margarine and fruit juice lids, used wrapping paper, ribbons, wood shavings, pasta dyed in a range of colors, dyed Popsicle sticks, yarn, leaves, bark, and sticks. It is important to use a wide variety of materials to invite sensory and language learning. Your own local area will yield many other examples.

Introduce a nursery rhyme orally; have the children repeat it aloud with you. When they are comfortable with the rhyme, improvise on how you say it:

> you say one line; children say the next
>
> boys say one character's part; girls say the other
>
> you act as narrator; children take the character parts
>
> clap the rhythm of the rhyme as all say it aloud
>
> clap the rhythm without saying the words
>
> accompany the words with percussion instruments

Write the rhyme on chart paper to help everyone remember it. Be sure to elicit the children's help with decisions about writing the rhyme — what to write first so that everyone knows the name of the rhyme, where to write next, what letters might be used in some of the words, and so on. In this way you are demonstrating to students a purposeful function of writing, an ongoing dialogue using metalinguistic terms in the context of their use, and a model of the writing process. As you create this classroom resource together, you are also giving the class a degree of ownership of the words as children help to create the experience chart.

Have the children work in small groups to create a collage to accompany the rhyme. As they work, encourage them to discuss the characters, what they say and do, and how they look. Display the pictures with the words and have the students say the rhyme aloud once again. You may wish to return to the earlier improvisations, this time using the print to identify the parts. For this reason, you might want to use different colors to signify verse and chorus or the words of different characters.

As each nursery rhyme is introduced, add the text and accompanying collages to your display until you have a nursery rhyme collage mural. This will be a valuable resource for children in activities involving word phrases and title matching, in choosing their parts in shared readings, for musical accompaniment, and as a general print resource for children's reading and writing.

What Else

Provide the children with the words and illustrations for several different nursery rhymes. Have them decide which words go with each illustration, thus giving insights into their present strategies for dealing with print. Copies of the pairs of nursery rhyme text and illustrations could be glued to sheets of paper and collated into personal books for the children to take home to share with their families. In printing the words, be sure to leave room for children to add their own writing. Alternatively, provide the illustrations only and invite children to write their own versions of the nursery rhymes.

Brenda Parkes, Brisbane College of Advanced Education, Mt. Gravatt, Queensland, Australia

All the Things We Can Do

Why

To heighten students' awareness of themselves as learners by incorporating and integrating cognitive, affective, and motor learning across the curriculum

Who

Kindergartners

How

To begin this unit, assemble the class outside or in the gym and talk about all the different ways we can move: running, crawling, sliding, hopping, and so forth. Encourage children to think about which parts of their bodies they use as they explore the different ways they can move. Set up painting, drawing, and writing areas nearby and encourage the children to write about and illustrate what they are doing. These might form part of a classroom display of "Things We Can Do."

If possible, take photos of the children as they move in different ways, and display the photos with the children's added captions. Later, collate the photos and captions into a book for the reading area. These books might be used for science activities by comparing and contrasting how animals and humans move.

Music

Start this session with a discussion about the ways we can use specific body parts, such as "We clap our hands," "We stamp our feet." Teach one of the favorite movement songs, such as "What Can You Do, Punchinello, Funny Fellow?" and invite the children to tell, in turn, what body part they are going to move. The other children join in by imitating the action.

For another version of the game, write the children's suggested actions on chart paper; then invite them to select an action to act out. Ask children to read aloud each written choice or to tell how they knew which action they were choosing. This gives insight into their knowledge about print.

Select another action song, such as "Clap, Clap, Clap Your Hands." Teach the song first; then write the words on a poster, discussing the words with the children as you write. With those words that are likely to have personal relevance for the children, you might say something like, "How do I start writing *clap?* It starts the same way as your name, Claire. What do you think comes next?" When you have finished writing, children may notice and talk about the repetition of many words. They may want to point to some of the words and phrases as they sing the song. Ask children what else they could do besides clap. Their action words can be written on small cards, and the children can take turns putting the new words over the word *clap.* Then they can sing and dramatize their new versions.

Leave the poster and sets of alternative action words where the children can explore them independently and use them as a print resource for personal writing. Many other popular children's songs, rhymes, and fingerplays lend themselves to this kind of treatment.

Physical Education

A well-planned outdoor area or physical education lesson provides another rich source of language. Set up a variety of equipment for the children to move over, under, in, out, through, along, and so on, and encourage them to verbalize what they are doing. Photos taken during this time can stimulate further discussion and can be added to the classroom display of "Things We Can Do."

Carpentry

Set up a woodwork area with such materials as nails of different lengths, polystyrene, wood, plastic bottle tops for wheels, margarine lids, and fabric scraps. Store the equipment in labeled containers. Have writing and drawing materials nearby for those who might like to draw plans, make lists, or record in writing what they have done. A simple plan for making an object could be introduced, and perhaps a parent could demonstrate how to build and use the object. If children show interest, a few very simple plans covered with clear adhesive-backed paper could be included in the area. Photos could be taken of the finished objects and made into a class book.

Cooking

Cooking can be a wonderful literacy experience. Prior to undertaking actual cooking, the children can practice pouring, measuring, beating, stirring, and mixing water and sand. At snack time they can help with the cutting, peeling, shredding, and serving of fruit and vegetables. This will give them experience with the concepts and the language that they will encounter in cooking. Explore samples of environmental print such as the containers for sugar, flour, and margarine, which the children are likely to encounter in cooking.

Introduce the cooking activity with a story such as *The Little Red Hen, The Gingerbread Man,* or *The Little Old Man Who Could Not Read.* You might improvise on *The Little Red Hen* so that she grew corn instead of wheat and wanted to make popcorn instead of bread. Explain how we find out how to cook something. Show the children a recipe book and how to use the index to locate a desired recipe. Read a simple recipe aloud to the children. Ask them to look for sample wrappers and containers of the ingredients in the class environmental print collection. Now write the recipe onto a poster, adding samples of environmental print alongside the words to serve as clues to their meaning.

Assemble the necessary ingredients and cooking utensils. Include a few items that you don't need. Now look at the recipe with the children and ask them to select only the necessary ingredients by matching the ingredients with the words on the recipe. Be sure to ask the children to tell you how they are making their decisions.

Follow the instructions on the recipe, taking photos to record the various steps. Display the photos as a story on the wall, and later collate them into a book for shared reading. Be sure to get a photo of the children enjoying the results of their cooking. Encourage them to write their own stories about the activity or to record the event with their own illustrations.

"We Can Write Lots of Things"

Spend some time looking at the wall displays together and encourage the children to recall all the "Things We Can Do." Suggest that they share their accomplishments by inviting their families and friends to visit the classroom. Ask the children to decide on the necessary information to include and the wording for an invitation to visit the classroom and see their work. Make copies for the children to take home, and place an invitation on the bulletin board. Leave a notepad and pencil by the bulletin board and set out a box for the responses from home. Each day the children can collect and read the mail. At the appointed time, the children can act as hosts and share a sample of their cooking and a copy of the recipe with the visitors.

Provide the children with folders and invite them to select the writings that they want to keep. Date the writings to record each child's development, and set a time for a weekly conference with each child about the selections, discussing the changes taking place in both the function and form of that child's writing. This folder can go home at the end of the year as a present to the parents, a lovely memento of a period in their child's development.

Brenda Parkes, Brisbane College of Advanced Education, Mt. Gravatt, Queensland, Australia

Nursery Rhymes for Oral and Written Language Use

Why

As adults, we all remember nursery rhymes we have learned. Though very simple and unsophisticated,

they are ingrained in our memories. Nursery rhymes are a welcome addition to the language arts curriculum because they (1) demonstrate a form of written language, (2) expand students' sense of language style and form, (3) provide patterns of our language, such as rhythm and figures of speech, (4) enable children to adapt these patterns for their own use, and (5) encourage positive interaction with one another.

Nursery rhymes provide excellent language experiences for several reasons. Children are able to identify with the characters and interpret the characters in different ways. By combining reality and fantasy, nursery rhymes feature such characters as people, animals, imaginary creatures, and inanimate objects that talk, wear clothes, and even dance. Nursery rhymes have a rich variety of language models — an extensive vocabulary of descriptors, modifiers, verbs, and nouns. Students respond to the magic language of nursery rhymes — rhyme, repetition, patterns, elements of poetry, figurative language — and enjoy exploring the variations in pitch and stress as they say or read the rhymes aloud. Children become more verbal as they become familiar with different nursery rhymes and are willing to take risks as they speak. They also begin to write with a more expanded vocabulary, perhaps incorporating the sentence patterns. Students are willing to take risks in reading because of the predictability of the language, and they develop confidence in themselves as writers. Nursery rhymes allow children to arrive at understandings concerning rules of language, thought, and behavior. Transfer takes place as students begin to recognize vocabulary terms in other reading material and to use them in writing. Finally, children love reading nursery rhymes over and over and find them meaningful and often humorous.

Who

Kindergartners and early primary students

How

Select a favorite nursery rhyme to initiate the first of many integrated language experiences. The following activity sequence might be developed for the nursery rhyme "Little Miss Muffet."

1. Introduce the nursery rhyme with a "Little Miss Muffet" bulletin board. Print the rhyme in large letters on chart paper and display it on the board. Have students recite the rhyme together and discuss its meaning.

2. Incorporate the characters into a craft experience. Make spiders, for example, from egg cartons. Paint the cartons black, cut them apart, and add pipe cleaners for legs.

3. Transform the spider into something different. Ask children to think of what the spider shape could be if it were not a spider. Children paste or draw the new shape on paper and answer this question: "When is a spider not a spider? When it's a ———."

4. Assemble a collection of books, magazine articles, pictures, films, or other resources that provide information about spiders. Ask students to consult the references and then to classify spiders by size, color, shape, or other characteristics. Students increase their vocabulary as they expand their knowledge and understanding of spiders.

What Else

1. Plan a "curds and whey" experience. Bring in cottage cheese or cheese curds for a snack. If equipment is available, make and then sample butter or buttermilk.

2. Plan additional literature experiences involving spiders. Read aloud *Spinning Jenny: A True Story of a Garden Spider* by Eleanor Clark, *The Very Busy Spider* by Eric Carle, or *Charlotte's Web* by E. B. White. Ask students to recite the favorite fingerplay about the "Incy, Wincy Spider."

3. Encourage writing experiences about spiders. Ask students to make a Spider Book, shaped like a spider, in which they can write about and draw spiders as they learn new facts and information.

Rebecca R. Montano, Tucson Unified Schools, Arizona

Peek and Describe

Why

To help students make use of the descriptive language they possess but use infrequently

Who

All elementary students

How

Choose a large colorful picture that easily lends itself to description in terms of color, motion, size, shapes,

details. Paste the picture on a piece of construction paper. On top of this, place a second piece of construction paper that is the same size, and tape the two together at the top. Cut small "windows" or flaps in the top piece of paper at strategic places that will give clues about what lies underneath. Number the windows in the order in which you want children to peek into them.

Gather a group of children for a discussion. Invite one child to peek into the first window and to describe to the group what he or she sees. The second child looks into and describes the second window, and so forth, until all the windows have been opened. As the children describe what they see, record their words or sentences on chart paper or on the chalkboard.

After all the descriptions have been recorded, the children use the descriptions on the board to dictate a group story about the picture. Write down their story, or ask a student to serve as scribe. Children read the completed story together or individually; then they discuss the story and predict what the mystery picture is. At this point the picture can be revealed.

What Else

Before the mystery picture is uncovered, children may write individual descriptions of the picture, make a prediction about it, and support this prediction.

Maudean Ruebling, Laquey R-V School, Missouri

A Day in the Life of . . .

Why

This lesson will help students discover that reading is part of everyday life and that it is not confined to reading a book. Students will use the cognitive skills of reading, writing, adding, problem solving, categorizing, and generalizing, as well as such social skills as cooperating, listening, being tactful, following directions, filling out forms, and ordering in a restaurant.

Who

With adaptation, all elementary students

How

Before the lesson, collect the items needed for the kitchen, the restaurant, and the shop windows, such as:

Popular cereal boxes (full)

Bowls, spoons, napkins, and half-pints of milk (one per student)

Place cards (one per student)

Typed memos, each pertaining to a different occupation (one per student)

Paper on which to respond to memos

Lunch menus from local restaurants (one per student)

Slips of paper for ordering lunch (one per student)

Sale signs, ads, fliers

Merchandise in boxes

Sealed envelopes, each containing a questionnaire and letter (one per student)

Textbooks or dictionaries (one for each pair of students)

Topics or questions corresponding to each book or dictionary

To do the many different activities in this "day" would take more than one class period, so either select a few activities or plan on spending several class periods.

Set up the front of the room to look like a breakfast nook — tables and chairs; a bowl, spoon, napkin, half-pint carton of milk, and place card for one student at each place; a box of cereal at each table; and any plants, pictures, curtains, and other details that make the room look like a real kitchen. Decorate one side wall of the classroom with sales signs, ads, fliers from churches and organizations, and perhaps merchandise so that it looks like a row of store windows in a shopping mall. Desks fill the rest of the room.

Announce to the students: "Today we are all working adults. It is Friday morning, and we just woke up. We are going to lead a typical day now. Remember to read *everything* you see as you go through the day."

The assignment sequence is as follows:

1. First everyone eats breakfast. Demonstrate how common reading is by reading the cereal box.

2. Time for work. Everyone sits at a desk and receives a memo, each addressed to a different occupation (such as "Dear Doctor," "Dear Carpenter," "Dear Bus Driver") and each presenting a work-related problem to be solved. Each "worker" must solve his or her problem sensibly and write a letter in response, incorporating standard letter format.

3. Announce that the work day is over; everyone will go to lunch together and then return home. For lunch, students sit at either the tables or the desks. Each student receives a menu and a blank slip of paper for ordering. Explain to students that there are no waiters or waitresses in this café. All customers must write their names and the date on the slip, list the names and prices of what they order (at least three items), add up the bill, pretend to eat, and leave the receipt at the front counter (i.e., your desk).

4. All the students then go window shopping on the way home. Demonstrate by walking slowly down the side of the room and reading all the signs, ads, and fliers. Discuss what you read with the students to encourage reading and remembering.

5. Home at last. Students arrive home at the same time and sit at the tables or desks. They read the day's mail, which consists of a note from a company whose product they recently purchased. Enclosed in the envelope with the letter is a questionnaire that must be filled out, including a written comment, and "mailed" back to you by replacing it in the envelope and putting the envelope on your desk. Students can receive the same letter and questionnaire, or these can all be different. Everyone finally has the chance to relax and read the day's paper. Students may read any section they want (comics, sports, news stories, features, ads) for about ten minutes.

6. As an optional activity, give half the students a textbook or dictionary with a paper that says, "You are a son or daughter who needs help with homework. Your assignment is to find all the information you can on ———" (a particular topic in the text). The assignment, for those receiving a dictionary, is to write the full word or name for a list of abbreviations you supply or to locate particular biographical or geographical information in the dictionary. The "sons" and "daughters" flip through their books and go to a "parent" for help. Every other student is a parent. The parent does not give the answers but refers the child to the appropriate sections in the book (the index or contents listing of the text; the abbreviations, biographical, or geographical sec-

tion of the dictionary) and suggests words that the child should look up for information on the topic (cross-referencing). As the child and parent work together on the assignment, they write down suggestions for locating the information needed to complete the assignment. Then it is time for the children to go to bed. Each parent selects a bedtime book to read with the child.

When the "day" is over, brainstorm with the students a list of everything that was read during the day — both the content and the source. Then students brainstorm a list of what else they might have read if it had been a real day (street signs, computer screens, paychecks, magazines, books). Students continue the activity by jotting down the source of all that they actually read during the next few days.

On another day you can review the brainstorming list and add items from the individual lists. Invite students to think about why they read each item. "Can someone find two things that two people read for the same reason? What was the reason?" The items can be put in categories according to reasons for reading. Students can think up other reasons for reading, giving examples from their own experiences or those of their classmates.

Elizabeth A. Jochum, St. Thomas More School, Chapel Hill, North Carolina

Reading Autobiography

Why

1. To provide an opportunity for students to indicate their attitudes toward reading
2. To give students practice in writing
3. To provide an opportunity for students to demonstrate their fluency as writers and readers

Who

Middle and upper elementary students

How

Display such reading materials as newspapers, magazines (for adults and children), trade books, textbooks, basal readers for several grade levels, and comic books, and allow students several minutes to examine and discuss these materials.

Then invite students to do a focused freewriting on the topic "The Strongest Memories I Have about Reading." After several students' writings are read aloud, distribute a reading autobiography outline, such as the following:

1. Preschool Years
   a. Favorite stories, books, rhymes
   b. Did my parents or other adults read to me much? What do I remember about those experiences?
   c. First book I remember
   d. Was I reading before I came to school? What did I read? How did I learn?
2. Early School Years
   a. What do I remember about learning or not learning to read? Who taught me? What did they do to help me learn to read?
   b. Favorite stories, books, activities
   c. What were my good and my bad experiences with reading?
3. On My Own in Reading
   a. When did I "take off" on my own in reading? Where? What book or story?
   b. When did I get hooked (or unhooked) on books? What book?
4. Now
   a. What's my favorite reading now? Books? Magazines? Newspapers?
   b. What's the best book I've read recently? Why do I like it?
   c. What kind of reader am I now? Do I enjoy reading? Why or why not?

Students discuss each point, suggest additional questions, and make brief notes. They then write their reading autobiographies. When the writing is complete, the autobiographies might be revised, edited, and shared with others.

What Else

1. Students may want to read their autobiographies to each other, to younger students, to teachers, to families, and to friends.
2. Autobiographies may be sent to a local newspaper or displayed in the hall or on bulletin boards.
3. Students may want to reread a favorite book from an earlier time in their lives and to respond to it now.

Frances E. Reynolds, Rock Bridge High School, Columbia, Missouri, and Annette Geary, Southern Boone County Elementary School, Ashland, Missouri

Reading and Writing Biographies of Important People in Our School

Why

Students can study the genre of biography by participating in activities that exercise and develop their language abilities. The general types of activities can include writing their reactions to books in their journals, making art displays to represent books of a particular genre, and presenting nontraditional book reports to classmates.

A month of biography activities provides students with opportunities to use and to develop a range of language strategies. Effective listening, speaking, reading, and writing are all essential to the successful accomplishment of the goal of producing accurate and interesting biographies. Not only do the students produce work of high quality, but they exhibit a commitment to their work and a sense of pride.

Who

Students in grades 4–6

How

An example of an appropriate activity is this fifth-grade biography project. After the students had read at least one biography and discussed the characteristics of this genre, the teacher announced that they would be writing biographies to read to the first graders, an activity that already was a popular and regular component of the reading program. There were five steps to the biography project:

1. *Choosing subjects.* The teacher explained to the students that they would be writing about people who worked in the school and who were familiar to the first graders. The fifth graders compiled a list of possible subjects, including other teachers, student teachers, custodians, administrative staff, and special teachers such as the physical education teacher and the librarian. The teacher wrote the names on the slips of paper, and the students drew the names of the subjects for their biographies.

2. *Generating questions.* The class brainstormed questions that might be asked of their subjects. All the suggested questions were recorded on the chalkboard. Then the class identified questions that might be too personal or that they would feel uncomfortable asking. The teacher typed the list of remaining questions.

3. *Conducting interviews.* The class talked about how to conduct interviews and made a list of interviewing do's and don'ts. Next, pairs of students role-played interviews, and the rest of the class critiqued the performances, according to the established rules. The group then developed a letter for making contact with the subjects and for setting up times for the interviews. As the students received replies from their subjects, they added each interview time and date to a master list. During the week in which all interviews took place, the teacher made a daily list of the interviewing schedule on the chalkboard. The teacher provided class time in which students could share interesting details from their interviews. For instance, one student could hardly wait to tell his classmates how his subject, a woman custodian, played quarterback on a football team.

4. *Writing biographies.* The young authors proceeded through several steps to turn the responses to their questions into polished biographies. First, they decided which information would be appropriate for the introductory section, which would compose the body of the biography, and which would be suitable for the conclusion. The class wrote and revised for an hour each day during one week. The revision process was conducted informally as students read their writing to one another, to the teacher, and to the student teacher. Students met individually with the teacher or student teacher to edit their work for spelling and grammatical errors. The class also discussed the nature of the audience so that the writing would be appealing to the first graders. One point that arose from this discussion was that first graders like illustrations. Students then had to decide where to add illustrations to their texts. The final handwritten copies of the biographies, complete with illustrations, were bound with a cover of construction paper.

5. *Reading biographies.* Before the students went off to read to the younger children, they discussed strategies for effective reading aloud. How could they be sure to capture and hold the children's attention? What should they say before reading? When should they show the illustration? Having

talked over these and other questions, the student authors were ready to share their work with the first graders.

Elizabeth Bondy, University of Florida, Gainesville

The Linguistically Different Child: How to Soften the Culture Clash

Why

Whether or not you have a foreign-language speaker in your classroom, sooner or later you will have a student who is linguistically or culturally different from the majority of the students. Some of the problems these students experience can be lessened by teachers who are willing to observe, learn, and adapt their teaching techniques.

A few years ago, when I was teaching an English class in a girls' college in Taiwan, I asked which students had completed their homework assignments. Not one raised her hand. I knew the diligence of my students and found it hard to believe that no one had done the work I'd assigned. Suddenly I understood. The girls who had done the homework wouldn't admit it for fear of embarrassing those classmates who had not completed the assignment. It was my first realization of how important it is for teachers to understand the values of their students. Not only were our cultures linguistically different, but our approaches to tasks were different. My lack of understanding caused a breakdown in communication and a potential break in the learning process.

Who

Teachers of children who are ethnically or linguistically different from the mainstream of Anglo-American society

How

Charlie, a sixth grader from an ethnic minority group, was labeled a slow learner. "Not only that," said one teacher, "but he is totally unmotivated to read or write." Charlie spent half of his time at school dozing.

As one of Charlie's teachers, I had a responsibility to learn not only about his cultural values but about his language as well. I needed to know if Charlie's first language differed enough in the surface structure from English to affect his reading. I also needed to find out what "turned Charlie on." I asked his parents to help me with motivation. As Charlie became more comfortable with his teachers, we began to work on building oral language as well as written language, the language of books.

Children learn from one another. Whole language activities combined with peer tutoring can provide a comfortable structure for learning. Children must come to the realization that reading is a matter of prediction and that the words written on paper already exist in their heads. For many children this concept can be especially hard to learn.

To acknowledge a variety of cultures, the entire class explored poetry in the language of their grandparents, neighbors, and friends. We talked about the "word pictures" in the sayings of different cultures. We spoke of our individual experiences with cultures different from that of our families. We talked about our favorite legends, stories, songs, and games. Once Charlie became more "alive" in our school environment, his daily program included the following activities:

1. Charlie wrote language experience stories with a trained peer tutor. The tutor was instructed not to change Charlie's language structure, but to encourage him to write for meaning from his personal experience.

2. Known words from the language experience stories were chosen by Charlie for his spelling words.

3. Several times a week Charlie wrote in his journal. He was told that no one would ever look at his journal and that he could write about anything he wished, including his frustrations and his angriest thoughts. Although Charlie kept his journal "a secret diary" when the activity was first initiated, he slowly began to share his writings with his teacher. Later he volunteered to read some of his works to the entire class.

4. Comic books and other motivational reading materials were kept within easy reach to encourage Charlie to read in quantity. Because he worked so slowly, some time was set aside for reading daily. It was important that Charlie learn not only to read, but to love reading. As he read, he acquired even more information for his experience stories and his journal.

Charlie's language arts activities were relevant to daily life. He made shopping lists for his family and began to write notes at home. His parents encouraged him to write letters for their family. At school we encouraged activities for Charlie that would be useful in life and that he would see as meaningful. In four short months Charlie had made significant gains in writing, in reading, and, perhaps most importantly, in enthusiasm to learn. Our attempts at being culturally attuned and flexible enough to make his language arts program meaningful made the difference. In doing so we discovered that what is most important for the child who speaks a variant of standard English and the culturally different child is what is important for all students — a feeling of security, acceptance, and caring.

Ann Powell-Brown, Kansas City School District, Missouri

Chapter 2:
Literature Points the Way

If one argues that story is basic to reading instruction, then one is also arguing that literature is basic. Literature becomes both a way to connect with the language strengths of children and to expand their world and abilities. It is a way of being sure that the initial school uses of literacy are meaningful and a way of demonstrating the possible rewards of learning to use language in written form. . . .

The literature we choose and present to children continues the socializing function of language so we need to choose wisely. If we want children to know what we value we can present them with literature that reflects our values. For example, if we believe in the importance of a pluralistic society we will present children [with] literature from diverse cultures reflecting linguistic variety. If we believe that good overcomes evil then we will present them with the high fantasy in which good does overcome evil. If we believe that the lives of great people and the lessons of history have relevance to their lives today we will present them with biography and history and historical fiction.

> — Rudine Sims, "Literacy, Literature and Power," presentation at the Center for Expansion of Language and Thinking Conference, College Station, Texas, 1983

This chapter is the bone and marrow of the language arts program. By sharing literature, teachers and students gain the basics for reading, writing, listening, and speaking. Activities invite children to sample all kinds of literature and to celebrate that literature by thinking, talking, drawing, and writing about it. Reading lists are included in some activities. See the Bibliography for additional titles.

Section A:
Themes and Organization

Literature Groups: Intensive and Extensive Reading

Why

Reading is a meaning-making process; learning to read is developmental and occurs over time. With this holistic, active approach to reading, students have constant opportunities to read both extensively and intensively.

Who

All elementary students

How

1. Provide Materials for Extensive Reading

Select books on the basis of children's interest and the potential the books hold for making meaning that is personal to the children and in keeping with the author's intent. Read or skim through all books before selecting them for the classroom. To create an environment that is conducive to reading and that supports student initiative, select books that are an extension of the students' previous experiences with literature, their desire to know, and their reading abilities. Very young readers may need familiar stories with a high degree of predictability.

The following books are appropriate for younger students. They were introduced during the first two months of school in Marilyn Harris Andres's first-grade classroom at Lee School, Columbia, Missouri.

Susan Blair; *The Three Billy Goats Gruff*

Norman Bridwell; *Kangaroo Stew*

Margaret Wise Brown; *Goodnight Moon*

Carolyn Burke and Jerome Harste; *All Kinds of Cats*

Polly Cameron; *I Can't Said the Ant*

Eric Carle; *The Very Hungry Caterpillar*

Bernadine Cook; *The Little Fish That Got Away*

Douglas F. Davis; *The Lion's Tail*

Paul Galdone; *The Little Red Hen; The Three Bears; The Three Little Pigs*

Janet L. Goss and Jerome C. Harste; *It Didn't Frighten Me*

Jerome Harste and Carolyn Burke; *Animal Babies*

Beth Hazel and Jerome Harste; *Icky Picky Sister*

Ezra Jack Keats; *Over in the Meadow*

Ruth Krauss; *The Carrot Seed*

Alan Mills and Rose Bonne; *I Know an Old Lady*

Phoebe Moore; *The Missing Necklace*

Maurice Sendak; *Chicken Soup with Rice*

Sharon K. Thomas and Marjorie Siegal; *No Baths for Tabatha*

Justin Wagner; *The Bus Ride*

Margot Zemach; *The Little Tiny Woman*

Books for older students might be selected from the following list. These books were introduced during the school year in Suzanne Davis's fifth-grade classroom at Lee School, Columbia, Missouri.

Louisa May Alcott; *Little Women*

Lloyd Alexander; *The Black Cauldron; The High King; Taran Wanderer*

Clyde Robert Bulla; *Shoeshine Girl*

Betsy C. Byers; *The Summer of the Swans; The Cybil War*

Beverly Cleary; *Ralph S. Mouse*

Vera Cleaver and Bill Cleaver; *Where the Lilies Bloom*

James Lincoln Collier and Christopher Collier; *My Brother Sam Is Dead*

Margaret Davidson; *Helen Keller's Teacher*

Marguerite de Angeli; *The Door in the Wall: Story of Medieval London*

Barthe DeClements; *Nothing's Fair in Fifth Grade*

Jeannette Eyerly; *The Seeing Summer*

Paula Fox; *The One-Eyed Cat*

Kenneth Grahame; *The Wind in the Willows*

Madeleine L'Engle; *A Wrinkle in Time*

C. S. Lewis; *The Lion, the Witch, and the Wardrobe; Prince Caspian*

Jack London; *The Call of the Wild*

Jane O'Connor; *Yours Till Niagara Falls, Abby*

Scott O'Dell; *Island of the Blue Dolphins*

Katherine Paterson, *Bridge to Terabithia; The Great Gilly Hopkins; Jacob Have I Loved*

Wilson Rawls; *Where the Red Fern Grows*

Willo Davis Roberts; *The Girl with the Silver Eyes*

Marilyn Singer; *Tarantulas on the Brain*

Doris Buchanan Smith; *A Taste of Blackberries*

Elizabeth G. Speare; *The Witch of Blackbird Pond*

J.R.R. Tolkien; *The Hobbit*

Jules Verne; *Around the World in Eighty Days*

2. Form Groups

Introduce five or six books to the students with a brief discussion of the title, author, plot, and characters. Invite the children, on the basis of their own backgrounds of experience, to select a title. Challenge students to explore new genres and subjects, thereby giving them practice at making meaning in unexplored territory.

The children form groups, depending on their first or second choice of books. There should be no more than seven or eight children in a group.

3. Read the Books — Extensive Reading

Assign a substantial number of pages to read, with the understanding that the children may read beyond the assigned number if they wish. Students are expected to read, read, read. "Living" the meaning and being one with the action are encouraged.

Students are invited to keep records of their reading and to make brief reactions to their reading in a journal or reading log. Compiling a personal literary history by exploring literary worlds is the chief goal of extensive reading. Reading independently, the children expand their knowledge of the world, its people, and what it means to be human.

4. Read the Books — Intensive Reading

Intensive reading is practiced in literature study groups, where students who have read the same book come together to study and discuss the book. To begin, encourage the students to share their impressions, ideas, and problems encountered in constructing meaning from the text.

When a topic surfaces that holds a common interest and has the potential for altering perceptions, shift the discussion from sharing to dialogue, a joint undertaking that encompasses critical thinking. Through dialogue in the literature study groups, the teacher and students work with one another to disclose and to construct meaning, thereby expanding the potential meaning of the text. Dialogue that draws on the elements of story is the chief means through which the intensive study of literature is conducted. It is not necessary to hammer away at the elements of literature or narrate their meaning. The elements surface naturally as the discussion focuses on the way the characters cope, the mood of a story, the ordering of time, the creation of place, the development of character, the story structure, and the use of language and symbols.

It is through dialogue that students learn to construct meaning and to practice this process. Dialogue slows down the process, externalizing the act of meaning construction, and confirms that the meaning a reader brings to a text is every bit as important as the text itself. Together, as a shared experience, readers reflect on the importance of events that pull the story forward, the meaning of symbols, the significance of place, the development of character, and how the structure contributes to meaning development. With practice, students learn to seize meaning, to project it into the dialogue, and to benefit from insights and perspectives of their own making and of the author's making as well.

Ralph L. Peterson, Arizona State University, Tempe

Text Sets

Why

To encourage students to share and extend their comprehension of two or more stories that have similar characteristics

Who

All elementary students

How

Two different procedures may be used that encourage children to share and extend their comprehension of text sets. For both procedures, select two or more stories that feature similar characteristics. See the suggested reading list at the end of the activity for examples of characteristics and text sets that feature the characteristics.

Procedure A

1. The set of texts is read by everyone for the purpose of identifying similarities across texts. Students may read the texts independently, or you may read a portion of the texts aloud to all the students and then ask students to read the remainder independently.
2. In a group, students discuss the texts' similarities (and differences, if appropriate). Questions to lead off the discussion should be deliberately open-ended, such as the following:

> What was the same about these stories? (narrative)
>
> What information did you find presented in more than one of the stories? (expository)
>
> What are the similarities in the way these stories were written? (expository)

3. After eliciting all possible thoughts about the similarities of the texts, ask the students to identify which of the similarities are of major importance. Ask if they have read or heard other texts that also share the major similarities. (The lesson may end here, or it may continue with steps four and five.)
4. Ask the students, individually or in groups, to write their own texts based on the major similarities in the texts discussed in class.
5. As children complete their rough drafts, ask them to share their new texts with others; invite group comments. Comments should focus on how the child has utilized the major similarities of the previously discussed texts in his or her writing.

Procedure B

1. Each individual in the group reads a single book from the text set and prepares to share what he or she read and learned from the text with other individuals in the group.
2. Ask each child in turn to relate to the other group members what he or she read and learned. Then invite the others in the group to ask questions, especially those that will help clarify what has been stated.
3. Encourage the children to discuss the similarities

and differences across texts as these become apparent.

Suggested Reading List

Books with Similar Stories

Variations of the Popular Folktale about the Three Little Pigs

> Barbara Brenner; *Walt Disney's The Three Little Pigs*
>
> Paul Galdone; *The Three Little Pigs* (multiple copies available in most libraries)
>
> Donivee Laird; *The Three Little Hawaiian Pigs and the Magic Shark*
>
> Eric Blegvad, illus.; *The Three Little Pigs*

Variations of La Fontaine's Fable about the Miller, the Boy, and the Donkey

> Mary Calhoun; *Old Man Whickutt's Donkey* (written in dialect)
>
> Roger Duvoisin; *The Miller, His Son, and the Donkey*
>
> Lloyd Alexander; *The Four Donkeys* (the book contains a different set of human characters than the two previous stories, but it has a number of interesting similarities, especially with regard to the donkey)

Variations of the Folktale about Jack and the Beanstalk

> Raymond Briggs; *Jim and the Beanstalk*
>
> Walter de la Mare; *Jack and the Beanstalk*
>
> Joseph Jacobs; *Jack and the Beanstalk*

Variations of the Folktale about a Large, Quarrelsome Family

> Ann McGovern; *Too Much Noise*
>
> Margot Zemach; *It Could Always Be Worse*

Variations of the Folktale about the Woman Who Swallowed a Fly

> Pam Adams; *There Was an Old Lady Who Swallowed a Fly*
>
> Steven Kellogg; *There Was an Old Woman*
>
> Alan Mills and Rose Bonne; *I Know an Old Lady*
>
> Nadine B. Westcott; *I Know an Old Lady Who Swallowed a Fly*

Books with Similar Themes

Understanding the Parts Requires Understanding the Whole

> Janina Domanska; *What Do You See?*
>
> Lillian Quigley; *The Blind Men and the Elephant*
>
> John G. Saxe; *The Blind Men and the Elephant*

The Value of Individuality

> Tomie de Paola; *Oliver Button Is a Sissy*
>
> Munro Leaf; *The Story of Ferdinand*
>
> Daniel M. Pinkwater; *The Big Orange Splot*

> Bernard Waber; *You Look Ridiculous Said the Rhinoceros to the Hippopotamus*
>
> Taro Yashima; *Crow Boy*

The Grass Is Always Greener on the Other Side

> Eric Carle; *The Mixed-Up Chameleon*
>
> Liesel M. Skorpen; *We Were Tired of Living in a House*

A Useful Resource for Locating Texts That Are Thematically Similar

> C. W. Lima; *A to Zoo: Subject Access to Children's Picture Books* (R. R. Bowker, 1982)

Books with Similar Structures

Characters Sequenced from Big to Little

> Marie H. Ets; *The Elephant in a Well*
>
> Alexi Tolstoy; *The Great Big Enormous Turnip*

Story Based on Repetition

> Paul Galdone; *The House That Jack Built*
>
> Rodney Peppe; *The House That Jack Built*
>
> Edna Mitchell Preston; *One Dark Night*

Similar Types of Books

"How" and "Why" Stories — Explanations for Natural Phenomena (Narrative "Text Types")

> Verna Aardema; *Why Mosquitoes Buzz in People's Ears: A West African Tale*
>
> Benjamin Elkin; *Why the Sun Was Late* (another version of the previous tale)
>
> Marilyn Hirsh; *How the World Got Its Color*
>
> Rudyard Kipling; *How the Camel Got His Hump; How the Leopard Got His Spots; How the Rhinoceros Got His Skin*
>
> David McKee; *The Day the Tide Went Out . . . and Out . . .*

Factual Accounts (Expository "Text Types")

> Eleanor Boylan; *How to Be a Puppeteer;* and Laura Ross; *Hand Puppets: How to Make and Use Them* (puppets)
>
> Eric Carle; *The Very Hungry Caterpillar;* and Marlene Reidel; *From Egg to Butterfly* (insects)
>
> Ruth Heller; *Animals Born Alive and Well; Chickens Aren't the Only Ones* (animals)

Texts Containing Stories about the Same Characters

> James Marshall; *George and Martha; George and Martha Encore; George and Martha Rise and Shine; George and Martha Tons of Fun*

Lynn K. Rhodes, University of Colorado at Denver

Thematic Reading

Why

Thematic units seek to build understanding of similar ideas found in different reading experiences.

Students learn to analyze similarities and differences in themes, characters, and events through well-designed activities, and critical creative readers are able to synthesize a personal response to the theme and to integrate the theme into their own lives. This process of synthesis is one of the higher forms of thought.

Who

Students in grades 4–6, including less avid readers

How

A thematic unit is simply a reading experience that involves using several books on the same theme. A suggested reading list appears at the end of the activity. Eager readers can be guided toward a few books that approach a theme from many different viewpoints; less avid readers can select books with less disparate viewpoints. After students have read their books, they share their reactions, feelings, and questions in small groups. Then each student selects an activity from the list below.

1. All of the characters are extremely resourceful in handling the tight situations in which they are involved. Construct a master list of those attributes essential to people who are "on their own."

2. Imagine that all of the characters reach their golden age and retire to a condominium development. They all gather on a community porch to brag about, bitterly remember, or thankfully reflect upon events that shaped their lives, problems that they faced, and how they became successful. Write a eulogy for one of the characters.

3. Write a dialogue between the main characters describing the behavior of one character during a certain event. Try to see that character as they would. How do they feel about him or her?

4. Courage comes in many forms, as demonstrated by the different characters. You are going to present an award at a writers' banquet to the author who created the character displaying the most courage. In a written speech you discuss your reasons for your selection.

5. You are a teacher. Each of the main characters is a student in your class, perhaps at a younger age. The characters' behavior in your classroom is similar to the way they behave in the story. Write a report to each student's parents or guardians explaining how some of his or her behavior is acceptable and how some is quite unacceptable.

What Else

1. After students take a close look at the individuality of the characters, an imagined conversation could be written involving all the individual characters in a particular category. Students could develop a discussion around:

> the relationship characters had with other family members and friends
>
> the person who suffered the most
>
> the person who helped others the most
>
> the person who made the biggest discovery
>
> the person whose invention changed the world the most
>
> the best ball player in the Hall of Fame

2. If students read several categories of biographies, a more demanding type of synthesis might be appropriate. All the different types of lives read about could be examined for common threads, as in the following assignments:

   a. Write a descriptive formula for becoming one of history's most notable people.

   b. Have several famous individuals reflect in writing on their accomplishments in light of the course that time and events have taken. (For example, I doubt if Orville and Wilbur had a *747* in mind.)

   c. Use the various categories to develop a hierarchy of most beneficial to least beneficial. Who are the most contributive types of people?

   d. From all the individuals studied, select one and nominate him or her for a special Nobel Prize for historical significance. Below are listed some possible categories and individuals in those categories:

   (1) *Explorers:* Christopher Columbus, Ferdinand Magellan, Admiral Richard Byrd, Meriwether Lewis and William Clark, Roald Amundsen

   (2) *Revolutionary figures:* Patrick Henry, Paul Revere, George Washington, Ben Franklin

(3) *Scientists:* Madame Marie Curie, George Washington Carver, Albert Einstein, Albert Schweitzer

(4) *Inventors:* Alexander Graham Bell, Orville and Wilbur Wright, Henry Ford

(5) *Artists* (music, art, sculpture, literature): Pearl S. Buck, William Shakespeare, Charles Dickens, Elizabeth B. Browning, Wolfgang Amadeus Mozart, Michelangelo

(6) *Sports figures:* Wilma Rudolph, Babe Didrikson, Jim Thorpe, Roger Bannister

(7) *People who have led unusual lives:* Dr. Tom Dooley, Anne Frank, Amos Fortune, Harriet Tubman, Martin Luther King, Jr.

(8) *People who have overcome unusual problems:* Helen Keller, Booker T. Washington, Jim Piersall, Henry D. Thoreau

3. After students have read several biographies in one category, plan activities requiring some analysis. The activities should cause a student to look for examples in the various books that illustrate the theme of the category, such as the following activities.

a. List/discuss/identify essential skills that lead to success in the particular field.

b. What personality characteristics did the individuals possess that contributed to their success?

c. Compare the educational and work experiences of the individuals.

d. What part did fate (accidents, incidents, strange occurrences) play in the development of the individual?

Suggested Reading List

Fantastic Adventuresome Journeys

Lloyd Alexander; *The Book of Three* and sequels
L. Frank Baum; *The Wizard of Oz* and other books in the series, including sequels
Susan Cooper; *The Dark Is Rising* and other books in the series
Roald Dahl; *James and the Giant Peach*
Norton Juster; *The Phantom Tollbooth*
C. S. Lewis; *The Lion, the Witch, and the Wardrobe* and sequels

Animal Stories

Fred Gipson; *Old Yeller*
Jim Kjelgaard; *Big Red*
Sterling North; *Rascal*
Wilson Rawls; *Where the Red Fern Grows*
James Street; *Good-Bye, My Lady*

Youth Alone

Robert Burch; *Queenie Peavy*
Felice Holman; *Slake's Limbo*
Scott O'Dell; *Island of the Blue Dolphins*
Conrad Richter; *The Light in the Forest*
Esther Wier; *The Loner*

Ken Cutts and Patricia Achey-Cutts, Area Education Agency 7, Cedar Falls, Iowa

Literature for Language Study and Play

Why

Children love to play with language. From their earliest ages, children repeat sounds, words, and phrases that they find interesting or funny, and soon they love to make up rhymes, jingles, and jokes. They are fascinated with puns, alliteration, and long, unique words. Teachers observing children engaged in language play can see that these children have developed the ability to stand back and look at language as an object of study. School lessons should be designed so that children find language interesting, fun, and open to discovery — rather than reducing language exploration to prescriptive do's and don'ts, workbooks, drills, and skill exercises.

Who

All elementary students

How

Authors and poets who write for children also enjoy playing with language, and there are many books written for children that focus on language play, puns, jokes, alliteration, the letters of the alphabet, and the sounds of language. It is through the creative energies of these authors that children can build on their own excitement and develop a lasting interest in the study of language. A partial list of children's literature useful for language study and play appears at the end of the activity.

The following description by Don Howard of his second-grade class at Miles School in Tucson, Arizona, illustrates what can happen in a classroom in which these books are used to heighten children's interest in language:

"Did you ever hear of the king who reigned for forty years?"

"What does *reign* mean?" asked Jody.

"Here's a picture, Jody," I said.

The class broke into giggles as I held up the cover of Fred Gwynne's book *The King Who Rained*, which shows the comical king floating in the air with rain pouring from his body. The next fifteen minutes were filled with smiles and laughter as we read about forks in the road, frogs in the throat, and fairy tales. After the first few pages I only read the captions and asked the children to describe what the picture should look like, a feat (feet) my K–3 class did with wonderful imagination and enthusiasm.

The next day we had more of the same with Fred Gwynne's *Chocolate Moose for Dinner.* After reading the second book, I asked if anyone could think of some other examples similar to the ones Fred Gwynne had written.

Silence.

We talked about how much fun it had been playing with the words of Fred Gwynne's books, and I suggested that we could make our own book with sentences like "My nose is running."

I asked again for examples and was greeted with puzzled looks, scrunched brows, wandering eyes, obvious frustration, and more silence. It was time to move on, so I closed with an open invitation for anyone to bring up examples whenever they thought of them. I consigned the invitation to the large stack of classroom ideas that didn't entirely work out. Oh well, I mused, we had a lot of fun with the books. The looks of delight on the faces of the children provided me with one of those golden moments that I will long remember.

A month passed. I was reading from Judith St. George's delightful book *The Halloween Pumpkin Smasher.* Mary Grace Potts and her imaginary playmate, Nellie, were huddled in the back of Mr. Simmons's Model T Ford. I was reading the following section from page 34: "I hoped he wouldn't see Nellie and me. I had never been horsewhipped and didn't want to start now. My knees were apple butter. . . ."

Gabriel raised his hand. *"Horsewhipped,* you know, Mr. Simmons carried a whip made out of horses like the coat made out of arms in the story you read."

It was as if an explosion of understanding took place as the members of the class caught Gabriel's meaning and roared with laughter.

Daniel said, "And he had a Model T car, a little car shaped like a *T.*"

Patrick turned to Gabriel and said, "The car could have a horn, like the horns on a bull, and he could blow on it."

Chester added, "Mr. Simmons was rich and had a lot of dough. You could show him making bread."

Zalman asked, "Have you ever seen people smoking?"

Andrew responded, "I saw people smoking pot. My friend said they were pot-heads."

I couldn't resist adding, "Kids from Miles really know a lot. No! No! No! No!"

Finally Gabriel called out, "What about the story? Read on, it's good." The mood shifted back to the Pumpkin Smasher, but not before Zalman volunteered to be the class recorder so we could make our own book.

Perhaps many lessons that we often dismiss as great tries do convey their messages only after children have time to think through the material and play with it in their minds.

Either the children or the teacher may initiate interest in any particular book, and often there is no need for an immediate extending activity. Before the class discusses the language issues raised by the book, it may be best to let the ideas incubate and to reread the book a week or two later. After the children talk about the book, listen to it being read a number of times, and read it silently, they might be encouraged to produce similar books of their own authored by a single child, a small group, or the whole class. (A small group of children in Don Howard's classroom selected Karla Kuskin's *Roar and More,* shared it with the class, and made a similar book using the sounds of their favorite animals and the sounds of vehicles they heard outside their classroom.) Teachers should discuss a variety of ways for writing such books so that the children's books are not virtual copies of the original. The idea is for children to learn how language can stimulate ideas and to expand on the ideas and creations of others.

There are many alphabet books that are not traditional but that stretch imaginations. The books are predictable to a point and then veer off into uncharted waters to help children think through some new notions about language and how it can be used. *Q Is for Duck* by Mary Elting and Michael Folsom and *Uncle Shelby's ABZ* by Shel Silverstein are two examples.

Homonym study is raised to a delightful level with Fred Gwynne's books, as well as with the *Amelia Bedelia* series by Peggy Parish. The very youngest child in school will love listening to the language in the books and talking about the incongruities in the language offers. As children gain more experience with the books, they will be able to generate their own originals. And once the children become familiar with a large number of these books, they may begin to categorize the books according to the language issues the books explore.

Suggested Reading List

Nicola Bayley; *One Old Oxford Ox*

Sara Brewton, et al.; *My Tang's Tungled and Other Ridiculous Situations*

Marilee Robin Burton; *Aaron Awoke*

Polly Cameron; *I Can't Said the Ant*

Eric Carle; *Catch the Ball*

Tomie de Paola; *Andy: That's My Name*

Fritz Eichenberg; *Ape in a Cape: An Alphabet of Odd Animals*

Mary Elting and Michael Folsom; *Q is for Duck*

Fred Gwynne; *Chocolate Moose for Dinner; The King Who Rained*

Jacquie Hann; *That Man Is Talking to His Toes*

Roger Hargreaves; *Albert the Alphabetical Elephant*

Richard Hefter; *An Animal Alphabet*

Karla Kuskin; *Roar and More*

Arnold Lobel; *The Book of Pigericks; On Market Street*

Betsy Maestro; *Busy Day — A Book of Action Words; Where Is My Friend? A Word Concept Book*

Betsy Maestro, and Giulio Maestro; *Harriet Goes to the Circus: A Number Concept Book*

George Mendoza; *A Beastly Alphabet*

Eve Merriam; *Ab to Zogg*

Jane Miller; *Farm Alphabet Book*

Sal Murdocca; *Grover's Own Alphabet*

Mary O'Neill; *Hailstones and Halibut Bones*

Helen Oxenbury; *729 Merry Mix-Ups*

Peggy Parish; *Amelia Bedelia* and other books in the series.

Ellen Raskin; *Figgs and Phantoms; The Mysterious Disappearance of Leon (I Mean Noel)*

H. A. Rey; *Curious George Learns the Alphabet*

Solveig P. Russell; *Which Is Which?*

Alvin Schwartz; *A Twister of Twists, A Tangler of Tongues*

Dr. Seuss; *On Beyond Zebra!*

Shel Silverstein; *A Light in the Attic* (selected poems); *Uncle Shelby's ABZ*

Peter Spier; *Crash! Bang! Boom!; Gobble, Growl, Grunt*

Robert Tallon; *Zoophabets*

Yetta M. Goodman, University of Arizona, Tucson, and Ann Marek, Department of Human Resources, Sparks, Nevada

Troll Tales: Cumulative Literary Experiences

Why

Cognitive psychologists have demonstrated that the quality of comprehension is determined, to a great extent, by the prior knowledge or schemata that the readers/listeners bring to the text. That is, readers/listeners generate meaning by bringing their knowledge of the world, language, and literature to the text and by building bridges between existing schema or prior knowledge and the new information in the text.

Recent studies of literacy development have also examined the interrelationships between reading and writing. After a review of the findings from correlational and experimental studies on reading/writing relationships, Sandra Stotsky concluded that "reading experience seems to be a consistent correlate of, or influence on, writing ability. Thus, it is possible that reading experience may be as critical a factor in developing writing ability as writing instruction itself." (Stotsky 1983, 637)

Objectives

1. In this activity the children will be invited to respond to each new literary selection in light of previous literary experiences. They will learn strategies for reactivating relevant background knowledge and for making connections between prior literary experiences and present ones, and they will learn to apply these strategies as they read independently.
2. The children will learn to use their literary background as a natural resource for composing their own narratives.
3. The children will move out from literature into drama, art, dance, and music in order to reconstruct or translate literary experiences into other forms of communication.

Who

Students in grades 1–2

How

Building the Literary Background and Making Connections between Diverse Texts

Read aloud *Trolls* by Ingri and Edgar d'Aulaire to introduce children to the world of trolls and their relatives. Ask the children to use the information in this book to generate a list of troll characteristics and habits as well as myths about encounters between trolls and humans. This list is recorded on chart paper, and it serves as the base from which to begin subsequent excursions into the troll world. Place a display table or shelf near the troll chart to hold the collection of troll tales that provide the literary context for this language arts activity sequence. (A suggested reading list of troll tales appears at the end of the activity.) Read several of the books aloud to the class and encourage the children to select one or more of these books to read independently or with a partner.

During the class story sessions, ask the children to consider each new story in light of those read or heard previously. That is, ask them to look for connections between the diverse tales in the troll collection. Guide this search by introducing questions into the class discussion of each story. These questions also serve as a model for self-questioning during independent reading. Below are examples of questions that can be used to stimulate children's comprehension.

1. What troll information found in the d'Aulaires's *Trolls* can also be found in this story?

2. What information is different than that found in the d'Aulaires's *Trolls*? How would you explain these differences?

3. What new information about trolls is included in this story and should be added to our wall chart about trolls and their relatives?

4. Authors have many different ways to tell a story. That is, they have different styles of writing. Compare this story with one or two other troll tales. What is special about the way each tale is told?

5. Artists also have many different ways to illustrate a story. That is, they have different styles of painting, drawing, and so forth. Look at the illustrations in three of the troll tales in our collection. How are they similar or different? Does each artist seem to have a special style?

6. What magic powers do trolls use against human characters?

7. In what ways do trolls respond to those who please them? Which trolls seem to have kind hearts? What clues in the stories help you answer this question?

8. What are some of the tricks used by human characters to outwit troll characters?

9. Which stories teach a lesson? Explain.

In this language arts sequence, the children undergo cumulative literary experiences in which they listen to, read, and compare the troll tales. Then they are invited to compose their own troll tales.

Using Literary Background as a Context for Composition

In preparation for the writing experience, invite the children to study the wall chart while one child reads aloud what has been recorded about trolls. By this time new items have been added to the original list, just as the children have been adding to their own growing store of troll knowledge. Then the children briefly review each of the troll tales read by individuals or heard in the group sessions. This review of the troll literature sets the stage for composition by reactivating and organizing information associated with prior reading experiences. The children bring their "troll schema" to the process of composing a troll tale.

To make the children feel comfortable about engaging in this independent writing assignment, reassure them that invented spelling is acceptable in their initial drafts. Some will find that drawing a picture of their story idea prior to translating it into written language is a helpful way to get started. Others will prefer to do the writing first and a picture later. Those whose literacy skills are very limited and who appear threatened by this assignment might dictate their story ideas to you or to an older student for transcription onto paper.

Children who are writing independently may be paired with a partner. During the course of the writing process, writers share their stories-in-progress with their partners and receive feedback. These writing-partner interactions are intended to help the children become aware of their potential readers and to become critical readers of their own writing.

As children complete their first drafts, they meet with the teacher to share their stories and to discuss necessary corrections and revisions. The final stories and accompanying illustrations are bound into individual books and read aloud to the whole class. Each book remains in the troll tale collection on display in the classroom and later is taken home.

What Else

To culminate the troll sequence, invite the children to select one of the tales from the troll collection and to re-create it through drama, dance, music, or art. The children may choose to work independently, with a partner, or with a small group to produce a play, a mural, a puppet show, a dance, a song, a poem, or other form of creative expression that would provide a format for re-creating favorite troll tales.

Work Cited

Stotsky, Sandra. "Research on Reading/Writing Relationships: A Synthesis and Suggested Directions," *Language Arts* 60 (May 1983): 627–42.

Suggested Reading List

Asbjornsen, Peter C., and Jorgen E. Moe. *East O' the Sun and West O' the Moon.* Macmillan, 1953.

Baker, Augusta, ed. *The Golden Lynx and Other Tales.* J. B. Lippincott, 1960. (See "Kari Woodencoat," 19–33)

Berenstain, Michael. *The Troll Book.* Random House, 1980.

Brown, Marcia. *The Three Billy Goats Gruff.* Harcourt Brace Jovanovich, 1972.

d'Aulaire, Ingri, and Edgar P. d'Aulaire. *Trolls.* Doubleday, 1972.

de Paola, Tomie. *Helga's Dowry: A Troll Love Story.* Harcourt Brace Jovanovich, 1977.

Fillmore, Parker. *Shepherd's Nosegay: Stories from Finland and Czechoslovakia.* Harcourt, Brace and World, 1958. (See "The Terrible Olli," 53–63)

Galdone, Paul. *The Three Billy Goats Gruff.* Houghton Mifflin, 1981.

Hatch, Mary C., ed. *More Danish Tales.* Harcourt, Brace and World, 1949. (See "The Seven Stars," 79–87; "The Princess with the Golden Shoes," 88–104; "The Boy Who Was Never Afraid," 182–98; and "The Golden Bird," 214–37)

Haviland, Virginia, ed. *Favorite Fairy Tales Told in Norway.* Little, Brown, 1961. (See "Boots and the Troll," 75–88)

Jones, Olive, and John Bauer. *In the Troll Wood.* Methuen, 1978.

Krensky, Stephen. *A Troll in Passing.* Atheneum, 1980.

Lobel, Anita. *The Troll Music.* Harper and Row, 1966.

McGovern, Ann. *Half a Kingdom: An Icelandic Folktale.* Warne, 1977.

Manning-Sanders, Ruth. *A Book of Ogres and Trolls.* Dutton, 1972. (See "Tritil, Litil and the Birds," 20–31; "John and the Troll Wife," 91–100; "The Troll's Little Daughter," 110–22; "Nils in the Forest," 123–27; "The Gold Knob," 38–43; and "Sigurd the King's Son," 53–65)

Marshall, Edward. *Troll Country.* Dial, 1980. (A beginning reader)

Minard, Rosemary. *Womenfolk and Fairy Tales.* Houghton Mifflin, 1975.

Olenius, Elsa, ed. *Great Swedish Fairy Tales.* Delacorte, 1973.

Stobbs, William. *The Three Billy Goats Gruff.* McGraw-Hill, 1968.

Torgersen, Don A. *The Girl Who Tricked the Troll.* Childrens Press, 1978.

Joy F. Moss, University of Rochester, New York

Survival Unit

Why

1. To improve students' reading and writing abilities by exploring a topic through all subject areas
2. To enhance students' concept development by actively involving them in the learning process from the beginning

Who

Students in grades 4–6

How

This unit involves the study of two or more of the following novels:

> Jean Craighead George; *Julie of the Wolves*
>
> Farley Mowat; *Lost in the Barrens*; also published in paper as *Two against the North*
>
> Scott O'Dell; *Island of the Blue Dolphins*
>
> Armstrong Sperry; *Call It Courage*

The unit lasts approximately three weeks and can be organized in the following ways, depending on the students' interests and the teacher's preference.

1. Four groups of students, each reading one of the novels
2. Two groups of students, each reading a novel from a contrasting region; for example, *Call It Courage* (the tropics) and *Lost in the Barrens* (the arctic)
3. The teacher reads either *Julie of the Wolves* or *Lost in the Barrens;* students read *Call It Courage* and/or *Island of the Blue Dolphins*

The unit described is designed for four groups, each reading one of the novels. Activities may be ordered so that daily plans include the following:

> reading the novel
>
> discussing the novel
>
> concept/label (vocabulary) study
>
> writing an assignment

If the groups are doing different activities at different times, then the teacher will be able to work with each group for part of the time each day. A detailed sequence of activities for this unit follows:

1. The teacher introduces the novels by reading aloud parts of each novel that show the character as lost or alone:

> *Julie of the Wolves,* pp. 5–6
>
> *Lost in the Barrens,* pp. 58–60
>
> *Island of the Blue Dolphins,* pp. 39–40
>
> *Call It Courage,* pp. 21–22

Each of the four groups of students predicts the items that its character will need to survive, and prepares a chart of the predictions. Students then classify the predictions under the basic needs of *food, clothing,* and *shelter* and prepare a second chart.

2. After students read the novels, they work in their groups to select details that reveal what the environment is like. Those details are charted under the headings of *plants, animals, climate,* and *geography.* Each group determines the setting of its novel and draws a map, using latitudinal and longitudinal lines. Next, students select details from the novels that reveal characterization and the plot. They discuss characterization through a list of directed questions and then write their responses to the questions.

3. The teacher demonstrates how to write "lone-thoughts" in the stream-of-consciousness technique, as demonstrated in "Lonethoughts" *(Manspace Teacher's Guide,* Nelson Stimulus Program, 96–100). Students discuss the loneliness of the main characters in the following sections of the four novels:

> *Julie of the Wolves,* end of Part I
>
> *Lost in the Barrens,* chapter 23
>
> *Island of the Blue Dolphins,* end of chapter 8
>
> *Call It Courage,* beginning of chapter 2

Each group dramatizes its character's thoughts. Students also write the character's thoughts in the stream-of-consciousness technique and arrange these thoughts into free verse.

4. To culminate the study of the novels, students work in groups to prepare and present the following:

   a. A list of survival items used by the character, ranked in order of importance. This chart is compared to the initial chart of survival items.

   b. A chart of basic needs and how the character met these needs. This chart is compared to the initial chart of basic needs.

   c. A map of the character's journey, located as accurately as possible.

   d. A drawing or model of the shelter made or used by the character.

   e. A time-line of events in the story.

   f. A mural of the environment.

What Else

1. Students research interesting animals, places, or ideas from the novel. The findings are presented orally, as a poster, or as a written report.

2. Students write another adventure for the main character.

3. Students take on the identity of one of the characters and keep a diary, presenting that character's feelings and his or her perceptions of people and events in the story.

Ruth Leblanc and Diane Schwartz, Edmonton Public Schools, Alberta, Canada

Animal Fantasy: Personification

Why

To acquaint students with the concept of personification

Who

Middle and upper elementary students

How

Many students enjoy reading fantasies that portray animals as having human characteristics. The authors of these works have carefully developed distinct personalities for their animal characters that appeal to youthful imaginations. This technique of creating characters can be a useful tool in constructing literature activities.

Read aloud a story or book, such as those on the suggested reading list at the end of the activity, in which animals take on human characteristics. Discuss personification with students, talking about the animal and human characteristics of the characters in these books.

Invite the children to imagine a new character in which there is a blend of both animal and human characteristics. As an aid to creating such a character, the children may want to make a list of their characters' animal characteristics, human characteristics, and those characteristics that both animals and humans might possess. Encourage them to think about what their new characters look like, are good at, need, like, dislike, and so forth. Once students have developed their characters, they may want to write plays or stories that involve these characters.

What Else

Invite children to draw a picture of their invented characters, perhaps depicting events in their plays or stories.

Suggested Reading List

Michael Bond; *A Bear Called Paddington* and sequels
Kenneth Grahame; *The Wind in the Willows*
Rudyard Kipling; *The Jungle Book*
Robert Lawson; *Ben and Me; Mr. Revere and I; Rabbit Hill*
George Selden; *The Cricket in Times Square*
Margery Sharp; *The Rescuers*
E. B. White; *Charlotte's Web; Stuart Little; The Trumpet of the Swan*

Ken Cutts, Area Education Agency 7, Cedar Falls, Iowa

Folklore from around the World

Why

1. To introduce students to folklore from various countries
2. To provide students with an opportunity to enhance a specific selection through puppetry

Who

All elementary students

How

Read or tell the children a folktale. Introduce other well-known tales by having students brainstorm a list of the folktales or fairy tales they remember from their earlier years. Explain that folklore originates in countries throughout the world and that different versions of the same tale might be told in several countries. You may want to introduce students to specific folklore selections from a country that is being studied in a social studies unit, selections that relate to a particular theme, or selections that are of particular interest to you.

A good reference in selecting folktales is Charlotte S. Huck's *Children's Literature in the Elementary School.* Three folktales I've used are listed below:

> Caroline Feller Brauer; "Fools in Folklore," *Cricket* 8 (April 1981): 20
>
> P. L. Travers; "Abu Kassem's Slippers," *Cricket* 10 (September 1982): 44–49
>
> "The Woman in the Waterpot," *Children's World* (March 1984): 7–9

See the Bibliography for additional titles.

Invite students to form groups and to select a story to perform for the others, using shadow puppets or stick puppets.

What Else

A learning center activity can be designed as a follow-up to this activity. Students review folktales they have heard or read by matching descriptions of characters and events with titles of folktales. Students can help set up the station by writing some of the descriptions that are to be matched with a folktale title.

Work Cited

Huck, Charlotte S. *Children's Literature in the Elementary School.* 3d ed. Holt, Rinehart and Winston, 1979.

Nancy Wiseman Seminoff, Winona State University, Minnesota

Fables and Folktales

Why

To encourage students to go beyond their present levels and boundaries of reading and to read more challenging literature

Who

All elementary students who need to branch out in new directions or who have difficulty going beyond the literal interpretation of a story

How

Invite each student to select and read a fable or folktale. Many of the traditional tales appear in anthologies of children's literature. (See the Bibliography.) Before, during, or after the reading, encourage students to find out, through research, as much as possible about the heritage of the tale, including the country of origin, the event or events prompting the tale, how the tale was handed down from generation to generation, and so forth. The students could report their findings and feelings about their tales in conferences or in writing.

Several students might undertake this project together. They might work individually on the investigation and then compare their findings. Students might analyze two tales from the same country for similarities and differences, or they might compare two tales from different countries. Students could illustrate parts of the tales and make a book depicting their version.

Ask questions that lead the students to critical thinking, such as the following:

What does this remind you of? (images)

How does it make you feel?

What can we learn from this tale?

What do you think it is trying to teach us?

What Else

In order to understand how oral language is transmitted and modified, students could play "Pass It Along." One student secretly tells a story to another student, who tells it to a third student, and so on until all children have heard the story. Ask the first child and the last child to tell their stories aloud, and have the class compare the two versions. It would also be interesting to see how the passage of time affects a story. One student could tell the same story over a period of hours, days, weeks, and months, and the other students could look for changes in the story over time.

*Karen Klepac, West Junior High School,
Columbia, Missouri*

Grow a Unit (From Turnips)

Why

A major underlying principle in planning language arts activities is that we want students to sense the wholeness of language, as one use of language grows naturally from another and leads to yet another. Too frequently, in contrast, children leave elementary school perceiving, albeit unconsciously, that the language arts are a random collection of isolated, unrelated activities. Using a book as a seed, we can grow an array of related activities, emphasizing the connectedness of the various language arts, as parts of a plant are connected to each other. The following description of a teaching unit is provided to show a process that teachers could use with many other books.

Who

All elementary students

How

Begin with an observing and describing activity to help develop children's abilities to use language for these two thinking purposes. A significant way we learn is by seeing how an unfamiliar person, place, object, or experience is like or unlike those we've encountered before. To foster such comparing and contrasting, bring a bunch of turnips, tops and all, to class. Encourage children to use their eyes to note color, shape, size; their fingers to note contrasting texture, resistance; their noses to note the varying smells of roots and greens. Then cut into the turnip so that the children can taste what is probably an unfamiliar vegetable. All the descriptive words students suggest may be listed on the chalkboard in categories according to the sense involved. Help children see that some descriptive words fit into more than one category — for example, some textures can be seen as well as felt. In the process, we are moving from sensory impressions to words, which will later be shaped into factual accounts of the activity.

Maintain the turnip theme by reading aloud *The Three Little Pigs*, a story in which turnips are integral. (I've found useful the versions by Lorinda Cauley and by Erik Blegvad.) Encourage the children to contribute their observations about the story line, the vocabulary used, and the nature of the illustrations. As students listen to each other and observe the teacher recording their comments in a list on the board, they have an opportunity to see the interrelatedness of the language arts. Again we are moving from sensory impressions through oral language into written language, as children may later follow up this step with compositions describing which of the versions they prefer and why.

The Cauley and Blegvad versions of *The Three Little Pigs* are effective since they offer some readily observable differences in language and visuals. There are myriad versions of the story available; in addition to differences in the text and illustrations, some also offer significant plot variations. The two editions recommended here include the trips to pick apples, harvest turnips, and visit the fair, details that are omitted in some other versions. With older children who can read fluently, four or more versions could be used as students meet in small groups to read a version aloud, analyze it, and report back to the entire class.

Include informal classroom drama activities with this unit. Many activities in this story can be mimed: the pigs building their houses, pulling turnips and picking apples, examining the churn maker's booth at the fair, and selecting a churn. There are also plenty of scenes for student-generated dialogues: the distraught mother pig bidding her sons farewell, the devious wolf beguiling the pig into going apple picking, the clever pig explaining his use of the churn to elude the wolf. Follow up the mimes and dialogues by inviting the children to write a narrative to link the scenes together in their own words. Then, put the various scenes in sequence and share the improvised presentations with other children to encourage their observing and listening skills.

What Else

1. Follow a suggestion offered by James Moffet and Betty J. Wagner (1983). In classes of older students, the student observers can take notes during the presentations and then write up their observations as factual accounts.

2. Other oral activities grow naturally: storytelling can follow watching a filmed version of *The Three Little Pigs*. (You might show the animated version by Disney Productions or a film using live animals, available from Cornet Instructional Films.) Let children view the film with the sound turned off, and tape-record their descriptions of the events. Students can illustrate some of the events in the story, working either in groups or individually. Then the illustrations can be shared with younger students while they listen to the taped versions of the tale.

3. Writing experiences evolve easily from this story.

Read the book to the point at which the wolf is threatening to jump down the chimney. Even if the children already know the usual ending, invite them to brainstorm as many other endings as they can think of. Generating ideas can serve as a prewriting experience, and the children can select from these ideas in later compositions. You might have each child choose one of the characters and rewrite the story from the point of view of that character. A group discussion can prepare students for writing these narratives. Some sample questions follow:

> What were the mother pig's misgivings as she sent her children into the world?
>
> How could the first two pigs have been so gullible while their sibling was more aware of what might happen?
>
> Why didn't the wolf anticipate a trap in the chimney?

Recasting a third-person narration into a first-person account helps children become aware of their own ethnocentrism and begin to explore, orally or in writing, the reasons why characters do certain things, how they feel about what they do, and what happens to them.

4. Try a story extension with your class. Invite students to write about what the third pig did the day after dining on boiled wolf. Introduce them to the assignment by asking such questions as "Where did the third pig go the following day? Whom did he meet? What did they do?" Arrange for students to read their stories to children in a younger class. Such cross-grade sharing provides a tangible audience for any writing task. This activity gives older students the opportunity to respond to and write about classic tales a second time, and students in the intermediate grades enjoy tales that they or the teacher might initially consider too juvenile.

5. But such an integrated unit need not be based only on traditional tales. If you're hungry, try growing a unit: lots of books contain seeds. For example, plant *Avocado Baby* by John Burningham in your classroom and see how it grows. It's a thoroughly charming, though somewhat improbable, contemporary tale of a puny baby who gathers extraordinary strength from eating an avocado. Many other children's books provide such organic opportunities as described here. Your language arts program will gather strength as you grow into wholeness from

such books as these and others that you can locate and nurture into a flourishing unit.

Work Cited

Moffet, James, and Betty J. Wagner. *Student-Centered Language Arts and Reading, K–13.* 3d ed. Houghton Mifflin, 1983.

John Warren Stewig, University of Wisconsin–Milwaukee

Section B:
Literature and Experience

Literature Response Logs: Making Meaning, Not Borrowing It

Why

Reading literature reflects experience and is an experience in itself. When the teaching of literature is approached as a meaning-construction process, readers take ownership of interpretation. If readers feel that the "true" meaning must be explicated to them by teachers and literary critics, they may abandon literature, feeling that understanding is beyond their grasp. In this activity young readers can examine their own perspectives in terms of other points of view.

Who

Upper elementary students who think that responses to literature in the classroom involve answering "comprehension questions," writing book reports, or trying to find the teacher's or the author's theme

How

The following activity sequence is used when a group of students reads the same piece of literature. The group can be the entire class or a literature interest group.

1. Each student keeps a reading response log — a notebook with blank pages.
2. The students look at the cover of the book and note its title, author, and illustrator. Then they make predictions about the book in their response logs during a five-minute sustained writing.

3. Ask students to read to a natural stopping point, such as the end of a chapter or scene. Encourage them to write for five to ten minutes on whatever they are thinking about: their feelings about the reading, questions stimulated by the reading, predictions about what they think will happen next, and so on. The following freewriting is in response to *Sweet Whispers, Brother Rush* by Virginia Hamilton. This response was written after a discussion of the scene in which Tree and Dab, the main characters, leave the apartment for the first time. Scenes from outside the apartment had been described, but except for fantasy travels in time, Tree and Dab had not yet left the apartment. Chris, a student described by many as being of "lower ability," suggested that this meant that Tree was growing up and going out into the world. John, another member of the group, thought that this interpretation made sense and elaborated on the idea in his response:

> I think that Tree is confused because she doesn't know her past and is finally realizing that she has needs and wants and is thinking Dab won't be there for her to take care of and that she has to make something of herself and get a little more active and establish some roots to grow with and expand her thoughts and actions till she realizes that nothing is permanent and that life just keeps on going and you can't afford to fall behind in it and she has to stay on top of things and that no one knows the future and that she has to make one for herself.

4. Students' responses are shared. This discussion helps readers get a sense of what others are thinking about the reading as well as demonstrating that the same text evokes a number of different responses. Accept all responses, but ask students to give reasons for their ideas. "I hate this book" is a legitimate response, but it is incomplete without substantiation.
5. Responses will vary in form as the group gets involved with the book. Questions will be raised, characters will take shape, themes will emerge. Specific topics for responses can be assigned to the group (such as a character's motivation for action). The goal is not consensus, but sharing and considering the ideas of others.
6. As a member of the group, the teacher can present a point of view. Students must understand that this is not the "answer." The teacher's new ideas might stimulate a dying discussion or contribute to a lively one.
7. A final synthesis paper might be written about the ideas expressed in the discussion.

What Else

1. After students finish reading the book, they reread their response logs and write a final entry in which they trace their thought processes, focusing on how their perceptions changed as the reading progressed. Talk about these entries and discuss what it suggests to students about the reading process.
2. Students keep response logs on books they read independently.
3. Keep a response log on books you are reading and share the entries with students.
4. Students publish a collection of their responses along with a synopsis of the book for the classroom or school library.

Paul Crowley, Jefferson Junior High School, Columbia, Missouri (adapted from an idea by Ben Nelms, University of Missouri–Columbia)

Tell Me about the Story

Why

1. To stimulate student discussion of books read for pleasure
2. To familiarize students with a variety of novels

Who

Students in grades 3–6

How

As students complete the reading of a novel, poem, or short story, ask them to record the title on a file card. After students have several entries on their cards, the class divides into small groups of four or five members and moves to different parts of the classroom. One student in each group starts the discussion by briefly retelling in his or her own words a story or poem listed on the file card. At any point during the retelling, other group members may ask questions. Often the students compare the characters, plot, or settings with other familiar novels, stories, and poems. Lively small group discussions follow as the students become acquainted with the procedures. Each member of the group has a turn retelling a story. Move around the classroom, joining each group for a short period of time. At the conclusion of the activity, the students form one group and discuss their findings.

Richard E. Coles, Givins-Shaw Public School, Toronto, Ontario, Canada

The Literary Journal

Why

To help students understand what they read and the levels of meaning they encounter

Who

All elementary students who are reading short stories, novels, and plays for class or personal reading

How

The following instructions are given to students for their literary journals:

1. Use your regular class journal, date each of your entries, and try to write in the journal after each reading session.
2. Without being overly concerned with organization, grammar, usage, spelling, punctuation, or other mechanics, write your personal *reactions* and *responses* to the novel or short story. State your thoughts, queries, and feelings on what you read concerning characters, ideas, actions, setting, symbols, plot, theme, and any other aspects of the story that interest you or hold some meaning for you. State what you like or do not like, what you understand or do not understand, what you can identify with, or what seems strange or confusing to you. Hypothesize what may happen or what something means. Draw on personal experiences that connect to the story. It is *impossible* to be wrong in your responses, so be bold, candid, and genuine, allowing your unique writing voice to emerge. Take risks with your responses.
3. *Avoid summarizing what goes on in the story.* Instead, react intellectually and emotionally to what you read; then write about it.
4. Occasionally, you may wish to make a drawing about an idea or cut out items from magazines or newspapers that you think relate to the story. If you wish to quote a section of the story and respond — that's fine; do it.

What Else

1. Suggest lead-in sentences only if necessary. My students have come up with the following:

> I'm completely lost at the beginning because . . . , but I will read more to. . . .
>
> I wonder what . . . means; maybe I'll find out later.
>
> I really don't understand what's going on here because. . . .
>
> I feel that character is just like . . . because. . . .
>
> I remember a time in my life that is similar to this situation in the story; it occurred when. . . .
>
> I can (can't) really understand or identify with what is going on here because. . . .
>
> I know (met) a person just like. . . .
>
> I like this section of writing in the story because. . . .
>
> This section of the story is particularly effective because. . . .
>
> I think the relationship between ——— and ——— in the story is interesting because. . . .
>
> I think this part is weird because. . . .

2. Students could later share their journal entries with groups or the whole class or use their journals to review past readings, to stimulate more formal writing, or to foster discussion in conferences.

Frances E. Reynolds, Rock Bridge High School, Columbia, Missouri

The Fifth Idea

"Well, we've all read *The Great Houdini* now. What did the author want us to know after we read the story?" the teacher, Jan Roberts, asks.

Jerry looks down at his paper; then his hand shoots up. "I think the most important thing was that the teacher cared — really cared — about his student."

Denise shoots back, "Nope, I don't think so. I felt more like the teacher is better and wants to prove it."

"My answer's completely different," Joan announces. "I thought the author was reminding us how dangerous the sea is — that you have to think about that when you're swimming."

"Yes, that makes sense," Roberts agrees. "And you may have been tuned into that because you swim and compete. You know we've talked about how we all bring our personal experiences into our reading."

"I think the author wanted us to know that you can be whatever you want," Matt adds.

After a brief discussion of these differing views, Roberts speaks, but not as teacher/leader, as in a typical classroom discussion. She is not offering students "the correct" interpretation. "You know, I had a different idea," she begins. "I thought it was more about learning about Houdini as a person."

Matt smiles, "So yours is the fifth idea."

"Yes."

The discussion continues with divergent answers to the questions, the teacher offering her viewpoint, but as a "fifth idea."

Ruth Hubbard, University of New Hampshire, Durham

Author! Author!

Why

1. To provide an opportunity for the entire class or for an interested group to study one author and all of his or her works
2. To refine students' language arts skills through self-selected activities

Who

All elementary students

How

The following activity sequence allows students to participate at their own level of interest and ability. Personal life experiences as well as experiences with various language forms should be put to use in these activities.

Assemble the collected works of a favorite author of the children and set up an attractive display in a designated area of the classroom. Accompany the books with any other materials related to the author — biographies, posters, book jackets, pictures, magazine articles, and so forth. On occasion, you might present filmstrips, videocassettes, or films of the author's books or about the author, such as an interview with Irene Hunt or a film describing the work of Ezra Jack Keats.

The activity sequence presented below was designed for fourth-grade students but could be adapted for use with students at other levels.

1. Introduce the activity by reading aloud a representative book or a chapter of a book. Encourage students to discuss the story and the author, and to recall any other books written by the author. Students will select and work at additional activities independently or in groups.

2. From various books, select colorful passages that lend themselves to illustration; type the passages on cards or on sheets of typing paper. Ask each student to read a passage and to assume the role of illustrator. Have a variety of art media available besides markers and crayons, such as paints, construction paper, magazines, wallpaper samples, old greeting cards, and yarn. Display and discuss the completed illustrations.

3. Invite students to make a chart that lists the featured author's books in order of publication. The chart might include book title, copyright date, illustrator's name, publisher, genre, topic, and the number of pages in the story.

4. Encourage students to write a letter telling the author what personal meaning the book held for them. The author's publisher will usually forward such a letter. Students might want to tell the author which of the published works they have read, which was a favorite book, which character they especially liked, and what they enjoyed most about the books. Suggest that students share an opinion or comment on story characters, story events, or the ending and ask for a reply from the author. They might inquire whether an autographed picture of the author is available.

5. Have students make a character study chart for the characters in a particular book. Students list each character on a separate sheet of paper and fill in information for each under the following headings: *physical description, personality description, character's background, relationship to others in the story.*

What Else

1. Ask students to prepare a short selection from a favorite story to read to the class. Suggest that they pick a section that will make others want to read the story for themselves. Tape-record a practice reading, or ask another student to do the taping. Then each student listens to his or her tape while following along in the book. Students keep practicing until the passage sounds smooth. When students are satisfied with recordings, play the final versions to the whole class.

2. Invite students to be pen pals with characters in the stories. They are to write a letter to a character, telling a bit about themselves and explaining what they enjoyed most about the story or how they might have solved the character's problem.

3. Encourage students to be problem solvers. Ask them to select a book and to state in one sentence the main problem or one of the problems. Have them explain how the problem was solved in the story.

4. Invite students to prepare a diary for a character who plays an active role in one story. Have them pretend that they are the character, starting with the beginning of the story and including as many days and events as possible. Students are to prepare a cover for the diary and to put it on display for others to read and enjoy.

Jane A. Romatowski, University of Michigan–Dearborn

Examining Illustrations in Children's Literature

Why

1. To develop students' understanding of picture book illustrations and their relationship to the story
2. To foster students' strategies of observing, comparing, classifying, hypothesizing, organizing, summarizing, applying information, and criticizing
3. To familiarize children with the methods and materials used by picture book illustrators through art experiences with various media
4. To integrate children's personal experiences into themes of picture books
5. To expand students' understanding of book binding and photocopying
6. To develop students' awareness of characterization

Who

Students in grades 1–3

How

For the activities that follow, collect a variety of picture books for children to examine, including such authors and/or illustrators as Ezra Jack Keats, Mitsumasa Anno, Jose Aruego, Marcia Brown, Raymond Briggs, John S. Goodall, Susan Bonners, Ed Young, Peter Spier, Leo Lionni, Gerald McDermott, and Wesley Dennis.

The following sample questions and procedures might be used in the three-week sequence of activities listed below as students examine illustrations in children's literature.

1. Observing
   a. What do you see in this picture that looks real or alive?
   b. What do you see in this picture that was made with paint?
   c. What do you notice in this picture that was not made with paint?
   d. What do you see happening?
2. Comparing
   a. How does this picture resemble that picture?
   b. How is this book like or different from that book?
   c. What changes have taken place in this story, considering the pictures only?
3. Classifying
   a. Would this picture book become one of your favorites? Why or why not?
   b. Is the mood of this story happy or sad? sad and lonely? sad and then happy? sad throughout? happy throughout?
   c. Which colors seem to express the sad parts of the story?
   d. Which colors seem to express a happier theme?
4. Hypothesizing
   a. What do you suppose this story will be about? Why?
   b. What kind of media did the illustrator use? Why do you think that?
   c. What kind of person do you think this character will be? Why?
5. Organizing
   a. Tell in sequence what the artist did to create this story.
   b. Illustrate an important part of the story using any media available.
6. Summarizing
   a. Dictate a summary of the story.
   b. Illustrate the theme of this story.
7. Applying
   a. Use a collage technique to illustrate something you experienced.
   b. Make a collage for one of these themes: a rainy day, playing with friends, a family event, being with animals, the scariest thing, the funniest thing, being lonely, getting hurt, growing, losing something, taking a trip.
8. Criticizing
   a. What do you like or dislike about the artwork in this book? Why do you feel that way?
   b. Do you think the illustrations do a good job of telling or helping tell what the story is about? Why?
   c. What do you think would have been a better technique for the artist to use in illustrating the characters in this story? Why do you think that?

Week One

Share the illustrations from a variety of picture books. Have children tell what materials and techniques they think were used by the illustrators. Then provide materials for painting. The children might want to experiment with tissue paper and water as a medium to create a wash effect on paper. Invite the children to write a story to accompany their paintings. Read aloud *The Snowy Day* by Ezra Jack Keats and discuss the artistic techniques.

Prepare a chart on the chalkboard for listing children's ideas regarding "How a Picture Book Is Made." Have children express their ideas about what tools and materials might be used, what procedures are undertaken by someone who wants to publish a book, and how ideas for stories and illustrations are decided upon. Present the filmstrip and accompanying tape by Weston Wood titled *How a Picture Book Is Made: The Island of the Skog,* which features the book by Steven Kellogg. Then have the children talk about which of their ideas were discussed in the filmstrip and tape. Keep the list posted for future reference and add ideas to it as children's knowledge grows.

Set up a book-binding work area, including such materials as different sizes and types of paper, magazines, wallpaper books, a stapler, yarn, metal rings, and chicken marking bands. Display resource and reference texts about book binding and the publishing industry. Children may bind blank books or may prepare books for specific writing projects. The work area becomes the place to go when other work is completed. If available, bring a spiral book-binding machine into class. After children are familiar with using it, they may want to write about how the machine works.

Share the illustrations in *Louie, Peter's Chair, A Letter to Amy, Goggles* and *Hi, Cat!,* all by Ezra Jack Keats. Have the children brainstorm a list of traits displayed by the characters and encourage them to share personal experiences that involve these traits.

Week Two

Set up a collage work area where children can mix paints, cut out designs found in fabrics, magazines, and wallpaper books, and glue materials to paper to express in pictorial form something they like to do. Invite them to write an accompanying story. Display the collages and ask students to read aloud their stories as the others in the class try to match the text to the picture.

Arrange to use the photocopier in your school. Bring children to the machine in small groups with their collages. Tape-record their comments as they predict what will happen when their illustrations are copied. Later, transcribe the taped comments and display them with the collages and the photocopies.

Read to children Tana Hoban's *Is It Red? Is It Yellow? Is It Blue?* Have children feel objects and materials in the room, and list their comments. Riddle form works well: "It's rough and has a point. It's a ———." Have children write their own books of sensory riddles. Older children may try their hand at writing sensory riddles about objects portrayed in such picture books as *Over in the Meadow* and *The Snowy Day* by Ezra Jack Keats, *Inch by Inch* and *Alexander and the Wind-Up Mouse* by Leo Lionni, *Anansi the Spider* by Gerald McDermott, and *The Very Hungry Caterpillar* by Eric Carle.

Share records and filmstrips of books like *Apt. 3, The Snowy Day,* and *John Henry: An American Legend* (all by Keats) and discuss the effect (or lack of effect) of the music on the story. Have children make instruments, or use available ones in your school, to accompany your reading of *The Winter Picnic* by Robert Welber, *We Came a-Marching . . . 1, 2, 3* by Mildred Hobzek, *Freight Train* by Donald Crews, and a version of *The Farmer in the Dell.* Tape-record each child's reading of a picture book, accompanied by an instrument or sound effects.

Visit the neighborhood library. In preparation, have children write a list of questions to ask regarding illustrators, types of illustrative techniques, standards for judging a picture book, and available resources for reviewing picture books. En route to and from the library, have children make chalk or crayon rubbings of objects they pass. Then cut the rubbings into shapes and invite children to glue the shapes into blank bound books in which they write about their trip to the library.

Week Three

Incorporate picture books into lessons and activities involving a theme or concept your class is studying, such as plants, eggs, sand, weather, or space. Display the books and have children vote for their favorite illustrators. Then bring in other books by the same illustrators and discuss with children the similarities and differences in technique, color, and overall format.

Set up a table containing paper, a pan of water, and two or three colors of enamel oil paint. Have children dribble oil paint into the water, swirl it gently, and lay a sheet of paper on top of the design. Carefully remove the paper by lifting a corner and dry the paper overnight. Then have children write the directions for making their unique designs.

Invite children to make hand silhouettes by placing their hands in front of the light of a projector and to make up a dramatization involving their silhouettes. Then have children cut out a person, some furniture, and a favorite object from black paper. Ask them to write about what the person will do with the object, who the person might be, and where the story is taking place. The cutouts are then arranged and pasted to the marbelized paper described above. (The reverse of this artwork can be produced by having the children make their cutouts out of the marbelized paper and glue these to black paper.)

Examine Leo Lionni's *Swimmy* with the children. Demonstrate how patterns can be repeated in illustrations by dipping such materials as doilies and rubber stamps in ink or watercolors. Let children try the technique and look for pages in *Swimmy* that may have been created in this manner.

Invite the children to make accordion-style books, illustrating each page with an animal that they know something about. Next, ask the children to write a factual piece concerning their animals. Have them share their writings with other students and request editing suggestions. On the final page, the children write a poem or story involving the animal.

What Else

Assemble *Louie, Peter's Chair, A Letter to Amy, Goggles* and *Hi, Cat!*, all by Ezra Jack Keats. Prepare five charts divided into thirds with these discussion headings: 1) *What is the main character like?* 2) *What are three important things he or she seems to be doing?* 3) *Would you like this character to be your friend? Why or why not?* Divide the class into five groups and request that each group choose a scribe who will write the group's responses on the chart. Distribute one chart and one book to each group. Announce that before reading the book the children are to examine each illustration and to discuss what the character is doing. Explain that after the group shares its thoughts about the character, the scribe records the group's responses to the three questions. Each group hangs its chart for the class to examine during the next few days. Later, the groups might switch books, repeat the activity, and then compare their thoughts to the previous group's responses.

Provide time for the groups to discuss personal experiences that were similar to the characters' experiences. Invite the children to write an individual account of what each thinks the group's story was about and to share their writings with other group members. Ask each group to compose a letter to the character telling what the children liked or disliked about the events portrayed, or to write a letter to the illustrator explaining what they think about his or her illustrative style. The class might start an adjective chart for character traits that are admired or disapproved of.

Bonnie Ivener, Albuquerque Public Schools and University of New Mexico

Chapters and Books

Why

1. To foster students' sense of accomplishment at finishing a reading assignment
2. To alleviate students' fear of a lengthy book by reducing it to manageable segments

3. To motivate reluctant and apprehensive readers to read

Who

Reluctant readers

How

Select a popular book of general interest to the class and locate a secondhand or inexpensive copy. (A photocopy might also be used.) Remove the binding from the book, assemble the pages into chapters, and rebind or staple the individual chapters. Each student is responsible for silently reading one chapter. More proficient readers might take longer chapters. If there are enough chapters, take one yourself.

To set the mood for reading, help students provide appropriate background information in an overview of the book. Then students retell their chapters in order and discuss how they knew the appropriate order. The children trade their chapters with other students, which usually happens spontaneously as the events unfold and the students want to read the remaining chapters.

What Else

1. Students write their reactions to the book, focusing on inferences and feelings about the content and their own reading. Group discussion might follow from the written reactions.
2. Students write a song, poem, or play that describes their feelings about the book.
3. Students paint or draw a picture related to the story.
4. In a more formal follow-up assignment, students write an expanded reaction paper that discusses their feelings about the book. Encourage them to consider the steps in the writing process (brainstorming, drafting, revising, editing, publishing). Collect the papers (making sure that no names appear on them) and redistribute them to the class. Each student reads aloud the paper that he or she has been given. Students discuss the papers in light of content, coherence, and use of the writing process, emphasizing the positive aspects of each paper. They discuss the book in relation to each reader's background and what they believe the author's intended meaning is.

Margaret Henrichs, Westminster College, Fulton, Missouri

The Decisions of Literary Characters: Using Flowcharts to Illustrate the Process

Why

1. To combine students' study of computer programming with their study of literature
2. To illustrate the decision-making processes of the major character in a story
3. To offer students a framework for examining how to make decisions
4. To expand children's ability to reason logically: to consider steps, consequences, and possible alternatives

Who

With adaptation, all elementary students who are familiar with basic computer programming

How

Using the flowchart format, the children map out the decision-making process faced by the main character in a recently read story or book. They choose and list in order the significant events of the story. The flowchart can become unwieldy if the children write down every event in the story, so they must select the most important details through group discussion. Also, they must pay particular attention to the sequence of events, especially if the author uses a literary device, such as a flashback.

The children diagram the events of the story on the flowchart and identify the points at which the character must make decisions about his actions. Sometimes the decision-making points are difficult to recognize, particularly when the character has considered only one outcome and has immediately acted. For children to recognize the decision-making point in such instances, they must backtrack to the point where the character first confronted the problem that resulted in his or her choice.

At each decision-making point, the children examine the main character's choices and the consequences of those choices. When appropriate, they discuss alternative choices not considered by the main character and what the consequences of those choices may have been.

There are three important aspects of the strategy: choosing the significant events of the story and listing them in an appropriate order; recognizing the points at which the main character must make decisions; and determining the reasons for and the outcomes of those decisions. The primary focus of the activity is not on flowcharts and programming, but rather on the decision-making process. The flowchart serves as a framework. Figure 2-1 shows a computer flowchart of *King Midas and the Golden Touch.*

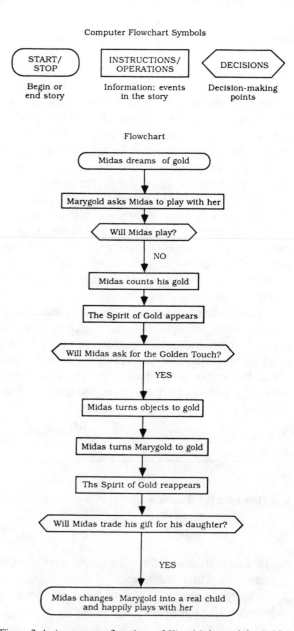

Figure 2–1. A computer flowchart of *King Midas and the Golden Touch.*

What Else

1. Students add to the flowchart by brainstorming other potential decisions that the character might make and by showing on the chart how these decisions might affect the outcome of the story.

2. Students generate the flowchart as they read the story. When the main character reaches a critical decision-making point, the children predict potential decisions and their outcomes. Students then read to find out what decisions the character actually makes.

Lee Ann Sinclair, University of Missouri–Columbia and Stephens College, Columbia, Missouri

Sorting

Why

To provide students with the opportunity to explore a variety of books, including different genres and books for different purposes

Who

All elementary students

How

Gather an assortment of books including folktales, picture books, textbooks, comic books, how-to books, and so on. Invite the children to look at and read through the books. Then have the students begin to categorize the books by asking them, "What kind of book is this? Shall I place the book here with the first book?" Continue discussing and placing books into piles according to the responses of the children.

The children often categorize on the basis of artwork, size, type of story, and use of characters. One second-grade class categorized books as *real with photographs, real with drawings, fantasy with drawings which were like real,* and *fantasy with cartoon drawings.* A kindergarten class labeled the same books as *books with animals* and *books without animals.*

What Else

Read aloud or have children read books from two or more of the categories; discuss the likenesses and differences. Ask students if they could recategorize books. Can one book go in more than one category?

Karen Sabers Dalrymple, Eagle Valley Elementary School, Eagle, Colorado

Understanding Literary Forms

Why

To help students understand literary forms and to discuss their characteristics

Who

Students in grades 2–6

How

Gather and read aloud several writings representative of one genre. Ask students to list some of the general characteristics of the stories or books, keeping the readings available for verification and clarification. Record the students' observations about the genre on a chart. As the year progresses and students have more opportunity to investigate and use the genre, they can add observations to the list. The chart could also include examples of students' writing within the genre.

One day, I asked a second-grade class to list all the story types they knew, and I wrote these on the chalkboard. Then I told the students that I was going to read aloud another type of story. I began reading from a group of fables I had selected. By the time I read the third, Nikki and Charles were ready to respond. "Oh, I get these. They are really short short stories," said Nikki. "Yes," added Charles, "and they have something at the end which you have to figure out what it means." "And it's about life," concluded Nikki.

Within the next few days I read many fables, and the children became more and more eager to talk about the stories and the form. After that, I selected fables occasionally and would sandwich them with many other read-aloud experiences. The students would say, "That's a fable," and would know there was a lesson about life implied in the story.

What Else

Invite the children to apply their knowledge of a particular genre by writing their own examples of the literary form. You will be impressed with the poetry, fables, tales, and so forth that they compose.

Karen Sabers Dalrymple, Eagle Valley Elementary School, Eagle, Colorado

Section C: Extended Literature

Shel Silverstein Is the Poet — I Am the Illustrator

Why

1. To promote an understanding of the relationship between spoken and written language
2. To use a simple drawing activity to demonstrate to students that they have something to say with their illustrations

Who

All elementary students, especially beginning readers who are making the connection between written and spoken language

How

Read aloud Shel Silverstein's poem "Eight Balloons" from *A Light in the Attic*. This poem is fun, predictable, and enjoyable to illustrate — a perfect choice for an activity to help students realize that groups of printed letters called *words* have meaning, just as spoken words have meaning. Encourage students to discuss their reactions to the adventures of the balloons.

Point out that author Silverstein is also the illustrator of this poem. Explain that many books have a separate illustrator. Using favorite books as examples (some with an author/illustrator and others with a different author and illustrator), explain what an illustrator does.

Read the poem again or invite students to do so. Have the class discuss how the poem could be illustrated. Assemble paper, crayons, felt-tip markers, or other appropriate drawing materials. Encourage students to illustrate the encounters of the eight balloons. Each student's drawings are bound into a book along with a copy of the poem and a title page listing Shel Silverstein as author and the student as

illustrator. Students may also include a page on which they dedicate their illustrations.

What Else

Illustrating other poems certainly might follow this activity. Care should be taken in selecting poems that are fun to read aloud and that contain numerous visual images.

Beth Arthur, Carbondale Elementary School District #95, Illinois

Looking at Things in New Ways: Poetry and Nature

Why

Poetry is an excellent medium for promoting close examination. Children carefully examine natural phenomena and then hear poetry that describes these phenomena. Using unusual imagery, the poetry confirms and extends children's original perceptions. Additionally, children develop their linguistic and cognitive abilities as they explore the environment from many different perspectives, using language functionally to accomplish these tasks.

The following activities invite children to hear and respond to a wide variety of poetry, thus experiencing how poets use language to express ideas. Rather than children imitating the form or style of the poetry, the emphasis is on savoring the rhythm, rhyme, and sensory images poetry can evoke. It is only after this observation, exploration, and "playing" with language that students are asked to express themselves in poetic form.

Who

Students in grades 3–6, with adaptation for younger children. Children who have difficulty or lack experience with poetry and writing might require more extensive work with word brainstorming and describing the concrete objects, and might initially prefer writing as a group or with partners.

How

Begin by placing an interesting or unusual object in each of several paper bags. (Possible items to include are rocks with unique textures, shells, particularly pungent smelling herbs, and sandpaper.) Pass each bag around, asking various children to describe the objects without displaying them so that others might guess their identity. Record the descriptive words and phrases. Discuss the various ways each object can be described.

Using books such as *Look Again* and *Take Another Look* by Tana Hoban and *Walk with Your Eyes* by Marcia Brown, ask children to brainstorm words that describe the various natural objects depicted in the photographs. Record their responses on the chalkboard. Discuss the various ways each picture can be described.

Read aloud poetry that describes various objects from nature using unusual imagery. Possible poems to include are "This Is My Rock" and "Tiger Lily" (David McCord), "Pussy Willow" and "Comma in the Sky" (Aileen Fisher), "Setting in the Sand" (Karla Kuskin), "December Leaves" (Kaye Starbird), "The Tree on the Corner" and "Crocus" (Lilian Moore), and "The River Is a Piece of Sky" (John Ciardi). Ask children to associate the images in the poetry with images from their experiences. Have them suggest other ways to describe these objects.

Next, share poetry that focuses on assuming the perspective of the object or animal being described. *Any Me I Want to Be* by Karla Kuskin and *Prayers from the Ark* by Rumer Godden are excellent collections of poems using this theme. Other poems appropriate for this activity include "Open House" (Aileen Fisher), "Reply to the Question: How Can You Become a Poet?" (Eve Merriam), "Chameleon" (Alan Brownjohn), "The Tickle Rhyme" (Ian Serraillier) and "Great Mouse" (Lilian Moore).

Share poems that associate various sensory images with one word. McCord's "Take Sky" and Kuskin's "Worm" and "Take a Word Like Cat" are good examples to use. Then ask children to create group or partner poems, creating as many associations as they can for one word.

Ask children (either individually or as a group) to go outside and collect their own interesting natural objects. Have each choose a favorite and write a detailed prose description of that object, carefully noting small details and distinguishing characteristics. Students who have difficulty moving beyond the obvious might find that the following guidelines help stimulate thinking:

It looks like. . . .

It feels like. . . .

It reminds me of. . . .

Before I found it, it traveled. . . .

It's as big (small) as. . . .

Poems that encourage children to think beyond the obvious include Merriam's "Cliche," "Associations," and "Reply to the Question." Children can use materials available in the classroom to illustrate their objects, paying close attention to detail. They could pretend to become the objects they've examined so closely, and write a poem from the perspective of the objects. (Some children may wish to write riddles and then ask classmates to guess the chosen objects.)

A similar set of activities can be completed using ordinary household and classroom objects like safety pins, buttons, paper clips, pads of paper, erasers, and so forth. Excellent poems that stimulate children to view these objects in new ways include "Flashlight," "New Notebook," and "Clockface" (Judith Thurman), "Safety Pin" (Valerie Worth), and "The Garden Hose" (Beatrice Janosco).

What Else

These ideas can be modified for use in examining other topics in unique ways, such as animals, buildings, and signs of the seasons.

Suggested Reading List

Brown, Marcia. *Walk with Your Eyes*. Watts, 1979.

Brownjohn, Alan. "Chameleon." In *Magic Lights and Streets of Shining Jet*, edited by Dennis Saunders. Greenwillow, 1974.

Ciardi, John. "The River Is a Piece of Sky." In *Piping down the Valleys Wild*, edited by Nancy Larrick. Dell, 1968.

Conkling, Hilda. "Dandelion." In *Piping down the Valleys Wild*, edited by Nancy Larrick. Dell, 1968.

Fisher, Aileen. "Comma in the Sky," "Open House," "Pussy Willow," and "Rain of Leaves." In *In the Woods, in the Meadow and in the Sky*. Scribner, 1965.

Frost, Frances. "Dandelions." In *Time for Poetry*, edited by May Hill Arbuthnot and Shelton L. Root. Scott, Foresman, 1968.

Godden, Rumer, trans. *Prayers from the Ark*. Penguin, 1965.

Hoban, Tana. *Look Again*. Macmillan, 1971.

———. *Take Another Look*. Greenwillow, 1981.

Janosco, Beatrice. "The Garden Hose." In *Reflections on a Gift of Watermelon Pickle*, edited by Stephen Dunning, Edward Leuders, and Hugh Smith. Scott, Foresman, 1966.

Kuskin, Karla. *Any Me I Want to Be.* Harper and Row, 1972.

———. "If I Were a . . ." and "Sitting in the Sand." In *Dogs and Dragons, Trees and Dreams: A Collection of Poems.* Harper and Row, 1980.

———. "Take a Word Like Cat" and "Worm." In *Near the Window Tree.* Harper and Row, 1975.

McCord, David. "Take Sky." In *Take Sky.* Little, Brown, 1961.

———. "This Is My Rock" and "Tiger Lily." In *Piping down the Valleys Wild,* edited by Nancy Larrick. Dell, 1968.

Merriam, Eve. "Associations" and "Cliche." In *There Is No Rhyme for Silver.* Atheneum, 1962.

———. "Reply to the Question: How Can You Become a Poet?" In *Rainbow Writing.* Atheneum, 1976.

Moore, Lilian. "Great Mouse." In *Think of Shadows.* Atheneum, 1980.

———. "The Tree on the Corner." In *I Thought I Heard the City.* Atheneum, 1969.

Serraillier, Ian. "The Tickle Rhyme." In *Magic Lights and Streets of Shining Jet,* edited by Dennis Saunders. Greenwillow, 1974.

Starbird, Kaye, "December Leaves." In *Don't Ever Cross a Crocodile and Other Poems.* Lippincott, 1963.

Thurman, Judith. "Clockface," "Flashlight," and "New Notebook." In *Flashlight, and Other Poems.* Atheneum, 1976.

Worth, Valerie. "Acorn" and "Safety Pin." In *More Small Poems.* Farrar, Straus and Giroux, 1976.

Amy A. McClure, Ohio Wesleyan University, Delaware, Ohio

Walking down the Street

Why

To encourage oral language, as well as reading and writing

Who

Students in kindergarten through grade 4

How

Bring to class a copy of Eve Merriam's poem "When You" from *The Birthday Cow.* Display the poem in a large format so that it can be read individually or as a group. Ask students to read the poem to themselves or aloud together, or read the poem to students. Encourage them to tell about what they meet when they walk down the street. Make a list of their ideas on chart paper and save it for later use.

Help the children become familiar with Merriam's poem through choral and individual readings. Ask them to compare how Merriam's walk is different from their walk. Review their ideas on the chart paper. Discuss possible settings on which students could expand:

How would the sights be different if you were riding in a car, on a bike, in the country, in the city, in a snowstorm, or on Halloween?

What are the sights you might really see walking down Eve Merriam's street?

What might you not see?

Why then did she include these in her poem?

Ask about the author's use of question marks in this poem. Discuss the concepts of reality and fantasy. Have students read the poem trying out various voice inflections to discover why the author chose the particular punctuation that she did.

What Else

1. Invite the children to use the pattern in Merriam's poem to write their own poems.
2. Use the poem in a social studies unit. Ask the children to create poems about children walking down the streets of distant villages and cities. The following two poems by students were written during a unit on Japan.

When you walk down the street,
what do you meet?
A bullet train,
Small red cars,
People walking in the street,
Fish market,
Tatami mats and low tables?
When you walk down the street,
what do *you* meet?

When you walk down the street,
what do you meet?
Different colored light shades,
Thong shoes,
Tatami mats,
Vegetables in gardens,
Kimonos?
When you walk down the street,
what do *you* meet?

Kathryn L. Taigen, Jefferson County R-1 School District, Lakewood, Colorado

Extending Children's Literature across the Curriculum

Why

1. To integrate classroom activities around literature
2. To extend students' frame of reference from their closest immediate experiences and to move through concerns of the classroom, family, neighborhood, community, geographical area, and state to national and larger cultural issues and concerns

Who

With adaptation, all elementary students

How

The teacher uses a web framework to explore the many paths that children might take after studying one work of literature. As the children and teacher work together to make suggestions for the web, the teacher gets immediate feedback on children's reactions to the particular activities suggested.

The web in Figure 2-2 is presented as a way of organizing children's experiences around Mercer Mayer's *What Do You Do with a Kangaroo?* The inner boxes list activities closest to the students' immediate experiences; the outer boxes involve more distant experiences.

Robert C. Wortman, Tucson Unified School District, Arizona

Pasta Potpourri

Why

This strategy orchestrates a variety of experiences across traditional subject-matter areas by integrating the book *Strega Nona* by Tomie de Paola into the curriculum. It provides a multitude of activities in language arts and other subjects, using the book in many different ways over a period of time. The continual repetition and focus on the semantic, syntactic, and graphophonic systems as well as the illustrations provide the teacher with the necessary options for choosing those strategies and concepts that best meet the individual needs of the students.

Who

Primary students; with adaptation, older students

How

Cooking

1. If cooking facilities are available, have students follow a recipe to make their own pasta. Cook the pasta and serve with butter and cheese.
2. Students follow a recipe to make alphabet soup with purchased alphabet pasta.

Math/Science

1. Students are given differing amounts of pasta shapes to make manipulative graphs, pictorial graphs, or abstract graphs.
2. The class works together to gather information on a topic and prepares a graph using pasta to present the findings.
3. The children string colored pasta according to a set pattern (such as red/red/blue, red/red/blue, red/red/blue).
4. Explain the concept of change by boiling pasta. Have students record their observations of the changes as the pasta progresses from rigid to bendable to soft to mushy.
5. As water boils, discuss the cycle of boiling water to steam to water vapor to condensation.

Fine Arts

1. Students use different types of pasta to create pasta collages or pasta people, and then write about their creations.
2. Students listen to "Capriccio Italian" by Peter Ilyich Tchaikovsky and discuss Tchaikovsky's perception of Italy.
3. Small or large groups of children can act out the following verse. Their movements reinforce the science concepts of cooking pasta.

Pasta Play

Be uncooked pasta.
Throw yourself in the pot.
Start to cook.
Start to boil.
Pour yourself on the plate.
Toss yourself with the cheese.
Wrap yourself around the fork.

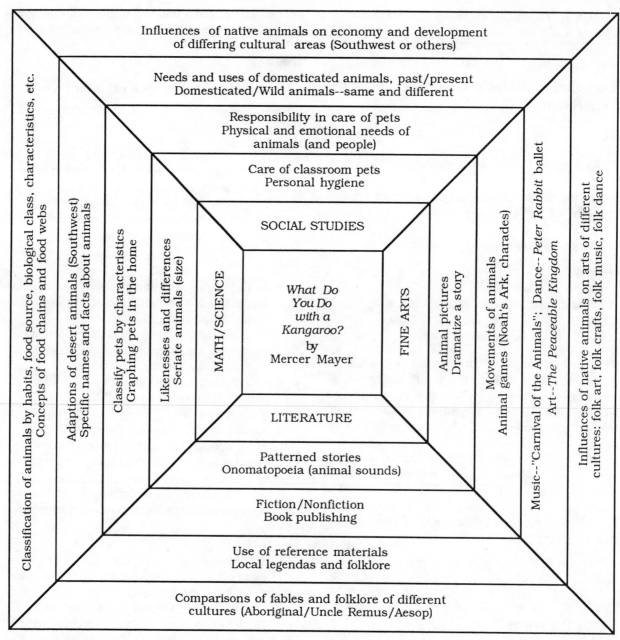

Figure 2–2. Web of activities originating from *What Do You Do with a Kangaroo?*

Get chewed up.
Be swallowed!

Social Studies

1. Discuss and compare the concept of *witch,* including cultural differences in the labels, expectations, and functions of witches.
2. Have students create imaginary potions for different occasions and write about their effects.
3. Discuss folk remedies of different cultures.

Language Arts

1. Children use different types of pasta to write their names or messages.
2. Use the chant below and have children clap,

snap, and slap to the pattern of the chant. Use a chart to emphasize, delete, or exchange specific words to change the rhythm and/or the meanings.

Bubble, Bubble, Pasta Pot

Boil some pasta nice and hot.
I'm hungry and it's time to sup.
Boil enough pasta to fill me up.

Robert C. Wortman and Jackie Wortman, Tucson Unified School District, Arizona

Bag It

Why

To develop listening and discussion skills by synthesizing ideas and writing them as clear, concise clues

Who

All elementary students, especially those in intermediate grades

How

Bring to class a copy of Shel Silverstein's poem "What's in the Sack?" from *Where the Sidewalk Ends* and enough small brown paper sacks to distribute one to each student. Read the poem aloud to the class; then lead students in a discussion of the poem's meaning and some of the items mentioned in the poem. Invite students to brainstorm other ideas and items that could have been in the sack. Write these suggestions on the chalkboard.

Have the class select one of the suggested items and write a class riddle about the item, being careful not to mention the name of the item in the riddle. Display the riddle on the chalkboard or using the overhead. Students now select an item from the list on the board, or choose other items, and write their own riddles. One student wrote the following riddle about a French pastry:

What's in My Sack?

Is it a ball, or is it a mouse?
Is it a poster, or is it a house?
Is it a brown and green tree?
No, it's a treat that's very sweet.

Austin Buchholtz

After the students edit and proofread their riddles, invite them to write their final copies on the paper bags, putting the answer under the folded-up bottom of the bag. Students enjoy reading their riddle bags in class and letting others try to guess the answers. Be sure to display the riddle bags in a prominent, well-traveled area so that students in other classes can read the riddles, make guesses, and check their guesses by peeking under the folded-up bottoms of the bags.

Shirley Terry and Della Fiske-Turner, Littleton Public Schools, Colorado

An Alexander Day

Why

To build student confidence by making connections between children's literature and children's own writing, and by developing a community of writers as the class comes to understand that everyone has Alexander Days

Who

Elementary students who need confidence and who think they have nothing to write about

How

Begin by writing on the board, "Have you ever had an Alexander Day?" To answer the question, read aloud Judith Viorst's *Alexander and the Terrible, Horrible, No Good, Very Bad Day.* Immediately, the children will respond with hilarious tales, their most embarrassing moments, and favorite signals of when it will be an Alexander Day. As the class members listen to their peers, they will laugh, groan, or nod in agreement. For those stories that produce the most response from the listeners, suggest, "That would be a good story to write."

Divide the class into small groups. Ask each group to select an example from the events previously recounted and to write it as the beginning of a whole day of Alexander episodes that might take place at school. For instance, one group might choose to write in response to the following: "What if you had arrived at the bus stop, like Brian did, with your sweater on wrong-side out? You might have the feeling this was going to be one of those days!

What else could go wrong throughout the school day?"

Invite the groups to read their stories aloud to the entire class. Then completely change the mood. Ask the students to relate examples of mornings when they wake up and know it will be a terrific day. Use their replies as beginning phrases, without developing them into full-blown stories. List the phrases on the board or on chart paper.

As children answer the question "When do you know it will be an Alexander-Terrific Day?" their responses may be revealing of their home and of our adult expectations of them. Below are some replies from sixth graders:

> "I know it is going to be a terrific, wonderful, beautiful, very good day when I smell blueberry pancakes for breakfast."
>
> ". . . when my sister stays overnight with a friend and I don't have to yell at her."
>
> ". . . when I have finished all my homework."
>
> ". . . when my baby brother sleeps late."
>
> ". . . when I have my glasses on and no one says, 'Michelle, I told you a hundred times you have to wear your glasses.' "
>
> ". . . when I have art class."
>
> ". . . when my lunch box is heavy."

The children may want to use the phrases as beginnings for their own stories. When given a choice of writing a story about an Alexander-Terrible Day or an Alexander-Terrific Day, many students choose to write both. The edited, published, and bound versions of Alexander Days seldom remain on the class bookshelves. Students keep them circulating.

What Else

1. To generate writing about a variety of settings, children can describe events that take place at the playground, on a typical Saturday, at a relative's house, or at a place in the community such as a fast-food restaurant.
2. To encourage writing from another's viewpoint, students may write stories about an Alexander-Terrific Day or an Alexander-Terrible Day as if they were famous people. Favorite characters selected by children range from Michael Jackson to Ronald Reagan to Larry Bird.

Shirley C. Raines, Northeastern State University, Tahlequah, Oklahoma

Dragons

Why

In this strategy students move from one communication system, such as language, to another communication system, such as drama or art. This allows students to take a new perspective on a text, thus enhancing and deepening their understanding of that text. The new communication system permits students to express new meanings that they were not able to express through language. Thus reading is enhanced by encouraging students to take varying perspectives through art, drama, listening, speaking, and writing. This unit also gives students a background for understanding the significance of the dragon in human experience and literature.

Who

With adaptations for age and interest, all elementary students

How

1. Brainstorm with the students about the word *dragon*. They are to call out anything they currently know about dragons, including the appearance of dragons, their habitats, and famous dragons from literature or movies. Simply list these without comment on a large chart or on the chalkboard. You may want to have students first do a ten-minute freewriting in which they write down everything they know about dragons.
2. Read aloud *Everyone Knows What a Dragon Looks Like* by Jay Williams. In this story, the residents of a city are in desperate need of a dragon to defend them from attackers. However, when the dragon appears in the form of an old man, no one except a small boy is willing to believe that he is the dragon.
3. After reading the story and discussing the image of the dragon in the story, invite students to close their eyes, and take them on an imaginary journey. Tell them that they are being sent into the deep, dark forest by the king to capture a greatly feared dragon. Include much imagery as you describe their journey through the forest and into a cave, where

they encounter the most terrible dragon they have ever seen. At this point, stop your description. Ask the students to open their eyes.

4. Invite the students to use such art materials as pencils, crayons, paint, torn paper, or modeling clay to create the dragon they saw in their minds. An alternative activity is for students to form groups of two or three and to create a dragon from newspapers and masking tape.

5. Have students take a second look at the brainstormed list of words and phrases about dragons. Ask them to add other items and to organize the list into categories. As the students continue to read and write about dragons, encourage them to add new items to categories or to create new categories as needed.

6. Involve students in writing either group or individual stories about the adventures of the dragons they have created. Students might dramatize these adventures as a prewriting activity or after the adventure writing is completed.

What Else

1. Read other stories about unconventional dragons such as *The Dragon of Og* by Rumer Godden, *The Knight and the Dragon* by Tomie de Paola, and *The Dragon Takes a Wife* by Walter Dean Myers. These stories are good for dramatizing.

2. Collect numerous books on dragons and examine the different ways dragons are illustrated. Have students categorize the types of dragons found in these books. Invite them to create murals that illustrate the different types of dragons found in the books.

3. Have students do a comparative study of dragon tales from various countries.

Kathy Gnagey Short, Goshen College, Indiana

Friends Can Help

Why

To stimulate students' flexibility in thinking and imagination in writing

Who

With adaptation, all elementary students

How

Amos and Boris by William Steig is a delightful story about a mouse who is saved by a whale and who is able to repay the favor years later when the whale needs help. Begin reading the story to the students, stopping at the point where Boris the whale rescues Amos the mouse and then swims to the Ivory Coast of Africa. Ask the children to think about how Amos and Boris might meet again, and to write an ending to the story. Invite them to share their endings with one another, and then read the ending of the story written by the author.

The following questions might be asked to stimulate discussion of *Amos and Boris:*

What kind of personality does Boris have? What is Amos's disposition like? How might the outcome of the story change if the characters were different? If you were Boris or Amos, do you think you would have acted in the same way? How do you know?

Does this story remind you of any other story you have read?

What are some of the problems that mice and whales have that people don't have?

Do you think Amos and Boris are real friends? Support your answer.

How would you feel if you were Amos before he is rescued by Boris, or if you were Boris before he is aided by Amos?

The following questions are appropriate for older students:

Examine the thoughts, statements, and opinions of Amos and Boris. Give examples of each and discuss.

What are the incidents in the story that are climactic?

What traits do Boris and Amos have that might cause conflict?

What is the major problem in the story? Is it the same problem or two different problems?

Could the same type of story be told about people instead of a mouse and whale?

What incidents demonstrate that Amos is definitely a risk taker?

What if Amos were prejudiced toward whales or Boris prejudiced toward mice? What effect might this have on their behaviors in a time of need?

What Else

1. Read *The Lion and the Rat* by Jean de La Fontaine. Ask students to discuss how it is similar to *Amos and Boris.*

2. Discuss fables with students, explaining that fables show animals acting like humans and express a moral. Ask students to compare the plot of *The Lion and the Rat* with the plot of *Amos and Boris.*

3. Invite students to write an original fable in which the characters get into a mess and are helped out by each other.

4. Encourage students to read other animal stories in which animals express their emotions and talk to each other. Discuss the concept of personification in literature. Some possible stories are: *Mr. Popper's Penguins* by Richard and Florence Atwater, *Miss Hickory* by Carolyn S. Bailey, *Rabbit Hill* by Robert Lawson, *The Borrowers* by Mary Norton, and *Charlotte's Web* by E. B. White.

5. Invite students to do a simple dramatization of *Amos and Boris.* Some students may want to prepare a tape of sound effects for the story. Share the tape with the class and discuss the sound effects that go with each incident.

6. Invite students to study William Steig's illustrations in *Amos and Boris, Sylvester and the Magic Pebble,* which won a Caldecott Medal, and his other children's books. Have students compare the style in each of Steig's books and compare his illustrations with those of other illustrators.

7. Suggest that someone write a newspaper report or develop a television or radio news brief about the human interest story involving Amos and Boris.

Maryann Manning and Gary Manning, University of Alabama at Birmingham

Alone and Together

Why

1. To encourage students to predict story events
2. To make stories more meaningful by relating them to students' experiences

Who

Primary students

How

Read aloud the beginning of *The 329th Friend* by Marjorie Weinman Sharmat. Encourage children to identify Emery Raccoon's problem and ask them to predict what Emery will do to solve his problem. Then read the end of the story.

During a retelling of the story, invite children to identify and discuss the feelings that they think Emery has at different points in the story. Ask the children to suggest things that they like to do alone, and list these on the board. Make a second list of things that they like to do with other people.

What Else

Invite children to draw a picture of something that they like to do alone and a second picture of something that they like to do with others. Suggest that they write about their pictures and explain whether they prefer the solitary activity or the group activity. The pictures and writings can be shared with other students.

Linda T. Sanders, Horace Mann School, Iowa City Community School District, Iowa

The Making of a Mystery

Why

1. To introduce students to mysteries
2. To encourage students to use mystery books as a model for their own mystery stories

Who

Middle and upper elementary students who are usually reluctant to read different types of books

How

Begin by reading a case (three to four pages) from one of the *Encyclopedia Brown* collections by Donald Sobol. These are well suited to classroom use because they are interesting and entertaining. The students are asked to listen for clues that help them solve the case. Prior to the conclusion of the story, students discuss the clues they spot, and suggest a solution before the ending is read.

Stories should be read for several days as an entertaining, nonthreatening introduction to mysteries. Then invite students to write their own mysteries for the class to solve. Three points to stress with the young writers follow:

1. Begin by making up the mystery to be solved.
2. Include clues in your story. Remember the reader must know everything the detective knows.
3. Have the detective solve the mystery.

Some children may enjoy writing a mystery using established characters. The following cast of characters might be incorporated into the students' mysteries:

> *Shady Sylvester* is a mysterious character who is always trying to trick people. He always wears a disguise and hardly ever wears the same one twice.
>
> *Miss Molly* is a sweet old woman who lives in a large house all by herself. She has all kinds of pets and is friendly to the neighborhood children, but she always seems to be hiding something.
>
> *Calamity Carl* is nice enough but leaves a trail of disaster wherever he goes. Buckets of paint, ladders, signs, and birds have been known to land on his friends.
>
> *Super Sleuth* has the remarkable ability to solve mysteries and is always hot on the trail of the latest crime.

Invite children to use these characters or to create other characters for their mysteries.

Discuss some of the special words or phrases found in mystery stories *(detective, mysterious, weapon, sneakily, vanished, confessed, clever, hidden, major mistake, suspect)* and how these terms help create a mysterious mood.

Encourage students to read aloud their completed stories, and ask the class to suggest solutions to the mysteries.

What Else

Ask the school librarian to inform students of mysteries that are available in the school library. Orally or in writing, students list the title and author's name and present a brief summary of mysteries they have enjoyed. Remind students to give only a brief background without revealing the outcome of the mystery.

Katherine Stroble, Shepard School, Columbia, Missouri

Discussions and Activities

Why

1. To encourage students to enjoy and discuss a humorous fantasy story
2. To help students share insights and opinions about events in the book
3. To have students design and dramatize some scenes related to the story
4. To give students practice at journalistic writing
5. To encourage students to write creative responses to characters and events in the story

Who

Students in grades 3–6

How

This sequence of activities is designed to provide a variety of book-related events. You might wish to select only some of the suggested response activities or to have your students offer suggestions that are more appropriate and suitable. Group discussions might include consideration of the characteristics of this type of fantasy, the style of writing, and the types and uses of humor in this and other stories.

Pique students' interest by writing on the chalkboard or in some prominent place the words *Find out!* Below this, list the following questions:

> Can a chicken be taught to heel?
>
> How high is fifteen feet?
>
> Is there such a place as Hoboken?
>
> Do chickens like french fries?
>
> How much is 266 pounds?

Introduce *The Hoboken Chicken Emergency* by D. Manus Pinkwater and read chapter 1 aloud. Discuss with the children how they think this story will develop. What will happen next? Is this going to be a real story or a fantasy? How can they tell? Next, children might dramatize the scene in which Arthur brings the chicken home to his mother or the dinner-table scene in which Henrietta is the subject of discussion.

Review chapter 1 briefly, and then read aloud or

invite the children to read silently chapters 2 and 3. The follow-up discussion might include consideration of the humor in these chapters and how people react to an unusual event before they know what is really happening.

Invite the children to write the story that the newspaper reporter might write to go along with the pictures he takes. This is a good place to discuss the form of a news article including the *who, what, when, where,* and *why* questions and the pyramid structure.

Review the first three chapters. Read chapters 4 and 5. Discuss the contents of the chapters, including why Henrietta has to be returned, the professor and his unusual animals, and why he leaves suddenly. You might also want to discuss the image of the scientist in our society and how Professor Mazzocchi fits that image.

Invite the children to create their own unusual animals. They are to draw a picture of the animal and to explain why and how it was created, just as the professor explains his rectangular goldfish.

Students could make up and write about another dream that Arthur might have about Henrietta, or students might write a description of Professor Mazzocchi, including what he looks like, how he talks, and what he is like. Ask students to pretend that Professor Mazzocchi keeps a diary about #73 and her problems, including her escape, and to write those diary pages.

Quickly review the previous chapters and read chapters 6, 7, and 8. The class discussion might include some consideration of the city's response to the chicken problem, Arthur's dilemma, and the preparations for Anthony de Palma. Students might take on the role of Henrietta and write about the events of her escape from the professor's apartment and her search for Arthur.

Other students might prepare and deliver a TV news report on the chicken emergency in Hoboken as it might have appeared on the local TV station the night before Anthony de Palma's arrival.

Quickly review the previous chapters and read chapters 9, 10, and 11. Discuss the events, focusing on the character of Anthony de Palma and his plans. Then divide the children into groups and let them plan, rehearse, and act out the scene in the mayor's office when Anthony de Palma makes his bargain with the city officials. An alternative plan might be to let each group create another famous chicken catcher with another idea for catching Henrietta.

Students could dramatize a scene where this character makes a bargain with the city officials.

Review the events from the last few readings and read chapters 12, 13, and 14. The follow-up discussion should include the events of these final chapters, such as who Dr. Hsu Ting Feng is, his plan for capturing Henrietta, the town's "Be Kind to Henrietta" campaign, the return of Henrietta, and the town's celebration. Invite the children to write a proclamation from the mayor of Hoboken to Arthur and Dr. Hsu Ting Feng, which is to be presented along with Henrietta's official license. Students might write another chapter to this story in which they imagine what might happen next to Arthur and Henrietta. Conclude the activity with a class discussion that summarizes the whole story and critiques the book.

What Else

1. Have students find out more about D. Manus Pinkwater and the other books he has written, including *Fat Men from Space, Attila the Pun,* and *I Was a Second Grade Werewolf.*
2. Ask students to prepare a chart showing the action or plot line of *The Hoboken Chicken Emergency.*
3. Select other books and plan comparable activities.

Kathryn E. Loncar, University of Missouri–Kansas City

Discussion, Drama, and Writing

Why

1. To promote the use of literature as a way to enter worlds far beyond the classroom
2. To encourage students to use their imaginations
3. To encourage students to follow reading with discussion, drama, and writing

Who

Middle and upper elementary students

How

Introduce *The Lion, the Witch, and the Wardrobe* by C. S. Lewis, perhaps by reading aloud chapters on a daily basis. Several copies of Lewis's other six books about the land of Narnia could be available in the classroom for students' personal reading. In lively discussions involving large or small groups, encourage students to examine the events of the story and to consider the conflict that takes place between good and evil, comparing it to real-life clashes.

Once the children are familiar with Susan, Peter, Edmund, Lucy, and the other characters, role-playing in character might precede written work. The children can assume roles and meet in small groups to act out a scene from the book. Simulated situations outside of the story give children a chance to create dialogue as a particular character would speak or react.

Drama and writing go hand in hand. Drama can lead to insightful writing, but writing from a character's perspective can also lead to an in-depth dramatic interpretation. The key to any successful experience is allowing the children to talk to each other prior to the writing or drama activity. Children experiment with language as they talk, and these interactions improve the quality of their work.

Children can use their discussions and dramatized situations as a springboard toward writing. *The Lion, the Witch, and the Wardrobe* lends itself well to viewing situations from different perspectives. Children may want to write about a particular incident through the eyes of various characters, perceiving a variety of viewpoints.

What Else

Other fantasy novels might be read and contrasted to the land of Narnia, such as Lloyd Alexander's books of Prydain, Carol Kendall's land of the Minnipins, or Mary Norton's adventures with the Borrowers. Students, working individually or in small groups, could examine and compare the settings, characters, means of entry to that fantasy or imaginary land, and conflicts.

Students might draw maps and chart the journeys of the characters. Some children may choose to illustrate the stories using a variety of available media. A large Aslan could be created using golden yarn. Turkish Delight, an integral part of the story, could be made, and children could dramatize the effects it takes as they eat.

Encourage children to bring together in their imaginations the characters from several fantasies. Depending upon the skills and interests of each child, the characters' interactions could be acted out, illustrated, or recorded in writing. Children could make puppets and put on a play for a younger audience. Invite children to imagine different ways of entering Narnia, other than through the wardrobe, and to write about or act out the adventures.

Susan Lehr, Skidmore College, Saratoga Springs, New York

Z Is for Father

Why

1. To encourage students to brainstorm book themes, to predict story events using pictures and text clues, to recognize patterns in stories, to develop themes, and to make inferences
2. To enhance students' vocabulary development and enjoyment of literature

Who

Younger students; with adaptation, older students

How

Discuss the title of the book *Q Is for Duck* by Mary Elting and Michael Folsom. Encourage students to predict why the title is not *D Is for Duck*. Read the story, pausing after each "Why?" to encourage students to predict the answers. (For example, "M is for cow because it moos.") Note the patterns.

Encourage the children to write their own stories. Point out that *Q Is for Duck* has the theme of animals. Ask students to brainstorm other ideas for a theme. Select one theme and ask the class to write an alphabet story on that theme. Include the children's names if possible. Have students revise, edit, and proofread the story as needed. Write or type the story, putting one letter of the alphabet on the front of each page. Be sure to put the reason for the letter on the back of each page, so that readers will be forced to predict as they read. Ask the children to illustrate each alphabet letter. Alphabetize the pages, make a cover, and bind the pages into a book.

Z Is for Father was the title of a book written by a group of third graders. Why *Z*? Because Father snores! The book was illustrated with *Z*'s coming out of Father's mouth.

What Else

Older students may want to make books individually for younger children.

Theresa Ihde, Owen-Withee Elementary School, Owen, Wisconsin

Adventures in a Hot-Air Balloon

Why

To encourage young readers to become actively involved with a story and to use their imaginations in both oral and written language

Who

Students in kindergarten through grade 2 who are beginning to read and write

How

Read aloud "Bear and Frog" by James Marshall in *Balloons* (Houghton Mifflin Reading Series, 1st grade level) and discuss the events in the story. Invite the children to make small paper hot-air balloons on which they write or dictate a sentence describing the balloon, such as "My balloon is red" or "Balloons can carry people." Pin these to the bulletin board along with photographs of colorful hot-air balloons. Students might also make their own hot-air balloons using nut cups, construction paper, and yarn, including a small passenger if they wish. Hang these balloons around the room from the ceiling. Encourage students to draw a picture about a favorite part of the story and to write or dictate a sentence telling about the picture. Assemble the illustrations in the order of events in the story to make a class book for all to enjoy.

What Else

1. Invite students to write or dictate personal stories about taking a trip in a hot-air balloon. Or each child might write and illustrate a page about what might be seen during the hot-air balloon trip. The pages could be assembled into a class book.
2. Play the record "Up, Up and Away" by the 5th Dimension. Write the words on chart paper so the class can read them aloud together.
3. Fill helium balloons with messages, including the child's name, school, and mailing address, and release the balloons together. While awaiting the return messages, students might write a story about where the balloons land and who finds them.

Jerri Deming, Columbia Public Schools, Missouri

Pooh Bear Visits

Why

1. To familiarize students with a popular work of children's literature
2. To encourage creative writing responses to a character in a story
3. To promote letter writing

Who

Students in kindergarten through grade 3

How

Introduce *Winnie the Pooh* by A. A. Milne by seating a stuffed Pooh Bear in a chair of honor in the classroom. On the board write a letter of introduction from Pooh informing the class that he will be visiting for awhile. Students will respond with many questions and much dialogue, and some will want to tell the class the Pooh stories that they know. Read aloud a favorite Pooh adventure and invite students to bring Pooh books and records from home or the library. Encourage students to write letters to Pooh. (I put a plastic pail under Pooh's chair with the word *Hunny* written on it. All letters went into the Hunny pot to be answered by Pooh Bear helpers — sometimes myself or a student teacher; sometimes other children.)

What Else

The sky is the limit. Pooh visited our classroom for nine weeks. He taught us to make a healthy honey breakfast, honey candy, and a honey snack. We became food critics and came up with adjectives to describe recipes. Pooh wrote the whole class a letter each Monday and individual letters on Friday. We drew Pooh illustrations and wrote stories about our bears. Students brought other favorite stuffed animals to school, making our room an exciting animal land.

Lynne C. Moore, Springfield Public Schools, Missouri

Carole Sue Gile, University of Missouri–Columbia

Idioms — Very Expensive Language

Why

To encourage students' understanding and appreciation of expressive language, particularly idioms

Who

All elementary students who are learning to distinguish literal and inferential interpretations of text, who have limited experience with idioms, or who enjoy wordplay and humorous literature

How

Read aloud *Amelia Bedelia* by Peggy Parish. Have the children discuss the story and the main character's interpretations of language expressions. Ask the students to volunteer idioms that would be humorous if put into a story similar to *Amelia Bedelia*. Similar books could be read to or by the children, further illustrating the meaning implied by idioms. Possible books are Parish's *Good Work, Amelia Bedelia* and *A Chocolate Moose for Dinner* by Fred Gwynne.

Encourage the children to make a list of the idioms most humorous to them. Have them illustrate the literal meaning and then ask others to guess the expression portrayed in the illustration.

The children could write a group story extending the Amelia Bedelia story, or they could create a new story utilizing the idioms they found or recalled. Working individually, children write stories based on their own plots and characters.

What Else

1. Examples of expressive language can be the object of a literature search. The examples found are copied on strips of paper and put in a box. Each child draws a strip from the box, illustrates the expression, and asks the other children to guess what the expression is.
2. The children may enjoy writing and acting out a play based on the fun-with-language concept presented in this activity.

Hatching Eggs and Ideas

Why

1. To use repetitious language and illustrations to enhance students' comprehension
2. To encourage students to make predictions as they read
3. To reduce students' apprehensions about reading by having them read a story in a group

Who

Reluctant readers, beginning readers who are having difficulty with reading and writing, or readers who are just beginning to integrate reading with writing

How

Write the title of the book *The Happy Egg* by Ruth Krauss on the board and read it aloud with the class. Show the book cover to the group and ask if anyone has heard the story. Ask what students believe the book will be about. Read the story as far as "So it got sat on and sat on and sat on and sat on. . . ." Pause and ask students to predict the text on the following page. Continue to read the story, pausing periodically to ask children to fill in a missing word or to predict the next illustration and its text.

Reread the story with the children joining in. Ask them to retell the story. Then discuss what the children already know about hatching eggs. Encourage them to think of clues in the story that indicate how long it takes to hatch eggs, and to remember what the illustrations show. Discuss what birds can do that eggs cannot.

Children may use flannel-board pictures to retell the story to one another. Working individually or in groups, they may write or dictate stories using the same format as *The Happy Egg* to show the development of other creatures, real or imaginary. Encourage children to make and use puppets to act out *The Happy Egg* or their own stories, or interest them in preparing and presenting a dramatized version of *The Happy Egg* to another class. Children might use toy birds encased in Play-Doh or L'Eggs hosiery containers as they retell the story.

What Else

1. Use the factual stories written by the children as additional reading for a science unit.
2. Plan a hunt for real eggs as a field trip. In advance, discuss where various nests are located and why they are not to be disturbed. Ask students to make notes or drawings of their discoveries.
3. When an active nest is visible from the classroom, *The Happy Egg* may spark discussion of comparisons and contrasts to the real nest.
4. Obtain a fertile egg of a reptile or amphibian. Contrast its development with the egg in *The Happy Egg*.
5. Collect various eggs or pictures of eggs and discuss their varying color, size, and texture.
6. Crack open an infertile egg and a fertile egg from hens and ask students to compare the two. Explain that eggs purchased at the store are infertile.
7. Locate factual information about eggs hatching. Ask the children to compare the two types of writing.
8. Plant beans; when they sprout, start incubating eggs and plant additional beans. Students can measure the bean plants on a regular basis and can compare and contrast the development of the animals and the plants.
9. Students prepare illustrations showing the passage of time.
10. Read aloud *Chickens Aren't the Only Ones* by Ruth Heller.

Mary R. Watson, Community Education Center, Columbia, Missouri

I'm as Quick as a Cricket

Why

1. To encourage students' use of oral and written language
2. To help students use their imaginations

Who

Prekindergarten through intermediate elementary students

How

Read aloud the book *Quick as a Cricket* by Audrey Wood. Have the children study the illustrations, which depict a child comparing himself (herself) to various animals. Encourage the children to ask questions for the others to answer, such as:

> How quick is a cricket?
>
> What does a cricket look like?
>
> Have you ever seen a cricket? Where?
>
> How does a cricket sound?
>
> How does a cricket move?

Allow sufficient time for the children to answer questions such as these and to talk about the appearance and characteristics of each animal depicted in the book. Then reread the book with the children joining in.

What Else

1. Read the book aloud again, this time encouraging children to supply the nouns: "I'm as quick as a ———." "I'm as slow as a ———." As the children dictate, write the new story on the board:

> Pete says, "I'm as quick as a fox."
>
> Sally says, "I'm as slow as a turtle."
>
> Tom says, "I'm as small as a mouse."
>
> Jo says, "I'm as large as a house."

Invite them to discuss and dramatize the new comparisons. Everyone then reads the statements aloud together. Recopy the story on paper and duplicate one copy for each student. Students make a cover for their books, and each child illustrates the comparison that he or she supplied. Children take the books home to read aloud to their families. Keep a copy of the story for the class library.
2. Encourage the children to write their own comparison stories in which they become the main character. (See Figures 2-3 and 2-4.)
3. Pantomime "slow as a snail" and ask the children to guess what you are pantomiming. Let them take turns pantomiming one of the animals, either from Wood's story or from the class comparison story.
4. Talk about animals: the way they look, their various sizes, and their different sounds.

Jill Janes, Hannibal Public Schools, Missouri

Figure 2–3. "I'm as sleepy as a baby bird" — Jennifer Roland.

Figure 2–4. "I'm as quiet as a clam" — Selena Wasson.

Chapter 3:
Making Sense by Reading

There is only one way to summarize everything that a child must learn in order to become a fluent reader, and that is to say that the child must learn to use nonvisual information efficiently when attending to print. Learning to read does not require the memorization of letter names, or phonic rules, or large lists of words, all of which are in fact taken care of in the course of learning to read, and little of which will make sense to a child without some experience of reading. Nor is learning to read a matter of application to all manner of exercises and drills, which can only distract and perhaps even discourage a child from the business of learning to read. . . .

. . . Children easily learn about spoken language when they are involved in its use, when language has the possibility of making sense to them. And in the same way children will try to understand how to read by being involved in its use, in situations where it makes sense to them and they can generate and test hypotheses.

— Frank Smith, *Understanding Reading: A Psycholinguistic Analysis of Reading and Learning to Read,* 2d ed., Holt, Rinehart and Winston, 1978, 179–80

The strategies in this chapter will create a literacy environment in which the child can, as Frank Smith suggests, "generate and test hypotheses." The suggestions must never become part of a skill, drill, and fill-in-the-blank routine that forces students through a prescribed reading program. The strategies will help students think and rethink the notions of (to use the words of traditional reading programs) main idea, characterization, context, following directions, sequencing, reading purpose, and all the other skills found in most reading instruction. But unlike most reading programs, these strategies promote the students' construction of meaning within the context of all the systems of language and within the context of what makes sense to them. Students are never asked to pretend that nonsensical materials and activities make sense. In another departure from most reading programs, many activities also involve talking, listening, writing, and thinking.

Section A:
Predictions and Expectations

Predictable Language Books

More and more teachers are selecting "predictable books" for reading instruction. What are predictable books? Why do teachers find them useful?

As our understanding of the reading process increases, predictability is a concept that is replacing the notion of readability. In the past, texts have been both written and selected for children on the basis of such factors as vocabulary difficulty and grammatical complexity, with little consideration of the role of the student in the reading process. For the most part, basal readers continue to be written in this tradition.

Basically, the greater the match between the

knowledge of the reader and the language and content of the text, the more predictable the reader will find the author's message and the form of the message. Goodman (1972) remarks that "A [text] will be easier to read to the extent that what the reader is most likely to predict actually occurs." Predictable texts are those that most closely match a reader's current knowledge of the world and language.

For beginning readers whose knowledge of graphophonics (letter-sound relations) is limited compared to their knowledge of syntax and semantics, various syntactic and semantic characteristics increase the potential of predictability. Such characteristics include familiarity of story, story line, concepts, sequences, repetitive or cumulative patterns, language rhythm and rhyme, as well as congruence between the content of the text and its illustrations (Bridge 1979; Rhodes 1979). Predictable books allow young children to use their syntactic and semantic knowledge at the same time they are increasing their knowledge of how print works, including graphophonics (Bridge et al. 1983; Bridge and Burton 1982). Predictable books allow beginning readers to utilize effective predicting and confirming strategies (Rhodes 1981; Tompkins and Webeler 1983), the same strategies used by proficient readers.

Predictable texts recommended for beginning readers are also useful for those children whose oral language is delayed (Rhodes and Shannon 1982) or is a variant of standard English (Tompkins and McGee 1983). Repeated and assisted reading of predictable texts increases the children's knowledge of language, which in turn increases the potential predictability of a wider range of texts.

Predictability of text is also important in the selection of reading material for use with older children often referred to as "word callers," students who read words without making sense of them.

The teaching ideas that follow will help you understand how predictable texts can be utilized when working with any student who needs more than minimal reading support. As you choose from among the recommended texts, remember that predictability is dependent on the transaction between text and reader; though we can recommend texts that have benefitted the students we've known, *you* must consider the match between each text and *your* students.

Works Cited

Bridge, C. "Predictable Materials for Beginning Readers." *Language Arts* 56 (1979): 503–507.

Bridge, C., and B. Burton. "Teaching Sight Vocabulary through Patterned Language Materials." In *New Inquiries in Reading Research and Instruction,* edited by J. A. Niles and L. A. Harris, 119–23. 31st Yearbook. National Reading Conference, 1982.

Bridge, C., P. Winograd, and D. Haley. "Using Predictable Materials vs. Preprimers to Teach Beginning Sight Words." *Reading Teacher* 36 (1983): 884–91.

Goodman, K. S. "The Reading Process: Theory and Practice." In *Language and Learning to Read,* edited by R. E. Hodges and E. H. Rudorf, 143–59. Houghton Mifflin, 1972.

Rhodes, L. K. "Comprehension and Predictability: An Analysis of Beginning Reading Materials." In *New Perspectives on Comprehension,* edited by J. C. Harste and R. F. Carey, 100–131. Indiana University, Monographs in Language and Reading Studies, 1979.

———. "I Can Read! Predictable Books as Resources for Reading and Writing Instruction." *Reading Teacher* 34 (1981): 511–18.

Rhodes, L. K., and J. Shannon. "Psycholinguistic Principles in Operation in a Primary Learning Disabilities Classroom." *Topics in Learning and Learning Disabilities* 1, no. 4 (1982): 1–10.

Tompkins, G. E., and L. M. McGee. "Launching Nonstandard Speakers into Standard English." *Language Arts* 60 (1983): 463–69.

Tompkins, G. E., and M. Webeler. "What Will Happen Next? Using Predictable Books with Young Children." *Reading Teacher* 36 (1983): 498–502.

Lynn K. Rhodes, University of Colorado at Denver

Sharing Stories with Repetitive Language

Why

1. To give students enjoyable shared reading experiences with highly predictable texts
2. To help students develop a positive feeling about themselves as readers

Who

Students, especially young children, who need to actively transact with print as they make sense of their reading in a relaxed, supportive environment

How

Assemble a collection of predictable books, such as *Brown Bear, Brown Bear, What Do You See?* by Bill

Martin, Jr., *Millions of Cats* by Wanda Gág, *The Very Hungry Caterpillar* by Eric Carle, and old favorites such as *The Three Billy Goats Gruff, The Three Little Pigs,* and *The Gingerbread Man.* (Other predictable books are listed in the Bibliography.) Through sharing these stories, children can discover how an author uses language to develop a story in a way that is quite different from the way they themselves use language.

Read the story *The Three Billy Goats Gruff.* Then reread it, encouraging the children to join in the repetitive parts. Let groups play the parts of different characters. (Some versions of this story print the repetitive parts in different type or color.) As children become familiar with the story, pause in the reading and let them take over.

What Else

1. Invite the children to illustrate a favorite part of the story, which encourages them to retell the story as they recall the events. Sort their illustrations according to the sequence of the story and then glue the artwork to a long strip of paper. As the class views the artwork, invite the children to write or dictate captions about the events depicted. Use different colors for the characters' dialogue, especially the repetitive parts. Display the wall story at eye level so the children can view it alone or with a friend.
2. Read other stories that begin "Once upon a time. . . ." Pause in the story after this opening phrase and ask the children to predict what kind of story it will be and to explain how they know this. Examine the illustrations and invite the children to predict the content and to give reasons for their predictions. Now read the story so they can confirm or disconfirm their predictions.
3. Invite the children to select wood blocks, castanets, drums, tambourines, or other instruments and to accompany a retelling of *The Three Billy Goats Gruff.* For example, a drum beat might be used for the big billy goat as he "trip traps" over the bridge.
4. Ask the children to form groups and to take the parts of the characters in the story. Each group could prepare cue cards of the dialogue, increasing the size of print and exclamation marks for the troll and the big goat. This provides an opportunity to discuss print as you and the children decide what to write and how to write it. Then narrate the story, with each group saying the lines of a particular character.

Brenda Parkes, Brisbane College of Advanced Education, Mt. Gravatt, Queensland, Australia

Readers Should Definitely Predict

Why

1. To stimulate students' imagination
2. To provide a structure for students to use when reading and writing

Who

Students who need the support of predictable language to help them read and to encourage them to write

How

Read aloud the story *Animals Should Definitely* Not *Wear Clothing* by Judi Barrett. Discuss the ways in which animals and people differ, and then invite the children to brainstorm other behaviors that animals shouldn't do. List them on a wall chart or chalkboard under the heading *Animals Should Definitely Not . . . ,* along with the corresponding reason:

> eat at the table — because they are messy.
>
> fly an airplane — because they don't know how.
>
> take a bath — because they don't need it.
>
> sleep in a bed — because they will get the bed dirty.

When the list is lengthy, ask each child to select one *should not* idea and to write about and illustrate it. The papers may be assembled into a class book.

What Else

1. The children could write stories about their own experiences when they helped a pet engage in some "human" activity, such as dressing in clothes or taking a ride in a baby carriage.
2. For further exposure to animals engaged in humanlike activities, read aloud *Corduroy* and its sequel, *A Pocket for Corduroy,* by Don Freeman. Students might want to use classroom art materials to make or illustrate their own Corduroy. Older children might enjoy listening to *Dominic* by William Steig, a hilarious story about the adventures and misadventures of a dog named Dominic.

3. Read the poem "Listen to the Mustn'ts" in *Where the Sidewalk Ends* by Shel Silverstein. Encourage the children to make a list of the *mustn'ts* and *shouldn'ts* that they've been told. Students could trade lists with partners and then discuss the similarities and differences.

4. For students who have a good background of experience but who have difficulty retrieving labels for objects, read a story about a common animal. Change the name of the animal to a nonsense word and ask the students to guess what animal the story is about.

Sarah W. Twaddle, Rock Bridge Elementary School, Columbia, Missouri

Predicting Who Lives There

Why

To encourage students to make reasonable predictions throughout the reading process

Who

Beginning readers who need to understand that reading is an active pastime rather than a passive activity

How

Read aloud *Who Lives There?* by John Hawkinson. Pause after each "I wonder — who lives there?" and encourage students to predict what animal will live in each place. Also encourage students to read with you the repetitive phrase "I wonder — who lives there?" Discuss other places where animals could live, and make a list on the board. Talk about why different animals live in different kinds of homes.

What Else

Make copies of the pages containing the descriptions of the places where animals live and the text ending with the phrase "I wonder — who lives there?" Make books for each student with a blank page after each description and invite students to draw pictures of animals that could live in each of these places. Ask for volunteers to announce their animals. Place the completed books in the class library or share with readers in another class.

Sandra J. Kinder, Central Methodist College, Fayette, Missouri

Creating a New Story from Picture Clues

Why

To aid students in predicting language from the content of pictures and in recognizing the relationship between oral and written language

Who

Students who need to become risk takers — who need to realize that they can create a story using such cues as illustrations and their own knowledge

How

Without revealing the printed text, show students the illustrations to a book such as *The Biggest Bear* by Lynd Ward. After students view the first illustration, invite them to dictate or write on their own papers the text to accompany the first page. Ask them to predict what is going to happen next, and record their predictions on the board. Read the text that accompanies the illustration so that students can check the accuracy of their predictions. Students view and discuss the second illustration, again predicting what will happen next. Continue until all the illustrations are discussed and students know the complete story.

Display the illustrations once again and then invite the children to write or to dictate to you or into a tape recorder their own story endings. Children may dislike the author's ending to *The Biggest Bear*, so the story encourages them to create different endings. Children might choose to illustrate their story endings. The written or recorded endings and accompanying illustrations are placed in the classroom library for listening or reading by others.

Kevin Lee Tyler, Indian Oasis Primary School, Sells, Arizona

Selections and Suggestions for Predictable Language Activities

Why

To extend reading by introducing activities involving the other language arts

Who

Kindergartners and primary students

How

Read aloud the predictable books listed below and invite children to partake in the suggested activities.

It Didn't Frighten Me by Janet L. Goss and Jerome C. Harste

1. Print the words on the chalkboard or on chart paper, or make a Big Book (see page 85). Invite students to read along.
2. The class paints a mural of all the characters in the story.
3. Each student makes a paper-plate puppet of one character. Students work in groups to create a puppet play of the story.
4. Each student makes a cut-and-paste picture of a character.
5. Using the authors' pattern, students insert new characters into the story and write new versions. Bind the stories into a class book.
6. Students write about things that might frighten them — or their teacher.
7. Students pretend to be one of the characters in the story and move about the room as that character.

I Was Walking down the Road by Sarah E. Barchas

1. Make a Big Book for a choral reading.
2. Students copy a favorite part of the story on a sheet of paper and illustrate it. Bind the pages into a class book.
3. Using the same pattern, students create a new ending, such as "I was walking down the road/Then I saw a *truck with a load.*"
4. Students brainstorm new language patterns, such as "I was sliding down the hill," "I was shopping with my mom."

The Runaway Bunny by Margaret Wise Brown

1. Children take turns playing the parts of the bunny and the mother and reading aloud their lines in the story.
2. Children make a mural illustrating the various things the bunny wished to become.
3. Students work in groups to prepare three or four illustrations of the story and to tell the story into a tape recorder. Bind their illustrations into a booklet for the listening center.

4. Students brainstorm a list of different things the bunny could be.
5. Children make up a new story using the same pattern.

Where's Spot? by Eric Hill

1. Make a Big Book so students can read along.
2. Children suggest other places Spot could hide. They follow the story format and make up questions for the hiding places, such as "Is he under the bed?"
3. Each child chooses one hiding place and makes a cut-and-paste illustration. Bind the pages into a class or group booklet.
4. Invite students to name some places they have hidden when playing hide and seek. Ask them, "Which places were good for hiding and which were not?" and "If you were the mother dog, how would you feel if you couldn't find your puppy?"
5. Children write or dictate another story using the same pattern, but they change the animal and the hiding places.

Joseph Had a Little Overcoat by Simms Taback

1. Make a Big Book so students can read along.
2. Children list all the things Joseph's overcoat was made into. Each child chooses one item and makes a cut-and-paste picture of it, attaching the caption, "So he made a ———— out of it," and filling in the appropriate word.
3. Students make up a different place for Joseph to wear the item they've illustrated.
4. Children make up a new story by changing the character, piece of clothing, and events. This could be a class effort or an individual book.

Rosie's Walk by Pat Hutchins

1. Invite students to discuss what is happening in this story, who has a problem, and how the problem is solved. Ask them to compare this story with another familiar story in which there is a similar problem.
2. Children use the same plot and suggest different situations Rosie might have experienced on her walk around the farm yard. Record their ideas on chart paper. Each child paints a picture to match his or her new situation. Bind several pictures together into a Big Book.
3. Make an accordion book containing four pages joined together, with each page illustrating an experience on Rosie's walk. The book folds at the seams and opens like an accordion.

B. Gail Heald-Taylor, Waterloo Board of Education, Ontario, Canada

Michael Reads and Writes Predictable Language Books

Why

The story *Brown Bear, Brown Bear, What Do You See?* by Bill Martin, Jr., stimulates writing because the literary form is simple, clear, and definite. The language is appealing for it has a definite rhythm and beat, and the words are predictable and repeated. When students model their writing after a reading selection with these criteria, they do not have to grapple with form, nor concern themselves with plot and character development. Additionally, using repeated language reduces some of the spelling frustrations that children might have.

Who

Students who need the support of predictable language and self-confidence in order to read and write; particularly beginning or reluctant readers and writers

How

One morning in summer school I decided to read my young students *Brown Bear, Brown Bear, What Do You See?* I passed out several copies of the book so that two or three students could share a copy. I began reading, "Brown bear, brown bear, what do you see? I see a redbird looking at me," finishing with "Children, children, what do you see?" At the children's request, I read the story aloud several times and then thought the children were ready to move on to another activity. I knew young children have short attention spans and could not sustain interest in an activity for long periods of time.

How wrong I was. One of the students asked if they could read the book themselves, and the others eagerly agreed. They read together and helped each other figure out words by using whole language and picture clues. Each child was absorbed in the reading task for the next ten minutes.

After storytime came writing time, when the children were to write on a topic of their choice using invented spelling. The children chatted as they usually did while writing, each sharing their thoughts and topic choices with other children at the table. Michael asked if he could write a "brown bear story," and I encouraged him.

Michael took his blank book, turned to the first page, and drew a bear. "How do you write *Brown bear*?" he asked. "Oh, I know. Where's the book?" Michael retrieved the book and then wrote, *Brown bear, brown bear.* "I'm going to leave out this part," he said, pointing to the words *what do you see*? "I'm just going to say it." Then he wrote, *I see a big ship looking at me,* using a space theme for his book.

It took Michael two mornings to finish his "brown bear story." He drew, chatted, brainstormed, looked in other books for the correct spelling of some words he needed, and wrote. When he read his completed story to the entire class, one student spoke for everyone by responding, "I like all of it!"

This example demonstrates how successful predictable books can be in stimulating young children to read and write. The following factors are instrumental in achieving success with these books.

Children select and explore their own topics. The opportunity to select and explore his topic through drawing and talking was an important process for Michael. He discovered what he wanted to say. He couldn't have written with voice unless he knew his topic.

Put mechanics in proper perspective. While drawing, Michael focused on making meaning and communicating, instead of on mechanics.

Integrate language learning. Although writing was the eventual outcome of the lesson, Michael engaged in listening, speaking, and reading activities before he actually wrote. He listened to get a general sense of the selection. He read to internalize how the author used language and form to communicate. He talked to clarify ideas grounded in his own wealth of experiences.

Sharing written work. Michael asked to read his story to the whole class. Through public sharing, he was able to see how his story affected others. Public sharing and public response, especially positive ones, are an impetus for more writing.

Yvonne Siu-Runyan, Boulder Valley Public Schools, Boulder, Colorado

Predictable Language Books for Upper Elementary Children

Why

To use predictable language books to encourage older students to interact with a text

Who

Upper elementary students

How

Because so many predictable language books rely on patterns and repetition or rhyme to tell their tales, they are often characterized as literature most appropriate for beginning readers. Predictability is a concept that can apply readily to older as well as to younger children. Upper elementary students have accumulated experiences with the world and want to read books that reflect their growing sophistication. They no longer need the close support of patterned stories and might complain if they think their reading material is too immature. Predictability, as it applies to older children, will reflect their more mature interests and language and provide them with an ever-widening source of good reading matter. (See the Bibliography for a list of suggested predictable language books for upper elementary students.) Five categories of predictable material for these readers are *life experience, alternate forms, serials, repetitive semantic structures,* and *guessing books.*

Life Experience

When older children read a published story dealing with a topic or issue that reflects their own lives, experiences, or concerns, the book acts much like the language experience stories written by younger readers. Topics such as relationships with parents or other adults, getting along with siblings, peer acceptance, and growing up are certain to find readers who bring both background and curiosity to the stories. The remarkable success of authors like Judy Blume can be attributed to the magnetism the audience feels in reading about people living through experiences similar to those of the audience. For example, a youngster with a demanding little brother will have no problem comprehending how Peter Hatcher (in Blume's *Tales of a Fourth Grade Nothing*) feels. If readers can identify with a protagonist, they can draw on their world knowledge to make inferences or understand motivation. "Higher-level" comprehension skill is little more than the ability to identify with a character or situation, and is a natural by-product of predictability.

Alternate Forms

A story that is first encountered through television, movies, or songs will be familiar to the reader of that story; one encounter provides background for the other. Many teachers avoid this category of predictable books and discourage students from reading or reporting on books based on available TV or movie versions. After all, they argue, how is it possible to be sure that the child has actually *read* the book and not relied only on the other form? There is evidence that children will choose to read these stories because the books are predictable (Bleich 1980), and will use their introductory experience only as a starting point for deepening their comprehension of the story through reading.

Books in a Series

Many young readers get hooked on reading about one character and will read through a series of adventures that features this hero. When a reader becomes familiar with a set of characters and their environment, lives, and problems by reading one book, other books about the characters become predictable. Serial stories are so popular with young readers that they might actually provide a "stage" in literacy development. Adults who have grown up to enjoy reading report that they went through a phase, often in their preteen years, during which they immersed themselves in tales of a literary hero, reading and rereading through long serials. This phase is always remembered as a keenly pleasant time, often among the most treasured memories the adult possesses (Atwell 1980).

Semantically Repetitive Books

When children read, they do much more than gain literal understanding about characters and plots; they also learn how stories are put together (Hansen 1983). Predictability, as it has been described for the beginning reader, is influenced by a repetitive structure as stories are often built on a recurring line or phrase. In a similar way, older children apply their developing internal structures, or schemata, in order to extend predictability across stories within a genre. Readers who classify themselves as sci-fi fans or mystery buffs are actually saying that they have discovered a basic generic pattern that they use not only to make sense out of the story at hand but to predict which stories they will read next. A student who has read and enjoyed one mystery will find the next one readable because the first provided a semantic structure that will be much like the next.

Guessing Books

In its most direct sense, predicting means guessing, and children often show a fondness for playing guessing games with and through language. Many books for older children build in formats that challenge readers to predict outcomes. Bantam Books' *Choose Your Own Adventure* series is a good example of this type of predictable book. In each of these, the readers actually create their own plots by selecting story options at decision points throughout the book. Although each book begins with a caution to the reader not to reread to select alternate paths, it is difficult to read straight through the book; it becomes a game of wits to guess the best path to victory. Other popular guessing books use a "minimystery" format that involves the reader in an active role. The reader is invited to put the clues together in order to solve the mystery and match the detective's ability. Riddles, puns, joke books, and other guessing books appeal to older children.

Works Cited

Atwell, Margaret. *Adult Reading Habits Survey.* Ph.D. diss., Indiana University, 1980.

Bleich, Linda. *A Study of Psychological and Social Characteristics of Adolescence in Adolescent Literature.* Ph.D. diss., Indiana University, 1980.

Hansen, Jane. "Authors Respond to Authors." *Language Arts* 60, no. 8 (1983): 970–76.

Margaret Atwell, California State University–San Bernardino

One-Sided Conversations

Why

To encourage students' interaction with a text by helping them predict what characters are going to say

Who

Students who fail to predict from semantic and syntactic cues

How

Give the student half of a conversation between two people, omitting the dialogue of one of the speakers. A sample one-sided conversation is given below.

> "Hello! Hello! This is Harvey."
> " . . . . "
> "I'm very well, thank you. And you?"
> " . . . . "
> "That's good. I'm glad to hear that because I've a favor to ask of you. . . . Hello?"
> " . . . . "
> "Well, that doesn't sound too friendly. Heh, heh. I'm only kidding."
> " . . . . "
> "Don't be so anxious. I'm about to tell you. I mean, to ask you. It's about that money I borrowed."
> " . . . . "
> "Well, no — I don't exactly have it. But I'm good for it. You know that."
> " . . . . "
> "Very funny. But seriously, just as soon as I get myself together, old buddy. . . . But about that favor — I was wondering, could I ask you for a wee bit more?"
> " . . . . "
> "Fine! I just knew I could count. . . ."
> " . . . . "
> "No, huh. By that, I guess you mean *No.* Well, it just goes to show you who your friends are!"

Invite the student to read the entire discourse before starting the predicting strategy. Then ask the student to read the conversation aloud and to predict the words, phrases, or sentences that would fit or make sense in the conversation.

What Else

1. Use conversations taken from a story that has been read recently. Again omit one side of the

conversation and ask the student to supply the missing dialogue.

2. Play "What If I Had Said This Instead of That" with the student. Ask how his or her responses might change.

3. Have a conversation between animals instead of people. The student again is to supply the missing dialogue.

4. Ask a student to attempt to complete the conversation without reading the entire passage. Stress that students should expect to have to make corrections.

Mary A. Evans, Columbia Public Schools, Missouri

Where Did the Bear Go?

Why

To aid children's language development by having them predict what could happen in a given situation

Who

Students in kindergarten through grade 2

How

Tape bear tracks made from construction paper or posterboard in a path along the floor leading to a window in the classroom. When the students arrive in the classroom, ask them to look at the path of the tracks. Tell them a story, such as the one below, about how the bear got in the room and left the prints.

> Last night after we all went home, the janitor said he heard something walking around in the classrooms. He walked down the hall and looked in our classroom window, and there was a big brown grizzly bear. He became so frightened that he ran back up the hall and shut himself up in the broom closet. He kept waiting for the bear to leave, but he fell asleep and woke up just before school started this morning. He remembered the bear, so he rushed back down the hall. The bear was gone. All the janitor found were these bear tracks and an open window. What could have happened to the bear? What was it doing in our room? Where did it come from?

Let about five students at a time follow the bear path. Ask them to look for clues (such as overturned books and cans of food that you've placed in the classroom). Explain that the clues will help predict what happened to the bear. Each student is to follow the path without talking and to predict what happened. After everyone has followed the path and drawn conclusions, the children volunteer what they think happened to the bear. As they tell their versions, write their predictions on the chalkboard. When everyone has given an opinion, read aloud all the versions. The students might want to read the predictions together a second time.

What Else

Have the class divide into groups to follow the bear tracks and to discuss the clues. Students in each group write a story about what happened to the bear. Compile the stories into a book for the class learning center or the library.

Reference

Rubin, Dorothy. *Teaching Elementary Language Arts.* 2d ed. Holt, Rinehart and Winston, 1980.

Lesia R. Lawson, Bluefield College, Bluefield, Virginia, and Richlands Elementary School, Richland, Virginia

Book-Jacket Predictions

Why

To encourage students to bring their own background of experiences to their reading

Who

With adaptation, all students who need help making predictions about reading material

How

Make copies of book covers or use the actual book jackets, covering up any description or summary of the book that may appear. Hold up or pass around one book jacket. Ask students to tell or write what they think the book is about and to support their predictions. Second-grader Bekah made the following prediction about *You Can't Eat Peanuts in Church and Other Little Known Laws* by Barbara Seuling:

I think that it is about A girl or a boy. That eats peanuts at church. And she or a he isent sasopst to. And he or she prabely does it at other palaes wen ther no saspost to.

Classmate Steven had a longer prediction about *Lost in the Devil's Desert* by Gloria Skurzynski:

I tiank that they were going on a vacashin and all the sudin they went over a clif and then they got out of the car and said What in the heic hapead the girl said we went over a clif then the son said ha dad why don't you fide a gass stashin he said ok then dad left When dad was gone a desrt King Cobra came by every body scremd then the king cobra left every body put a bandeg on there leag then a truck came by and said do you want a ride shire said the son the man who asked the peple if they can have a ride said come on were going to fide a gass stashin so we went to the gass stashin and we saw dad.

the end

Encourage students to compare their predictions. Then read aloud the description given on the inside of the jacket and ask students to compare their predictions with it. Next, read aloud the first chapter so that students can confirm or change their predictions.

What Else

1. Repeat the activity with other book jackets. This time ask students to make their predictions based only on the jacket photographs — cover up the title, author's name, and any descriptive information. Or ask the students to make predictions based on just the title or the name of the author. Talk about how each item provides clues to the content of the story.
2. Have students form groups and then give each student a different book jacket. Each student is to write his or her predictions for that jacket. Students rotate the jackets and make predictions for the other books. When the jackets have rotated around the group, one student reads aloud all the predictions for a single jacket, and the other group members try to match the correct title to the predictions.
3. Reverse the procedure somewhat and ask students to design book jackets for their favorite books. The jackets might be displayed on the classroom door or bulletin board, and other students could predict what the books are about. Encourage the children to obtain copies of the books that interest them and to verify the accuracy of their predictions as they read.

Dorothy J. Watson, University of Missouri–Columbia, and Pamela Thomeczek, Missouri Valley College, Marshall, Missouri

The Case of the Missing Word

Why

1. To encourage students to take risks as they read
2. To interest students in exploring the reading process

Who

Students who are not linguistic risk takers and who feel that they have nothing to bring to the reading process

How

Using a modified cloze procedure, I pass out the following activity to the children, who work individually or with peers to solve the mystery. If students have trouble reading the story, they can underline the difficult words and try to identify them along with the crossed-out words.

The Case of the Missing Word

Jacob is a famous detective. He has solved many important cases. One day, Michele came to see Jacob. She said, "I have a case for you."

Jacob said, "What is it?"

Michele showed Jacob a book. She said, "I wanted to read my book, but my dumb brother crossed out some words. Now I can't read it. Can you help me?"

Jacob said, "Did your brother say anything about the words?"

"Yes," Michele said. "He said it is the same word. He said it is a word he doesn't like."

Jacob said, "I think I can solve this case."

Here's what Jacob saw on page one of Michele's book:

> Hi. My name is Jim.
> I have one brother and one **xxxxxx**.
> My brother is Sam. My **xxxxxx** is Lisa.
> I am ten years old, and my brother is twelve.
> My **xxxxxx** is a baby. She is two.
> I like my brother, but my **xxxxxx** can be
>   a real pest.

What is the missing word? _____

The detective theme allows us to talk about the

clues (or cues) that readers use. Ask students to tell how they could solve the case of the missing word. List their responses on the board and later record them on an ongoing list titled "Reading detectives use clues when they read."

What Else

1. This activity can be repeated by developing a variety of personalized stories requiring different types of cues, including rhymes, first letters, and patterns. "The Case of the Messy Hands" or "The Case of the Sloppy Eater" might involve smudged words. In "The Case of the Torn Page," shown below, words at the end of lines have been ripped from the page.

The Case of the Torn Page

Jacob was a famous detective. He had solved many important cases. One day Michele came to see Jacob. She was holding a book.

"Not again!" Jacob said. "What did your brother do this time?"

Michele shook her head sadly. "This case may be too hard for you," she said.

Jacob said, "*No* case is too hard for me! Tell me about it."

Michele said, "Well, I was reading my book, and that horrible brother of mine tried to grab it right out of my hands. I held on to the book and ran away from him. But he tore one of the pages."

"Let me see the book," Jacob said.

Michele opened the book up to the torn page. She said, "Most of the sentences are missing the last word."

Jacob looked at the torn page. "This may take time," he said, "but I think I can help you read this page."

Here's what Jacob saw on the torn page in Michele's book:

> Ten Little Squirrels
> Ten little squirrels played in a tree.
> The first one said, "What do I see?"
> The second one said, "A man with a
> The third one said, "We'd better ru
> The fourth one said, "Let's hide in
> The fifth one said, "I'm not afraid.
> The sixth one said, "Don't make a sound
> The seventh one said, "He's looking all
> The eighth one said, "Let's run to our n
> The ninth one said, "No, staying here is
> The tenth one sneezed . . .
> "Ker . . . ker . . . ker . . . KERCHOO!"
> Then BANG went the gun,
> And ten little squirrels, how they did

As the missing words are determined for these stories,

continue to develop the list of reading clues. This discussion can be repeated at the finish of other types of strategy lessons as well.

2. Return to the list of reading clues and help students categorize the clues. For example, there are meaning clues (semantic cues), language clues (syntactic cues), graphic or sight clues (letters and forms), and picture clues.

3. Another useful ongoing list for students is titled "When we read and we come to something we don't know, we can. . . ." As students supply endings for this statement, their responses become a list of actual reading strategies, such as "think about what might make sense," "read ahead for more information," and "reread to see if we can gain more meaning."

Debra Goodman, Detroit Public Schools, Michigan

The Sprinkled Script

Why

Practice with a modified cloze procedure can be an effective method for increasing risk-taking behavior in readers with limited vocabularies and readers who are overly dependent on substituting the word *blank* whenever they feel uncertain of a word. However, being faced with blank lines where words are expected may seem unnatural or threatening to some students. It may even seem that the teacher is testing them, as if this were a fill-in-the-blank exam. A reassuring explanation to the contrary may convince readers who are sophisticated enough to grasp the rationale behind a cloze procedure.

Who

Younger or more suspicious students who feel ill at ease with a cloze procedure

How

Write a short play based on the interests and reading abilities of the students who will be using this procedure, or find an appropriate play already in print. Periodically throughout the script, select a predictable word to omit. But rather than having a blank line fill the space, cover the word with a drop of iodine. (Or if the play is written with a felt-tip marker, a drop of water might be sufficient to smear the word.)

Next, tell the students that they are players in an outdoor summer theater and that they have been handed a script that was written in nonpermanent marker. It is starting to sprinkle outside, and wherever a raindrop hits the paper, the marker runs, making the word become a brown splotch. But they are not worried because they know how to ad lib. (This activity should follow previous creative dramatics activities.) Explain to students that any word can be used where they see a splotch, as long as it makes sense and sounds like normal talking. Tell them that the audience in this fantasy hasn't seen the original script and will never know that they are creating dialogue.

What Else

If the students feel comfortable with this activity and are able to ad lib as needed, explain that this same kind of pretending can be a great help to them when they come to unfamiliar words in reading. (They can just pretend that they are in a play and need to ad lib, putting in a word that makes sense and sounds normal.) Provide some supervised practice with oral reading, in which praise and encouragement are given for students' attempts to ad lib difficult words. Then they can be encouraged to use this same strategy in their silent reading.

Margaret Berger, Columbia, Missouri

Jack and Jill Were Risk Takers

Why

To help students become aware of the process of predicting, confirming, and constructing meaning as they read

Who

Young readers who need to be encouraged to become risk takers

How

Use this procedure with the entire class so all children can become comfortable with predicting (taking a risk). Ask students to say various nursery rhymes aloud together. Pick out a favorite, such as "Jack and Jill," and print this on the chalkboard. As you point to the rhyme, say the beginning and let the children fill in the last word or phrase. Pick out other favorites and proceed in the same fashion.

Using the song "Old McDonald Had a Farm," pick out individual children to fill in the animal name. Continue until the children feel comfortable trying this. Then select or write a predictable passage involving a topic or characters that children are familiar with, such as the following:

> Tom and Jerry are my favorite cat and mouse. Often they get into terrible fights. One day Tom was asleep on his favorite rug. Suddenly a loud crash woke Tom up. He saw Jerry hanging by his ———. Tom chased Jerry around the ———. Tom soon tired out and went back to sleep on his ———. Soon Jerry was hanging by his ———. Because they are so funny, Tom and Jerry are my favorite ——— and ———.

Hand out written copies and ask the children to supply the missing words.

What Else

Students might want to write their own stories with missing words, such as the one below:

> One spring morning I wanted to walk to school. I kissed my ——— goodbye. I opened the front ——— and walked outside. I looked up in the big tree and saw a little ——— singing. A dog ——— at me as I walked by. I saw some pretty ——— growing by the side of the road. Just then I felt a drop of rain hit my face. I didn't have my ——— with me so I got wet. I dropped my books and they got ——— too. I started to ——— fast. All at once it stopped ——— and the sun came out. Then I heard the bell ring, and it was time for school to begin. What a fun ——— I had.

Make copies for the other children and explain that they should predict any reasonable response for the blank spaces. Emphasize that many responses will be appropriate, not just one right answer.

After students fill in the blanks, display the text on an overhead projector and ask for volunteers to read their word choices aloud and to indicate how and why they chose these words. Encourage students to discuss the different meanings created by the different choices of words.

Jill Janes, Hannibal Public Schools, Missouri, and Doloris (Dee) Campbell, Columbia Public Schools, Missouri

Section B:
Reading Awareness and Control

Here's What I Do — What Do You Do?

Why

To help students become aware of self-initiated reading strategies

Who

Students who are unaware of the need to adjust speed of reading

How

There are many personal and common strategies readers use to make sense of what is being read. Depending on the complexity of the text and the reader's familiarization with the format, genre, or content, the variety and necessity of reading strategies change. By discussing and comparing the strategies each child uses, students' confidence in using certain strategies will increase. During a reading period or whenever you encounter a text segment that warrants using a specific reading strategy, you might introduce the idea of reading strategies by explaining,

> When I am reading, sometimes I slow down or reread. I do this when I am reading material such as tests or taxes, or when I want to back up or reread parts of a mystery to figure out "who done it." Other times I speed up or read through a hard word in order to keep going and to make sense of what I am reading.

Invite students, in small groups or in the class as a whole, to discuss how and when they vary their reading speed. As students hear about and discuss these strategies, they become more aware of reading strategies available to them.

Richard Thompson, Columbia Falls Elementary, Montana

Going Ahead by Thinking Back

Why

To enable students to use meanings of known words from one part of a passage as an aid in understanding unfamiliar words in succeeding parts of the passage

Who

Middle and upper elementary students who need to sharpen their use of semantic cues in reading in order to assure meaning and to increase rate, and those students who rely too heavily on phonic cues to the detriment of reading for meaning

How

Use passages taken from materials that students have been or will be reading, such as instructional reading materials, literature, content-area materials, newspapers, magazines. These passages should contain words whose meanings students already know but whose written forms may be unfamiliar, or words that students can pronounce but whose meanings are unknown.

Begin by using passages whose content (topic) is familiar to the students. This facilitates using the semantic (meaning) cues that words will convey to them. After students have developed facility in using anaphoric (pertaining to a previous reference) semantic cues in such materials, the teacher can present passages in which the content is less familiar. Whether using passages from published materials or teacher-constructed texts, the words in the passage (except for the word to be identified through semantic cues) should be familiar to the students.

In the following example, the unfamiliar word is *condiments*. The anaphoric semantic cues in the preceding sentence are *mustard, ketchup,* and *relish*.

> At McDonald's, you can get mustard, ketchup, and relish to put on your hamburger. These are the kinds of <u>condiments</u> that most kids like.

In this second example, the unfamiliar word is *astronauts*. The anaphoric semantic cues are *space program, men and women who fly into space,* and *space flights*.

The United States has had an active space program for some time. One of the important factors in the program has been the selection of the men and women who will fly into space. They are selected very carefully and are then given special training. The success of our space flights depends a great deal on these <u>astronauts.</u>

Present one passage at a time. You can use the chalkboard, chart paper, or a transparency for doing group work. Ask the students to read the passage silently, trying to figure out the meaning of the unknown word from other words in the preceding sentences of the passage. Ask volunteers to tell what other words in the passage helped them determine the meaning of the unknown word.

If no one is able to recognize the unfamiliar word, ask students to reread the passage orally, one sentence at a time. Discuss with them what each sentence is about. Then, use their understanding of the sentences to help them arrive at the cumulative meaning of all the sentences (this enables them to "get a handle" on the topic of the passage). Next, ask the students to look for specific words or groups of words that they know and that belong with the topic of the passage. Finally, ask them to use the known topical words to figure out the meaning of the unknown word. In instances in which this closely directed strategy does not result in successful understanding of the unfamiliar word, point out the cue words and show how these preceding words suggest what the unfamiliar word might mean.

What Else

1. For those students who need additional help, provide duplicated passages of texts taken from a variety of sources. Ask the students to circle all the words or word groups that help them determine the meaning of the underlined unfamiliar word in each passage. If students have difficulty locating such semantic cues, discuss the cues in the passage and show how they help identify the unfamiliar word.
2. Ask students to write their own passages in which the last sentence contains a word whose meaning can be figured out by words included in preceding sentences. Students may share their papers with a partner or in a small group, and the other students can try to determine the meaning of the unfamiliar word.
3. Show students passages in which semantic cues appear in sentences *following* the one in which an unfamiliar word appears (cataphoric semantic cues).

Have them go through the same procedures to determine the meaning of the unfamiliar word.

Laura Bursuk, York College, City University of New York, Jamaica

Question the Text

Why

Reading with comprehension involves making predictions, asking questions, and then reading to confirm or negate these predictions. When some students are confronted with especially difficult material, they stop active reading — that is, they stop questioning and stop making associations with their own lives. This strategy encourages questioning and active reading, and can also be helpful as a method of notetaking.

Who

Upper elementary students who are encountering difficult reading material

How

Discuss the reading process with students. One way to do this is to read difficult material aloud and to discuss with students how they can ask questions during the reading. Vary the kind of questions you demonstrate; include statements like "I don't understand the idea of. . . ." Show students how some of these questions can be answered by simply reading further in the selection.

Ask the students to take a piece of paper and to fold it vertically. They are to label one side of the opened page *Questions I have,* and to label the other side of the page *Answers I can give.* At the top of the page, they list the page numbers of the material they will be reading.

Students begin reading the selection. As they come to things they do not understand or have questions about, they jot down questions in the first column. Encourage them to finish the paragraph or page they are reading before jotting down questions, so that their writing will not interrupt the flow of the reading.

After they have finished reading the entire selection, students return to the questions. Now that they have more information, can they answer any of their questions? Can they answer any by looking at another text? Encourage them to answer as many of their original questions as they can.

What Else

Students meet with a partner and trade question sheets. First they attempt to answer any of the questions that stumped their partners. Then the paired students look to see if they have any questions that are the same. If so, it may indicate that the author did not do a good job of presenting the material.

This strategy works well both as a beginning for a discussion and as a way to take notes. The class can discuss similar questions and try to brainstorm answers, which may lead students back into the text or to other resource books. Students could keep their pages as notes for reviewing for tests or as notes for writing future papers.

Carol Gilles, Jefferson Junior High School, Columbia, Missouri

Get the Point? The Author's and the Reader's

Why

Often the expectations of readers do not match the intentions of the author. Students need to know that it isn't a matter of "missing the point," but that their interpretations are valid and might be developed more clearly through discussion with other readers. This discussion may help students recognize the differences and similarities between the intentions of the author and expectations of the reader.

Who

All elementary students who need encouragement in recognizing their own ability to construct meaning from text

How

Have students read a story orally or silently. Encourage them to discuss the events that take place in the story. Write their responses on the board or on the overhead projector. As the list develops, question where each event fits — before or after items already listed.

When the list is complete, pick two events from the list and question the author's intentions. Ask students questions such as the following:

> Why do you think the author chose to put in this event? Why did the author put it in at this point?
>
> Is there anything you want to ask the author about any of these events? Is there something that is not written in the story that you thought might or should happen?

As students talk about the story, encourage them to focus on any difference in their expectations and the author's intentions.

What Else

Students may wish to take notes on the story and use these notes as they write their own takeoffs on the original story. These writings could be shared with other students to see if they as readers get or miss the point.

Richard Thompson, Columbia Falls Elementary, Montana

Purposes for Reading

Why

To give students an awareness of the different purposes for reading

Who

Upper elementary students

How

Collect several articles (ranging from paragraphs to chapters) that contain information about a topic — for example, information about nutrients in vegetables, vegetable gardens, colors of vegetables, and so forth. Make copies of the information for the students and prepare questions related to the reader's purpose for reading the information.

Ask students to read the selections. Then ask, "If you were a scientist, how could you use this information?" Repeat the question several times, substituting *computer analyst, vegetarian, artist,* and so forth for *scientist.* Encourage students to think of all the various people who might read the articles, and to discuss their purposes for reading.

Karen Sabers Dalrymple, Eagle Valley Middle School, Eagle, Colorado

Reader-Selected Vocabulary Procedure (R.S.V.P.): An Invitation to Natural Vocabulary Development

Why

Words are labels for ideas, and an "unknown word" encountered in reading may actually be an unknown label for a familiar, thoroughly understood idea. But many readers, when confronted with such a word, focus on features of the label in an effort to identify or recognize it. In doing so, they neglect both context and their own knowledge, which can often make the underlying idea clear. Such readers need to develop new strategies and to experience the success those strategies afford. The Reader-Selected Vocabulary Procedure (R.S.V.P.) is intended for those readers.

Who

Elementary students whose reader-selected miscues usually include individual words that interfere with their understanding because they have not yet developed effective strategies for dealing with the words

How

Review the directions for Reader-Selected Miscues (see page 218). Before students begin reading, explain that if they encounter any unknown words, they should mark those words with a check and then promptly resume reading. At the end of the reading time, students are to look over what they have read and to make some judgments about the words they have marked. As students read, watch for those who may need a reminder or some encouragement to just mark and keep going. When students have completed the reading, hand out copies of a reading activity sheet, which consists of a sheet of paper that has been divided into four columns headed *Words I Know after Reading, Important Words I'm Not Sure About, My Best Guess,* and *Reference.* This sheet serves as a guide for evaluating the words

students have marked and for discovering an effective strategy for handling unknown words.

Ask students to look back at the words they have marked, and to note first those whose meanings they now know. These words are to be simply listed in the first column, headed *Words I Know after Reading.* The next step is to examine the remaining words, whose meanings are unknown, and to judge whether the words are important to understanding the reading selection. If so, words are listed at the top of the second column, marked *Important Words I'm Not Sure About.* If there are some words that seem less important, students may list them at the bottom of the second column under the heading *Other Words I'm Not Sure About.* Students then jot down in the column labeled *My Best Guess* what they think each word in column two means. The final step is for students to use such references as a dictionary, textbook, atlas, map, globe, encyclopedia, another student, or a teacher to confirm their best guesses. As words are looked up, a check mark is placed in the *Reference* column when the student judges a guess to be "on target." If a guess is incorrect, students enter the correct definition in the *Reference* column in their own words and note its relationship to their best guess. When all the definitions have been verified, students choose one of the words on their lists. Without referring to the activity sheet, they explain to their classmates what the word means.

A follow-up discussion can help students realize that the "mark-it-and-keep-going" strategy of R.S.V.P. pays off in terms of learning new words in an efficient and natural way. Students can also understand that the words labeling key ideas occur repeatedly and in contexts that make these ideas clear, while word meanings that are not made clear by the total context are usually not critical to understanding the selection. By waiting to consult the dictionary or other reference until they complete their reading, students will have a shorter list of unknown words; they will have at least some idea of a word's meaning and will be more apt to understand the dictionary entry.

Over time, students can realize that everyone — even successful readers — is occasionally puzzled by an unfamiliar word. Students can gain the confidence to keep going, to make tentative decisions about meaning that they can modify and refine as the reading progresses. They can become better readers who are more aware of the reading process and whose vocabularies grow as a natural by-product of that process.

Like any strategy lesson, R.S.V.P. should be used often enough for students to develop and gain confidence, but it should not be overused to the point of suggesting to students that the purpose for reading is to learn new words.

John C. Stansell, Texas A&M University, College Station

Schema Stories

Why

1. To convince students that they possess knowledge about the organization of written text and that they should apply this information to the material they are reading
2. To encourage students to become comfortable when reading, to predict the course of the text, and to monitor their own reading

Who

Students in grades 2–6

How

By listening to stories of all kinds, children become familiar with story structure (text schema). As they read stories themselves, they bring their own general frame of reference (personal schema) to each new passage. Select passages that have easily identifiable organizing structures, such as beginning, organizational sequence, plot development, climax, ending. Science, social studies, and math materials may be used as well as stories from newsmagazines such as *Scope, Sprint,* and *Weekly Reader.* Each section must be long enough to give students something substantial to read.

Cut the passage into three to six sections, depending on its length and complexity. Break the story at highly predictable points so that the student will have schematic and semantic support from the text on which to predict what the next section will be.

If working with a small group of children, give one section of the story to each member. Ask the students to read their sections silently and to think about what must have happened before or after that particular excerpt. Encourage them to think about the similarity of the material to other stories or texts they have read. Is it like a science or social studies text, a play, or a fictional story?

Ask who has the beginning section. That student reads the excerpt aloud and explains why it seems like the beginning of the story. (You may want to leave the title on the section.) Other students indicate whether they agree, perhaps suggesting another section as the beginning of the passage. Proceed through the entire passage, with students making and testing predictions and discussing decisions.

What Else

1. Individual students receive all the sections of the passage and then reconstruct the entire text.
2. Duplicate copies of the passage and give each member of the group all the excerpts to reconstruct. Invite the students to compare the order in which they placed the sections. Discuss how students might come up with more than one acceptable organization for a story.
3. Ask each student to prepare a schema story for the group to reconstruct. The passage may be written by the student or taken from a book or magazine. The student determines appropriate places to break the text into sections.
4. Students use the schema-story procedure as a review of the content-area material.
5. Encourage students to compare the organizing structures of fiction and nonfiction works, possibly written on the same topic.

Dorothy J. Watson, University of Missouri– Columbia

Sorting Events of a Story

Why

To determine important and not-so-important parts of a story

Who

Upper elementary students

How

Read aloud a story to the class; then have the students form small groups. Give each group a set of cards on which are written important and not-so-important events of the story. Invite the children to discuss the events and to sort the cards into two piles: important and not-so-important events. Each group reports to the entire class on how it categorized the events, perhaps sharing the most interesting point discussed in the group.

What Else

Students might use the pile of important events to retell the story, arranging the events in proper sequence. Or students might arrange the events from most important to least important. Invite students to prepare their own cards for other stories or for content-area materials.

Karen Sabers Dalrymple, Eagle Valley Middle School, Eagle, Colorado

Whole Text Awareness: Structure of Nonfiction Writing

Why

To help students understand the use of textual prefaces, bold type, titles, subtitles, indexes, content pages, and so forth as a guide to comprehending the text

Who

Upper elementary students

How

Select a chapter in a nonfiction work that students have not read. Ask them to page through the chapter, reading only the bold print. Encourage them to discuss the information they gathered in that perusal. Explain that paging through a text prior to reading it gives them an advantage because the bold print helps develop a framework for the reading. Select another chapter and again ask students to read and to discuss the bold type.

Following this same procedure, have students examine other aspects of the text — chapter titles, subtitles, table of contents, indexes, and so forth. With each aspect, ask students to discuss the information they found and how it helped them understand the text.

Karen Sabers Dalrymple, Eagle Valley Middle School, Eagle, Colorado

The Study of Word Origins

Why

To help students become aware that words are "a language invention of man" (Jacobs 1969, 298)

Who

Middle and upper elementary students

How

Evolution of language

1. Discuss early picture writing and alphabet symbols. Invite children to formulate their own secret code systems to communicate with others.
2. Students engage in classroom or library research to find out what their first names mean. They may want to illustrate the meaning of their names.
3. Students participate in role-playing to understand the reasons that last names came into being. Explain to them that they are to imagine that all the students in the classroom have only first names. They are to develop ways to differentiate between students with the same first names.
4. Next, students research the origin of their surnames, using the library or information from family members. Students may wish to design a coat of arms reflecting the meaning of their surnames.

Countries of Origin

1. Students are invited to cut and paste pictures of their favorite foods. The dictionary or library research will help them discover where the food originated. Older students might make a list of English words that originated in the country of their surnames.
2. A bulletin board game helps students learn the origins of some English words. Place a world map at the center of the board. Students select a picture card from a pocket on the board and match the picture card to a corresponding word card on the board. Students extend a length of yarn from the word card to its country of origin. Older students might use the dictionary to determine the origin,

while younger students could read the place of origin on the back of the picture card.

Creating an Etymological Dictionary

1. Use an overhead projector or chart to display a sample entry in either a standard dictionary or an etymological dictionary. Explain how to read the entry and where to find the explanation of abbreviations. Give students word entry forms on which they are to fill in the following information:

> Word:
>
> Place of origin:
>
> Original meaning:
>
> Does the word mean the same today?
>
> If not, how has the meaning changed?

Working individually or in small groups, students complete an entry form for a particular word.

2. Students complete entries for an etymological dictionary. Younger students might work in groups to organize, by countries, entries that include the word, place of origin, definition, and illustration, if appropriate. Older students might select a word from a box and work individually to complete the entry data. The finished entries can then be compiled into one classroom dictionary.

Associating Countries and Language

1. Students develop a list of foreign languages and a coordinating list of countries in which the languages are spoken.

2. Students locate on a world map the countries in which particular languages are spoken. They might use a length of yarn to connect a card listing the name of the language to the countries where the language is spoken.

3. Students may be introduced to vocabularies of foreign languages by learning how to count or how to say the names for family members, school objects, or body parts.

4. Games such as Bingo, Concentration, and Simon Says may be used to teach foreign languages.

Standard English and Slang

1. Discuss with students standard English and slang. Help them learn to distinguish between the two.

2. List some slang words or phrases on the chalkboard. Invite students to explain the meanings and to speculate how the slang expression began.

3. Students might suggest current slang words and phrases. These are best discussed if presented in a contextual manner.

4. Conclude the study of words and word origins by asking students to coin their own words. Students might present their new words in riddle fashion for others to guess.

Work Cited

Jacobs, Leland B. "Teaching Children More about Words and Their Ways." In *Elementary School Language Arts: Selected Readings,* edited by Paul Clay Burns and Leo M. Schell, 297–304. Rand McNally, 1969.

References

Alexander, A. *The Magic of Words.* Prentice-Hall, 1962.

Childcraft Annual: The Magic of Words. World Book–Childcraft, 1975.

Dale, Edgar, and Joseph O'Rourke. *Techniques of Teaching Vocabulary.* Addison-Wesley, 1971.

Epstein, Samuel, and Beryl Epstein. *The First Book of Words: Their Family Histories.* Watts, 1954.

Hodges, Richard E., and E. Hugh Rudorf. "Searching Linguistics for Cues in the Teaching of Spelling." In *Elementary School Language Arts: Selected Readings,* edited by Paul Clay Burns and Leo M. Schell, 358–66. Rand McNally, 1969.

Sarnoff, Jane, and Reynold Ruffins. *Words: A Book about the Origins of Everyday Words and Phrases.* Scribner, 1981.

Tompkins, Gail E., and David B. Yaden, Jr. *Answering Students' Questions about Words.* ERIC Clearinghouse on Reading and Communication Skills and National Council of Teachers of English, 1986.

Susan M. Jones, Wake County Public Schools, North Carolina

Figurative Language

Why

To encourage students' understanding of figurative phrases or sayings

Who

Upper elementary students

How

Introduce figurative language to students with some common examples, such as "green thumb," "let the cat out of the bag," and "dead as a doornail." Encourage them to think of other common sayings. Students discuss the expressions in small groups and then write the sayings in their own words. The rephrased expressions are read aloud, discussed, and compared.

What Else

1. Present some examples of figurative language, such as the following:

> He who locks himself into the arms of Morpheus promptly at eventide and starts the day before it is officially announced by the rising sun excels in physical fitness, increases in economic assets, and cerebrates with remarkable efficiency.

> It hath been deemed unwise to calculate upon the quantity of junior poultry prior to the completion of proper incubation.

> Plumed bipeds of the same genus and species assemble in multitudes.

As a class, students look up the unfamiliar words and discuss what is being said in each example.
2. Students find or create their own examples of figurative sayings and then work in groups or individually to put the sayings into their own words. Students may choose to illustrate their sayings.
3. Students discuss whether figurative language aids or hinders clarity.
4. Students construct complete sentences containing figurative expressions, such as the following:

> John is not yet dry behind the ears.

> Lillian had two left feet.

> She may be the last rose of summer, but there is a lot of vinegar in her yet.

Students rephrase their own sentences, or they exchange papers and rework their partner's sentences.

Joy Sherard, Rolla Junior High School, Missouri

Introducing the Encyclopedia

Why

1. To help students understand the format and type of information contained in an encyclopedia article
2. To give students practice in obtaining information from encyclopedias
3. To encourage students to summarize information in the form of an encyclopedia entry

Who

Elementary students who are not familiar with the encyclopedia or who have difficulty using it

How

Have the class visit the school library to see different encyclopedias, or bring a variety to the classroom. Discuss with students how encyclopedias are organized and what kind of information they contain. Encourage the children to sample several encyclopedias. Ask students to suggest a subject that they might like to know more about. Read aloud several entries on this topic.

Students then brainstorm their impressions of the way the information is presented in an encyclopedia. The list may include the name of the item, size, where it is found (or habitat), when it started, how it lives, what it eats, and so forth. If the entry is about a person, students might include the name of the person, chronological events in the life of the person, greatest accomplishments, famous sayings, physical description, and so forth. Encourage students to return to the encyclopedias to see if most follow a general pattern or format.

Ask students to choose a topic they know very well and to write about that subject in the format of an encyclopedia entry. Entries are read to classmates for suggested revisions and polishing. The final versions of the entries might be collected and bound as a mini-encyclopedia for the classroom.

What Else

1. If the students' encyclopedia entries are bound in a loose-leaf notebook, additional entries can be added as students learn new information. This gives them an ongoing opportunity to summarize the facts they encounter. The information is readily available to other students, and the encyclopedia becomes a class resource book the following year.
2. Students enjoy comparing their entries to those in a standard encyclopedia.

Robin Hill and Carol Gilles, Jefferson Junior High School, Columbia, Missouri

It Happened This Way

Why

To help students develop a story schema that will aid them in comprehension and retelling

Who

Elementary students who find it difficult to retell or write stories in a logical sequence

How

Read aloud *Little Red Riding Hood, Goldilocks and the Three Bears,* or other familiar stories that have an obvious problem and resolution. Discuss the story schema with students by drawing a large square on the chalkboard and by dividing it into four parts labeled *Characters and setting, Problem, Events* (what happened — attempts to resolve problem), and *Resolution* (of problem). Discuss each part separately and have the class write one or two sentences for each part, such as in the following example.

Characters and setting	*Problem*
Little Red Riding Hood was going to take a basket of goodies to grandmother's house.	On the way to grandmother's house Little Red Riding Hood met a wolf. The wolf ran to grandmother's house, put grandmother in the closet, and dressed in her clothes.

Events	*Resolution*
The wolf tried to fool Little Red Riding Hood by pretending to be grandmother. When it didn't work, he jumped out of bed and chased Little Red Riding Hood.	A woodcutter came to the cottage and chased the wolf away. The woodcutter, grandmother, and Little Red Riding Hood had a celebration.

Students may take this story schema, fill in any other details they care to add, and retell the story.

What Else

1. Show the story schema through the illustrations in the book.
2. Students write "take-turn" stories in which each student contributes a sentence.
3. Students apply the schema to stories they've written.
4. The headings can be changed and the schema applied to nonfiction works. For example, the instructions for an art project could be divided into the following four categories: *Materials, What we're making, Directions, How it should look.*

Jolene M. Davis and Karen Shroyer, Montgomery County R-II, Bellflower Elementary School, Bellflower, Missouri

Words Are Never Alone

Why

1. To encourage students to play with words both orally and in written form
2. To encourage students to develop and maintain an appreciation of the power and magic of language
3. To strengthen students' self-expression
4. To help students be aware of the importance of context in assigning meaning to a word

Who

All elementary students, from proficient to reluctant readers and writers

How

To introduce younger students to the idea that words can have several meanings, ask a student to look up the word *run* in the dictionary and to note how many different ways the word can be used. Help students develop a list of other familiar words with multiple meanings, such as *time, down, side, set, back,* and *out.* Be careful to explain the different meanings and the different ways the words can be used. Then ask students to select one word from the list and to write a class story using the word in as many different ways as they can.

With older students, begin (without comment) a bulletin board labeled "What's Up?" Each day, add a new phrase using the word *up,* such as *move up, light up, up to par.* After a few days, discuss why the board has been set up, and talk about the expressions on it. Encourage students to add their own *up* phrases and to explain to the class what their expressions mean. Expand the discussion to include other words that can be used in various expressions and that have numerous meanings. Write the words on the board as students suggest them. Then ask students, working alone, in pairs, or in groups, to select one word from the list and to write a story, poem, or paragraph in which the word is used in as many different ways as possible. One sixth-grade student came up with the following imaginative uses of the word *out:*

"OUT"

Out is odd, you hear it all the time, but with<u>out</u> noticing!

You can be out to lunch, which most people don't think is far-out.

You can also be out of luck which makes it hard to knock out someone while out-patients watch you box.

(I don't think I'll ever be <u>out</u> of ideas)

If you are in an <u>out</u>rage, you might get kicked <u>out</u> of the house, outside.

If you throw a football out of sight you'll get thrown out of a game.

If you think you outclass someone they'll think you don't produce enough output, so they'll outdo you, and send you out to an outpost! After that you'll have an outburst and say they're outlaws. Then they'll outnumber you, then you'll stop your outcry, so they will outdistance you, and they'll outcast you.

John's friend's outfit is outdated. So you outline a shirt and make him one, by plugging the sewing machine into the outlet!

(OUT of paper)   THE
                        N
                        D

Students read their papers aloud, and the class discusses the different usages of the selected word. All the papers might then be displayed on the board.

What Else

Students choose one word and illustrate one of its uses or meanings. The illustrations are compiled into a class book.

Elizabeth M. Baker, Columbia Public Schools/ Gifted Program, Missouri

The Great Cookie Chase: Following Directions to Find the Gingerbread Boy

Why

To give students practice in reading and following directions

Who

Primary students

How

Read aloud to the class *The Gingerbread Boy.* Encourage students to talk about the story and to list main events in sequential order. If cooking facilities are available, ask students if they would like to bake their own Gingerbread Boy. Call for volunteers to bring ingredients from home. Enlist an adult volunteer to help on baking day.

Involve children in reading directions, measuring, mixing, and shaping on the day of baking. Students return to class while the Gingerbread Boy bakes. Before the children go back to the kitchen, the adult volunteer removes the Gingerbread Boy from the oven and hides him in a previously determined place somewhere in the building. A note is left in the kitchen that instructs the children to go to a certain location, where another note is found. Depending on the maturity of the students, they continue following directions until they reach the fourth or fifth place, where they find the Gingerbread Boy. Students may celebrate the discovery by eating the cookie.

What Else

1. Students work individually or in groups to write a story about a cookie person.
2. Divide the class into small groups. Let each group hide a prize for another group and write a series of messages directing the students to the prize.

Beverly Simpson, Hannibal–La Grange College, Hannibal, Missouri

Punctuation Please

Why

To help students realize the importance of punctuation in conveying meaning when reading or writing

Who

Elementary students who seem to ignore punctuation when reading or writing

How

Provide children with two copies of a short, familiar story. One copy should be written with punctuation and one without. Read both versions aloud so students can compare how the two sound. They discuss the differences in sound and in meaning, which leads to discussion of why punctuation is used.

Hand out copies of another story, again with and without punctuation. Ask students to work with a partner and to take turns reading aloud the copy of the story written with punctuation. Encourage them to discuss the possible meaning of the story.

Have the entire class look at their copies of the story without punctuation, or write the story on the board or on an overhead projector. Ask a student to read the story aloud. Again explain how the lack of punctuation makes the story hard to read and the meaning unclear. Encourage students to supply the missing punctuation without the aid of the punctuated copy. Then compare the two copies and have students point out where their suggested punctuation differed from the author's.

What Else

1. Ask the students to recopy a story they have written, without inserting the punctuation. They exchange stories with a classmate and punctuate that person's story. The punctuated story and the other student's original version are then compared and discussed.
2. You may want to focus on one type of punctuation at a time, especially with younger children. For older students the lesson can be a review of all types of punctuation.

Kathleen A. Carter, Van-Far R-I, Wellsville, Missouri

Retelling as a Learning Strategy

Why

Retelling a text is an activity that taps directly into the comprehending process. Over time, written retellings can be used to evaluate the developmental link between students' natural competence in oral language and their developing competence in written language.

Who

With adaptation, all elementary students

How

Prepare for the activity by making copies of a story, article, or passage. Fold and staple the text so that only the title is visible. Have students form groups of four or five, and then hand out one copy to each student.

Follow the activity sequence given below, modifying the audience, purpose, focus, and materials to match the students' age and competence. Students' predictions and retellings may be oral or written.

Predicting (5–10 minutes)

1. *Predict a plot.* On the basis of the title alone, each student writes one or two sentences on what the story might be about. They are to work quickly, making spelling and neatness of minor importance.

2. *Predict some words.* Next, students predict some words or phrases that they expect to encounter in the book.

3. *Read and listen.* Students read aloud their predictions about the plot and their predicted word lists. As the other group members listen, they look for similarities with their own predictions.

4. *Make a comment.* Each student makes one comment about one other group member's written predictions. Emphasize that students are to be positive in their comments.

Everyone Reads (3–5 minutes)

Students unstaple their stories and are given instructions about the purpose for reading the material. They might be told to read the story as they would read a newspaper or light story. Then they are to think about how they would describe the story to someone who hasn't read it. Or students might be told that the material will be covered in a future examination and that they are to read the passage thoroughly.

Retelling (10–15 minutes)

Next, students are to retell the story or passage in writing, according to the directions given prior to reading. They are to write from memory on the back of the story, without referring to the text. Stress that the writing should be readable, but that students should work quickly, without worrying about neatness or spelling.

Share and Compare (time varies)

Students pair up with a partner, exchange papers, and compare their retellings.

1. *How are our retellings different?* Students identify material that they chose to include but that their

partner omitted, and vice versa. They talk about why each included or omitted the material.

2. *Muddled meanings.* Students comment on whether the partner's story changed or affected the original writing, whether due to omission, addition, or rewording.

3. *Paraphrase power.* Students identify and discuss any words or phrases in the partner's story that are different from the original version but that still mean the same.

4. *Borrow a bit.* Students then look for a portion of the partner's retelling that they would like to borrow and add to their own stories. They explain why they would do so.

Brian Cambourne, Centre for Studies in Literacy, University of Wollongong, New South Wales, Australia

Open Retelling Response

Why

To help students develop their abilities in retelling a story

Who

All elementary students

How

As a beginning-of-the-year activity, assemble a collection of art materials, puppetry materials, hats, old clothing, and assorted props. Mention the titles of several read-aloud stories or invite students to think about a story they've heard, read, or seen. Then ask students to retell the story silently to themselves. When they've had time to retell the story several times, explain that they are to retell the story orally to the entire class, making use of assembled art materials and props. Provide sufficient space and time for the retellings. Open responses of students allow for their personal reactions to literature.

What Else

Repeat the activity throughout the year. As students share their open responses to literature, encourage them to experiment with new art materials, theatrical techniques, and visuals as vehicles for retelling a story.

Karen Sabers Dalrymple, Eagle Valley Middle School, Eagle, Colorado

Read and Respond

Why

To enhance students' comprehension by encouraging them to respond to what they read

Who

All elementary students

How

Have students select reading materials that interest them. If necessary, review the guidelines for silent reading time:

1. No one talks.
2. No one gets up.
3. Everyone reads.

Have students read for a set period of time. Then students choose or are assigned partners for shared reading. During this time students read to each other or describe their selections, ask questions, and express their feelings about either selection.

What Else

1. Invite students to respond in writing to either of the reading selections, their own or their partner's. Responses may be in the form of feelings about either book, stories based on ideas from one of the books, evaluations of the book, and so forth.
2. Students form groups of four or five to share written responses. Encourage group members to ask questions about the books or the responses.
3. Students are encouraged to revise their written responses.
4. Students write questions about their partners' books. In small groups, partners then respond to the questions orally or in writing.

Bill Searcy, Northeast Missouri State University, Kirksville

Section C: Invitations to Read

Big Books

Why

To stimulate students' reading

Who

Elementary students, especially early readers, who need the support of both predictable language and group effort

How

When literature is used as instructional reading material, it is a delight to become a reader. Children learn to read with ease as they read along while a favorite literary selection is read to them. Several commercial Big Books that are available have print large enough for a class to read. The following instructions can help you turn other selections into Big Books.

At the beginning of each week, choose a work of literature that has a predictable pattern. Print the text with a bold black marker at the top of large manila sheets (12″ × 18″). The pages are assembled in order but not attached.

Read the original book to the children and show them the illustrations. Then read the printed story in the Big Book, one page at a time. As you read, encourage children to read along with you. Discuss the story by asking such questions as "What is the story about? What do you like best about it? How could it have ended differently?" Invite individual children to read a page as the story is read aloud one more time.

Each page of the Big Book is to be illustrated by one child. (Not all books will be long enough for every child in the class to illustrate a page. Keep a record of the illustrators for each book so that each child has an opportunity to be an illustrator.)

Big Books can be bound with a heavy-duty stapler, and the stapled side reinforced with library tape.

Individual pages may be bound with masking tape for longer wear. Large metal rings can be used to join Big Books if the left edge of each page is reinforced with masking tape so that the pages don't pull out. Big Books can also be stitched together with heavy cord or wool.

For ease in reading Big Books, construct a reading stand that can be kept in the reading corner. The stand can be made from a piece of plywood and should be large enough for a Big Book to rest on with the covers opened.

Some pattern stories lend themselves to personalization by a group of students. *Brown Bear, Brown Bear, What Do You See?* by Bill Martin, Jr., is such a book. The original pattern can be used as a model for creating a new story. The following story excerpt, based on a spring theme, was created by first graders:

> Red tulip, red tulip, what do you see?
> I see a yellow worm looking at me.
> Yellow worm, yellow worm, what do you see?
> I see a purple crocus looking at me.

B. Gail Heald-Taylor, Waterloo Board of Education, Ontario, Canada

Wordless Picture Books to Support Reading in the Upper Elementary Grades

Why

1. To emphasize to students that books have meaning and that reading can be enjoyable
2. To provide students with the opportunity to view themselves as successful readers
3. To enhance students' sense of story through oral, artistic, and written experiences
4. To increase students' knowledge of how to handle a book (i.e., reading from left to right on the page, from the front to the back of the book)

Who

Upper elementary students who are having difficulty learning to read

How

Become thoroughly familiar with *The Silver Pony,* a wordless picture book by Lynd Ward. (The book is divided into chapters, so it's less apt to be labeled "babyish" by the students.) Form your own opinions about the book and decide how to introduce it to your students. (I have often begun by stating, "This is a book that tells an intriguing story through the use of beautiful pictures. Let's look at the first chapter together to see how *you* like it.") Because the major purpose of the activity is to enhance children's understanding and enjoyment of books, discussion of the story will revolve around children's feelings, impressions, and ideas. This focus will be one of encouraging the aesthetic response to literature or reading for the sheer enjoyment and beauty of the story.

Encourage students' responses to the story at the outset by asking, "What can you tell us about this story?" Or students may wish to start looking at the pictures in the book and to respond when ready.

The responses will help determine the form of the accompanying lessons, which may include discussing and responding to one or more of the seven chapters through music, art, or writing.

The Silver Pony is such an intriguing book that small groups of children reading it together will respond with little encouragement from the teacher. Children talk freely about their feelings and ideas when there is an atmosphere of respect for these feelings.

To extend students' responses to the book, many expressive activities are possible, including the use of music, art, writing, and dramatics. After students observe the style of art in the book, they may create their own pencil drawings of what they believe will happen next or illustrate a new chapter. Students may want to write a script and present one-act plays to correspond with individual chapters. They may work together to find background music appropriate for their presentations. Students may want to use drawing or painting to express how each chapter makes them feel. Students may choose to write the dialogue, including characters' thoughts, for each page of the book. The dialogues might be clipped to the book for others to read.

What Else

1. Students look at other wordless picture books and share one with younger children. (See the Bibliography for a list of other wordless picture books.)
2. Students discuss the genre of fantasy and select other fantasy books to read.
3. Students familiarize themselves with the style of art in the book and look for other artists using a similar style.
4. Students may be interested in the warfare depicted in the final chapter and may decide to learn more about such weapons, which could lead to a research unit.
5. Students discuss the settings depicted in the book and extend their knowledge of farm life, city life, life in Antarctica, or life in any of the other locations.

Myna M. Haussler, Tucson Unified School District, Arizona

Encounters with Wordless Picture Books

Why

Wordless picture books are effectively used to extend both oral and written language. These books provide a story structure that allows children to verbalize at their own level, ranging from unrelated descriptions of pictures to connected discourse integrating all the elements of narratives. Wordless picture books also help children bridge the gap from pictures to print and promote book-handling abilities, such as reading from front to back and left to right.

The wordless picture story allows children to create an oral or written text using their own expectations of stories, background experiences, sense of events, theme, sequence, character continuity and development, as well as their abilities to predict and confirm.

Who

Elementary students at different levels of oral and written language development

How

Encourage students to look through a wordless picture book from beginning to end to familiarize themselves with the story. Then invite them to put the story into words. Each child's narrative is a creative experience, guided by the illustrations but involving no right or wrong judgments. Tape-record the students' stories so that they can hear themselves as authors and can monitor, elaborate, and confirm their narrations. Taking dictation of children's stories helps them connect spoken language with written language and furthers their pride in becoming authors. Both the written and taped stories provide a permanent record that can be returned to, appreciated, and perhaps reviewed.

Although time consuming, it is rewarding to use an opaque projector to enlarge the illustrations to produce a Big Book (see page 85) for a shared storytelling time. An overhead projector and duplicated copies of the transparencies provide another way to share the pictures with the class. Each child's contribution in the group storytelling enhances other children's narrative sense. A child who easily creates dialogue for characters is balanced by other children who attend to detail in setting, sequence of events, or feelings and motivations. Group storytelling also stimulates children to put words to the wordless picture books they read independently.

What Else

1. Once children are familiar with wordless picture books, extend their understanding of story schema by removing the binding of a book, separating the pages, and inviting a group of students to organize the picture story in a logical (sensible, workable) sequence by drawing on their predicting and confirming skills.
2. Wordless picture books also can be photocopied and laminated onto sheets of tagboard. Leave adequate room for students to write accompanying text. Use of transparency pens allows for revision and editing, and the same sheets can be reused throughout the year. Transparency pens, photocopied transparencies, and an overhead projector allow teachers to make group storytelling into a writing experience.

Wilma J. Kafora and Sandra J. Simons-Ailes, Albuquerque Public Schools, New Mexico

Attending to Print

Why

Current research into the reading process indicates that fluent readers use three cuing systems simultaneously: the semantic system or meaning of the language, the syntactic system or structure of the language, and the graphophonemic system or sound-symbol relationships of the language. The proficient reader samples from the print while relying heavily on the semantic and syntactic cuing systems. Occasionally, we encounter students who do not attend to print, often because they have had limited experience with books and thus are at the early stages of development in the reading process. The following teaching strategy is designed to give these students more experience in attending to print.

Who

Elementary students who need additional help in attending to print

How

The following activity sequence develops a large cadre of familiar print materials. Each step builds on the previous one, increasing the amount of print processed but always blending this with meaning and the flow of language. Print awareness is increased through the production of student-made, teacher-made, and classroom materials. Throughout the sequence, provide daily opportunities for students to transact with print — both through the language of personal experience and the more standard language of print.

1. Observation and Teacher-Child Interaction

As a preliminary step, observe the students in various settings to learn more about their interests and the important events in their lives. Then, in a one-to-one conference with the student who needs to attend to print, talk about these personal events or interests.

2. Bookmaking

Prepare an "I Can Read" Book for the student by folding four sheets of 8½″ × 11″ paper in half and stapling them in book form. As the child watches, write the title "I Can Read" and the child's name on the book. Help the child select eight words for the book that are meaningful and significant to that child. Previous conversations or interactions will help identify appropriate words. Print one word at the top of each page, encouraging the child to read along and to predict what the word or next letter might be. Help the child use each word in a sentence and print the sentence underneath the word. The following is a sample of one girl's "I Can Read" Book:

> Natasha
> My name is Natasha.
>
> Tyrsa
> I play with Tyrsa at my babysitter's.
>
> Aretta
> Aretta always plays with us.
>
> Ballet
> Tyrsa, Aretta, and I go the ballet on Thursdays.
>
> Mommy
> My Mommy is a teacher.
>
> Daddy
> My daddy plays squash.
>
> King
> King is our big noisy dog.
>
> Baba
> On Sunday we visit Baba [grandmother] Halayda, or Baba and Dido [grandfather] Powlowski.

4. Reading

When the "I Can Read" Book is completed, encourage the student to read the book often. Be available to listen to the reading and to help out if needed, or ask another student to assist.

5. Word Awareness

When the student feels confident about reading the book, ask him or her questions about the print, which helps the student focus on it. For example, the teacher working with Natasha might say, "Where is the word *Natasha?* What other word starts with the same letter as *Natasha?* Show me the word." Be aware of the child's word usage at other times as well. Some of the child's more meaningful words may be used in writing times — one indication of becoming more aware of print.

6. Experience Charts

Use the information in the "I Can Read" Book as a basis for a discussion with the child. Help the child expand the ideas, incorporating more of the child's background or experiences. Make an experience chart by printing the ideas, in sentence format and one sentence per line, on a sheet of chart paper. As you put these ideas into print on the chart, encourage the student to watch and to predict the message. The student confirms or rejects the predictions by utilizing prior knowledge, the context of

the writing, and the letters and words being printed. The significance in this approach to teaching print awareness is that the meaning is paramount. At no point is print separated from meaning and relevance to the child's experiences.

Natasha's experience chart might look like this:

> My name is Natasha.
> I am four years old.
> Tyrsa and Aretta are my friends at my babysitter's.
> They are sisters.
> I play with Tyrsa.
> Aretta plays with us.
> Tyrsa, Aretta, and I go to ballet on Thursdays.
> We each have a black leotard and pink tights.
> We like to dance.
> My mommy is a teacher.
> She teaches nursery school and kindergarten.
> My daddy plays squash.
> He likes baseball, too.
> On Sundays we visit Baba Halayda or Baba and Dido Powlowski.
> When we go out, King watches our house.
> He is our big noisy dog.

For approximately a week after making the experience chart, encourage the student to reread it and the "I Can Read" Book often. Be available to help the student with the reading if necessary. When the child is comfortable reading the chart, cut the sentences into strips and scramble them into a random order. Invite the student to sequence the strips in a logical order and to read the assembled strips.

7. Favorite Chant

Move away from personal experience texts to help the child gain control of familiar chants, poems, songs, even jump-rope rhymes. Select a chant that is a favorite of the student's and print it on chart paper. The student follows the same procedures as with the experience chart: reading the rhyme daily, finding significant words, locating words that look the same, and so forth. When the student has become familiar with the chant, cut the chant into strips and scramble the pieces. Ask the student to put the strips in the proper order.

In this activity it is important for the student to internalize the flow of language. Present the chant in various print forms so that the student has an opportunity to examine the chant printed in a book, handwritten on chart paper, typed on a sheet of paper, and, occasionally, printed or handwritten as a musical score. Encourage the child to write his or her own version of the chant. One first grader created this variation of Dennis Lee's "Alligator Pie":

> Alligator purse, alligator purse,
> If I don't get one,
> I think I'm gonna curse.
> Give away my teacher,
> Give away my nurse,
> But don't give away my alligator purse.

8. Favorite Story

The last step in gaining independence in attending to print involves the use of good literature. Select a predictable book of interest to the child. *Brown Bear, Brown Bear, What Do You See?* by Bill Martin, Jr., and *The Little Red Hen* are favorites. (See the listing of predictable books in the Bibliography.)

First read the book aloud to the student. Then reread the book, encouraging the child to read along. Continue rereading the story until the child can read it independently. Repeat the procedures involved in the "I Can Read" Book, the experience chart, and the chant to foster print awareness. Next, ask the student to use the format of the predictable book to produce a personal book, recording one idea per page and including an appropriate illustration. The text of Natasha's book shows how she has reworked the pattern of the *Brown Bear* story:

> Natasha, Natasha, who do you see?
> I see Tyrsa looking at me.
> Tyrsa, Tyrsa, who do you see?
> I see Aretta looking at me.
> Aretta, Aretta, who do you see?
> I see Mommy looking at me.
> Mommy, Mommy, who do you see?
> I see children looking at me.
> I see Natasha, Tyrsa, and Aretta looking at me.
> That's who I see.

Orysia Hull, Child Care and Development Branch, Manitoba Education, Winnipeg, Canada

Skinny Books

Why

To provide students with interesting, relevant, and manageable reading materials

Who

All elementary students, especially those who are hesitant about approaching a long text or who need background information before reading a more difficult text, and those who are interested in reading about a special topic

How

Assemble a large collection of Skinny Books in the classroom library. These books are short in length (under one hundred pages), pertain to one topic, and are interesting reading. Skinny Books can be written by professional authors or by students.

A good story taken from such sources as old basal readers, magazines, or newspapers can be made into a Skinny Book. Assemble the pages, add a cover of construction paper, and write the title and author's name on the cover. Invite children to write a book-jacket summary or to illustrate the cover.

Skinny Books can also be made by removing chapters from old, well-written textbooks that contain information still current and accurate. Students can make Skinny Books from excerpts taken from the encyclopedia and other reference books, or they can research and then write their own factual Skinny Books. Short accounts on the same topic could be grouped into one Skinny Book. Conceptually or thematically related books could be placed together in the classroom library.

Dorothy J. Watson, University of Missouri–Columbia

Reading Novels to Children as They Read Along

Why

1. To promote the reading of good literature
2. To provide an opportunity for reading to lead to process writing
3. To provide an opportunity for teachers to use their own creative ideas for teaching language arts

Who

All elementary students, especially those who need an extra boost in order to attend to story and print

How

To get started, a team of teachers and students might set up criteria for selection of books and submit possible titles. Work through your media center specialist to order classroom sets of chosen novels. Begin with a minimum number of sets and add to your supply as needed and as funds are available. Inexpensive racks for storage are available, though not essential.

Introduce books to your class in a variety of ways: simply begin reading as students follow along in their own books, provide background material to whet their interest, or present a map pointing out the setting of a story. Pictures of the Metropolitan Museum of Art in New York City help students relate to Claudia and Jamie's adventure in *From the Mixed-Up Files of Mrs. Basil E. Frankweiler* by E. L. Konigsburg. A bulletin board of actual pictures of Laura Ingalls Wilder and her family (available at a nominal cost from the Laura Ingalls Wilder museum in Mansfield, Missouri) can interest students in any of the *Little House* books. Pictures of New York City's Times Square area take children into the world of Chester Cricket, Harry Cat, and Tucker Mouse in *A Cricket in Times Square* by George Selden. Try to set aside time each day to continue the reading.

After the first chapter or two have been read aloud, students might discuss story elements such as setting and character development. Some books are more appropriate for a particular focus than another. *Caddie Woodlawn* by Carol R. Brink can be effectively used to examine the character traits of Father or Indian John. Robert Lawson's *Rabbit Hill* is perfect for teaching paraphrasing, using Father's big words. Predicting outcomes provides fun as students try to decide what will happen to Claudia and Jamie in *From the Mixed-Up Files of Mrs. Basil E. Frankweiler*. Children may learn to face their own fears and be more tolerant of others by reading *A Dog Called Kitty* by Bill Wallace. Invite your students to read some passages of each book orally for expressive language.

Developing concepts with related vocabulary is possible, but avoid becoming tedious and using the same technique over and over. Lead the children in constructing meaning by using their own backgrounds of experience and by using the dictionary when appropriate. Allow for independent, partner, and group work. Encourage interaction among students as they work. Occasionally use a matching exercise you have created.

What Else

As you progress through a novel, look for opportunities for children to write reflexively from personal experience in connection with the theme of the story. As they read *Caddie Woodlawn*, children may recall stories their own grandmothers have told them, and they may want to record these stories in writing. Writing of a time they tried to run away from home may be appropriate after *From the Mixed-Up Files of Mrs. Basil E. Frankweiler*. Personal fears may be more easily expressed in writing after reading *A Dog Called Kitty*.

When you finish reading aloud the last chapter, wait before making a writing assignment. Remain quiet, allowing children their private thoughts. If children are eager to respond, let the conversation flow naturally, without teacher direction. Let this be a special time for your class. A concluding paper or other book-related activity could wait until the following day.

Nancy Thrasher, Anderson Elementary School, Conroe, Texas

Look What We Know — Then and Now

Why

To recognize and build upon children's prior knowledge of a topic

Who

All elementary students, especially those who feel insecure about their learning

How

Before beginning a lesson or unit, ask students to write down everything they already know about the topic. For example, Chad wrote the following about sound:

> Sound can bounce off of things. We can make sound. It can be heard from pretty far away if it is loud. Ripping things can make sound. Everything can make sound.

Encourage students to read aloud and to discuss what they have written. You might make a list on the chalkboard or on chart paper so students can visualize how much they already know and to reinforce this knowledge. Then proceed with the particular lesson or unit.

When the lesson or unit is completed, give students several small sheets of blank paper stapled together to form mini-books. Invite them to make concept books by writing what they *now* know about the topic. Here is what Chad wrote about sound after the science lesson:

Sound

Sound can bounce off of things. The thing that causes sound is vibrate. How does sound travel? It can travel through solids, air, under water. Differint sounds are made by the pitch. We can make sound. It can be heard from pretty far away if it is loud enough. The less room sound has to vibrate the higher it gets. Almost everything can make sound. Sound is very useful. A bell after it rings will vibrate for a little bit and you can hear it. Sound travels faster through water. Sound is very important. "I am glad we have it!"

Have students compare their original writings to the concept books. Working in groups, students might discuss what they originally knew, whether that knowledge was correct, what they learned, and what else they would like to know about the topic.

What Else

1. Kindergartners can do their own writing (and drawing) or can dictate information.
2. In addition to writing what they already know, students can predict what they will learn.
3. At the culmination of the lesson or unit, ask students if their predictions have been confirmed and if their questions have been answered.
4. Groups of students or the entire class can combine ideas from the individual concept books into one larger book, to be placed in the class reading center or in the school library for others to check out.

Jolene M. Davis, Montgomery County R-II, Bellflower Elementary School, Bellflower, Missouri

---

E.R.R.Q.: Estimate, Read, Respond, and Question

Why

To enhance students' reading comprehension by encouraging them to link the new information in a text to their own backgrounds of experience

Who

Elementary students who give up reading materials easily, who do not personalize their reading, or who have difficulty asking and answering probing questions

How

1. Explain to students that they are going to do something called E.R.R.Q., which stands for Estimate, Read, Respond, and Question. Ask them to select something they want to read, to look it over, and to *estimate* how far they can read with understanding, how far they can "stay with" the text. Ask them to mark that place lightly in pencil in the margin or to record the page number.
2. Next, students *read* the text, either silently or orally. As they read, ask the students to think about how the text makes them feel. Do any images or words come to mind? Does the text remind them of anything from their own lives? Does it remind them of anything they have read earlier?
3. After reading, ask students to *react* to the reading. What came to mind as they read the article? Did images or memories flash in their minds? How did it make them feel to read the article? Then, ask them to *retell* everything they can remember about the article. Both the reacting and retelling are done rather quickly.
4. Invite students to ask themselves *questions* about their reading. These questions can involve a stating of facts (such as "What is the main idea?") or can involve prediction or interpretation ("How will the book end?" "Why is it so sad?" "How can I find out more about that?").

What Else

This procedure is not a recipe. It is meant to be modified, depending on the needs of the students.

1. The form can be modified. Students can do the *response* and *question* sections orally or in writing, depending on the size and age of the group and the purpose of the reading.
2. In a content-area class the teacher might select the reading materials. For leisure reading, the choice will be the students'.
3. The *reaction* portion of the *response* can lead naturally into the *retelling*. Many students begin reacting and end up retelling. Usually, the better the

reaction, the richer the retelling. Depending on the quality of the reaction and the teacher's purpose, the *retelling* need not be done every time.

4. The *questioning* portion can be modified. If students have great difficulty asking appropriate questions as they read, provide some sample questions as a model for students to follow. If the *questioning* process is a written activity for students, the questions can serve as the opening of a dialogue or written conversation between the teacher and the students.

Dorothy J. Watson, University of Missouri–Columbia, and Carol Gilles, Jefferson Junior High School, Columbia, Missouri

Giving Gifts to Story Characters

Why

1. To intensify students' interest in a book *while* they are reading
2. To help students understand the relationships between characters in the story and become involved in some way with the characters

Who

Lower and middle elementary students who have difficulty understanding the relationships of characters in a story and those whose interests sometimes stray while reading a story

How

Select a photo or illustration showing a birthday party or a holiday scene. Through discussion, students identify people in the picture and their relationships to one another. Select one person in the picture and have students speculate about the presents that this person might have given to one or more of the other people in the photo.

Refer to a story that the class has recently read or heard. Select characters from the story and invite the students to speculate on the gifts those characters might receive and give.

Ask students to select a character from the books they are currently reading, to make a list of people to whom this character would be giving gifts at holiday time, and to identify what those gifts would be.

What Else

After the book is completed or at any time the students feel they are well enough acquainted with the characters, students might discuss or write about a special holiday the characters might celebrate, including who would be there, where they would gather, what they would do.

Margaret Essig, Grain Valley R-5 Schools, Missouri

L.E.A.D. to Read

Why

To produce reading material for students that consists of their own ideas expressed in their own ways

Who

Elementary students who are beginning to read in English and whose first language is not English — students labeled bilingual, speakers of English as a second language (ESL), or limited English proficiency (LEP) students

How

The technique of Language Experience Approach Directions (L.E.A.D.) works best with small groups and with individuals. It involves thinking, discussing, writing, reading, and copying.

Think. Help students commit themselves to topics based upon their interests. Next, they are to decide on a purpose and an audience for the ideas they will record. You may suggest a purpose, such as "Do you want to make a book of your stories?" but when students decide on their own purposes, the material will be more authentic and readable.

Discuss. Encourage students to discuss and decide what to write. This vital step is closely related to setting purpose and audience and is often carried out at the same time. It is essential to the writing and shouldn't be skipped.

Write. Serve as the scribe for students as they dictate what to write. Use an overhead, the chalkboard, or newsprint so that students can see what they are dictating. As you transcribe each sentence, read it aloud quickly, pointing to the sentence. Oral reading should be fast enough to sound like language, not like a word list.

Read. Read the full text aloud, asking if there are any changes. Sometimes students suggest sweeping revisions, sometimes only minor polishing. Major revisions may require scheduling time to work on the piece again. With group transcriptions, one student will sometimes want to alter a sentence dictated by someone else. The original author needs to be consulted and must give permission before any changes can be made.

Copy. When the writing is as complete as it can be at this first meeting, it should be copied onto appropriate paper. Some texts will be complete at this point. If, for example, the purpose of the writing is to develop a Chore Chart indicating which child is to perform which classroom chore on which days, then that chart is the final text. A large, neat copy of it will be placed where the students can easily refer to it. Other texts should be typed and duplicated. Copies of a report of a group's science project, for example, should be made for each member of the group, for the teacher, and for other interested readers, both in and out of the classroom.

Remember to write what the students say, not what you want them to say. Remain silent except when reading aloud dictated sentences. ESL students may dictate ungrammatical sentences and may use some vocabulary incorrectly, but it is important for several reasons to write what students say without making any corrections or comments. First, the purpose of this lesson is to produce materials that the students can read easily, by using their ideas expressed in their own way. Changing the students' writing makes the reading more difficult for them. Second, the purpose is reading and creating reading material; it is not a grammar lesson. Changing the students' language focuses the students' attention on form rather than on meaning, which again makes the reading more difficult for them. Third, writing down students' exact words produces an excellent record of their proficiency and their progress in English, and helps you plan appropriate lessons in grammar, concept building, and vocabulary building.

What Else

1. *Chance It.* Copies of the L.E.A.D. text can be changed in a variety of ways. Individuals can rewrite, incorporating new ideas or new phrasing. The original group can review and edit, incorporating suggestions from classmates who have read and reacted to the material.

2. *Cloze.* Recopy the L.E.A.D. material, inserting blanks for a few words here and there. Ask students to suggest what words would make sense in each blank. This helps students increase their vocabulary in English as they are improving their reading.

3. *Cut Up.* If it appears that students have memorized the L.E.A.D. piece and aren't really reading it, cut a copy of the text into its different sentences, put the sentences on 3″ × 5″ cards, and ask a pair of students to put the text back in the appropriate order.

4. *Show You Know.* Using a copy of the L.E.A.D. text, the students underline every word they can read. They will probably underline almost every word, but be aware that being able to read these words in the L.E.A.D. material does not mean that students can read them out of context, such as on a card or list. (That's not reading, anyway.)

5. *Write It Yourself.* A pair of students can work together to create their own L.E.A.D. text, following the same procedures described above. Because the students will be their own scribes, their spelling, handwriting, punctuation, and capitalization may be far from conventional. What is important is that students are reading and writing.

Pat Rigg, Consultant, American Language and Literacy, Tucson, Arizona

Print We Can All Read

Why

Environmental print is a vital resource for early literacy learning. Students learn to read this form of text as they observe examples around them — no one deliberately sets out to teach them "how." Children learn because the print occurs as an integral part of the situation in which it is found, and because it provides important and useful information to them and to others involved with them in the situation. A driver stops when there is a *stop* sign. A parent reminds a child, "Brush your teeth and don't forget the toothpaste." *Toothpaste* is a word that appears on the tube the child uses.

Who

All elementary students, especially beginning readers

How

One way to invite children to be aware of environmental print is to capitalize on the print found on the packaging of food products that are used in homes every day. Make an environmental print collection that can be used for making posters and books, as a resource for writing, and as a "home corner."

Attach four or five large sheets of paper to the wall or display area, labeling one chart for each meal time and snack time. Discuss with the children the various times of the day when they eat and drink. Have the children take turns selecting a carton or packet they have brought to school. They are to read the label aloud and to explain to the others when they eat that particular food. The children then cut out the print sample, attach it to the appropriate chart, and write their names on the chart beside the print sample. Other children can also add their names if they eat that type of food too.

Discuss with children individually and in small groups the items from the environmental print collection. As they identify the products, ask them how they know what the print indicates.

Invite the children to make information booklets titled The Food We Need and Like, incorporating cut-outs of environmental print and their own functional writing. The children can extend their writing by referring to the environmental print incorporated in the charts.

What Else

1. If all or some of the children are still exploring the relationships between spoken and written language, make twelve large cards (roughly 3″ × 9″). On four cards print the words *I like;* on the next four print *I don't like;* and on the remainder print *I need.* Have each child select several cutout words from the environmental print collection that he or she can read. Then, using a flannel board or similar display area, show the children how to combine the language cards with items of environmental print to compose sentences that are true. For example, one child might wish to write

I like	ice cream

while another may attempt

I need	apples

Have the children take turns making a sentence on the board and telling the others why it is true: "I like ice cream. It is yummy." "I don't like peas. They stick in my neck."

2. The environmental print collection can also be used as a basis for writing advertisements, similar to those the children see around them on billboards or on television.

Judith Ann Smith, Brisbane College of Advanced Education, Mt. Gravatt, Queensland, Australia

Baseball Made Easy: Reading for Meaning

Why

1. To reinforce the value of reading for meaning
2. To demonstrate to students how incorrect information causes the reader to reread, rethink, and, if possible, correct the passage

Who

Middle and upper elementary students who value flawless oral performance above constructing meaning, or students who read for extrinsic reasons and have no personal interest or investment in the process

How

Begin by displaying baseball cards, a baseball, a bat, and other materials associated with baseball. Suggest that students guess the subject of the reading material. Talk about the game. Find out who the experts in class are.

Ask the students to form groups of three or four. Give each student a copy of the following material to read. Observe students' reactions to the information.

Baseball Made Easy

Chapter 1: How to Choose a Bat

The best bat for you will be the easiest one to swing, so be sure to pick a bat that is light. With a light bat you can swing faster, and the ball will not go as far.

Chapter 2: Batting Stances

You will have to decide for yourself which is the best way to stand. Choose the way that is most natural to you. Everyone is different, so it is important to try and copy someone else.

Chapter 3: Base Hits

It is very hard to hit a baseball. Since it takes a lot of practice, you should not expect to get a base hit every time. The secret is to hit the ball where it is easiest for the fielders to catch.

Chapter 4: Running the Bases

In most Little Leagues, you can't steal bases, lead off, or run before the pitch reaches home plate. However, there are three things to remember:

1. Never run when you hit the ball.
2. Run to first base outside the foul line.
3. Always run past first base. You can't be tagged out as long as you stay in foul territory.

Chapter 5: Your Glove

Your glove helps you catch hard-hit balls. With a glove there is no reason to be afraid of the ball. Your glove is meant to catch the ball all by itself. Even the worst fielders need to use only one hand.

Discuss the information given, both accurate and inaccurate. Then ask the groups to rewrite the baseball passage, deleting or changing the false statements. If there are experts in the group, they are to expand the information. Students may want to illustrate their copies of the revised passage.

What Else

Extend this lesson by asking students to select other topics and to write their own short texts containing misinformation. Students exchange papers with another student or in their groups and correct the false statements.

Laura Kinder, Columbia, Missouri, and Shirley R. Crenshaw, Webster University, St. Louis, Missouri

Potato Poetry

Why

1. To help students observe that oral language can be manipulated, with results that are sometimes rhythmic and rhyming
2. To help students discover that writing and reading are a symbolic language process

Who

Kindergartners, beginning readers in primary grades, and hesitant readers in upper elementary grades

How

To prepare for this activity, visit the grocery store and purchase some russet or Irish potatoes, some sweet potatoes, and some yams. (You may run into some horticultural controversy about the difference between sweet potatoes and yams. For purposes of this activity, a sweet potato is the larger, light-colored potato with a light yellow meat, while yams are more elongated and have a smaller circumference, a darker reddish-brown skin, and a dark orange meat.) You'll need about a dozen of each variety.

Begin this activity by informing the children that you're going to teach them to read potatoes. This is usually met with skepticism, but ask the students to trust you. First, establish the vocabulary by naming each of the items to be read, that is, *white potatoes, sweet potatoes,* and *yams.* This is your reading vocabulary. (For younger children, you may want to bring in extra potatoes so that samples can be hefted for weight, cut in half, described, and tasted.) Once students can recognize and name each variety, show them how to construct and read a potato sentence. Arrange potatoes in a random order and then read the sentence by pointing to and naming each variety from left to right; for example: "white potato, white potato, yam, sweet potato, white potato, sweet potato." Repeat the sentence, asking the children to read along with you. After constructing and reading a second example, encourage one of the children to put some potatoes together into a sentence for you to read. At this point children will generally begin to catch on to the process. Ask another student to construct a potato sentence, and select a third child to read it. If the children can successfully do this, divide the class into pairs for some potato-sentence practice, with students trading roles of writer and reader.

When students are able to create and read potato sentences, explain that they are now ready for a real challenge — the writing of potato poetry. Arrange your potatoes appropriately and have students read the first line of the poem, perhaps "White potato, white potato, sweet potato, yam." Read it again, this time clapping the rhythm as you read. Ask for a volunteer to supply the next line, perhaps "White potato, white potato, yam, yam, yam." Then read the whole couplet. Encourage other students to come up with different rhythms and rhymes. Usually students' enthusiasm, creativity, and delight in the potato poetry are spontaneous and contagious.

What Else

Young children will want to repeat the activity several times. Older children can be encouraged to listen for the rhythmic and rhyming qualities of other common items and might contribute a poem like the following:

> White potato, salt shaker, pat of butter, knife, napkins, salad bowl, Mr. Morton's wife.

On a subsequent day, suggest some potato poetry without potatoes. Instead, have an envelope containing colored shapes of paper that represent the potatoes. Explain how potatoes, after all, are bulky, heavy, and dirty, and tend to spoil or dry out; colored paper shapes have none of these shortcomings. The whole previous activity can be repeated with pieces of paper serving as symbols for the potatoes:

$\triangle$ = white potato
$\bigcirc$ = sweet potato
$\square$ = yam

The first line of the potato poem could be written in symbols as:

$\triangle\ \triangle\ \bigcirc\ \square$

These manipulatives have some problems for both writing and reading, and these shortcomings can be discussed. Explain that one answer is to replace the colored paper with an even more convenient symbol system — written letters.

By the time the activity has been worked through this far, children have begun to internalize several important concepts related to language and reading.

1. Writing must start with "languaging." Ideas and objects are thought and expressed, and then represented in some way with visual symbols.

2. To write and read about objects, it's not necessary to have the real object at hand; they can be represented by shapes of paper or by written symbols.

3. Once we know the symbol system, we can share writing and reading with any other person who also knows the system.

4. Writing and reading are fun.

Leonard Breen, University of Oklahoma, Norman

Section D:
Music, Drama, and Reading

Sing Along with Reading and Writing

Why

Many authors and illustrators of children's books take advantage of the rich folk-music tradition in English and in translation from other languages as they introduce folksongs, game songs, and songs of historical significance — but always songs that children love. The study of song can be an exciting language arts experience for students as they discover ways of gathering and presenting new material, as well as ways of updating and categorizing existing material in new and different ways.

Who

All elementary students

How

Assemble a collection of books based on songs, such as those listed on the suggested reading list at the end of this activity. Additional titles are listed in the Bibliography. A number of the books might be accompanied by film strips or cassette tapes and might be made into Big Books (see page 85). Children can sing along and become comfortable with the songs. As they get to know the songs well, children can experience the folk process themselves by adding verses to fit some controversial issues, to focus on a political event, or to fit the song into a social studies, science, or math unit.

Songs help students expand their vocabulary and knowledge about particular issues or problems. For example, not all children know the difference between sheep and goats, but the illustrations and different sound effects with songs like "Old Mc-Donald Had a Farm" and "The Old Woman Who

Swallowed the Fly" will help provide children with the experiences needed to differentiate between the two animals.

By comparing two or more books based on the same song but written and illustrated by different authors, artists, and composers, children can explore the folk tradition. "The Old Woman Who Swallowed the Fly" is an excellent song to use, since the reading list suggests four different books about this song. Students can discover why each book has a large amount of the same language, though a certain amount of the language is different. As they examine the illustrations, they might discuss the different kinds of personalities the artists have given the characters of the song or the reasons for choosing different settings. Children might explore questions such as the following:

Who is the real author of the song?

When was the song originally written?

How and why do the songs change?

How can we find answers to these questions?

Students could interview parents, grandparents, and neighbors to see if the songs are known in different versions, or if similar songs exist in other languages used in the community.

All these aspects of exploration lead to more knowledge about language, as well as to critical and interpretive reading and listening. Many of the songs, such as "Yankee Doodle," "Sweet Betsy from Pike," "Casey Jones," and "The Erie Canal," provide interesting information about historical and political themes and issues. Children can be encouraged to discover other songs from these periods that may represent different views. This will lead children to find collections of songs rather than books about a particular song. Students can begin to categorize the songs into divisions such as the following: children's songs, historical songs from particular periods, songs about political issues such as war and peace, songs related to elections of presidents, work and union songs, or songs about particular geographic regions.

Suggested Reading List

Fred Burton of Ohio State University began the following list of books based on songs, and we have added to his list. A collection of this sort should be continuously updated with the help of children's librarians as well as the children in your classroom.

(For additional books based on songs, see the Bibliography.)

Adams, Pam. *This Old Man.* Grossett and Dunlap, 1975.

Aliki. *Hush Little Baby.* Dutton, 1975.

———. *Go Tell Aunt Rhody.* Macmillan, 1974.

Bangs, Edward. *Yankee Doodle.* Parents Magazine Press, 1976.

Chase, Richard. *Billy Boy.* Golden Gate Junior Books, 1966.

Conover, Chris. *Six Little Ducks.* Crowell, 1976.

Crane, Walter. *The Baby's Opera.* Simon and Schuster, 1981.

de Paola, Tomie. *The Friendly Beasts: An Old English Christmas Carol.* Putnam, 1981.

de Regniers, Beatrice S. *Catch a Little Fox.* Seabury, 1970.

Emberly, Barbara. *Simon's Song.* Prentice-Hall, 1969.

Emberly, Barbara, and Ed Emberly. *One Wide River to Cross.* Prentice-Hall, 1966.

Emberly, Ed. *London Bridge Is Falling Down.* Little, Brown, 1967.

Gauch, Patricia L. *On to Widecombe Fair.* Putnam, 1978.

Hart, Jane. *Singing Bee: A Collection of Favorite Children's Songs.* Lothrop, Lee and Shepard, 1982.

Hazen, Barbara. *Frere Jacques.* Lippincott, 1973.

Hurd, Thacher. *Mama Don't Allow.* Harper and Row, 1984.

Jeffers, Susan. *All the Pretty Horses.* Scholastic, 1974.

Keats, Ezra Jack. *The Little Drummer Boy.* Scholastic, 1968.

———. *Over in the Meadow.* Four Winds, 1979.

Kellogg, Steven. *There Was an Old Woman.* Scholastic, 1980.

Kennedy, Jimmy. *The Teddy Bears' Picnic.* Green Tiger Press, 1983.

Kent, Jack. *Jack Kent's Twelve Days of Christmas.* Parents Magazine Press, 1973.

Langstaff, John. *Frog Went a-Courtin'.* Harcourt, Brace and World, 1955.

———. *The Golden Vanity.* Harcourt Brace Jovanovich, 1972.

———. *Hot Cross Buns and Other Old Street Cries.* Atheneum, 1978.

———. *Oh, a-Hunting We Will Go.* Atheneum, 1974.

———. *Ol' Dan Tucker.* Harcourt, Brace and World, 1963.

———. *Over in the Meadow.* Harcourt, Brace and World, 1957.

———. *The Swapping Boy.* Harcourt, Brace and World, 1960.

Nic Leodhas, Sorche. *Always Room for One More.* Holt, Rinehart and Winston, 1965.

Parker, Robert A. *Sweet Betsy from Pike: A Song from the Gold Rush.* Viking, 1978.

Paterson, A. B. *Waltzing Matilda.* Holt, Rinehart and Winston, 1972.

Price, Christine. *Widdecombe Fair.* Warne, 1968.

Quackenbush, Robert. *Clementine.* Lippincott, 1974.

———. *She'll Be Comin' 'Round the Mountain.* Lippincott, 1973.

———. *Skip to My Lou.* Lippincott, 1975.

———. *There'll Be a Hot Time in the Old Town Tonight.* Lippincott, 1974.

Rounds, Glen. *Casey Jones: The Story of a Brave Engineer.* Golden Gate Junior Books, 1968.

———. *Sweet Betsy from Pike.* Childrens Press, 1973.

Rourke, Constance. *Davy Crockett.* Harcourt, Brace and World, 1955.

Spier, Peter. *The Erie Canal.* Doubleday, 1970.

———. *The Fox Went Out on a Chilly Night.* Doubleday, 1961.

———. *London Bridge Is Falling Down.* Doubleday, 1967.

Stanley, Diane. *Fiddle-I-Fee.* Little, Brown, 1979.

Westcott, Nadine Bernard. *I Know an Old Lady Who Swallowed a Fly.* Little, Brown, 1980.

Yulya. *Bears Are Sleeping.* Scribner, 1967.

Zemach, Harve. *Mommy, Buy Me a China Doll.* Follett, 1966.

Zemach, Margot. *Hush Little Baby.* Dutton, 1976.

Zuromskis, Diane. *The Farmer in the Dell.* Little, Brown, 1978.

Yetta M. Goodman, University of Arizona, Tucson, and Ann Marek, Department of Human Resources, Sparks, Nevada

---

Reading by Singing

Why

1. To help students learn the rhythm of language and articulation through music
2. To help students attend to print through the support of music

Who

With adaptation, all elementary students

How

Write the title of a sing-along book on the chalkboard, such as *The Little Drummer Boy* by Ezra Jack Keats. (Other titles are listed in the Bibliography.) Read the story aloud as the children follow along on their copies. Then invite the children to

sing along as you sing the song. Play a record or tape of the song if a recording is available; if not, invite some of the children to prepare a tape of the song.

What Else

1. Students write and draw what they might give to a religious figure or a member of royalty. Ask them to explain to the class why they would give that gift.
2. Students illustrate what they think *The Little Drummer Boy* or another song is about.
3. Students prepare a dramatization of a song. They present it to other classes or invite their parents to watch and listen.
4. Select other books to read by singing. Students might practice in small groups and then sing to the entire class.

Jennifer W. Paschall, Tazewell County Schools, Tazewell, Virginia

---

Top Twenty Tunes in Our Classroom

Why

As a teacher and a music lover, I have always been fascinated by the fact that my students and friends can easily forget simple directions, daily procedures, or some of the content of almost any lesson; yet they appear to have no difficulty remembering most of the lyrics to many popular songs. Listening to music, attending concerts, collecting record albums, and watching musical videos are an important part of the lives of children and adults. This activity utilizes this common interest in music to promote class discussion and to develop students' abilities to read and compare survey information, to conduct a survey, and to apply the necessary math skills to tabulate survey results.

Who

Students in grades 4–6

How

Ask a student to bring to class a current list of the "Top Twenty" songs. These lists can be found in many local newspapers on a weekly basis. The top twenty songs are listed on the chalkboard or on chart paper. Then everyone selects ten favorite songs from the list and writes the names on a piece of paper. A committee of several students makes a master list of the top twenty songs. The committee collects the lists of favorite songs and records the students' votes on the master list. Before the results of the survey are read to the class and displayed on the bulletin board, students predict which songs will be selected. They enjoy discussing the results of their class survey and comparing their own selections with the final list.

By continuing this activity over several weeks, each student is able to participate in tabulating the survey results. The survey promotes classroom discussion as students compare their favorite songs and musicians and explore current trends in popular music.

Richard E. Coles, Givins-Shaw Public School, Toronto, Ontario, Canada

Read It with Music

Why

Songs are a natural for classroom language development: they are enjoyable and require no explanation or motivation. The rhyme, rhythm, and repetition of verse and chorus heighten the predictability of the language. Reading songs becomes highly successful because students have the opportunity to read and reread predictable and familiar language. Song reading is a natural way to introduce print without any picture cues.

It is important to remember that songs will aid reading growth even if they are not read, since they expand the language base of the reader. However, there are many ways to use songs *with* print in order to take advantage of an enjoyable activity and make it a literacy experience.

Who

All elementary students

How

Various activities that integrate music, reading, and writing are described below. The following guidelines will enhance each activity.

1. Songs invite repetition. Use them again and

again. With younger children, repeat them daily.

2. Introduce songs by singing them. Let the children read along as they are learning the words, but don't make the reading a chore. It's easier for them to read a song *after* they have learned it.

3. Always focus on the whole when using song sheets or posters. Point to entire sentences during a sing-along, rather than pointing at each word.

Shared Songs

Write the words to a simple, repetitive song on the board. Sing the song with the group several times, focusing on the written words as you sing, until the children are familiar with the song. Continue to sing the song each day, allowing students to take turns being song leader and guiding the singing. Copy the song onto chart paper or posterboard so that it can be used over and over. The pages might be illustrated and bound into a Big Book (see page 85) for the classroom. Some appropriate songs to use are "I Love the Mountains," "Hush Little Baby," and "If You're Happy and You Know It."

Individual Student Books

As a perfect follow-up (suggested by author Bill Martin, Jr., in a workshop at Oakland University) to the shared books, prepare small books for students to read at the reading table or reading corner. Using half sheets of typing paper, type or write one line of the song on each page and staple the pages inside a cover made from cutting a file folder in half. For longer songs, put one verse on each page. Decorate and laminate the cover. The pages may be illustrated or left plain, providing a pictureless reading experience. Older students can prepare their own books.

Singing Signboards

Signboards can be made for any repetitive song, such as "She'll Be Comin' 'Round the Mountain," "I Love My Rooster," "There Was an Old Woman Who Swallowed a Fly," and "If You're Happy and You Know It." Write each repetitive phrase or verse on small strips of tagboard and the chorus on larger sheets of tagboard or on posterboard. Use the signboards in the following activities:

1. Hold all the cards (or ask a student to) and

turn them over as the song is sung, or place them on a chart board, allowing children to read the words as they sing. Later make this a sort of guessing-song game, silently holding up the next verse to be sung.

2. Ask students to hold up signboards as the class sings a song. Each student holds his or her card down until the class sings the verse on the sign. This activity is a natural to share with another class once students have rehearsed it several times.

3. Establish a place where students can use the signboards with another student or as an independent activity. Children can repeat the class activities or invent their own.

Using the Listening Post or Tape Center

When students know a song well, the words can be tape-recorded for the class listening post. Students use the tape as a read-along with books made in the classroom or trade books. To make the tape, assemble a book, a tape recorder, a blank tape (preferably a ten- or twenty-minute cassette so both sides can be used with a minimum of rewinding), and a clicker, a pair of rhythm sticks, or other noisemaker. After students rehearse singing the song with one student using the clicker to indicate when to turn the page, tape-record the song. This is a perfect time to talk about record and tape production. The classroom becomes a recording studio, and several "takes" might be needed before the recording is acceptable. Older students might work individually or in groups to tape-record a book for younger students.

Writing Song Books

Many songs suggest original verses. Some, such as "Put Your Finger in the Air," are very simple and work well with younger students. Others, such as "Hey Lolly," are more complex. Other songs can also be rewritten and personalized. Use these invented songs to make illustrated class books, with a verse on each page. These songs can also be tape-recorded for the listening post.

Song Sheets

Older students will enjoy classroom song sheets. Start with one page and add on as the year continues. Several songs can appear on each page, perhaps grouped by theme. Song sheets are versatile — they can be used daily in a self-contained class and are also wonderful for a substitute teacher. Don't worry if young children don't really read the words at first. They will be reading the lyrics before long.

Extending Song Sheets

1. Many records come with printed song sheets. Make a tape recording of the song and add it and the song sheet to the listening center. Ella Jenkins, a children's folksinger, is ideal for listening-post sing-alongs. Tapes and song sheets of some popular music might also be added to the listening center.
2. Invite children to prepare song sheets for some favorite works of popular music. This is a complex literacy task that children will enjoy.
3. Invite children to construct scrapbooks to serve as class songbooks. The songbooks can be a year-long project used for sing-alongs, or they can be an end-of-the-year collection of favorites.

Song Bees

Song bees are an old camp game. Divide the class into teams and select a word. In turn, each team sings a song that contains the word. A team is eliminated if the students cannot think of an appropriate song, and the game continues until only one team remains, as in a spelling bee. Thematic words work best, or give students a general concept, such as *water,* and let them use variations of the concept, such as *rain, snow, ocean, sea, cry, tears.*

Expand the song bee into a literacy experience by giving the teams time to list their songs in advance of the bee. Or announce a theme at the beginning of the week to give teams time to look for songs. On the day of the bee, teams sing the songs they have found.

Debra Goodman, Detroit Public Schools, Michigan

A Change of Tune

Why

Early readers often do not expect what they read to make sense. Many times they read word for word or sound by sound and seem unaware of the relationship between oral and written language. This lesson will help students read in "meaning segments" by showing them the importance of grammatical and semantic structure in written language. Their reading will improve as they use the natural flow and rhythm of language.

Who

Kindergartners and primary students

How

Write the words to a favorite song, nursery rhyme, or poem on the chalkboard, overhead projector, or chart paper. Select a song that would be easy for students to modify. Discuss the verses or lines as separate parts that are connected in some way. For example, in "The Farmer in the Dell," each verse is about a different person or animal, but that character adds a new character who then takes over in the next verse.

Erase or block out all the nouns or verbs (or both elements) in the selection. Have the class read or sing the song and discuss how it does not make sense without the missing words. Talk about what kinds of words would or would not make sense in the blanks.

Students could make up new verses by inserting new words in the blanks and could read or sing the new verses aloud. For example, "The whale in the sea" might replace "The farmer in the dell," and "The whale eats a shark" might replace "The farmer takes a wife."

What Else

After students become adept at working together to transform the lyrics to popular songs, invite them to work individually or in pairs to transform song lyrics. The new words and appropriate illustrations are bound into a book for the classroom library.

Charla Lau, Royal Oak, Michigan, with Diane DeFord, Kathleen Evans-Bates, and Jane Robertson

Using Music to Predict Written Language

Why

To make language more meaningful for students and to help develop their language proficiency by combining language with an art form meaningful to them

Who

Upper elementary students who are deeply involved in music

How

The student strums a guitar (or plays another appropriate instrument) and sings a favorite song. Listen and give objective positive feedback. As the student again sings and accompanies the song, tape-record the performance. Tape or print a script from the tape of the performance. (Students can observe the preparation of the script or make their own scripts.) Designate the chord changes on the script.

The student gives a second performance, this time reading the script aloud to the accompaniment of the guitar, rather than singing the song. The student repeats reading the song with accompaniment until he or she becomes comfortable with the print alone. Then the student reads the words of the song with no accompaniment.

What Else

1. Students create the words and music for their own songs.
2. Students compose musical chords to accompany the reading of a favorite poem, or they might compose a melody and rhythm for singing the poem.
3. Play a song on the piano while students associate words with the melody.
4. Students compile books of song lyrics and chords.

Glen R. Anderson, Central Missouri State University, Warrensburg

Let a Puppet Do Your Talking

Why

To motivate children to tell stories to one another with the use of puppets

Who

All elementary students

How

Select a puppet that will appeal to the class. Younger students might enjoy a puppet made from an old stuffed animal — simply cut a slit in the bottom and remove the stuffing. Older children might prefer a more sophisticated puppet. Use the puppet to encourage oral language by having it tell tall tales, tell fish stories, tell ghost stories, or retell a favorite story. Or play a game based on *Brown Bear, Brown Bear, What Do You See?* by Bill Martin, Jr. Have the puppet ask, "Crystal ball, crystal ball, what do I see?" The children take turns responding, giving such answers as "I see a spooky ghost looking at me."

What Else

Invite students to make puppets for their own use. Then provide an ample supply of paper — and time — so students can write their own puppet stories.

Carmen Kennedy, Saints Peter and Paul
Elementary School, Boonville, Missouri

Drama-Based Comprehension

Why

To use drama as an effective springboard for comprehension

Who

Kindergartners and primary students

How

Discuss with students the components of every story: location or setting, characters, action, and problem or conflict. Ask students to brainstorm a list of different characters and locations. Then have the class select one setting and several characters, perhaps by voting. Choose children to play the characters, and have them stand together at the front of the classroom. Remind everyone of the imaginary location. Ask the students at their desks to develop a problem or conflict to be resolved and to give directions on how to carry out the action to those students playing the characters. It is a good idea to have a bell or some other system to freeze the action while the students agree upon the next move. The student actors continue the action until the problem or conflict has been resolved.

Next, seat the children around you and have them help write down the story that has been dramatized. Slow the writing process down so children can see how to record their ideas. Draw attention to skills involved in writing when appropriate, but be careful not to emphasize skills over the content of the story. Ask for volunteers to read aloud what has been written, and encourage students to make revisions and to select a title. Type the final version of the story, putting one or two sentences at the top of each sheet of paper. Duplicate the story, bind the pages into booklets, and distribute a copy to each child in the class. Encourage the children to make illustrations for each page of the book. Students read their books each day, either aloud as a group or silently to themselves. As appropriate, discuss skills that will help them construct meaning from the text.

Sandra Lee Smith, Phoenix Elementary School
District #1, Arizona

PART 2

Nov. 26
happinD

I'am gonea Be a writer and this is how it The Sorning I thote to my Sellf. if I want to Be fameoueS. I Shound Do itnow. BeCoues if I Do it, when I'am old and Grey. coues I might Die from a heart atac. and if I do it when I'am miDill aGe'D. I'll Be marryD. and I have kid's of my own. and I'll have to take them. to the movie's all the time. and the Park. and I won't have time to Write. So I thote when I'am in my childhood it would Be BESt. So I'am going to write a Story. and See what my mom and DaD think of it. and if they think it's good. I'll SenD it. to tronto and Get it PuBlish?

Nov. 26
Josh M

Chapter 4:
Writing for Self-Expression

... some writing ... not only communicates information, it makes the reader care about that information, it makes him feel, it makes him experience, it gets under his skin. That is what we call creative writing. The writer simply calls it good writing, writing that works. And if it gets under enough people's skin, generation after generation, it is art.

— Donald M. Murray, *Learning by Teaching: Selected Articles on Writing and Teaching* (Boynton/Cook, 1982), 136

The theme of the writing experiences in this chapter is personalization within a social setting. Included are activities that evoke the single, clear, imaginative voice of each child within the group setting.

A Writing Inventory

Why

To assist students in establishing a bank of ideas that they can draw upon for writing topics

Who

All elementary students

How

Ask students to think about the many things that they could tell someone about. Brainstorm with them as a group, if necessary, and list on the board all the topics that they feel they know something about. Then ask students to make their own lists of ideas and to record the topics on paper. The following is Shawn's list:

I no about Stars.
I no about basketball.
I no about book.
I no about list.
I no about Pac Man.
I no about letters.
I no about Rules.
I no about notes.
I no about hockey.

The lists later serve as an inventory of writing ideas. Students can keep their lists in their writing folders and continue to add topics.

Linda I. Inglis, Consulting Services, Edmonton Public Schools, Alberta, Canada

---

I-Searching

Why

This activity adapts Ken Macrorie's *Searching Writing* (1980) to the elementary grades. Students choose a topic that they truly care about and then find out more about it — hence, *I-Search*. I-Searching differs from traditional researching in that it is a student-centered, rather than teacher-centered, project. The secret to successful I-Searching is two-fold: students must have a genuine interest in their subjects (no pretending interest just to please the teacher), and they must talk to people in the course of their search. Macrorie's I-Searchers interview "experts." For elementary students, interpret the term *expert* loosely to ensure that each student has the opportunity to interview someone.

Students see a real-world function of writing when they I-Search, and they enjoy sharing their papers with one another. I-Searchers learn how to interact with information, explore many resources, and discover that people are resources, too.

Who

All elementary students

How

Topic selection is the key to I-Searching. Ask students to suggest all the topics that they personally would like to know more about. Cover the board with their responses, which will range from computers to soccer to ballet. Explain that in I-Searching students will become detectives investigating their subjects. Let students think about possible topics for a few days, and then each student chooses his or her own topic. Macrorie recommends the cooling-off period before the final topic selection to give students time to change their minds and to discover new possibilities.

Explain that the form for presenting the research is a first-person narrative. As the students write and think "I," they take full responsibility for their own search. The paper will contain four general sections:

1. What I already know about my topic and why I chose it.

2. What I need to know.

3. What I did to find out the information.

4. What I discovered.

This progression is vital because it gives the student a clear way to organize and present a variety of information.

The first section, listing previous knowledge about a topic, can be written in class. Some students may need gentle prodding before they realize that they already know something about their topics. Most students move easily from the first section to the second section, where they list everything that they would like to find out about their topics, but they will need varying degrees of help in generating this list of questions. Here is what one third grader wanted to find out about computers:

1. Where do computers come from?
2. Where can I get a computer?
3. Where can I get a apple 2-e?
4. Where can I get a game computer?
5. How can they help me with school?
6. Where can I get discs?
7. Where are computers made?

At this point, call for assistance from parents and from the community at large. Send a letter home to parents listing all the topics that students have selected and explaining the project itself. Ask parents to volunteer to serve as experts on any of the topics and to list names and phone numbers of other possible resource people. Librarians, resource specialists at local schools or businesses, and friends and acquaintances are possible sources of information.

The interviews are conducted outside of class. In advance, arm students with as much information as possible. Help students find books, pamphlets, articles, and brochures about their topics, and encourage them to do some reading prior to the interview. From the list of possible resource people, help each student locate the name of an appropriate specialist to interview. Talk about interviewing techniques and help students develop a list of questions to ask. The success of the project does not depend upon the richness of the resources or the amount of information gathered — in I-Searching the *process* is as important as the *product*. After the search is completed, students describe in writing how they acquired the information to answer their questions.

The last section of the paper, in which students describe what they discovered, is the most difficult for them. They need to interact with their processes and to decide what they have learned as a result of the I-Search. They cannot simply review the information that they gathered. Here is what one second grader discovered about playing soccer:

How to play Soccer
(my book)
I learned that you have to stay in shape for Soccer. You have to excersise! I also learned the official Soccer Signals.

The teacher's role throughout has been more coach than judge, and the I-Search papers are not evaluated like traditional research papers. I-Search papers are to be shared. The sharing makes all the hard work, from interviewing to editing the paper, worthwhile. Each student is the resident expert on his or her topic and has real-world information to share with the class. Michael is the only one who knows whether or not he should buy a home computer, and only Sarah knows which sticker club is best for her. Josh becomes the person to see about major league baseball, and Chris knows all about dog training.

What Else

Adopt some of the I-Search procedures in other teaching activities. At the outset of a lesson on a new topic, ask students to write about what they already know about the topic. When the lesson is completed, have them write what they have learned from the lesson. The writing reinforces the lesson and incorporates writing across the curriculum.

Reference

Macrorie, Ken. *Searching Writing.* Boynton/Cook, 1980.

Suzanne L. Noble, Pines Elementary School, Magalia, California

Ask the Author: Author as Authority, Author as Resource, Author Unavailable

Why

To help students strengthen the connection between reading and writing by developing inferential comprehension

Who

All elementary students

How

Ask the Author (A.T.A.) is a three-phase strategy for teaching inferential comprehension in classrooms where children are taught writing as a process. The process approach to writing involves blocks of time forty-five to sixty minutes in length several times a week when children choose their own topics, revise and edit their pieces, and, most importantly, share their writing with other students. It is during the sharing of written pieces that the teacher implements A.T.A.

To help readers make inferences at necessary points, teachers need a clear idea of what an inference is, and which inferences are the important ones to make. Help students make inferences that are both text based and relevant: information implied by the text but not directly stated, and information important to the progress of the narrative. Practice applying these criteria to questions asked during reading lessons. At several points during A.T.A., model the asking of inference questions. Good inference questions can be explained to students as being "hinted at but never really said in the writing" (text based) and "needed for the story to make sense" (relevant).

The *first phase* of A.T.A. is "Author as Authority." (It is not at all necessary to label the phases of A.T.A.; the labels merely help in outlining the strategy.) "Author as Authority" should last two to three months in most classrooms. As children finish writing pieces and are ready to share them, set up a time when each author reads his or her piece to the rest of the group. Experiment to decide if "the group" should be the whole class or a smaller group. Each group member has a copy of the author's text, either a photocopy of the author's original or a copy of a typed version.

After the author reads, the other children are encouraged to respond in a concrete, positive way to the content and style ("I liked the part about scaring your little brother," or "The way you described the airport made me feel like I was there"). Then children are to read back over their copies and ask questions of the author. Encourage good inference questions by such comments as, "Yes, your story hints at that but doesn't really tell us, and we need to know the answer." If important inference questions are not asked, ask them, modeling the technique. You may want to present one or more sessions on asking good questions, during which the student criteria for text-based, relevant inferences are emphasized.

The author is the first and final authority on all questions. Readers may have different opinions of what the text means to them, but the author knows what was intended. During this phase, writers become aware of their audience and of what questions might be asked. They begin to see that what they imply when they write must be inferred by their readers. Writers also experience success at answering inference questions, the vital first step in inferential comprehension.

The *second phase* of A.T.A. is "Author as Resource." When readers have learned to ask good inference questions and writers have learned to answer them, help students focus on the text, rather than on the author. Each group member again has a copy of a student text. The author is present for discussion of the text, but is not called on until the end of the discussion. The group designs and answers questions about the text, again with encouragement and guidance from the teacher in focusing on text-based, relevant inferences. Guide the students in forming hypotheses, referring back to the text, and reaching consensus on possible answers. The emphasis should be on the process of making inferences; there may be more than one plausible response to any question.

The author is called on as a resource to confirm or refute answers. The author should also be encouraged to listen to and respond to the process the group uses. An author might say, "I see how you thought that, but I meant. . . ." During this phase, readers learn a process for answering inference questions, and writers receive feedback on the clarity of their writing.

The *third phase* of A.T.A. is "Author Unavailable." It is similar to "Author as Resource" in procedure, but the material is no longer written by students from the class. The text may be stories written by students in another school, basal stories, or library books. Again, students work together to ask good inference questions and reach consensus on plausible answers. Now, however, students must be content with their answers, because the author is not available to verify their conclusions. In this phase, the process of posing and answering inferential questions is transferred to the ordinary demands of school reading and reading done outside the classroom. Occasionally, the group might want to write authors with particularly perplexing questions, such as:

> Dear Mr. Sendak,
>   We can't figure out how Max's supper could still be warm. Was he dreaming? Was it a daydream? Did he go upstairs early and sleep, and his mother brought dinner later?

For the most part, however, readers learn to rely on their own inferential ability.

Move to the "Author Unavailable" phase after students become proficient with posing and answering questions. However, "Author as Authority" and "Author as Resource" can be used effectively throughout the year in combination with "Author Unavailable." Interspersing the three phases will add variety to the development of inferential abilities and will emphasize the natural connection between being an author and understanding an author.

JoBeth Allen, University of Georgia, Athens

Written Conversation

Why

This strategy reinforces the usefulness of writing as a means of communicating. The language user's own language resources are used and fostered. Conventions are learned in a purposeful context, and an interest factor is inherent. Success with written conversation can lead to further interest in writing as well as be a meaningful way to practice and use written conventions. This strategy will help students realize the relationship between oral and written language.

Who

All elementary students; with adaptation for different ages and developmental levels

How

Students conduct written conversations as they would an oral conversation. Have students work with a partner; older students might work in groups of three or four. Explain that the partners are to communicate, but that no talking is allowed. Everything they want to say to one another is to be written. Students take turns writing, just as they would alternate in oral communication.

As written language is produced, conventions in spelling or punctuation might be transmitted from one student to another. In the following example, note how one second grader conventionalizes his spelling:

> Do you want to make cookies today?
> *Yes!*
> Do you want to EAT cookies today?
> *Yes! Why do y ask such eesee questins?*
> Because. What kind of cookies shall we make? That's not such an easy question! You like them all!
> *I want chockletchip cookies and that is an easy question.*

Specify the content of the conversation and use the written conversation as a study strategy, or let the students choose the topic of their conversation. In the following example, two eighth graders discuss solving this math problem: Jake bought some donuts at 10¢ each. He ate 4 and sold the rest at 15¢ each. His profit was $2.40. How many donuts did he buy?

> I wish this wasn't about food.
> *Yes, I'm starving. I only ate about 5 minutes ago. I think a variable should be used for the number bought. X.*
> The number sold was 4 less than X then, X−4. So X−4 times 15¢ = $2.40. Right?
> *I think there's more to it. $2.40 is the profit. Profit equals selling minus buying. Right? So how does [(X−4)15] − (X10) = 240 seem?*
> Too hard! Why didn't he just sell them all?!
> *Would be the same process.*
> (15X−60) − 10X = 240. How the h--- do you get those ( ) out?
> *You don't need to.*

In the written conversation given below, the fifth-grade participants are having a friendly argument.

> did you eat? did you get Fat?
> *How about you? Did you get fat?*
> No. I did not get Fat.
> *Yes you did.*
> No! Where do you see it?
> *But you are still fat.*
> NO NO I am not fat.
> *Yes you are!*
> I tell you I am not fat dummy. Look at me I am Not Fat!
> *O.K. youre not fat.*
> Thank-you for telling me I am Not Fat.

What Else

1. Put a written message on the board, such as "Please return to your seats; we are going to have social studies now." Do not respond to any questions or comments. Just look pleasant or mysterious. Have an overhead projector ready and several prepared acetate sheets on which further information is written. Begin by using a sheet explaining the activity. For example, "For the next 30 minutes you are invited to communicate with each other in writing only. If you have a question, a comment, or a problem, you will have to tell me or a classmate — in writing." Continue to write the directions for a familiar type of assignment for the class. Roam around the room, exchanging written communication with the children as they are working, or remain at your desk and invite children with questions to come to you. Remember that no verbal communication is to be used.

2. Divide the class into groups of three to five students. Allow them to work together on a content-area assignment for a short time, again using just written communication. Each group has a leader who is responsible for seeing that all group members have a chance to participate as much as possible in the nonverbal communication.

Adapted by Dorothy F. King, Office of Indian Education, Chinle Agency, Chinle, Arizona; "What Else" by Heather Hamlin, Harrisburg Elementary School, Missouri

Dialogue Journals: A New Tool for Communication

Why

Dialogue journals are a natural way to engage students in using reading and writing. They require no commercial materials, diagnostic tests, or teacher training. They are completely individualized, with topics of particular interest to each student and text adapted to each student's reading level.

Who

All elementary students, from beginning readers to upper-grade students, and including special populations such as children learning English as a second language, deaf children, and special education students

How

Dialogue journals are a long-standing means for teachers (especially in elementary classes) to carry on private, written conversations with each student in a bound journal on a daily basis. The writing is *functional;* that is, students and teachers write directly to each other, using language to get things done in an active way. Students ask questions, complain about lessons, describe what happened on the playground or at home, reflect on why things happen, express personal feelings, and even argue with the teacher about the fairness of assignments — in other words, they are using written language in all the ways they use their oral language.

The teacher writes a direct, personal response to

the *content* of the student's writing, rather than commenting on form or style, and also brings up new topics of interest for discussion. The teacher's responses are natural elaborations and extensions of the student's thinking about issues and experiences. For young learners, this provides the best kind of language modeling about topics in which they are interested, and teachers can easily adapt their writing to a reading level that is just slightly challenging to the student. The informal conversational style means that a student must often reread his or her own entry to understand the teacher's response; the bound form of the journals makes rereading easy.

There are logistics in the keeping of a dialogue journal. Most teachers have found that the following procedures work best for elementary students.

1. When you introduce dialogue journals, explain that they are a way for you and your students to talk to each other. Stress communication, privacy, and honesty.
2. Small, bound journals (not spiral notebooks) with covers that can be individually decorated are most appropriate. Students are impressed when they fill up a whole book and get a new one.
3. At the beginning literacy levels, set aside one specific time during the day for dialogue journals, with other times optional if students have more to say. It may be helpful to set a *minimum* length for each entry — such as one, two, or three sentences — so that no one can complain about having to write "too much" on those days when there just isn't anything to say. This keeps the dialogue going over dry spells. But don't get hung up on length; it's the content that counts.
4. In upper elementary classes, journal writing should be allowed to occur at free times or transition times all during the day, rather than only at one assigned time. Older students need to be able to write as soon as questions, ideas, or problems pop into their heads; they may forget what they really felt and wanted to say if they have to wait until a set time.
5. Establish a regular place and time for journals to be turned in and handed back. They should not be "collected" like other papers. A special place in the room or a "journal bag" can be used.
6. Write responses in the journals the same day or evening. Short, brief exchanges seem to work better and are easier.
7. Return the journals to students at the beginning of school each morning. Allow time then for students to read your responses and to write in return.

Just as important as the logistics are your responses. They will help students "dig deeper" into themselves and express more of their ideas, opinions, feelings, and values. Some tips for responding follow:

1. Repond to their topic first, acknowledging the importance of what they are writing about or commenting on their topics, before you introduce a new or related topic of your own. The more interesting your comment, the more you'll give them to talk about.
2. Ask only genuine questions, ones that you want answered with their ideas and personal opinions. Be careful not to ask two or three questions consecutively, implying that you are quizzing them.
3. Make your response interesting by talking about how *you* feel, about your opinions and concerns. As you develop greater rapport with individual students, share some personal experiences and fears, just as you would with a close, trusted friend.
4. Write about as much as the student writes, not more. This is important to equalize the power between you, an experienced writer, and the student, a beginning writer.
5. Use a direct, informal style of writing — write what you would say if you were responding orally, including phrases and exclamations, such as "That's great!" "OK!" "Ouch!"
6. Be patient. It may take a month or two for students to become comfortable with putting their ideas and feelings in writing. The following excerpts from two young students' dialogue journals demonstrate their ability to express themselves:

> I had eggs and toast. I have soccer tomorrow.
> *What color is your uniform?*
> Blue and white.
> *Can you draw me a picture of it?*
> No.
> *Why not?*
> I don't know what it looks like.
>
> I saw Peter Pan and I saw it with my Grandma and Grandpa and Jessica.
> *Did you like it?*
> *Did anyone fly besides Peter Pan?*
> Yes.
> *So tell me who!!*
> Michael, Wendy and John.
> *I enjoyed seeing it a long long time ago.*
> of course.

Jana J. Staton, Virginia Polytechnic Institute and State University, Blacksburg

The Kindergarten Journal: First Things First

Why

The kindergarten journal provides a tool that allows children to communicate effectively, with all their developmental inconsistencies and within the framework of a large class. They can achieve success and growth daily in a noncompetitive, self-gratifying activity, utilizing their own strengths and interests — the perfect motivational tool. Children work at their own levels of written communication: drawing, labeling, and using inventive spelling, sentences, and story structure. This gives each child a sense of achievement, which permeates the whole classroom atmosphere. Children provide supportive responses to one another's "authorship" because written communication is viewed so positively.

The daily journals are a good medium for establishing communication with the parents about the child's personality and background. Journals provide children with a means for expressing their unspoken thoughts and can often evoke humor — an invaluable ingredient in a parent-teacher conference.

Who

Kindergartners

How

Begin by preparing the journals. Fold eight sheets of 12″ × 18″ paper in half, add a cover of heavier paper, and staple the pages, preferably so the pages lie flat when the journal is opened. The covers might be of index-card stock, perhaps color-coded for each month, or you might laminate children's illustrations for each month's journal.

Introduce the activity by explaining that the students will be keeping a monthly journal. After they open the journal to the first page and write the page number and date in the top right-hand corner, ask the children to think of any story they wish and to write it in the journal by recording the sounds of the words they wish to use. Stories might be personal anecdotes, fictional accounts, or summaries of a science or social science project. Then children are to read their stories aloud to you or to a teacher aide or volunteer, who also could take dictation from those students reluctant to write with inventive spellings.

Make no value judgments, but do encourage those who wish to edit and revise their stories. For those students who finish their journal stories before the others, provide additional paper for writing a story to take home. Writing time should be special, and no alternative activity should be allowed until at least half of the group finish their journal stories. If time allows, ask volunteers to "publish" their stories by reading them aloud to the class. Encourage positive comments from the others.

Have students keep a separate journal for each month of the school year. The journals remain in the classroom until the end of the year, but they are available for students to refer to and for parent-teacher conferences. For those parents who are concerned about encouraging incorrect spellings, I offer this anecdote.

When a Japanese girl who spoke no English joined our class, she readily took to the journal. Atsuko loved to draw in the journal, and the children admired her pictures and communicated with her in the beautiful nonverbal way that young children have. I wished to learn the name of the animal she often drew, and played charades with her to guess the name. "Bow-wow?" "Meow?" No response. I pantomimed "big ears," and immediately Atsuko responded, "Oosagee! Oosagee!" My first Japanese word was *rabbit*. I wrote it on the chalkboard — "oo-sa-gee," to reinforce it in my vocabulary. At that moment I realized I was using inventive spelling of my own.

What Else

1. At parent-teacher conferences, use the series of journals to demonstrate the child's progress. Point out the child's level of language development by his or her use of drawing, labeling, sentencing, sequential storytelling, and beginning reading skills. The journals might prompt the parents to share anecdotes from home about such topics as children's fears or imaginary playmates. Encourage parents to refrain from making negative comments about the journals and to keep journals themselves, providing an opportunity for children to see their parents as writers.
2. Children might write their own books based on stories in their journals. This could be an ongoing activity, with the stories kept readily available in writing folders. Periodically, children could select a story to publish and could illustrate the cover. The cover might include a short description of the author

and his or her photograph. The "About the Author" text might be dictated to the teacher or into a tape recorder.

3. Make transparencies of the children's stories and ask them to illustrate the transparencies with special markers. As each child's story is displayed on a screen with the overhead projector, tape-record the child "reading" the story. A variation of this activity is to take slides of individual children as they are writing. Project the slide on one screen and the story on another screen while playing a tape of the child "reading" the story.

4. As an end-of-year activity, children make and decorate large envelopes on which they write, "I Am an Author." Fill each child's envelope with his or her journals, published and unpublished books, and transparency drawings. Send the writing collection home for the children to share with their families.

Shirley L. Murray, Journal Consultant, South Burlington School District, Vermont

Guided Fantasy Stories

Why

Guided fantasy evokes an imaginary story from young children that uses their creative minds and personal imagery. By fantasizing the whole story in images, students need not worry about how it is going to end, but concentrate on how to communicate what happened in their minds. The emphasis is on communication and reconstruction rather than construction. The integration of the four language arts processes occurs as the children orally share their journeys before writing and reading about the journeys.

Who

All elementary students, particularly young learners and remedial learners who need to proceed from thinking in pictures to thinking in words

How

Guided fantasy begins with a teacher-directed journey eliciting vivid imagery about an imaginary trip. After the journey is complete, students share their journeys in pairs, allowing them to verbalize the inner experience immediately. Remind the children that words signify the pictures and feelings they had when their eyes were closed. After the immediate oral sharing of the story, students may want to write a group story or to write individually.

Create an atmosphere of multisensory experience. Ask students to close their eyes to decrease their reliance on visual stimuli. Suggest the setting and characterize the traveler in the journey. Then present some type of calming action, which allows the imagery of the setting to unfold naturally, according to the personal experiences of the students. When the students are in this relaxed state, develop the action of the adventure. Unusual and strange actions are often more effective for young children. Interweave the various actions with calming statements and pauses to maintain a relaxed, image-making, dreamlike state. To personalize the fantasy experience, leave the action incomplete so that students can finish the journey on their own. Then direct their thoughts back to the classroom in order to connect the fantasy with reality.

The following is an example of a fantasy experience. Read it aloud in a calm, serene voice, inserting many pauses so the imagery of the journey can flow through the conscious mind of each child.

1. Sensory-Awareness Statement

> Close your eyes and relax in your chair.... Now listen to the noises in the room.... Can you hear them?... Feel the temperature of this room.... Is it hot or cold?

2. Setting Statement

> Now turn the sounds of this room into the sounds of the meadow.... Listen to the sounds of the meadow.... What kind of day is it?... Sunny? ... Cloudy?... Hot?... Cold?... Imagine that you are walking on a narrow pathway toward a mountain....

3. Calming Statement

> A calm breeze is blowing gently on you as you walk down...down...down...a pathway.... With each step the mountain comes closer...and closer...and closer....

4. Action Statement and Calming Statement

> As you reach the mountain you begin to climb up...up...up and around and around the side of the mountain.... Through the clouds...you climb up...up...up....

5. Imaging and Action Statement

> As you reach the top of the mountain, you enter a cave where you see a wise old man sitting in front of a fire. . . . You approach the wise man . . . and sit down with him. . . . He has lived a long time. . . . He can answer any of your questions. . . . Ask him about something you want to know. . . .

6. Closing and Separation Statement

> I will leave you here. . . . You can finish the journey in your mind. . . . When you have finished your journey . . . you may return to the classroom and open your eyes.

After this fantasy experience, a group of twenty-five beginning first graders wrote the following story.

The Wise Old Indian

We were marching to a mountain. We went up a rocky mountain. When we got to the top of the mountain, we took off our shoes at the door of the temple. We saw a wise old Indian. We asked the Indian a question. We asked him what life was about. He said life was about love. The end.

What Else

Children discuss how the written story reminds them of what happened when their eyes were closed. This discussion strengthens the concept that written language is a communication of an author's feelings and imaginations through linguistic symbols. It further emphasizes that the language system is a means of communicating the inner thoughts of one person to another.

Barbara J. Walker, Eastern Montana College, Billings

Decision Stories

Why

1. To give students an opportunity to become involved in personalized learning experiences in which their ideas can be freely expressed and valued by others
2. To enable students to internalize patterns of thinking about reading as ideas that can be spoken, written, and read
3. To encourage students to read as a consequence of increased sensitivity to their environments, their language, and their personal needs
4. To encourage students to take risks, clarify values, consider different ideas, and generate material from their own background of experience

Who

Middle and upper elementary students

How

Read aloud or invite students to read a decision story such as the following:

Andy's Dilemma

Andy is an eleven-year-old only child whose parents were divorced last spring. His mom and dad live in the same town, and he spends a lot of time with each of them. Andy's father wants Andy to go to a professional football game in Chicago over a long weekend. His mother wants him to go to a family birthday dinner that will be attended by many relatives. His grandmother and cousin, both very important to him, will be there. Andy has never missed a family birthday dinner. He always looks forward to the dinners and hates to disappoint his mother and his grandmother. Yet Andy would love to spend the weekend in Chicago with his father and see a professional football team. He doesn't want to disappoint his father either. His parents have left the decision entirely up to him.

What should Andy do and why?

Ask students to write their reactions to the decision story, indicating what the character should do and why. Organize students into small groups so they can discuss their reactions. Ask them to decide on the best possible actions, giving supportive reasons, and to present their conclusions to the entire class. Ask students to summarize the various points of view, not necessarily trying to reach a consensus.

Invite students to write decision stories that include the following components: title, situation, characters, facts, events, conditions, and major questions. Suggest outlining to help students organize their thoughts. Ask students to exchange papers for reading, constructive feedback, and suggestions. Establish and maintain a positive atmosphere for talking and writing. Have students use the following guidelines for composing and analyzing the stories:

1. Does the situation pose a "fuzzy" or perplexing problem?

2. Has enough information been included to present the realities of the situation?

3. Has enough information been included to describe the characters adequately (such as personality traits, role, job, responsibilities, relationships)?

4. Is the issue obvious in the situation?

5. Have all the facts and events been presented?

6. Does the title suggest the nature of the situation?

Give students an opportunity to incorporate their classmates' feedback in a final draft of their decision stories.

What Else

1. Use the decision stories as occasional activities to provide purposeful writing throughout the year.
2. More ideas for decision stories can come from diaries and journals, from interviewing students and adults, or from other stories.
3. Decision stories could be expanded into short stories or role-playing experiences.
4. Decision stories could be assembled into class booklets.

Reference

McWilliams, Lana, and Dennie L. Smith. "Decision Stories: Language Experience for Adolescents." *Journal of Reading* 25, no. 2 (November 1981): 142–45.

Barbara Halliwill Bell, Columbia Public Schools, Missouri, and University of Missouri–Columbia

Celebrate the Birthday Child

Why

1. To encourage students to see writing as a functional tool that is used to express ideas and thoughts
2. To help students build self-esteem

Who

Lower and middle elementary students

How

Trace the birthday child's body on newsprint and cut out the figure. Ask this child to sit in a special chair at the front of the room while the other students write on the cutout one positive sentence about the birthday child. Younger children might dictate their statements. The birthday child might invite others in the school (such as principals, other teachers, the librarian, secretaries, or other school personnel) to add a sentence to the cutout. Roll and tie the birthday picture with a colorful ribbon, and then send the cutout home as a reminder of how important the child is to others in the class.

What Else

The idea of celebrating a child can be applied to older children by creating a V.I.P. book of positive statements about the child.

Nancy Fritsch, Parkade Elementary School, Columbia, Missouri

Living, Loving, and Writing Poetry

Why

Reading poetry is teaching poetry. As in any literary genre, language users develop through experience a familiarity with the sounds and feelings that are unique to poetry. Louise Rosenblatt stresses that the literary experience is the "lived through" experience in which a personal, visceral meaning is evoked for the reader rather than the reader being concerned with what is to be learned (to be taken away) from the event. Poetry celebrates itself.

If teachers want students to enjoy poetry, poetry must be enjoyable. When students hear and read poetry and sense the teacher's love of poetry, they often want to write poetry themselves. The following activity sequence helps stimulate that desire to write poetry and helps students learn how to write poetry.

Who

All elementary students, especially those who have a desire to write poetry but who are having difficulty getting started

How

Reading Poetry

Begin by reading a poem to the class every day. Read poetry *you* enjoy and think children will like as well. Choose poems from a variety of styles about a variety of topics by a variety of poets, including poetry by and about minority and ethnic populations. Invite students to select from a collection of poetry books in the classroom library those poems that they would like to read or to have you read aloud. Read aloud poems that you have written, and then describe the process you went through to create the poem. Encourage students to write their own poetry. Read these poems aloud and ask if children want their poems displayed in the classroom.

Writing Poetry

Ask the students what a poem is. Help them brainstorm ideas about what makes a poem different from other literary forms. Discuss which of these ideas relate to all poetry and which relate to some poetry. Find poems that exemplify each of the categories listed. Return to the discussion of what poetry is and isn't. Have the class agree upon a definition of poetry.

Encourage students to experiment with poetry whenever they feel the desire. During writing conferences, suggest poetry as a possible choice of genre if the student's topic lends itself, as most do, to poetry. Encourage students to re-create images or repetitive patterns that they enjoy in the poems they read. One student, who was fond of hearing Nikki Giovanni's "Ego-Tripping (There May Be a Reason Why)" over and over, was inspired to write his first poem:

> My mind is like a bird it soars higher and higher and never falls.
> The trees in my mind never die.
> My mind can go anywhere,
>   it has no limit.
>   There is life in my head it never stops!
> I am the UNIVERSE!
>   When my body is gone my mind is EARTH.
>   Gregg Ketchie

The following suggestions might encourage prospective, though insecure, poets in your classroom. The amount of direction or structure can vary according to the needs of the students. The focus of the activities should be on helping students become poets, but they should maintain ownership of their writing.

1. Ask students to add one or more stanzas to an existing poem, either a poem in a book or one written by another student. The structure of the poem will provide direction. Poems with highly predictable structures (such as repetitive language) might be the easiest for students to add to.

2. Students may build a poem around a line from another poem. To do this, they must come to terms with the imagery. Chris, who was having trouble starting out, wrote the following poem based on the line "Zero makes me hungry" from Aliki Barnstone's poem "Numbers."

> Zero makes me hungry when I'm riding my
>   motorcycle.
> I'm fast real fast
> I like to feel the wind.
> I like to fly over jumps.
> But when it is just sitting when the speedometer
>   is on zero
> It eats me up.

3. Two or more students might collaborate to write a group poem.

4. Remember not to grade students' poetry — just enjoy it.

What Else

1. Make anthologies of student poetry for the classroom library or the school library.

2. Ask students to read or write poetry that relates to different content areas, such as math, social studies, and science.

3. Invite students to bring in the lyrics to favorite songs. Make a copy for each student and have the class read the words aloud.

4. Students put poetry to music.

5. Invite students to illustrate poems found in books or student-authored poems.

6. Present literary terminology naturally, as the concepts develop. For example, children often use similes before they know the term *simile* or what it means.

Paul Crowley, Jefferson Junior High School, Columbia, Missouri

From Images to Poetry

Why

1. To provide students with guidance in writing poetry without inhibiting them by demanding adherence to exact forms

2. To help students create poetry that connects to images from their real lives

Who

Middle and upper elementary students

How

Guided Imagery

Begin the activity sequence by guiding students back to some meaningful memory. They are to close their eyes, relax, and focus on the memory. Read aloud, in a calm, serene voice, a passage designed to conjure up memories. A sample passage follows:

> You are going back to that place where you will see, hear, and feel everything again. Choose a time and place that has stuck in your memory. Perhaps it is a place where you enjoyed doing something. It might be a soccer field, a secret hiding place in a tree, a pet store where your family first saw its puppy, a fishing boat where you struggled to catch a big fish, or you might have an entirely different kind of special place in mind. Now write the name of your special place on your paper.

At this point check that each student has identified and written down a place so that no one will be left behind when the imaging begins. Then continue with the guided imagery.

> Close your eyes and sit back in your chair with your hands loosely on your lap and your feet on the floor. Try not to make any sounds or to move around because that might interrupt someone else's imagery. Breathe slowly in and out. Feel your neck relax.... Now the relaxation spreads into your shoulders...down your back...through your arms.... You feel comfortable and relaxed as you breathe slowly in and out.
>
> In your mind's eye you are back in the place you wrote on your paper. What do you see?... What colors?... What shapes?... What's happening?... What are you doing?... Watch yourself moving.... Are there other people there? What are they doing?... What are you thinking?
>
> Get really close to something and look at it carefully, as if your eyes were magnifying glasses.... You see every detail.... Reach out to touch something or let something touch you. What does it feel like?... Listen. What do you hear?... Are people talking? What are they saying?... What are you saying?... What are you thinking?... Sniff the air. What do you smell?... Can you taste anything? What is it like?... You're getting ready to leave. You're above the place looking down.... What do you see?... What are you thinking?... Now come back to this room. Open your eyes.

Freewriting

As soon as students return from their mental journeys, ask them to write about their memories and to continue writing until you tell them to stop. Explain that they are not to worry at this time about spelling, complete sentences, or even making sense. They are not to stop to erase or reread, but they may want to cross out words or to start over on a new line. The idea is to write spontaneously and continuously.

Students stop writing after five to seven minutes. Expect their drafts to be between one and two pages in length and to vary in form. Some will be lists; others will contain mainly phrases; a few will be organized narratives. All will contain vivid sensory specifics; most will show reflections and honest feelings.

The Composing Process

Students' freewritings contain a rich deposit of recorded information that they can draw on for composing. Now students can experiment freely, almost playfully, as they select one word, phrase, or line and reject another. To help students experiment, you might ask them to underline the phrases or words that they like best and to read these words to a partner. Or suggest that students arrange phrases or words from the freewriting in the shape of a long, thin poem and then rework the verse into final form. Here is a verse created by one third grader:

> At North Carolina Beach
> Under a house I hear the wind blowing.
> I sit and hear the waves breaking
> See gulls and baby crabs all over the sand
> I pretend to work at a soda shop.
> Nice and cool.
>
> Johanna Kroenlein

What Else

1. Write on the chalkboard the following sample sentences from Alan Ziegler's helpful book, *The Writing Workshop:* "As I look outside, I can see the trees sway. They look like dancers. There are also flowers that climb quietly as the kind rain falls" (53). Then copy onto the board some of the ways this paragraph could be put into verse, minus connective words and punctuation. The following examples are also from the Ziegler book (54):

> outside
>
>   trees sway like dancers

```
            flowers quietly climb
            kind
            rain
            falls
            outside
trees sway       dancers
            flowers quietly      climb
            kind
                rain
                    falls
```

Encourage students to select a paragraph or section of their freewritings, to eliminate unnecessary words and punctuation, and to reposition the words to create poems.

2. Question students to help them be more explicit with their vocabulary: "What does a 'cute' puppy look like?" "You say it was 'spooky.' Make me see exactly what you saw so I feel the spookiness." "You say it was 'fun.' The word *fun* means winning at tennis to me. What does it mean for you?" "What sound did the water make? Did it trickle, sprinkle, gush? Can you use a word that will make me hear what you heard?"

3. Provide samples of a variety of poetic forms, such as haiku, cinquain, triolet, and the villanelle. Encourage students to experiment with verses patterned after the samples.

Work Cited

Ziegler, Alan. *The Writing Workshop.* Teachers and Writers Collaborative, 1981.

Adele Fiderer, Curriculum Center, Scarsdale Public Schools, New York

---

Stories from the Past

Why

To help develop students' interviewing skills

Who

With modification, all elementary students

How

Prewriting

To motivate students for this assignment, begin with a session of shared inquiry that involves questions of fact, interpretation, and evaluation. The class is not grouped for prewriting — students are seated informally as they would for storytelling. Ask questions about storytelling, such as: "Do you have a grandmother or grandfather, or an aunt or uncle, who is very old and who loves to tell stories about the way things were a long time ago?" Encourage volunteers to talk about their storytelling relatives, and then ask students to make a list of questions about the old days, such as the following:

What was your school like?

Where did you go when you went out?

How much did a soda cost?

What kind of rules did your parents set for you?

Ask students to tell some of their own stories from as far back as they can remember — from first grade or perhaps preschool. Ask why storytelling was so important to them then. Is it just as important to them today?

The Writing Assignment

1. Students are to interview the oldest person they know — a grandparent, great-grandparent, or friend of the family who is age seventy or older and who can talk about life in another era. If it is not convenient for them to talk with a person of this age, they may interview the oldest person in the household or in the neighborhood. Younger students may need some practice at interviewing in advance of the assignment. Encourage students to convey their interest in what the person being interviewed is saying, and to ask questions and make comments that promote discussion. They are to take notes, without being concerned about grammar and spelling. Students who wish to use a tape recorder must get permission from the person being interviewed.

2. Immediately after the interview, while the conversation is still fresh in their minds, students are to write a character description. Suggest that they begin with a physical description of the person and include details that reflect something about the personality of the person. Encourage students to appeal to the senses and to use comparisons. Where appropriate, they should include quotations from the interview. Remind them to concentrate on an effective opening and an ending that is natural and satisfying. Display the finished papers so that students may share their character descriptions. Each student has selected a different person to interview,

which reduces competition and provides a wide variety of subjects.

Rebecca Brantley Corbett, Franklin County Schools, Louisburg, North Carolina

---

Spin a Space (or Earth) Story: "Life in 2091"

Why

To help students prepare speculative writings based on imaginative details and sensory impressions

Who

Upper elementary students

How

Prewriting

Ask students to imagine themselves in the twenty-first century, in the year 2091. What has changed, and what has remained the same? Are they living on Earth or on some other planet? Ask them to imagine what changes may have taken place, such as interplanetary travel, as well as what changes they would like to see, such as teachers being replaced by computers. Encourage students to discuss these changes and to establish categories, such as *Education, Public and Private Transportation, Home Life, Job Life, Social Life,* and *Local and National Government.* Ask students to write these categories on paper and to list details about their future worlds in each of the categories. For example, *Home Life* might include fully automated underground apartments with indoor gardens lit by skylights.

Next, in a freewriting, students conjure up sensory impressions they have of life in the twenty-first century — sounds, sights, smells, and tastes that they would expect to encounter. Students share their drafts to see if the sensory impressions convey the tone they want to establish in their futuristic descriptions. This freewriting might become the first paragraph in their papers.

Lastly, students decide on characters they want to include in their writings about the future — parents, children, teachers, public officials, robots, space creatures, and so forth. Students jot down bits of possible dialogue and decide on a setting (Earth, some other planet, a planet in another galaxy).

The Writing Assignment

Give students the following directions:

Look over your lists of details, your freewriting based on sensory impressions, and your dialogue notations. Then write about life in 2091. You may want to show your audience what life is like in this new world by describing how you spend your day, from morning until evening. Try to depict the setting vividly, employing sense impressions to establish the tone of the paper in the opening paragraph. The tone of the paper may be witty, ironic, or serious. What would visitors to the scene see when first arriving? How would they feel about what they saw? Write using first-person point of view (*I*) and active verbs in the present tense. Your purpose in this piece of descriptive writing is to make the reader *see* the world you have created, by depicting one day of your life in this new world. Your audience will be your friends and peers, so you will want to focus on scenes, objects, characters, and situations that will appeal to them.

Here is how one girl described life in 2091:

Today my mother has ordered me to do the shopping. It takes me about ten minutes to accomplish. I just go to the video terminal in our living room and attach the terminal to our selectavision set. I flip the switch and punch into the computer the various articles my mother has requested. About half an hour later a tram will pass by our house and drop off our packages. We receive delicious soybean meat and fresh synthetic vegetables from the tram. The packaged vegetables come from new organic gardens that have been tested for radioactivity.
Hilda Cordani

What Else

When the papers are completed, ask students to form small groups, to exchange papers, and to use the following questions to guide their discussion:

Can you tell where the events take place?

Are the details concrete and vivid? What part of this paper was most vivid?

Can you picture this place — its setting, its characters, and their habits?

Does the writer use lively words to describe this place and its people?

Did the writer capture your imagination?

Was the tone of the writing established in the first paragraph? Is it consistent throughout?

Is more description needed?

Is the description clear enough to be comprehended?

Can you tell who is speaking when dialogue is used?

Is there anything that should be omitted because it detracts from the paper?

Did the reader (temporarily) convince you that this is a real place?

Do you have in your mind a clear picture of the action?

Is the order of the action clear?

Anna Wooten-Hawkins, St. Mary's (Junior) College, Raleigh, North Carolina

Thumbkin Thoughts

Why

To develop students' creativity in art, conversation, and writing

Who

All elementary students

How

Provide lots of paper, pencils or pens, and ink pads (or substitute tempera paint on a sponge). Ask children to make several thumbprints on a page and to turn the prints into animals, people, or plants by drawing arms and legs, stems, or other details. Below are some sample Thumbkins:

Encourage conversation while students are working. You might ask, "What do you call an alligator who is a Thumbkin? A Thumgator," to inspire the children to develop names for their creations.

Next, students brainstorm a list of possible writing topics about Thumbkins and choose one topic to work on, either individually or with a partner. Some possibilities follow:

1. a book of Thumbkin characters and their names
2. an adventure story involving Thumbkin characters
3. Thumbkin comics
4. holiday Thumbkin stories
5. an advertisement for a Thumbkin product, such as a breakfast cereal
6. Thumbkin greeting cards
7. a Thumbkin recipe book

Carmen Kennedy, Saints Peter and Paul Elementary School, Boonville, Missouri

New Directions in Writing

Why

To help students explore the precise language needed for writing directions

Who

Upper elementary students

How

Prepare kits containing various objects and general instructions about what to do with the objects. Place each kit in a manila envelope, a shoe box, or any other creative container. Three possible kits are described below:

Kit 1: The G.I. Can Opener

1 G.I. can opener [available at a military surplus store or where camping provisions are sold]
1 clean, empty can with the bottom still intact

Instructions:
1. Figure out how to open the can.
2. Write directions for someone else to do it.
3. Share your directions with a friend. See how they work!

Kit 2: The Light Bulb

1 D-cell battery
1 piece electrical wire, 4″ long, ends stripped
1 flashlight bulb

Instructions:

1. Figure out how to light the bulb.
2. Write directions for someone else to do it.
3. Share your directions with a friend. See how they work!

Kit 3: The Airplane

1 sheet blank paper, any size

Instructions:

1. Make a paper airplane with the paper.
2. Write directions for someone else to do it.
3. Share your directions with a friend. See how they work!

Students work with a partner or in a small group and follow the instructions in each kit. Partners or groups exchange and carry out the written directions. In doing so, they develop an awareness for the intricacies of writing good directions.

What Else

1. Students examine the written directions on boxes of food, shampoo labels, toy assembly kits, computer software manuals, and the myriad of things around home and school that include directions.
2. Older students might wish to explore the profession of technical writing and to talk to a person who does this kind of writing for a living.

Wendy C. Kasten, University of South Florida at Sarasota

Adopt a Tree: Observing Nature through the Four Seasons

Why

To provide a record of students' observations of how a tree changes during its life cycle

Who

Students in kindergarten through grade 4

How

At the beginning of the school year, invite children to observe a nearby tree in its summer greenness. Explain that the class will be following the life cycle of the tree throughout the school year by drawing pictures and writing about the tree. Encourage children to bring from home storybooks about trees so that the class can learn more about trees. A suggested reading list appears at the end of the activity. Ask students to write a description and make an illustration of the tree in summer foliage. Date and save the writings and illustrations.

In the fall, observe the tree again for color changes in the leaves. Invite a forrester to talk to the students about trees and why the leaves change colors. Have students write about the tree and make another illustration. Date and save the writings and illustrations.

On a cold, snowy day, take the students outside to observe the tree in the starkness of winter. Discuss their feelings about the tree. Invite students to write about the tree and make another illustration. Date and save the writings and illustrations.

As the tree begins to bud or flower in the spring, have more observing sessions with discussion of the changes in the tree. Have students write about the tree and make another illustration.

Each student puts his or her written and illustrated pages together to form a book, adding a cover, title page, dedication page, and table of contents. Students share their books with each other.

What Else

1. In place of a tree, substitute any living thing that changes during the seasons.
2. The art media used for the illustrations may be different for each season.
3. Students might write poems or stories about the tree rather than descriptions.
4. Brainstorming activities may be used as a prewriting activity before each writing assignment.
5. Kindergartners may dictate their first two observations to the teacher or aide.
6. Class books or experience charts may be made using the language experience approach in which the entire class contributes to the writing of one description, poem, or story.

Suggested Reading List

Longman, Harold. *The Wonderful Tree House.* Parents Magazine Press, 1962.

O'Brien, Thomas M. *To Know a Tree.* Holt, Rinehart and Winston, 1963.

Tresselt, Alvin. *The Beaver Pond.* Lothrop, Lee and Shepard, 1970.

Zim, Herbert S., and Alexander C. Martin. *Trees: A Guide to Familiar American Trees.* Golden Press, 1952.

Sandra J. Wanner, Mobile College, Alabama

Chapter 5:
Learning to Write by Writing

The rules and formulas that govern the paragraphing practices of professional writers have yet to be discovered. Let us, therefore, focus our students' attention on what they have to say — on the arguments they want to present, the points they want to make — and not on the number of indentations they should use in saying it. Let us make them think about the topics they plan to discuss rather than about the "correct" location of their topic sentences. Let us, in other words, make our teaching discourse-centered.

> — Arthur A. Stern, "When Is a Paragraph," in *Composition and Its Teaching,* edited by Richard C. Gebhardt (Ohio Council of Teachers of English Language Arts, 1979), 113

The activities in this chapter provide varied opportunities for beginning writers to experiment with the many forms that writing may take. The focus is first on building confidence and fluency and secondly on learning about the unique conventions of written language: using left-to-right movement, developing focus for related sentences, organizing and sequencing ideas, using quotations, creating and punctuating dialogue. If writing activities begin with the students' own messages, the conventions of writing will be encouraged in nonthreatening ways, allowing beginning writers to build schemas for many writing formats.

Personalizing a Famous Quotation

Why

To encourage students to use their own life experiences in order to make language come alive

Who

Upper elementary students who need to use their own backgrounds to make their writing rich and who need help with writing

How

Read aloud several quotations that relate to your own life, and share a personal anecdote that reveals why the quotation is so memorable. Next, read several student-authored paragraphs in which students have applied quotations to their lives. Two examples are given below.

Our Hidden Side

"Everyone is a moon and has a dark side he never shows to anybody." This quotation by Mark Twain says that everyone has a part of himself that he keeps to himself. Even though this quotation was written by an older male, I, a young female, still understand what he meant. For example, I have many dreams and goals for my life that I don't share with anyone. They are a special part of me I can't share. No matter who you are, or what your age may be, everyone has a side that he or she keeps a secret, just like Mark Twain and me.

Jennifer Downey

Be Prepared (The Worse Is Yet to Come)

"Dig a well before you are thirsty." An unknown Chinese writer composed this proverb. It means that you should think ahead to the needs you will have; to be ready before it happens you must be prepared. This quotation has been passed down through many generations in the Orient, but even today its message is still relevant to modern life. This is true and can be proved, such as last month I went camping with some younger boys. After setting up, while it was still light, I unstuffed my sleeping bag. When we all went to bed, the younger campers struggled around in the dark trying to unpack. I just hopped into my warm sleeping bag and dozed off. So remember, always be ready for the fall before you trip.

George Brickhouse

Students discuss *how* these paraphrases are structured: the writer first copies the quotation, acknowledging its source; second, the writer explains the quotation by paraphrasing it; next, the writer relates the quotation, which may have been written long ago, to the present; then, the writer gives an example from his or her own life; finally, the writer ends by rephrasing the quotation, asking a question, or providing some other clincher.

Make available copies of Bartlett's *Familiar Quotations* or similar books of quotations, as well as greeting cards, morals from fables, *Reader's Digest* "Quotable Quotes," and other resources. Allow plenty of time for students to find quotations that appeal to them. They may want to ask parents and friends for their favorite quotations. Students write drafts and then exchange papers with a partner or in a small group. Peers suggest revisions or may propose titles, which usually turn out to be the main ideas. After students have revised their papers, display the paragraphs on the bulletin board.

Nancy H. Banks, Martin Middle School, Wake County Public Schools, Raleigh, North Carolina

You and Your Autobiography

Why

1. To increase students' knowledge about themselves
2. To produce an autobiography that students can add to over the years and share with children and grandchildren
3. To encourage students to study contemporary or historical figures

Who

Upper elementary students

How

Give students the following instructions about preparing their own autobiographies:

1. Choose and read an autobiography of a person now alive or a historical figure. The librarian might suggest books within a particular subject area.
2. To prepare for writing your own autobiography, read through and answer the following questions, adding any additional information that these questions bring to mind:
   a. When and where were you born?
   b. Is there any unusual circumstance or interesting story surrounding your birth? (premature? born at home?)
   c. Describe your brothers and sisters. Where are you in the birth order?
   d. What do you remember about your family in your early years? (customs or talents in your family, visits to relatives)
   e. What do you remember about your early neighborhood? (playmates, games, schooling, church)
   f. What were your favorite nursery rhymes and bedtime stories and songs?
   g. What were your favorite toys? foods?
   h. What chores did you do at home? What were the rules for your behavior?
   i. How were holidays celebrated by your family?
   j. Describe the house where you spent your early childhood.
   k. Describe your first school or classroom.
   l. Do you remember what you wore on your first day of school? Do you remember how you felt about school?
   m. What were your feelings about your first teachers?
   n. What subjects do you remember?
   o. What were disappointing times you remember from your early years? happy times? scary times?

3. Use these facts and impressions from your early life as you write your own autobiography. Pattern your writing style after the autobiography you read, or create your own style.

4. Include a poem about yourself on the first page. It can be written by you, a parent, a sibling, a grandparent. If no one feels poetic, ask a relative to write a descriptive paragraph about you.

5. Include photos and, if you wish, scrapbook mementoes from your early years.

6. Prepare a copy of your family tree as an appendix to the autobiography.

7. Cover your autobiography with some material that has a special meaning or sentiment for you, such as one of your baby blankets, a favorite T-shirt, wrapping paper from a special gift, an old dance-recital costume, or fabric from clothing worn by your parents or grandparents. Explain the symbolism of the cover material on the inside front cover.

8. When you've completed preparing the autobiography, tape-record a song that either your mother or father remembers singing in childhood. Tape yourself singing the song or, even better, record one of your parents singing it. Write a simple introduction to the song, which you may tape or present orally before playing the tape to the class.

9. Share with the class a family craft, heirloom, story, recipe and a sampling of the food, artwork, souvenir, or other object associated with your family. Plan a two- to three-minute presentation. If you have a grandparent who likes to weave stories, you might invite him or her to visit the class for some storytelling.

Encourage students to continue writing sections for their autobiographies over the years and to add additional photos or mementoes. The autobiographies will provide fascinating reading for their own children and grandchildren.

Esther V. Dunnington, Grandview High School, Missouri

Write about Me

Why

To motivate students to write stories by modeling writing behavior for them and by presenting a possible story structure

Who

All elementary students, especially beginning writers who are insecure about the writing process

How

Ask children to take out their journals for sustained silent writing. They are free to write about whatever they choose. In the beginning, set a timer for five minutes. Later, as the children become more comfortable with writing, the writing time may be increased.

While the students write, you also write, creating a story about one of the children. The story should always have the same structure: an introduction that identifies the setting and the main character or characters (perhaps several classmates), a simple problem, an attempt to resolve the problem, and a conclusion. A sample story follows.

> Once upon a time there was a little boy named Randy. Randy lived in Bellflower with his mom and dad.
>
> One day Randy's mother asked him to go to the store to buy some bread and some ice cream. Randy went to the store for his mom.
>
> On the way home, he saw Jerrod and Jackie playing in the park. Randy stopped to play with them. He set his bag of groceries on the picnic table.
>
> The boys played baseball. Then they played tag. Then Jackie said, "I'm hungry. I wonder what Mom is fixing for lunch. I'm going to go home and find out."
>
> Randy went to the picnic table to get his bag with the bread and ice cream. When he picked up the sack, the bottom fell out. The sack was all wet. The ice cream had melted and was running all over the inside of the sack.
>
> Randy threw away the sack. He carried the bread home in one hand and the drippy ice cream in the other. When he got home, he asked his mother what they were having for lunch.
>
> His mother answered, "From the looks of that ice cream, I guess we are having ice cream soup."

When the timer goes off, read your story aloud and encourage the children to share their writing, too. Never suggest that students write about themselves nor point out the structure of the stories. As the activity is repeated, students naturally begin to write stories about themselves and their classmates, possibly following the structure of the stories that you read aloud. Teresa's story appears below.

> There once was a girl named Linda. She liked

candy. She ate too much candy one day. Her mom said she had to go to the doctor.

The doctor said, "You will be put in the hospital and you will eat through a needle and you will get a shot night and day and mornings."

"Oh, no," said Linda, "I won't eat any more candy."

What Else

Bind together copies of your stories and keep them in the classroom library for the students to read. Make additional copies for the main characters to take home and share with their parents.

Karen Shroyer, Montgomery R-II, Bellflower Elementary School, Bellflower, Missouri

"Once Upon a Time . . ." and Beyond: Using a Word Processor

Why

1. To use a word processor in integrating the language arts
2. To help students develop a sense of story and recognize the conventions that various stories employ

Who

All elementary students who have access to a word processor

How

To begin the story process, students spend several days telling stories, which you or another student tape-records. The oral storytelling allows students to express their ideas without experiencing writing constraints. When students feel satisfied with their collections of stories, each selects one story for transcription with a word processor.

It is helpful if several students assist while each student writer transcribes a story. One student can operate the cassette recorder while others assist with spelling, punctuation, and accuracy of the transcription. This first draft is saved on a disk for future revisions. Figure 5-1 shows Melissa's original transcription.

Ask students, "What are some important things that should be in a story?" or "What makes a good story?" and note their knowledge about story conventions. Then each student's transcription is shared with the entire class or a small group of students. After some positive comments, ask each student, "What would you do to change your story?" Note the student's observations, which generally reflect rather vague notions about punctuation, words, characters, and capitalization. Discuss and categorize these observations, as well as the symbols used to note the changes. The student later marks these changes on the printout (see Melissa's changes in Figure 5-2) and revises the story on the computer disk accordingly (see Figure 5-3). As students develop an awareness of language conventions, they keep a file of their categories on a disk and update it periodically.

Following further discussion, students revise their stories, incorporating several language and story conventions (see Figure 5-4 for Melissa's final changes). This revision allows students to orchestrate the language subsystems, as well as attend to spelling and punctuation, while constructing meaningful texts. Moreover, as other conventions, such as time sequence or cause-effect relationships, are introduced and discussed, and as students read stories that illustrate these specific conventions, they begin to include these conventions in their categories and in their revisions.

When students feel satisfied with their revisions, their stories are shared, and the meaning, plot, flow, and so forth are discussed. Students may then make further revisions if they wish, and decide on the final presentation of their stories — in a book, in a group sharing, in a story file, and so on. Finally, each student retells the story into the tape recorder, which demonstrates whether he or she, through the manipulation and generation of language and ideas, is producing and using language that reflects what he or she has learned.

As students become more proficient in generating stories, introduce story genres. This is important for moving students beyond openings such as "Once upon a time" or endings such as "They lived happily ever after" or simply "The end." Students select and read stories from a specific genre, such as fairy tales, mysteries, biographies, or character sketches. When students feel somewhat confident in recognizing some of the conventions of a specific genre, each selects a story from his or her story file that has the possibility of being reworked in a particular genre. The story process begins again.

```
ONCE UPON A TIME THERE WAS  A L ITTLE GRIL NAMED SARA.SHE
LOVED CANDY  ANDSHE HAD A LITTLE  CANDY HOUSE .SHE GOT IN
IT ONE DAY .AN D SO HER MOM SPANKED HER.AND THEN THE NEXT
DAY WHILE HER MOM WAS SLEEPING SHE GOT IN IT AGIAN.  SO THEY
HAD TO PUT THE CANDY HOUSE UP HIGER AND AFTER THAT SHE
CLIMBED TO THE HOUSE AND AFTER THAT SHE GOT IN IT AND SO
THEY HAD TO MOVE IT HIGER AND SHE STILL GOT INTO IT AND SO
THEY HAD TO THOW IT OUT. AND THAT DAY WHY THE TRASHMAN WAS
COMING SHE GOT INTO THE TRASH  AND GOT IT. AND SHE HID IT
IN HER ROOM AND AFTER THAT SHE ATE IT EVERYTIME HER MOM WAS
ASLEEP. AND AFTER THAT HER MOM FOUND OUT AFTER THREE OR
FOUR DAYS AND SHE TOOK IT AND HID IT SOMPLASE AND SHE WAS
GOING TO THROW IT OUT.AND SO ONE DAY THE TRASHMAN CAME AND
THAT WAS THE NEXT WEEK AND THE CANDY HOUSE HER MOM SAW THEM
COME AND GAVE THE CANDY HOUSE TO HIM. HE DIDN'T SMASH IT
BUT HE KEPT IT AND THEN THEY HAD THE SAME THING WITH THERE
DAUGHTER THEY HAD THE SAME TROUBLE. SO AFTER THAT  'THEY
GAVE /IT TO THE LADY AGIAN AND SO SHE GAVE IT TO ANDTHER
LADY AND SHE HAD A KID AND THE Y DID THE SAME THING SO THAT
LADY JUST THROW IT OUT.AND THAT'S THE END.
```

Figure 5-1. Melissa's original transcription.

```
ONCE UPON A TIME THERE WAS  A L ITTLE GRIL NAMED SARA.SHE
LOVED CANDY  ANDSHE HAD A LITTLE  CANDY HOUSE .SHE GOT IN
IT ONE DAY .AN D SO HER MOM SPANKED HER.AND THEN THE NEXT
DAY WHILE HER MOM WAS SLEEPING SHE GOT IN IT AGIAN.  SO THEY
HAD TO PUT THE CANDY HOUSE UP HIGER.AND AFTER THAT SHE
CLIMBED TO THE HOUSE.AND AFTER THAT SHE GOT IN IT.AND SO
THEY HAD TO MOVE IT HIGER.AND SHE STILL GOT INTO IT.AND SO
THEY HAD TO THOW IT OUT.AND THAT DAY WHY THE TRASHMAN WAS
COMING SHE GOT INTO THE TRASH  AND GOT IT.AND SHE HID IT
IN HER ROOM.AND AFTER THAT SHE ATE IT EVERYTIME HER MOM WAS   whenever
ASLEEP.AND AFTER THAT HER MOM FOUND OUT AFTER THREE OR   X
FOUR DAYS.AND SHE TOOK IT AND HID IT SOMPLASE AND SHE WAS
GOING TO THROW IT OUT.AND SO ONE DAY THE TRASHMAN CAME.AND
THAT WAS THE NEXT WEEK.AND THE CANDY HOUSE HER MOM SAW THEM   X
COME AND GAVE THE CANDY HOUSE TO HIM. HE DIDN'T SMASH IT
BUT HE KEPT IT.AND THEN THEY HAD THE SAME THING WITH THERE
DAUGHTER THEY HAD THE SAME TROUBLE. SO AFTER THAT  THEY
GAVE IT TO THE LADY AGIAN AND SO SHE GAVE IT TO ANDTHER
LADY.AND SHE HAD A KID AND THE Y DID THE SAME THING.SO THAT   X
LADY JUST THROW IT OUT.AND THAT'S THE END.

CATEGORIES AND SYMBOLS
Words I am Curious About (Spelling)--circled
It Doesn't Sound Very Good (Sentence Structure)--X
Take Out all the Ands--crossed out
Move Once over (Indentation)
Use Capitalization at the beginning of a sentence
```

Figure 5-2. Melissa's changes on the printout.

```
     ONCE UPON A TIME THERE WAS  A LITTLE GirL NAMED SARA.
SHE LOVED CANDY  AND SHE HAD A LITTLE  CANDY HOUSE.  SHE GOT
IN IT ONE DAY.  SO HER MOM SPANKED HER.  THEN THE NEXT DAY
WHILE HER MOM WAS SLEEPING SHE GOT IN IT AGAiN.  SO THEY HAD
TO PUT THE CANDY HOUSE UP HIGhER.    AFTER THAT SHE CLIMBED
TO THE HOUSE.  AFTER THAT SHE GOT IN IT.  SO THEY HAD TO
MOVE IT HIGhER.  SHE STILL GOT INTO IT.  THEY HAD TO THrOW
IT OUT.  THAT DAY WHY THE TRASHMAN WAS COMING SHE GOT INTO
THE TRASH  AND GOT IT.  SHE HID IT IN HER ROOM. AFTER THAT
SHE ATE it whenever  HER MOM WAS ASLEEP.  AFTER THAT HER
MOM FOUND OUT AFTER THREE OR FOUR DAYS.  SHE TOOK IT AND
HID IT SOMePLAcE AND SHE WAS GOING TO THROW IT OUT. SO ONE
DAY THE TRASHMAN CAME.  THAT WAS THE NEXT WEEK.   THE CANDY
HOUSE HER MOM SAW THEM COME AND GAVE THE CANDY HOUSE TO
HIM. HE DIDN'T SMASH IT, BUT HE KEPT IT.   THEN THEY HAD THE
SAME THING WITH THeir DAUGHTER THAY HAD THE SAME TROUBLE.
SO AFTER THAt THEY GAVE IT TO THE LADY AGain.  SO SHE GAVE
IT TO ANoTHER LADY AND SHE HAD A KID AND THEY DID THE SAME
THING. SO THAT LADY JUST THReW IT OUT. AND THAT'S THE END.
```

Figure 5-3. Melissa's revised story.

```
     ONCE UPON A TIME THERE WAS  A LITTLE GirL NAMED SARA.
SHE LOVED CANDY  AND SHE HAD A LITTLE  CANDY House. She ate
the coconut grass ONE DAY.  SO HER MOM SPANKED HER.  THEN
THE NEXT DAY WHILE HER MOM WAS SLEEPING SHE she ate the mm
chimney.  SO THEY HAD TO PUT THE CANDY HOUSE on a high
shelf.    AFTER THAT SHE CLIMBED up on the couch TO THE
HOUSE.  AFTER THAT SHE GOT IN IT.  SO THEY HAD TO MOVE IT
HIGhER.  SHE STILL GOT INTO IT.  THEY HAD TO THrOW IT OUT.
THAT DAY WHY THE TRASHMAN WAS COMING SHE GOT INTO THE
TRASH  AND GOT IT.  SHE HID IT IN HER ROOM. AFTER THAT SHE
ATE it whenever  HER MOM WAS ASLEEP. After three or four
days her mom found out.  SHE TOOK IT AND HID IT SOMePLAcE
AND SHE WAS GOING TO THROW IT OUT. SO ONE DAY THE TRASHMAN
CAME.  THAT WAS THE Next week.  HER MOM SAW THEM COME AND
GAVE THE CANDY HOUSE TO HIM. HE DIDN'T SMASH IT, BUT HE
KEPT IT.   THEN THEY HAD THE SAME THING WITH THeir DAUGHTER
THEY HAD THE SAME TROUBLE.  SO AFTER THAt THEY GAVE IT TO
THE LADY AGain.  SO SHE GAVE IT TO ANoTHER LADY.  SHE HAD A
KID ANd  THE SAME THING happened with the candy house. SO
THAT LADY JUST THReW IT OUT. AND THAT'S THE END.
```

Figure 5-4. Melissa's final version.

Clearly, this process of writing and revising stories cannot be completed in a short period of time. Using a word processor helps students accept revision more readily than if they were rewriting the story each time in longhand, and students enjoy the challenge of operating the word processor.

Marie Ice, California State College, Bakersfield

The Shell: A Game of Description

Why

To help students learn to write an accurate description

Who

All elementary students

How

Begin by helping students explore by using their five senses. You might put various objects in a feeling box and ask students to reach in without looking and to identify the objects. Or take a listening walk and encourage students to identify the different sounds that they hear.

If possible, plan a trip to the beach to collect seashells of varying size, shape, and color. Back in the classroom, ask students to sort the shells by such categories as size, shape, color, texture, or other appropriate characteristic. Brainstorm descriptions of a sample shell, listing all the answers on the chalkboard. Ask students to decide which descriptions are most helpful for identifying the shells.

Pass out a shell to each student, who writes a description of that particular shell. Collect the shells and the descriptions. Each student is then handed another student's description, while the shells are grouped on a table where everyone can view them easily. Each student reads his or her new description, selects the shell that best fits the description, and returns to his or her seat with the shell. Next, the students take turns reading aloud their descriptions and holding up the shells they selected to match the descriptions. Then, the original author of each description announces whether the correct shell was identified. If not, students discuss what went wrong in the writing or the reading of the description.

What Else

Use rocks, oranges, apples, leaves, flowers, or other objects in place of shells and repeat the activity.

Alice Ganz, Ridge Elementary School, Shoreham, New York

Show, Don't Tell

Why

To demonstrate to students that good writers make the reader feel and think by filling their writing with specific, honest information that shows, rather than tells, the reader what is happening

Who

Young writers who need help showing their audience what is happening

How

Demonstrate the difference between writing that shows and writing that tells. One teacher did so by writing on the chalkboard, "The teacher was angry." Then she said, "I'll *show* you what the teacher did." Pantomiming the actions of an angry person, she slammed the door, stomped to the front of the room, scowled, and flung an eraser onto the floor. The teacher asked the students to describe what they had seen, as she wrote their comments on the board. She then read aloud their descriptions of her actions: "The teacher slammed the door and stomped into the room. Her mouth twisted down. She grabbed an eraser and threw it on the floor so hard the dust flew out."

The students compared this description to the sentence "The teacher was angry" and concluded that a good writer usually tries to show the reader what's happening. The teacher then suggested that when students read something like "I was mad" or "I was happy" during a writing conference, they should remind the writer to "Show, Don't Tell."

What Else

Select excerpts from popular works of literature to demonstrate how professional writers show the reader what is happening. Read a few excerpts aloud, such as Beverly Cleary's description of Ramona's embarrassment in *Ramona the Brave* when she has to apologize to another student in front of the whole class:

> Ramona felt as if she were walking on someone else's feet. They carried her to the front of the room, even though she did not want them to. There she stood thinking, I won't! I won't! while trapped by twenty-five pairs of eyes. Twenty-six, counting Mrs. Griggs. Her cheeks were hot. Her eyes were too dry for tears, and her mouth too dry for words. The silence was terrible. The click of an electric clock finishing off a minute. Ramona looked desperately at Mrs. Griggs, who smiled an encouraging but unyielding smile. There was no way out. (115-17)

Ask students how a writer who doesn't know the "Show, Don't Tell" technique might describe this same scene. Then encourage students to discuss the differences between writing that shows and writing that tells.

Adele Fiderer, Curriculum Center, Scarsdale Public Schools, New York

Let's Go Shopping: Using Catalogs

Why

To expand students' oral and written language through the use of catalogs

Who

Primary students

How

Pass out mail-order catalogs to students, inviting them to make a list of what they would like to buy. Explain how to match the picture with the text. Ask children to list the price of each item and to explain why they would like it.

Children might start with a list of ten items they want. Through discussion they narrow this list to five. Then they narrow the list to one item and explain why they chose that item.

Students might write their own descriptions for catalog items, which could be compared to the actual text. Or children might choose an item and write one description that would appeal to them and a second description of the same item that would appeal to their parents.

What Else

1. Students could pretend to shop for items for a particular room, making a list of items that are needed and their prices.
2. Children could use their math skills to figure out how much money they would spend on their pretend shopping trip.

Pamela Shriver, Cedar Rapids Schools, Cedar Rapids, and Linn-Marr Schools, Marion, Iowa

Epitaphs: Graveyard Images

Why

1. To focus students' attention on writing concisely (How many words can you fit on a tombstone?) and on using humor (especially puns), rhyme, or gimmicks in making their points
2. To encourage students to use descriptive modifiers and verbs and to avoid such overused words as *good, nice,* and *is*

Who

Middle and upper elementary students

How

Prewriting

Read aloud selections of epitaphs from Giles Brandreth's book *871 Famous Last Words* or any other book of tombstone sayings. Brainstorm a list of elements that seem common to many of the epitaphs read. Another way of looking at this step is to ask students to list all the habits, traits of personality, and physical descriptions for which folks are remembered.

Ask students to list the traits for which they would like to be remembered. They should include in this list any personal or professional goals they hope to achieve, and should keep this list to hand in later. Ask students to write down any traits they have that someone else might notice and use in writing an epitaph. These traits may be serious or humorous, and a few should be negative or in some way considered flaws. Share the lists students have made, and allow students to add to their lists if they desire.

The Writing Assignment

Students are invited to write their own epitaphs on a handout sheet containing the outline of a tombstone. Here are the directions I give them:

> You are to write two epitaphs: one that glorifies your best trait and one that pokes fun at a personal flaw. The audience for your epitaph is posterity — all those people who will read your tombstone. You want them to understand what kind of a person you were. Your epitaph may be in the form of a poem or lyrical saying. Your name may be contained within the epitaph as a regular word, a rhyme, or part of a pun. If it is not used within the epitaph, it should be added just above or just below the actual writing on the tombstone. Copy your final drafts in ink on the tombstone form provided, which will be mounted on black paper.

My students have created the following epitaphs:

> Here lies Meredith Griffin
> Died at age 12½
> Came in,
> looked about,
> had some fun,
> went out.

> Here lies John,
> the respected actor.
> He led a good life
> till he got run over by a tractor.

> Kathy was kind.
> Kathy was nice.
> Kathy crossed the street
> but didn't look twice.

> In his grave
> lies Allen Hill.
> He was an angel
> And he is still.
> R.I.P. (Real Interesting Person)

What Else

Students read aloud their epitaphs. The discussion that follows is guided by the following questions:

1. Does each epitaph focus on one of the personal characteristics of the author?

2. Does the writer use descriptive adjectives and verbs, avoiding the use of *good, nice, bad, sad,* and other overused words unless they are part of the humor or pun?

3. What are some other words you might suggest to the writer to replace dull words?

4. Does the humor or gimmick fit the epitaph well?

5. Is the epitaph short enough to fit onto a tombstone, yet complete in its thought?

6. What do you like best about each epitaph?

Work Cited

Brandreth, Giles. *871 Famous Last Words.* Sterling Publishing, 1979, and Bell Publishing, 1982.

Lea Sage, Martin Middle School, Raleigh, North Carolina

Chapter 6:
Writing for an Audience

You can't get an audience to listen and hear you till you have something to say and can say it well. Yet I think the process by which people actually learn to speak and write well is often the other way around: first they get an audience that listens and hears them (parents first, then supportive teachers, then a circle of friends or fellow writers, and finally a larger audience). Having an audience helps them find more to say and find better ways to say it.

— Peter Elbow, *Writing with Power: Techniques for Mastering the Writing Process* (Oxford University Press, 1981), 179

The activities in this chapter encourage students to write for real and fictional audiences so that they learn to vary form and voice as they adjust to varied audiences. Revision exercises focus on peers as the most immediate and responsive audience for children. The chapter concludes with activities that encourage students to write messages, notes, and letters.

Section A:
Developing a Sense of Audience

Two Approaches to a Topic

Why

To make students aware of the concept of audience by providing practice in manipulating various aspects of written language to accommodate a specific reader

Who

Upper elementary students; with adaptation, younger students

How

Provide each student with a specific essay topic and with a specific audience that is familiar with the topic. A list of sample assignments follows. In all cases, the first audience listed is familiar with the topic, the second is not.

1. Describe your favorite or least favorite room for someone who
   a. has seen or been in the room
   b. has never seen or been in the room
2. Describe your oldest or youngest relative for someone who
   a. has seen or met the relative
   b. has never seen or met the relative
3. Describe your first or last trip to the office of a doctor or dentist for someone who
   a. was present during the visit
   b. was not present during the visit
4. Describe your first or last argument with a good friend for someone who
   a. was present during the argument
   b. was not present during the argument
5. Describe your usual approach to doing homework for someone who

a. has seen you doing homework
b. has never seen you doing homework

6. Explain your usual method of planning weekend activities for someone who
   a. has seen or heard you planning weekend activities
   b. has never seen or heard you planning weekend activities

7. Explain whether your neighborhood needs improvement to someone who
   a. lives or has lived in your neighborhood
   b. has never lived in your neighborhood

When the essays are completed, divide students into small groups. Each group should be composed of students who are unfamiliar with the topic on which the other group members have written; that is, no group should include members of the actual audience to whom individual essays were initially addressed.

Ask students to take turns reading their essays aloud to the other group members. Students then comment on those aspects of the essays that seem to be incomplete or irrelevant. Each student should have the opportunity to develop varying perspectives on the writing process by serving as author, audience, and critic.

Then ask students to rewrite their essays for an audience similar to the audience who has just heard their essays; that is, for an audience unfamiliar with the topic. Ask the class, especially those students whose first and second essays differ markedly, to attempt to explain why they needed to make such extensive changes.

What Else

1. Once students have gained skill in manipulating various aspects of written language to accommodate individuals who are present in the immediate environment, they can begin to broaden their concept of audience to include persons who are not readily available for comment, as in the following sample assignments:
   a. Describe your first day of school this year for a first grader or for your principal.
   b. Describe your first or last argument with someone over the age of twenty-one for a stranger who is either under the age of thirteen or over the age of twenty-one.

c. Explain your approach to taking multiple-choice tests for a very young relative who admires you or for an adult whom you admire.
   d. Explain to all students attending your school or to your school's PTA whether you feel students and teachers have rights as well as responsibilities.

2. Teachers wishing to coordinate writing activities with activities in other subjects might consider providing audiences that vary over time and place, as illustrated below:
   a. Describe an automobile or bus for a contemporary of George Washington.
   b. Describe your last trip to an amusement park or a fair for a contemporary of Henry VIII.
   c. Explain your method of making a phone call for a native of the Amazon jungle.

Allison Wilson, Jackson State University, Mississippi

The Lead: How Writers Attract Readers

Why

Perhaps the single most important part of any piece of writing is its lead or beginning. The reader skims the first few sentences and passes judgment whether to read on or to put the article or story aside. We can help our students make their leads more effective if we share with them the following two facts about writing leads.

1. Writers do not come up with masterful leads as soon as they begin to write. In fact, many writers write their leads last. Good leads usually are the result of brainstorming and experimentation by writers who create several leads and try them out on a reader. Occasionally, a lead is found somewhere in the middle of a composition — in an exciting action, unusual image, or an interesting bit of dialogue. The writer can extract the line or paragraph, put it up front, and with some deletions and additions, connect it to the body of the piece so it makes sense.

2. Reading, hearing, and discussing good leads focuses the attention of student writers on the importance of leads. They learn that the opening line or lines have three basic purposes: to spark interest, to set the mood or tone, and to lead into the main focus or idea of the piece, which can be established a bit later. To spark interest, writers may try to tease

the reader with an unusual image ("At 8:00 every morning, Mom and I go turtle-hunting") or startling statistics ("Ten-year-olds spend one third of their waking time watching television"), or they use interesting dialogue or action, or even a provocative question, to entice the reader.

Who

Middle and upper elementary students

How

The following activities rely on leads written by professional and student writers to help students become aware of the importance of leads and the strategies used by the writers to develop them.

1. Excerpts from Literature

To demonstrate the importance of a lead that grabs the reader's attention, read aloud several strong leads from a newspaper or magazine article or from popular works of literature, such as the two following leads:

> *Olga da Polga* by Michael Bond
>
> From the very beginning there was not the slightest doubt that Olga da Polga was the sort of guinea pig who would go places.
>
> *The Shrinking of Treehorn* by Florence Heide
>
> Something very strange was happening to Treehorn. The first thing he noticed was that he couldn't reach the shelf in his closet that he had always been able to reach before, the one where he hid his candy bars and bubble gum.

Ask students which leads they like best and why. Take students to the library for a "Lead Hunt." Ask students to share their favorite leads afterwards.

In group discussions or in writing conferences, ask questions that encourage student writers to experiment with leads, such as "What new leads can you try?" or "How can you make your lead more interesting?"

2. Examples of Students' Experiments with Leads

To show how leads can capture the reader's attention and reflect the mood of the story, read aloud the following leads or show them on an overhead screen. Ask children to discuss which of the two leads in each set they prefer. Ask them to use the second of the two leads to guess what the mood of the rest of the piece must be, such as scary, exciting, and so forth.

Space Mountain

Lead 1. When I got to Disney World my best and scariest ride was called Space Mountain. Space Mountain is a very, very scary roller-coaster.

Lead 2. When I saw Space Mountain at Disney World I began to shiver. Once I got inside, it looked like I was in another dimension. There were screens all over the place. One screen I was looking at showed what the ride would be like. After I saw it, I said to myself, "Am I going to really go through with this?"

The Noise

Lead 1. Yesterday I went to my friends house and ate lunch over and just then when we were going to leave we both heard a noise it came from upstairs. The noise sounded like footsteps. We went upstairs to investigate.

Lead 2. One dark spooky night I heard a thud while watching the movie Young Frankenstein. I thought it came from upstairs and I went to investigate. I could not find a thing, so I went to the attic.

The Lost Turtle

Lead 1. My pet turtle gets lost a lot, and we have to look for him.

Lead 2. At 8:00 every morning, Mom and I go turtle-hunting.

They Tease Me

Lead 1. There are these three kids in my class who tease me.

Lead 2. "Hi, Bobafette:" Tom, Pete and Arthur made that up to tease me.

As your students get more adept at writing attention-grabbing leads, use examples from their writings in this activity.

Adele Fiderer, Curriculum Center, Scarsdale Public Schools, New York

Guidebook for Newcomers

Why

1. To encourage students to become better acquainted with their own school building
2. To put the school "rules" and guidelines into words for a real audience

Who

Upper elementary students

How

Explain to students that they are to produce a school guidebook for new students. Discuss what a guidebook is, and pass around some sample guidebooks. Children form committees and brainstorm topics to include in their guidebook.

Once the topics have been determined, help students divide the tasks into workable parts (such as a map of the school, schedules, a list of teachers, the nurse's hours, a welcome from the principal), and assign a task to each committee. Meet daily with each committee to review accomplishments and to offer suggestions. After each section of the guidebook is read and proofread, students assemble the parts into a booklet that is then duplicated for each student in the class and for new students.

What Else

Parents and new students will enjoy seeing the final product. Post a guidebook in the hall for visitors' reference as well.

Ann Ballin, Blue Ridge Elementary School, Columbia, Missouri

Sell a Friend

Why

1. To provide students with experience in a variety of communication skills: viewing, listening, writing, speaking, persuading
2. To increase students' awareness of media techniques used to sell goods and services
3. To aid students' understanding of how writers manipulate their audience through words

Who

Middle and upper elementary students

How

This assignment might be coordinated with an assignment to view a television program (for example, a play or some other program tied to classroom literature). However, the lesson can be used independently at any time and takes advantage of an activity — TV watching — for which students need no prompting. Tap students' creativity by allowing and encouraging them to be as elaborate as they desire in producing this assignment.

Ask students to keep a log of eight commercials seen on television, in which they list the name of the product and record the ad format (story, testimonial) and brief, key bits of script (such as "McDonald's and you" or "Where's the beef?"). An example of a student's commercial log is shown in Figure 6-1.

Students use their observations and analysis of commercials to "produce" their own commercials — a thirty-second script designed to merchandise a friend. Students are to advertise this friend as if he or she were a real commercial product, such as a soft drink or a sandwich. Bits of dialogue from actual TV ads may be freely borrowed or adapted for student scripts. An example of a sell-a-friend script follows.

Announcer: Today we're visiting with people in Bangor, Maine, where the winters can get very long and depressing. Here's what Mrs. John Smith, a lifetime resident of Maine, has to say about how Ellen has helped her.

Mrs. Smith: For years, the winters in Maine really got me down. I had these awful headaches, my nose was stopped up, and I felt depressed. I tried everything. Then finally my doctor told me I should try Ellen. I felt better right away! Now I'm never without her. A day without Ellen is like a day without sunshine. She brings long-lasting relief from winter misery.

Neighbor: Where's the sunshine? I don't think there's any of it back there (*pointing to winter clouds*).

Mrs. Smith: Relief is just a friend away. What you need is Ellen — recommended by nine out of ten doctors for relief of winter misery.

Neighbor: Ellen? What is Ellen?

Mrs. Smith: The winter remedy most doctors recommend. Ellen's kind of people never have to ask, "Where's the sunshine?"

Neighbor: (*Smiling*) Don't gimme that same old gloom . . . I wanna Ellen!

Commercial Log

Product	Format	Dialogue
1. Shasta	Song–skit	"Don't gimme that same old cola . . . I wanna pop"
2. Wendy's	Short story	"Where's the beef?"
		"I don't think there's anybody back there."
3. Anacin	Testimonial	"Nine out of ten doctors recommend . . ."
4. McDonald's	Short story	"Break it to me gently."
		"McDonald's and you."
5. Skinner's Noodles	Testimonial	"Never gets lost in the sauce."
6. Coke	Short story	"The one that never lets you down."
		"Coke is it!"
7. Campbell's Soup	Short story	"Soup is good food."
8. Hallmark Cards	Short story	"What I'm really sending is a part of me."
		"When you care enough to send the very best."

Figure 6–1. Student's log of television commercials.

Announcer: Remember — for fast relief of the midwinter blahs, try Ellen . . . the one that never lets you down.

Give each student the option of videotaping his or her commercial, tape-recording it (as if for a radio commercial), or reading the script "live" to the class. For any of these options, encourage the use of background music, props, or other features that might enhance product appeal and add effectiveness. Prior to the actual production of student commercials, you may wish to ask students to turn in the TV logs and copies of their scripts to screen out any objectionable material.

Laurie E. Holder, Jr., Millbrook Senior High School, Raleigh, North Carolina

Read a Picture, Write a Summary, Convince a Reader

Why

1. To help students create an image of a story they have read
2. To help students use their illustrations to prompt classmates to read new stories

Who

Middle and upper elementary students

How

After the class has studied a wide variety of literature, invite each student to select a book from the bookshelf. As students read, ask them to pay attention to any illustrations accompanying the story. Then students meet in peer groups and talk about the stories they read.

Next, introduce the writing assignment by discussing book jackets or movie ads that capture the interest of an audience by showing an inviting scene from the story. Without copying an illustration from the book, students are to illustrate their own interpretations of a scene from the story they read. Encourage students to capture the characters in the scene and to show what they are doing. Stress that students need not be artists to convey the action of the story. Then students write a one- or two-sentence summary that describes the interpretation and that would interest another student in reading the story. Remind students to include the title and author of the story, and suggest that they refer to the following checklist as they work on their illustrations and summaries:

1. I have selected and illustrated a scene from the story I read.

2. I have a one- or two-sentence summary describing my scene that would encourage someone else to read the story.

3. I have shared my illustration with my peer group.

4. I have considered the suggestions made by members of my peer group and have made the revisions that I feel were necessary.

5. I have included the title and author of the story in my finished paper.

Students meet in peer groups and share their illustrations and summaries with one another. Suggest that they keep the following guidelines in mind as they review a classmate's work:

1. Does the illustrator illustrate without copying from the book?

2. Describe, in your own words, the scene that is illustrated.

3. Does the summary tell about the scene, and is it motivating to the reader?

4. What aspect of the illustration is your favorite?

5. Have the title and author been included with the summary?

6. What suggestions, if any, do you have to make the summary better?

Students revise their summaries in response to suggestions from the group. The final versions of the summaries and the illustrations are then displayed on the class bulletin board.

Gayle A. Glover, Angier Middle School/Harnett County, Dunn, North Carolina

Points of View

Why

This activity is appropriate to use with students as they encounter points of view in literature or discover the need to incorporate a point of view in their own writing. Each student participates in imaginative writing, reads his or her writing aloud, hears responses from peers that express the different outlooks held by each student, and is able to respond immediately to other students' writings. Students discover on their own that a reader's knowledge of a scene or an event is limited by the point of view from which it is told.

Who

All elementary students

How

To introduce the concept of point of view, tell a story, such as the one below, as the class begins the day's activities.

> Today as I walked to class I noticed a squirrel busily searching in the snow for any tidbits he might find to eat. He was so used to pedestrians that he wasn't alarmed at all at my approach. I walked cautiously just to see how close to him I could get without disturbing him. I was actually within touching distance when I stopped to enjoy watching him. But when I stopped, he did too. He looked up just as curiously at me, and we had several moments of real eye contact. I had this insane desire to talk to that squirrel; he honestly looked more intelligent and alert than some people I've had trouble making eye contact with. How I wished we could talk together.

Invite students to write from three points of view, using this episode as stimulus for their thinking. I give students the following directions:

> *Writing 1.* Put yourself in my place as I stood there on the sidewalk looking at the squirrel. Give us a movie of what might be running through your mind as you look at him. What would you say to him, if you knew he would understand? If you could ask him a question, what would it be? Would you tell him anything about yourself?

(I wrote along with the students, indicating the question that I would just have to ask: "Does your bottom get cold when you sit in the snow like that?")

> *Writing 2.* Put yourself inside the squirrel. What is your reaction to that person who has stopped to stare at you? What do you make of him or her? What would you like to say to him or her?

(One student quipped something, through the squirrel's mouth, about the leather, fur-lined coat I was wearing that day. Students may describe themselves, of course, as the person who has stopped.)

> *Writing 3.* Pretend that you are sitting in a car across the street, watching the squirrel and the person. Describe the scene you witness.

After writing, students form groups of four or five and share what they've written. Ask each group to choose one writing from each of the three points of view and to read their selections aloud to the class.

What Else

1. After each group reads aloud a favorite writing in each category, students vote for the class favorites.

Winners are printed in a booklet for the entire class to read the next day.

2. Students discuss books they've read that were written through an animal's point of view. They might talk about other animal books that would be fun to rewrite from the animal's point of view.

3. This activity might serve as a prewriting exercise to prepare students to rewrite a scene in a novel from a different character's point of view.

Elizabeth D. Nelms, Hickman High School, Columbia, Missouri

Pointing

Why

To demonstrate to students the power of words in their writing

Who

Middle and upper elementary students

How

Pointing is a strategy suggested by Peter Elbow in *Writing without Teachers*. Begin the activity by displaying a set of pictures in the classroom. Students are invited to select one picture and to write a description of it. The pictures may be discussed in small groups before the writing begins, or they may simply be introduced as an impetus for writing.

Students form groups of three or four and bring their first drafts to share with the other group members. As each student reads his or her paper, the other group members listen carefully to *point* out words that have impact — words that "stand out" or "penetrate the skull" of the readers — and make a list of these words.

Then students use this group list to try to identify the picture described by the student in the writing. The student author confirms or refutes the group's selection. The discussion that follows centers on the words chosen by the group members and how the words are effective in generating a mental picture. If the author discovers that readers are unable to create an accurate mental image of the object or picture being described, then the author has gained valuable insight about the need for clear, precise

descriptions. The writer does have the option of ignoring the comments of the group members and leaving the paper as is, or of making changes in word choice to make the image more clear or more accurate for the reader. An important lesson that the writer can learn is that editing and revision can be easily accomplished to make the piece of writing draw the intended picture in the minds of the readers.

Work Cited

Elbow, Peter. *Writing without Teachers.* Oxford University Press, 1973.

Sharon Lee, Texas A&M University, College Station

An Oral Revision Strategy Using the Typewriter

Why

As an infrequent approach, this strategy seems to be of benefit in a variety of ways: as a model for revision, as an aid to editing, as an incentive for careful rereading, as a chance to "use" the teacher without relinquishing ownership, as a lesson in paragraphing or mechanics, and as a source of spelling help. Each child gets a longer than usual session with the teacher on a one-to-one basis. Furthermore, it makes children eager to learn to type.

Who

Students in grades 4 and 5

How

The strategy can be used for its novelty effect several times a year and can occur at any point in any draft a child is working on. Take the role of the class secretary, wheeling in a typewriter and inviting one child to dictate, while you type, as much as he or she has written of an ongoing writing project. Assure the writer that he or she can make any changes during the dictation, including revisions that "mess up" the parts already typed. Small changes are crossed out or inserted with carets. Double-spacing and wide margins provide enough room for most changes. Major revisions are accommodated as well. Show the child how to use symbols, such as $, #, and *, to indicate such changes as "Insert $ at point $."

As the child dictates, react by laughing or nodding or responding specifically to an event or statement ("Oh no, not having to baby-sit again!"). You might hint at confusing statements or missing information by stopping and looking back at the earlier text with an expression of puzzlement. Sometimes the child catches on right away: "Oh, I forgot to mention that I went home and got my glove by then." If not, express uncertainty with a question.

Children whose drafts are fairly well polished at the dictation stage can be asked to "read in" the punctuation verbally. Thus, a child who wants the teacher to type a period or question mark would have to say so. Some children can supply much of the punctuation by this method, even when their drafts contain none. If a child is distracted by such a task, fill in the punctuation by pencil at the end of the session, with the child's help.

Some children may be ready to begin work on paragraphing. You might suggest, "Oh, since this is the next day, would you like to start a new paragraph?" The basic technique of dictating and typing remains the same for all children, but the content of the "lesson" can easily be tailored to each child.

The typed version replaces the "sloppy copy," making it easier for the child to continue the revision and to reread the copy to check the tone and overall structural attributes.

Usually seven children can dictate their writings during a fifty-minute session, even including an occasional "emergency consultation" with those children working independently. In three or four days, all the students can have a turn.

What Else

A fringe benefit is that the typed segment functions as a dictionary. When children write on a given topic, many words recur frequently. As they continue their writings, students can refer to the typed copy to check on the spelling of some of these words.

Mary M. Kitagawa, Richey Elementary School, Tucson, Arizona

Wesley Davis serves as mail carrier in the photograph at right.

Section B: Messages, Notes, and Letters
Compiled by Patricia Jenkins, Columbia Public Schools, Missouri

Classroom Post Office

Why

To encourage students to communicate with others in writing

Who

All elementary students

How

Each child is assigned a mailbox in one central location (such as shown in the accompanying photograph), or children might decorate individual desktop mailboxes. Encourage them to write letters and notes to one another about people and events of importance to them, about their feelings, or about school activities, or to comment on or ask questions about assignments or information discussed in class. Students will naturally pay some attention to spelling, punctuation, grammar, and penmanship so that their readers can understand the message.

Each day a different child serves as mail carrier.

This child picks up all letters and notes left in the location designated for mail collection, sorts the mail by name or number, and delivers the mail to the appropriate mailbox.

Send a letter home to parents, explaining the class post office and encouraging them to write letters to their children. Other children in the family might also like to participate in the letter writing. Four-year-old Chad wrote his brother the following letter by dictating it to his first-grade cousin.

> Dear Joey
> Haw r you Brthr
> I m fin
> By
> Lave
> Chad

The younger boy wanted to send the message to his brother and insisted on visiting the school to leave the letter at the school post office. The letter demonstrated that the boys had learned that they could produce written language for the purpose of communication.

Seven-year-old Andrea helped her two-year-old sister, Jenny, "dictate" the following letter to Renea, a friend of Andrea's.

> Dear Renea
> Merry Christmas Renae
> I like your mom
> I like you
> Do you like me
> My mom like you
> Do you like my mom
> My mom like your mom
> Jenny like you
> My dad like your dad
> Andrea like you
>   Love
>   Jenny

Andrea revealed that she composed the letter, asking young Jenny if she wanted to say each sentence. Jenny's reply to each question was "Um hummm."

What Else

1. Students write letters and notes to absent classmates, perhaps designing and illustrating cards.
2. Each Friday send each student a personal note, commenting on particular successes of the week and offering suggestions for the following week. This is an opportunity to provide examples of traditional spellings and standard grammatical structures for individual students.

Karen V. Packard, Education Consultant, Ketchikan, Alaska

Mailboxes

Why

Mailboxes turn classrooms into interactive communities, generating enthusiasm and interest in writing. Mailboxes put variety into a composing program that is usually dominated by the writing of narratives. Children who use mailboxes develop a writing habit they can continue at home.

Who

All elementary students

How

Establish a mailbox for each child and for yourself. Initiate communication by writing a note to each child in the classroom and explain that you will respond to all notes that the children send you. From there, the fun of communicating takes over.

In a preschool classroom, it took fifteen children less than two weeks to learn to read each other's names and to locate the appropriate mailbox. They sent each other scribble messages and pictures and signed their names. Most notes were not legible, but that hardly mattered. They were having fun with the process of communicating. One day when the teacher was absent, the substitute was amazed that the children spent a large portion of their "free time" drawing pictures and writing notes to their teacher. By the time the day was over, the teacher's mailbox was literally stuffed with messages from the children.

A kindergarten teacher received some heartwarming messages in her mailbox. One girl wrote, "I AM SRE TET I FRI IN THE MORNES. I LOVE YOU. I HOP TAT YOU RELE LOVE ME." This student was still adjusting to attending school and used the mailbox as a vehicle for venting her emotions. Her teacher spent about twenty minutes each afternoon, during rest time, writing notes to children who had written to her, and to those from whom she had not heard in some time. One child wrote a whole page of mostly repeated "I love you's." At the end she said, "I ROTE A HOLE PAGE. NOW YOU HVE TO RITE A HOLE PAGE BACK!" The children also wrote interesting notes to each other. By the middle of the year, they had mastered on their own the letter-writing form of "Dear ———," with a comma after the greeting.

The first-grade children were a bit more bold in their messages to the teacher. She told the class that she would respond to any of their questions, so one student immediately asked, "How old are you?" Like the kindergarten children, they wrote many short "I love you" notes. Several wrote in memo form: "To: Sarah, From: Latash." Some wrote about their fears or things going on in their lives outside of school. They felt free to communicate some of their deepest thoughts to the teacher.

Third graders asked real questions of each other, such as what would they do during recess or after school. They were intensely curious about their teacher and each other and used the mailboxes as a way to explore this curiosity. The third-grade teacher used mailboxes as a vehicle to promote good feelings within the room. She designed projects that could be accomplished through the mail. For example, each child drew from a hat the name of a secret pal, and then the children were encouraged to write notes to their secret pals each day. After a week of writing to each other, they tried to guess the identity of their secret pals.

A fifth-grade teacher used mailboxes to return children's work. She also wrote notes to the children from time to time. The class had a "Dear Abby" type of mailbox into which the children could place questions or notes describing problems that were bothering them. Working in teams of five, the children took turns discussing these issues and formulating responses. This mailbox allowed for anonymity on sensitive issues and was the teacher's way of tapping the children's real interests and concerns for a problem-solving unit.

Mailboxes can be constructed in a variety of ways. One teacher made a classroom mailbox out of wood, with hinges for each door and magnets to hold the doors up. A kindergarten teacher used the children's cubbies as mailboxes. A first-grade teacher found that a liquor box with cardboard divisions was appropriate for mailboxes. A third-grade teacher attached large frozen-juice containers to a shelf with Velcro. And a fifth-grade teacher used a metal shelving unit with slots in it, the kind that might be used for filing papers.

Mailboxes are most successful in the classroom when the teacher models their use by writing often to the children, when children have sufficient time to write, and when there is a purpose for communicating.

What Else

After children develop the note-writing habit within the classroom, extend their writing by finding pen pals outside the classroom or by encouraging them to write to friends and relatives.

Linda Leonard Lamme, University of Florida, Gainesville

We Write Letters

Why

1. To provide an opportunity for students to engage in meaningful and purposeful writing
2. To expand students' uses of written language
3. To promote interaction and communication between students and a wide range of audiences

Who

All elementary students

How

Rather than a brief unit on letter writing, establish letter writing as a year-long activity, which will encourage students' interest in this lifelong activity. Begin by asking students to make a list of all the people who work and help them at school. The list might include the following personnel:

> principal
> secretary
> teachers
> custodians
> parent volunteers
> bus drivers
> assistant principal
> receptionist
> classroom aides
> cafeteria workers
> P.T.A. officers
> P.T.A. committee members

Encourage students to write letters to the people on this list, showing appreciation for some task or favor or developing friendships with those outside the classroom. Here's what one student wrote to her principal:

> Dear Dr. Moss,
>   I colored my eggs on Friday of last week.
>   I have a brother, a mother, a step mother, a father, a step father, and a step sister. I live with my real mother. I visit my real father. You are my best friend. Thank you for your note.
> > Love,
> > Kelly

This list could be expanded to include other audiences. For example, letters might be written to congratulate winners of a school contest or fair, to explore the activites of school clubs, and to develop friendships with children in other classrooms.

R. Kay Moss, Southeastern Louisiana University, Hammond

This Summer I . . .

Why

To establish correspondence with students in advance of the school year

Who

All elementary students, especially those new to school

How

Sometime during the summer, send postcards to students who will be in your class in the fall. Describe your summer activities and ask students to write you about their summer fun, perhaps inviting them to enclose schedules of ball games or information about other activities in which they are involved. Students might put their descriptions in narrative form, and these narratives might be expanded into books once school starts. Invite students to suggest classroom activities for the fall. Ask them to keep a list of books they read (and loved) during the summer, which could become the basis of a class list of favorites in the fall.

What Else

Send along the names and addresses of any students new to the school and invite the "oldtimers" to send a welcoming note to the newcomers.

Jolene M. Davis, Montgomery County R-II, Bellflower Elementary School, Bellflower, Missouri

Letters of Advice

Why

To encourage students to learn how to *use* language appropriately (rather than just being taught *about* language)

Who

All elementary students

How

To integrate reading and writing across the curriculum throughout the school day, students write a letter of advice about a particular subject area to students in a lower grade or to those in a different class in the same grade. Students might write a letter of advice about getting a good grade in a specific subject area, or about carrying out a specific assignment in a subject area, or about getting along with a particular person or group, such as a bus driver, the janitor, the principal, peers, younger children, or older children.

The full composing process should be employed for the activity. During a planning period, students can work as a class, in small groups, and individually as they plan their letters. Children can move from one draft of a letter to another as they frequently share their drafts with you, another student, or the whole class and ask for suggestions. The introduction, body, and conclusion of a letter could be discussed as separate components, as well as the salutation and closing.

A certain number of pieces of advice or hints might be specified for the letters. For example, the children might be asked to include five tips for completing a science project or for keeping a journal. Such letters encourage children to think about what steps or information would be important to do or know, and reveal this thinking process to the teacher.

What Else

Children might write letters to authors and publishers about a particular book. The letters can help a child who is having trouble reading and remembering the book, and demonstrate how well the child can evaluate the book. In addition, authors and publishers may appreciate getting a child's perspective on the book.

Avon Crismore, Indiana University–Purdue University at Fort Wayne

Chalk Talk

Why

To help students see that reading and writing are communicative activities

Who

All elementary students

How

Write a message on the chalkboard while the students look on. The message should have personal meaning for the class, such as the following example.

Dear Boys and Girls,
   Today the baby chickens started to hatch. I think we could sit in front of the incubator all day and watch them trying to peck their way out of their shells. It takes a long time, doesn't it? The chicks are working very hard and they must stop often to rest.
   Love, Mrs. S.

As I am writing the message, the children are busy reading and predicting what I am going to write next. After I have finished my message, a few volunteers read the complete message to the class. Then the class reads the message in unison. A brief discussion usually follows.

What Else

Encourage students to write responses or original messages. Frequently I receive notes in my mailbox responding to the daily chalkboard message.

Karen Shroyer, Montgomery R-II, Bellflower Elementary School, Bellflower, Missouri

PART 3

The Anasazi

No one can
exsplae about
the Anasazi.
But Sum Peepoul
Can give you
an Il deu.
The Anasazi
ate turkey
and and Pumpkin
corn.
The Anasazis
white black and red
Pottery Stil rumanes.

Matthew King

Chapter 7:
Reading, Writing, Listening, and Speaking across the Curriculum

---

. . . into every act of knowing there enters a passionate contribution of the person knowing what is being known. . . .

— Michael Polanyi, *Personal Knowledge: Towards a Post-Critical Philosophy* (University of Chicago Press, 1958), viii

---

The activities in this chapter focus on writing, reading, listening, and speaking as a way to personalize and integrate the content of social studies, math, and science. The last part of the chapter is devoted to activities that invite students to read, discuss, and write newspapers.

Section A:
Language Arts across the Curriculum

What Students Know and What They Write: Ways to Focus a Writing Conference

Why

This strategy focuses on the writing conference that takes place when the student is engaged in some form of informational writing. It examines ways in which personal knowledge about a topic affects the language, organizational structure, and coherence used by particular writers.

Writing across the curriculum as an approach to learning suggests that activities in writing cannot be isolated from the subject matter the student is writing about. Because the student's personal knowledge so directly helps shape the paper, the teacher's understanding or assessment of what a student knows about a topic will shape the writing conference and eventually shape the paper as well.

Who

Students in grades 3–6

How

An examination of student papers demonstrates that when students know a good deal about a topic, the language, organization, and coherence of their writing are likely to be good; conversely, when students know little about a topic, their language, organization, and coherence are likely to seem tight, restricted, and contrived, or to fall apart altogether.

Students Who Know a Little. When students have little knowledge or are unwilling to risk stating the ideas they do have, they may voice gross generalities or abstractions without examples or enriching illustrations. At other times their writing is fragmented; they often write their associations, examples, and descriptions in the form of lists with few explicit connections between their ideas. Students who know little about a topic need a special kind of conference, one focusing directly on building ideas or concepts for the paper. Such students may need a conference that is primarily concerned with the presentation and development of new information. In the course of this conference, it may become apparent that a student knows so little that simply amplifying the topic will inevitably prove futile. In such cases the teacher may need to suggest sources of further information for the student to consult before even attempting to revise the writing. Sources might include direct instruction, another student, a film, or particular books or magazines in the library. In some cases it may even be more productive to suggest an alternative topic.

Students Who Know Some. When students do know something about a topic but haven't thought it through thoroughly, the first draft often serves as a way to develop ideas. Students seem to know some of the attributes and can cite examples associated with the topic, but they are not sure if or how the parts fit together. In this case a productive conference might focus on what the student knows about the topic and how aspects of that knowledge are related to each other. In this type of conference the teacher needs to help the student think through the major topic, identify some interweaving details, and imagine how all the pieces fit. While this type of conference deals with topic-related knowledge, the teacher can also help the student begin refining that knowledge with the specific writing task in mind. Since the first draft in this case is a productive step in becoming aware of available knowledge and relationships, it is important that the student reflects on the conference and applies insights gained from it in refining the paper.

Students Who Know a Lot. With students who know a good deal about a topic and have thought it through already, a conference focusing on the linguistic or organizational aspects of the paper can be helpful. Their knowledge will usually lead them to make good use of examples and associations in their writing, providing the elaboration and embellishments necessary to make a paper work well. For them the conference can focus on teacher and student judgments about how the details might best be organized, which words or phrases might be changed for specificity and impact, and what might be changed for coherence.

A consideration of how thoroughly the writer has thought through the material can help both the student and the teacher focus the conference on one particular aspect of the paper — either the topic or

the manner of presentation. It helps students think about what they know, what they think is important to write about, and how they think things are related. It also encourages them to give examples and descriptions of what they mean to say. Such considerations can change the conference from teacher "telling" to student "showing." Similarly, the teacher's role changes from a "teller" to a "concerned other" who helps the student reflect on, expand, and evaluate what is known and how to write about it.

This type of conference can be particularly freeing for both teachers and students. With the teacher as "teller," students are often uneasy. In informational writing they often hold back information. They hesitate to give examples or share their associations when they aren't absolutely certain whether or where things fit — when they're still thinking things through. Unfortunately, these are the kinds of ideas that need to be explored because they have the potential to provide clarity for the writer and can help the paper become more interesting, more alive.

If conferences are approached with these distinctions in mind, the teacher may have a clearer understanding of where to focus the student's attention, and the student may emerge with a clearer idea of what to do next.

Judith A. Langer, State University of New York at Albany

Making Connections between Prior Knowledge and New Ideas

Why

Students need to make connections between what they already know (prior knowledge) and new ideas presented in class. Expressive writing is one tool that students can use to begin to make these connections. Expressive writing, informal in nature, reflects the learner's attempts to make sense of new ideas, to seek clarification, and to raise additional questions about concepts discussed in class.

Who

All elementary students

How

For students who have no prior experience using expressive writing as a tool to aid learning, begin

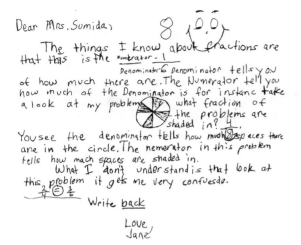

Dear Mrs. Sumida,

The things I know about fractions are that this is the numerator-1 of how much there are. The Numerator tell you how much of the Denominator is for instanc take a look at my problem what fraction of the problems are shaded in? 4

You see the denominator tells how much spaces there are in the circle. The nemerator in this problem tells how much spaces are shaded in.

What I don't understand is that look at this problem it gets me very confuesdo.

Write back

Love,
Jane

Figure 7-1. Jane's math learning log.

with a structured learning log. For example, whenever new ideas have been introduced during a math or social studies class, provide ten to fifteen minutes of class time for students to respond to the following questions about the ideas discussed in class:

1. What is clear?
2. What is confusing?
3. What do you want to know more about?

Figure 7-1 shows a second grader's entry in her math learning log. Jane reviewed what she knew about fractions and then stated what she didn't understand.

Ann Shea Bayer, University of Hawaii, Honolulu

Learning Logs

Why

Much learning remains at the tacit level. When students write about their learning, they prove to themselves that they are indeed learning. In addition, when learning logs are used on a regular basis, students begin to search for the learning potential in any activity they encounter.

Who

All elementary students

How

At the end of an activity, a morning, or an entire day, give students half sheets of paper, pens, and

pencils. Ask them to write down something they know now that they didn't know when they came to school in the morning, or something they can do that they couldn't do yesterday, or something they can now do better. For students who can't think of anything to write, ask them to write a brief description of an activity, to react to the activity ("Did you like it?"), and then to speculate why the teacher provided the activity.

After about ten minutes invite students to share what they wrote in their learning logs. This gives students a chance to hear ideas they hadn't thought of, and it reinforces ideas that they themselves recorded in their learning logs.

Repeat the activity frequently, perhaps daily. As students become familiar with writing in their learning logs about what they now know or now can do, they will need less direction.

What Else

1. Compile each child's learning logs into a booklet for the week or month to provide a record of important accomplishments, as a review for the child and a means of sharing these accomplishments with parents during conferences. At the end of the year, students might be asked to write a learning log for the entire school year. Encourage the children to write about several special accomplishments, perhaps categorized by subject matter.
2. Learning logs can also be completed by the entire class on chart paper or easel paper and then compiled into a class book for the classroom library. Even less proficient readers will enjoy reading and rereading about accomplishments of the class throughout the year.
3. Some students find that language alone is insufficient to represent what they have learned, and they incorporate in their logs art and nonprint graphic symbols, such as arrows, mathematical symbols, charts, and graphs. A classroom rich in various ways of presenting ideas supports students in making shifts between systems.

Kathryn Mitchell Pierce, Webster University, St. Louis, Missouri

Science Logs

Why

Like professional scientists who keep written logs of their experiments, students can record in science logs as they investigate and explore science materials in the classroom. The logs provide a meaningful context for writing, as students maintain accurate records of experiments and results.

Who

All elementary students

How

Develop a science center that includes hands-on materials from commercially published kits and found objects brought in by students and teachers. Batteries, light bulbs, wire, small electric motors, beakers, harmless chemicals and household products, measuring containers, earthworms, seeds, soil, and so forth might be assembled over time. Include in the center the task cards from the science kits and other suggestions for performing simple experiments.

Have students form small groups, and invite one group at a time to work in the science center. As students explore the materials, ask open-ended questions, such as "What do you think will happen?" "Why do you suppose it did that?" or "Is there any other way to do that?" Encourage students to come up with their own questions that can be answered only through experiments. Ask them to think through their intended experiments and to list the necessary equipment and supplies.

Also ask students to record the steps they would go through in conducting the experiment and to predict what will happen. Upon completion of the experiment, students write their actual findings and any ideas for future experiments.

The science logs can be kept in the science center for other students to use when looking for experiments to try or for ways of improving experiments they have underway. The logs also provide a valuable record of each child's science activities, which can be presented at parent-teacher conferences.

What Else

Science logs can form the basis of science stories in the class newspaper. Several students might work together to report on an experiment for the school newspaper.

Catherine Copeland, Stephens Elementary School, Columbia, Missouri, and Julia K. Crisp, Stephens College, Lincoln, Nebraska

Writing to Learn: Content and the Research Process

Why

1. To help students improve their reading, research, and writing skills as they develop concepts in science
2. To help students understand that they have something to say that is of value and interest to others

Who

Students in grades 3–5

How

Ask students to select a science topic to write about by looking through books in the classroom, in the library, or at home. They might talk to other students for ideas or brainstorm a list of possible topics on their own. Once they have narrowed their lists to one topic, students choose an audience for their project (parents, classmates, or the whole school) and decide on a format for presenting their information (a booklet, a wall display, or another format). By making these decisions, students develop the notion that they have things to say, and assume responsibility for what they say in their writing.

Students prepare a first draft on their topics, writing what they know, what they think they know, what they would like to know. Even though this early draft may contain meager content, it helps students see what they already know, and they begin to discover their points of view.

Next, students do research on their topics, keeping a bibliography of sources they consult. They read books, magazines, pamphlets, and newspapers. They review charts and maps. They talk with people who know something about their topics and make their own personal observations.

At this point students talk with a friend or in a small group about what they have learned. They rehearse their new information and thus gain authority or voice as they make the new information their own. Talking in the presence of others also gives the student writers a sense of how readers will respond to their information. When the students return to their drafts, they see a difference between what they wrote and what they now have to say. They revise this draft as they wish, adding, deleting, or changing information.

After the draft is revised, students read their writing aloud to a classmate or the teacher. Then the writers and listeners talk about the content, using questions such as the following:

Who is this for?

Why are you writing this?

What is the most important thing you are telling about?

Is there more you could tell about that?

There is no prescribed series of questions that dictates what the discussion will be. The talk begins with what the writer has included in the writing and moves to what he or she has not included. The writer then decides what changes, if any, he or she will make in the content of the writing and returns to the reference materials if necessary.

The teacher might help with the organization or structure of the writing. As students talk about their topics, the teacher makes a list. Students can compare the list with their writing to see if they have the writing organized the way they want. The teacher asks questions about grouping together sentences and paragraphs on the same topic and about the order of these topics. Students examine the organization of their writing to see if it matches the organization they've developed with the teacher.

Students prepare the table of contents with a concern for how titles of chapters are worded and the order in which topics are presented to the reader. Students revise their papers to match their tables of contents and make any other final changes.

Constance W. Bataller, Barrett Elementary School, Arlington, Virginia

"I Can't Write It All Down": Notetaking Help

Why

1. To encourage students to become active learners and to assume responsibility for their own learning
2. To help students learn to take effective notes

Who

Upper elementary students

How

Discuss specific problems that students are currently having with taking notes in content-area classes. Encourage them to express some of their notetaking problems in question form, such as the following:

What is the best way to organize my notes?

Should I write down everything the teacher says?

How can I incorporate outside readings and textbook readings into my notes?

Ask students to write down three questions that they would like to have answered. Write down three questions of your own and then record students' questions on the board. Ask students to identify any that are the same or closely connected.

Discuss notetaking strategies with the students. Successful note takers could share their strategies and show samples of their notes. Practice together on a content-area chapter or text. Discuss what you are doing as you take notes and make decisions about what to include.

What Else

This lesson can be used in a variety of situations. The basic format is as follows:

1. Students identify a problem.
2. Students generate questions for which they want to find answers in a variety of texts.
3. Students seek answers to those questions in the texts.
4. Students evaluate answers to determine which will be most useful in answering their questions.
5. During the follow-up sessions, students and teacher evaluate which answers were effective.

Encourage students to comment on any changes they made in their notetaking habits and on how effective these changes have been.

*Marion Carroll, John A. Logan Community
College, Carterville, Illinois, with help from Jessie
M. Brooks, Harrisburg, Illinois, and Pat Rigg,
Tucson, Arizona*

Peer Paraphrasing: From Listening to Writing in the Content Areas

Why

Gaining meaning through listening to informational material and then summarizing information in personal language are two important content-area skills. Students remember what they have talked about when they translate from text language to their own language.

Who

Upper elementary students, especially those who rely on copying answers from printed text without processing the information or those who tend to include unnecessary details in their answers

How

When beginning a new topic of study, invite students to share any knowledge of the topic that they already have. Then explain that you will read them information on the topic and that they must listen carefully because they will be unable to read the written text themselves. Reassure them that it is common for students to feel apprehensive about this process at first, but that they are to keep trying to make sense of what they hear.

Hand out to students a question outline of the material to be read and ask them not to write on the outline. Read the first question aloud and tell students to listen for the answer to that question in a section of text that you read aloud. During the first reading, students are to listen only. During the second reading, students are to write what they think is the answer. When you read the text a third time, students are to listen and polish their answers. Do not answer any questions at this time, but ask for three volunteers to share what they have written. After the students read aloud their answers, ask if any additional information needs to be added and if anyone wants to comment on the three ways of answering the question.

Then ask for student reactions to the process. Students may find the activity frustrating at first, but stress that it gets easier with practice. Explain that they can't and don't need to write down every word — they must summarize as they write. Point out that they must pick out what is important from what is read and must distinguish between important and unimportant parts.

Ask if anyone still needs information to answer the question. If so, again ask for volunteers to read their answers. When everyone knows the answer, discuss any underlying ideas or concepts. Then go on to the next question and repeat the process. Students will gain confidence in their ability to grasp meaning from oral language and to translate it to their own written language. After several questions, three readings probably will not be necessary, and most students will want to share their answers. Also, students will find that notes in their own words are easier to remember and to study from.

What Else

1. Students can use their answers to write a paper on the topic being studied. The information is in their language and is already sequenced; all that is needed is an introduction, transitions, and a conclusion, which can be worked on as a group. Students might work in small groups to write sections of the paper. The whole class could suggest final revisions.
2. Write a question outline for a passage of written text. Ask students to read the text and to write in their language what they think the answers are. Invite volunteers to share their answers as above.

*Elizabeth M. Baker, Columbia Public Schools/
Gifted Program, Missouri*

Artifact Collections for Literature and Content-Area Reading

Why

This strategy is designed to increase students' interest in and comprehension of works of literature and content-area reading selections. This activity is a pedagogical interpretation of schema theory applied to reading. The theory suggests that comprehension is highly dependent upon the background knowledge that the reader brings to the reading act. Artifact collections attempt to develop the reader's background for particular readings.

Who

All elementary students

How

Artifact collections are groupings of various objects that pertain to or are in some way related to a book, a story, a content-area chapter, or any other text that children read. Items that might be a part of an artifact collection include the following:

1. Clothes of particular characters in a book, represented through cutouts from a catalog, paper dolls, or photographs.
2. Songs or music from a place or period of time depicted in the text.
3. Recipes and prepared food typical of the location or time period of the story.
4. Dioramas illustrating certain events from the story.
5. A map showing the locations and journeys depicted in the book.
6. Selected poems that reflect the theme of the reading.
7. A biographical sketch of the author.

The collections can be made up of widely diverse and unusual objects. The only criterion is that the objects be related to the reading selection in some way.

Artifact collections work well when reading literature aloud to the class. At a part of the story where an artifact is appropriate, the teacher or a student can pull the item out of the box, talk about it, and pass it around for everyone to see and touch.

When the class or a group is reading a story together, the artifact collection can be placed in a reading corner for the children to explore on their own. The collection can help satisfy questions that arise when children read, such as "Where is this place?" or "What did that look and feel like?" The collections help bridge the gap between the concrete and abstract.

Several artifact collections can be displayed together in the reading corner with multiple copies of the accompanying books. This can serve as an attractive bait to lure children to books they might not otherwise tackle.

What Else

1. As children become familiar with artifact collections and their corresponding books, they may want to add items to existing collections. Some students may wish to assemble their own collections for books that are personal favorites. This would be an excellent alternative response activity for literature reading, and one that makes the response as fun as a scavenger hunt. Asking students to assemble artifact collections is an alternative way to check their comprehension since they can't prepare the collection unless they've read the book, understood it, and can explain why they selected certain items for their collections.
2. Older students might enjoy making artifact collections for children in lower grades. This activity would be particularly helpful in getting older, less proficient readers involved in books in a purposeful way.
3. Artifact collections could be used to stimulate student writing. Students might be given a particular set of objects from the collection and might be asked to write a story that somehow uses the various objects in an integrated way. Students may wish to compare their completed stories with the text that accompanies the collection.
4. For those classrooms that have separate instruction for spelling, words associated with the artifacts will form a natural spelling unit. In addition to just knowing and spelling the words, the students have the opportunity to touch, see, smell, listen to, and maybe even taste the items associated with those words.

Timothy V. Rasinski, University of Georgia, Athens

Writing to Learn in Social Studies

Why

1. To encourage students to utilize a variety of resources in researching a topic
2. To encourage students to respond personally to what they are learning

Who

Middle and upper elementary students; with adaptation, younger students

How

In the following research activity, students are not writing research papers that will be read only by the teacher. They go public during the research and writing stages, and at the end of the activity they select a way to present the information they've gathered.

Before drafting papers on various topics dealing with colonial life, students read and take notes, talk to a friend about what they have learned, and participate in a journal dialogue with the teacher. Talking or rehearsing enables them to get an idea of what is interesting about what they are learning. They become authorities on their subjects.

After preparing a first draft, students read their writings to several classmates. Talking with their classmates helps students find out what they didn't include in their drafts and what they want to find out. Classmates' questions (such as "Was Paul Revere a dentist, too?" and "Did he make his ride alone?") might send the students back to do further research. They return to reference materials and dig into previously unused sources. What they are looking for is important to them.

During the three weeks that students spend on the activity, they record in their social studies journals their notes about the topic, their plans for how to share the information they assemble, and a written conversation about the topic with the teacher. The journals allow the teacher to express excitement about what the students are learning, to model making connections between what they are finding out and what they need to know, to give them new information that they might find useful, and to help them locate sources of information. The journals allow students to ask for specific help, to raise questions about their topics, and to talk informally about new notions or ideas and about what surprises, puzzles, or delights them. The following journal excerpts show some examples of these conversations:

Dear Ms. B,
    Instead of finding out about what goes on in the home back then, I'll be working on what the woman's chores were. OK?
                Sincerely,
                Jenny

Dear Jenny,
    Yes, tomorrow you can get information about the chores women had to do. Have you used the book *Rural Reflections?* It has some detailed information about all the chores women did.
                Sincerely,
                Ms. B

Dear Ms. B,
    My dad told me that Paul Revere was a dentist for awhile. Is that true? I am going to look in books about Paul Revere that I haven't read yet to find out if he was a dentist. One clue that he may have been a dentist for a short time is that he did make silver and gold teeth at this work.
                Sincerely,
                Mike

Dear Mike,
    That could be true. I've never heard or read that before. I'll do some reading on that and let you know what I find out. You're doing some good detective work.
                Sincerely,
                Ms. B

Dear Ms. B,
    I am studying food and cooking. I'm learning how the Indians learned how to cook, how they ground corn, how they ate, etc. There is still a lot more to look at, too. I wonder how it would be like if we ate that way! There is really a big difference in today's and yesterday's cooking. Have you ever really thought about how little meat, liquid, food, flour, and sugar they had?
                Sincerely,
                Lisa

Dear Lisa,
    You got a lot of information today. Good job of note taking. How right your are when you say they had very little to cook with. Sugar was especially valuable to colonists because it was shipped from far away. (Sugar cane only grows in warm, moist places like Cuba.) Usually they sweetened foods with maple syrup.
                Sincerely,
                Ms. B

Students revise by adding new information to their drafts and seek additional responses until they are pleased with the content of their papers. After editing, they prepare their final copies. Students might choose to present their information to the class by role-playing, by writing plays and poems, or by preparing demonstrations of what they have learned.

Constance W. Bataller, Barrett Elementary School, Arlington, Virginia

An Economics Lesson on Scarcity

Why

Scarcity is a basic premise for understanding economic systems. The following activities are designed to follow a progression of understanding on the topics of scarcity, needs, wants, and decision making. Reading and writing will support economic learning.

Who

Primary students; with adaptation, older students

How

Scarcity

Begin the lesson on scarcity by presenting to the class the following problem: "We have twelve apples and thirty students. Are there enough apples for everyone to have one?" Divide the class into four groups and give each group three apples. If available, have an aide or parent serve as group leader, or select a student leader for each group.

Ask each group to brainstorm ideas for solving the problem and to list the ideas on paper. Students are to analyze each solution, discussing whether it is fair or possible. Students in each group decide which solution they like best and select a reporter to announce this decision. The full class reassembles to hear and discuss each group's decision. Steer the discussion back to the original problem and explain that it has a name: *scarcity.* Then give every child an apple and ask if there is a scarcity now. Explain that when there is no scarcity, objects are found in abundance and are sometimes free.

Scarcity can also be demonstrated in a game that is the reverse of Musical Chairs. Begin with an equal number of chairs and children, perhaps six. When the music stops, each child sits in a chair. Explain that all the children have their needs satisfied. Then add one child and resume the game. When the music stops, one child cannot sit in a chair. Explain that this child's need is not satisfied. Ask children for possible solutions. They might suggest that two children share a chair. Play the game a few more times, each time adding one child. Ask students to

observe whether their solutions will work and to identify what was scarce during the game.

Use Mother Goose rhymes and other favorite children's tales to reinforce the concept of scarcity. For example, "Old Mother Hubbard," *The Three Billy Goats Gruff, The Lion, the Boar and the Vultures, Jack and the Beanstalk, The Bean Boy* by Joan Chase Bowden, and *Socks for Supper* by Jack Kent all present situations where there is a scarcity. Read aloud *Stone Soup* by Marcia Brown and ask children to bring in things to make stone soup in the classroom.

Needs

To introduce the concept of needs, bring to class a plant and an animal (such as a gerbil, rat, hamster, or fish). Explain that both the plant and animal require certain things to stay alive. These are called *needs.* Ask children to suggest what the plant will need and what the animal will need to stay alive. As children brainstorm, write their suggestions on the board. Invite students to compare the two lists of needs.

Next, children might brainstom a list of their personal needs, such as food, shelter, clothing, and love. If students mention things that are not a necessity, explain that these items are called *wants.* Ask children to review and compare the lists of needs for the plant, the animal, and themselves.

Needs and Wants

To compare needs and wants, have students form small groups and ask them to brainstorm a list of all the things they want but don't need. Students discuss why they don't have all of these things, suggesting limited income, limited raw resources, limited time, and so on. Next, ask children to draw a picture of themselves and to make a collage of the things they want by cutting and pasting pictures from magazines and catalogs. Then they write about what they want and why.

Display the group lists and ask students to determine the ten most popular wants. List these items on a survey sheet and ask the children to select their own favorite item or perhaps two items. Pair children with partners and let them survey each other. Graph the results for all to see. Students might then survey other students in the same grade in the school. Graph these results and ask the class to compare the two graphs. You might break down the results by first and second choice or by sex, asking children to draw conclusions and inferences as to whether boys and girls have different wants.

Decision Making

Assemble colored squares of construction paper about one inch square and assign one color to different kinds of desserts (such as pie, cake, cookies, ice cream) or main dishes (pizza, hamburgers, tacos, hot dogs) or even vegetables (carrots, peas, broccoli, corn). Prepare a chart on the bulletin board listing the four food items.

Ask students to hypothesize which items will be the two most popular choices in the class. Then ask students to take turns making a selection by putting a paper marker on the board in the appropriate category. (Markers might be attached with push pins or tape.) Discuss the results and the accuracy of students' hypotheses.

Initiate another decision-making activity by reviewing the concept of a want and by explaining that students are to make a class collage of wants. Review the concept of scarcity, reminding students that they cannot have everything they want. Ask students to select from a catalog or magazine a picture of one item that they want. Students glue the pictures to butcher paper to make a class collage of wants. Students might also examine the choices that others make by asking a partner what item he or she selected and why. Students announce their partner's choice and the reason, such as "John wants a football because it is his favorite sport." Discuss how individuals have different wants because each person is unique.

What Else

Read fairy tales or wishing stories to the class to illustrate the economic conflict between unlimited wants and limited resources. Some possible stories are listed below:

> Aesop; *The Goose That Laid the Golden Egg; The Grasshopper and the Ant*
> Lorna Balian; *Sweet Touch*
> Dick Gackenbach; *Hattie Rabbit*
> Brothers Grimm; *The Fisherman and His Wife; The Golden Goose*
> Leo Lionni; *Alexander and the Wind-Up Mouse*

Additional economics materials, including filmstrips, are available from the Center for Economic Education, College of Education, Room B 209 Payne Education Building, Arizona State University, Tempe, AZ 85281 (602/965-6062); and the Arizona Council on Economic Education, 1130 East Helen Street, Tucson, AZ 85719 (602/626-5357).

References

Gray, Polly. "Why Can't I Have It?" *The Elementary Economist* 1, no. 1. The National Center of Economic Education for Children, Lesley College.

Kniep, Willard M. *Economics Exchange: Teaching Economics in Elementary School,* 12-13. Kendall/Hunt, 1981.

Willard Kniep, Global Perspectives in Education, New York, New York, and Sandra Lee Smith, Phoenix Elementary School District #1, Arizona

Group-Authored Books on a Social Studies Topic: The Westward Movement

Why

In the activity described below, students compile a group-authored book as a follow-up to a social studies unit. The activity utilizes a complex series of language strategies: concept retrieval, idea organization, labeling, dictionary and reference research, composition on a topic, copy reading, building a table of contents, and writing an introduction summarizing the project. All work is done by the students with the teacher serving as guide.

Who

Upper elementary students

How

After students complete a social studies unit, in this case a unit on the Westward Movement, ask them to brainstorm all the words that they can remember about the topic as you list the words on the chalkboard: *derringer, buffalo chips, beef jerky, quirt, Nez Percé,* and so on.

Next, students decide on a way to group the words, and transfer them to appropriate columns on a long piece of butcher paper hung horizontally. Students might decide to relocate some words to a more appropriate category and to discard other words as inappropriate to a study of the Westward

Movement. New columns might need to be started to accommodate additional words. Some words might be placed in more than one category. When all the words are categorized on the chart, students determine a heading for each column. The completed chart might look something like the chart in Figure 7-2.

Next, each student selects a topic of interest from the chart and writes a composition for the class book. Students might select one of the general topical headings or one of the original words. They might choose one of the historical characters and write biographical sketches. The writings are to relate some factual information, so if remembered information is sketchy, students might do more research in reference books or social studies textbooks. Students could coach each other and cooperate on projects.

Peer readers suggest spelling corrections and additional information, as do other students in group question sessions. When students finish writing or want assistance, they read aloud their papers and field questions from other students. Then the student writers make the revisions that they feel are necessary. Some students might wish to prepare illustrations to accompany their papers.

Help students develop an outline to organize their collection of essays. For simplification, designate each major topic as a chapter, with special items appearing as subheadings. Students work in groups to produce an introduction summarizing the project from start to finish and an introductory paragraph for each chapter. The book might conclude with a copy of the wall chart.

Photocopies can be made directly from the students' papers. If only a ditto machine is available, parents might volunteer to help type the papers onto ditto masters. Duplicate enough copies of the completed booklet so that each student has a copy and copies are available in other classrooms. Students are to collate and assemble their own books. Encourage them to make a special cover and to title the book appropriately to reflect the scope of the material.

The project will take over two weeks. It will give the student participants pride in their writing and will elicit a range of language usage from each student who helped, as well as from those with whom it is shared: classmates, teachers, and family.

Martha L. Eshelman, Knob Noster R-VIII School District, Missouri

Take Time in History

Why

To help students use writing to learn about a particular person and a specific time period in history

Who

Upper elementary students

How

Have copies of *Time* magazine available, including the issue with the Man or Woman of the Year on the cover.

Ask each student to select a personality in American history, to research this person, and to plan a cover story about him or her for an issue of *Time* magazine. Explain that students will write about

Equipment	Animals	People	Places in Town	Territories Traveled
Cowboys	Cowboys	Sam Houston	newspaper office	mountains
wagons	hogs	General Custer	ice house	steep hills
saddles	oxen	Davy Crockett	general store	lakes
canteen	dogies	Capt. Meriwether	blacksmith shop	plains
Indians	horses	Belle Starr	church	valleys
tepee	Indians	Chief Sitting Bull	jail	Mississippi
arrowhead	dogs	Crazy Horse	cabins	mountain passes
	horses	Geronimo	trading post	Death Valley
	Wild			
	puma			
	horses			
	buffalo			

Figure 7-2. Chart of words pertaining to the Westward Movement.

their historical figures from the viewpoint of the time in which the people lived. Students are to choose a specific month and year during the person's lifetime. They are to include the following items in the issue, written in magazine format:

1. an interview with the personality
2. three to five ads for items recently invented or frequently used at the time
3. a biographical sketch of the president at the time
4. a "news in brief" account of what was happening in the country at the time
5. a poem about the person or a narrative describing an incident in the person's life
6. any other items or articles of interest that students want to write and include

Students assemble their completed magazines, perhaps including a cover photograph or illustration. They might do a "Read-Around" in which they read each other's magazines and write what they liked on a comments page.

What Else

As an alternative to the magazine, give students the following options for preparing a report on a historical person:

1. Write a report using fictional eyewitnesses to talk about the event or person. Headlines like "Janitor Tells All about Secret Meeting in Philadelphia" (1787) or "Bird Sees Men Fly through Air" (1903) might give you inspiration.
2. Use the point of view of a minor character to write the report. For example, one of Washington's soldiers might discuss crossing the Delaware; a soldier might talk about being a patient of Clara Barton's; or the boy who tended to Lee's or Jackson's horses during the Civil War might comment on his interactions with the general.
3. Determine five questions that you would ask the person in history if you could talk to him or her today. Write the questions and responses in an interview format.

Elizabeth M. Baker, Columbia Public Schools/ Gifted Program, Missouri

Thanksgiving Web

Why

To encourage students to make use of what they know about Thanksgiving while learning more about the holiday

Who

Primary students; with adaptation, middle and upper elementary students

How

Follow the six steps outlined in the Thanksgiving Web shown in Figure 7-3. Select activities from those suggested or substitute related activities of your own choosing.

Three first graders created the following turkey recipes.

Jamie's Turkey Recipe

1. Go to Lucky's and buy a turkey that weighs 200 pounds.
2. Make stuffing with 15 hot dogs, 14 hamburgers and cranberry sauce. Put inside turkey.
3. Put the turkey inside the oven at 200 for 4 days.
4. Serve with mash potatoes, ice cream, raspberry and salad.

Trevor's Turkey Recipe

1. Go to Sears and buy a turkey that weighs 6 pounds.
2. Make stuffing with 5 pieces of meat, 6 potatoes and catsup mix and put inside turkey.
3. Put turkey inside oven for 6 minutes and set oven for 7.
4. Serve the turkey with pork chops, hamburgers and mash potatoes.

Celina's Turkey Recipe

1. Go to Lucky's and buy a 3 gallon and 1/2 turkey.
2. Put in 3 gallons of salad.
3. Put it in the oven for 2 minutes.
4. Serve it with forks and ice cream.

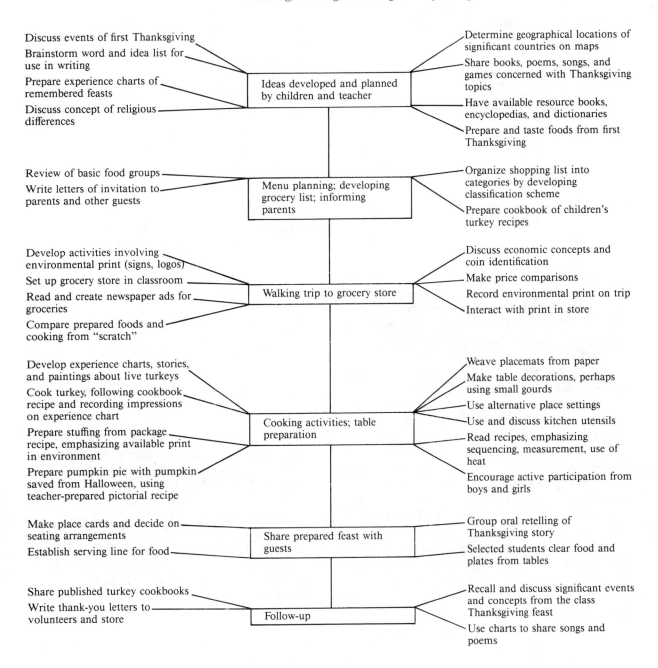

Discuss events of first Thanksgiving

Brainstorm word and idea list for use in writing

Prepare experience charts of remembered feasts

Discuss concept of religious differences

Ideas developed and planned by children and teacher

Determine geographical locations of significant countries on maps

Share books, poems, songs, and games concerned with Thanksgiving topics

Have available resource books, encyclopedias, and dictionaries

Prepare and taste foods from first Thanksgiving

Review of basic food groups

Write letters of invitation to parents and other guests

Menu planning; developing grocery list; informing parents

Organize shopping list into categories by developing classification scheme

Prepare cookbook of children's turkey recipes

Develop activities involving environmental print (signs, logos)

Set up grocery store in classroom

Read and create newspaper ads for groceries

Compare prepared foods and cooking from "scratch"

Walking trip to grocery store

Discuss economic concepts and coin identification

Make price comparisons

Record environmental print on trip

Interact with print in store

Develop experience charts, stories, and paintings about live turkeys

Cook turkey, following cookbook recipe and recording impressions on experience chart

Prepare stuffing from package recipe, emphasizing available print in environment

Prepare pumpkin pie with pumpkin saved from Halloween, using teacher-prepared pictorial recipe

Cooking activities; table preparation

Weave placemats from paper

Make table decorations, perhaps using small gourds

Use alternative place settings

Use and discuss kitchen utensils

Read recipes, emphasizing sequencing, measurement, use of heat

Encourage active participation from boys and girls

Make place cards and decide on seating arrangements

Establish serving line for food

Share prepared feast with guests

Group oral retelling of Thanksgiving story

Selected students clear food and plates from tables

Share published turkey cookbooks

Write thank-you letters to volunteers and store

Follow-up

Recall and discuss significant events and concepts from the class Thanksgiving feast

Use charts to share songs and poems

Figure 7–3. Web of activities related to Thanksgiving feast.

Robert C. Wortman, Tucson Unified School District, Arizona

All about Radio for All

Why

To provide a meaningful context for content writing of all kinds

Who

With adaptation, all elementary students

How

Children plan, discuss, research, and then write short reports on a topic related to a particular subject area. Each student reads his or her report aloud while another student records the report onto an audiocassette. Another class hears the recording as a news break during snack time or some other quiet period of the day.

The reports need not be recorded all at once. Several can be recorded during the week, with a narrator providing continuity. While a student plays a musical theme in the background, the narrator can introduce the news report by identifying the radio call letters chosen by the class and then introduce each student's report. The stories can bring to life topics being studied in social studies, science, or health. Commercials as well as featured entertainment specials can be written by individuals or small groups.

Students might want to focus on one event or topic they are studying and to produce a dramatization with sound effects. For example, students could improvise a scenario in which Christopher Columbus tries to talk the king and queen of Spain into giving him ships to sail west in search of Asia.

This activity can be a one-time project, or it can become a regular weekly or monthly feature of one class or group of classes. When several classes exchange radio programs, students have added motivation, knowing that other students are listening to their reports and are actually learning about events and topics through the reports. The activity can also encourage interaction between different grade levels.

What Else

Students might want to write about problems to a fictitious Ann Landers in another class. Students in the second class work in groups to suggest solutions and then prepare a radio program in which they read aloud their responses.

Diane R. vom Saal, University of Missouri–Columbia

Bubbles Throughout: A Week-Long Integrated Learning Experience

Why

Bubbles are a part of science and mathematics; they encourage curiosity and invite investigation and discovery. Curiosity encourages questioning and answering and lots of discussion. Bubbles can flow through all areas of the curriculum.

Who

Students in kindergarten and grade 1

How

Day One

Assemble dishwashing soap, cups, straws, buckets, pouring and measuring equipment, a water table (if possible), egg beaters, towels, and a mop.

Present *Bubble, Bubble,* a wordless picture book by Mercer Mayer, by first just showing each illustration to the children. Then "read" the book, with children supplying the story text.

Lead a few children to the water table, where there is a bucket of soapy water and various water-play equipment. Scoop about ½ inch of water into a cup for each child; give each child a straw; and remind the children to blow out the soapy water, not to suck it through the straw. There will be a profusion of bubbles in the air and many comments, which are recorded on chart paper as the children talk ("Rainbows," says one child; "Look, ice cream," says another). At circle time talk about the experience and read aloud what the children said about their bubbles as they worked at the water table.

Day Two

Assemble 2-inch circles cut from construction paper, sheets of 8½″ × 11″ paper, butcher paper, glue or rubber cement, crayons, a record player or tape deck, and records or tapes of "bubbly" music.

Start by reading *Leo the Late Bloomer Takes a Bath* by Robert Kraus et al. After talking about Leo's bathing experience, suggest that it might have helped if Leo could have turned the bubbles into something else. Hold up a circle, blow on it, and let it float to the floor. Then ask, "What else could this bubble be?" Encourage the youngsters to pretend that bubbles can become something else and to glue the circles (the bubbles) on paper to form other objects, adding details with crayons.

Prepare a cover page with one circle and the words "Once this was a bubble. . . ." As children finish their pictures, take their dictation, leading them into a language pattern by asking, "What is it now?" Students respond, "Now it's a nose," "Now it's a traffic light," "Now it's a Ford 4 × 4," or some other object containing one or more circles.

Assemble the picture and text pages together in an accordion book, made by taking a length of butcher paper, folding it in half lengthwise (for strength), and then folding the paper accordion style. Glue the children's pages to the folded butcher paper. At circle time each child can read his or her own page. Later this durable book may be displayed so that several children may read it at one time.

When the book is completed, students dance to the "bubbly" music. You may want to suggest some body movements, such as "Make your body into a bubble and roll around"; "Blow up bigger, bigger, bigger"; "Float away . . . Pop!"

Day Three

Assemble 1½-inch circles in any two colors, 6-inch green circles, paper fish about 4 inches long, dots made by a hole puncher, paper bathtubs about 6 inches long, a large bathtub cut from butcher paper, glue or rubber cement, and marbles.

At circle time make a people graph by asking, "Who takes a bubble bath? Who does not?" Children line up on the floor according to their answers. Discuss which line is longer, and count the children in each line. Give each child a small circle of any color, representing a bubble. Each child writes his or her name on the circle and tapes or pins it on the large paper bathtub. The tub is divided in half, with one end labeled "I take bubble baths" and the other end labeled "I do not take bubble baths." Children discuss the concepts of more and less and count the bubbles on each side of the tub.

Children move to number stations where a particular number concept is highlighted; for example, *six.* At one table children may place six bubbles (small circles) on a small paper bathtub. They dictate how many of each color they've used: "Four pink and two blue, six bubbles in my tub." Children may make several tubs, varying the number of each of the two colored circles but always using six circles. At another table, children glue a fish onto a 6-inch circle (a fish bowl?) and glue six paper-punch dots near the fish's mouth, dictating something like, "One fish blows six bubbles." As time allows, work on invariance of number concepts with individual children by hiding and counting marbles.

Day Four

Assemble small balloons, vinegar, baking soda, a clear plastic bottle (such as the one the vinegar comes in), paper, crayons, lemonade and limeade, cups, spoons.

At circle time reread the accordion bubble book. Then students form small groups and discuss what is a solid, a liquid, and a gas. Perform the following experiment for each group. Pour ½ inch of vinegar into the plastic bottle. Place a heaping teaspoon of baking soda into the bottle and immediately put the mouth of a balloon over the top of the bottle. The balloon inflates. When it is fully inflated, carefully pull the balloon off and knot it.

Later, mix the lemonade and limeade for snack time and give each child a cup of juice. Carry around a bowl containing the baking soda and let each child place a teaspoonful of the baking soda into his or her cup, instantly producing lemon-lime soda. Ask the children to draw something about the experience and to write (or dictate) what they are drawing. Write the soda recipe on chart paper.

Day Five

Assemble a copy of *Billy Balloon,* salt, flour, blue coloring, water, oil, a toaster oven (if possible), aluminum foil, soap, cups, and straws.

Read *Billy Balloon* aloud and encourage the children to read along during a second reading. Talk about how balloons are like bubbles. Ask them to look around the room for things that begin with the letter *B*.

Make a batch of blue clay (another *B* word) with the salt, flour, blue coloring, and oil, or bring in blue Play-Doh. Encourage students to make *B* objects, such as birds, boats, bananas, and butterflies. Let each child make one item to keep. Place these on foil and bake them in the oven.

Wind up the activity by getting out soapy water, cups, and straws and by going outside to blow bubbles. Encourage children to talk and think about the other bubble activities and to review their completed bubble projects.

Wendy Hood, Hollinger Elementary School, Tucson, Arizona

A Trip into Space: Writing in Science

Why

To stimulate students' imaginative exploration based upon a foundation of knowledge

Who

Middle or upper elementary students

How

Prewriting

Students read and write about the solar system, with a great deal of discussion of factual information. Plan a bulletin board that shows the planets and moons in relative size in orbit around the sun. Children make crayoned drawings painted over with black paint to give the look of outer space, and they make mobiles using different-size styrofoam balls or papier-mâché. They listen to the music from *Star Wars* and, if possible, take a trip to a planetarium.

The Writing Assignment

Read aloud the following instructions to students:

> We have learned many facts about our solar system, but we know that scientists are learning more each year as information is gathered from huge telescopes, satellites, and spacecraft. By the year 2000 there may be space shuttles taking passengers, like you, back and forth into space. Where would you like to go?
>
> Close your eyes. Imagine you are taking a trip into space. What does it feel like as you take off from the ground? Are you getting dizzy going so fast? Is it noisy? What do you see out the window? How would you describe the planet Earth as you look back? As you leave Earth's atmosphere and gravity, are you floating around in the spacecraft? How does it feel? When you land, what do you see? What's the surface like? Do you land on sand, on clay, on slushy ice, in water, on a mountaintop, or in a volcano? What is the weather like? Are

> there clouds? Is it hot or cold? Do you see any living creatures? Do they look like human beings? Can you communicate? How? What else do you see? How are things different from Earth? What do you do while visiting this planet? Do you want to leave and return home, or stay? Why? What do you want to bring back to Earth?
>
> Now open your eyes and describe in writing what you saw in your "mind's eye." Give specific details of what you saw, heard, and touched, and how you felt. Pretend you are telling your parents or friends about your trip. Don't forget, this is make-believe. Use your imagination. Have fun!

What Else

Students may want to ask themselves the following questions when they complete their papers. They might then read their papers aloud to a partner and ask the partner to answer the same questions about their papers.

> Did I tell what I saw and heard, and how I felt?
>
> Did I pick the best describing words?
>
> Did I put my ideas in an order that makes sense?

Janet S. Cumbee, Wake Forest Elementary School, North Carolina

It's So Nice to Have a Pet around the House: Learning about Animals

Why

1. To encourage students to explore interesting animals in science class
2. To help students use close reading and observation to write a persuasive argument for owning a very unusual pet

Who

Middle or upper elementary students, especially animal lovers

How

Prewriting Activities

Invite students to read articles on or descriptions of unusual animals, such as the squid, aardvark, koala bear, armadillo, bat, platypus, sloth, boa constrictor, and kangaroo. Ask them to locate pictures and descriptions of these animals in the encyclopedia, wildlife books, zoo books, science texts, and so forth. After students have read about their animals, divide the class into groups of three or four, with each group member focusing on a different unusual animal. Strive to have some of the same animals represented in more than one group.

Within the groups, each student shares the information he or she has gained, while group members take notes on the characteristics of the animals described. Then two groups join and share notes. If some of the same animals have been chosen by both groups, students gain more information that they can use for elaboration. Through discussion, students gather and pool enough information so that they understand the unusual habits or appearances of certain animals.

Ask students about the animals they have at home as pets. Invite them to share stories about the behaviors of their pets, what their pets eat, and how they take care of these animals. Help students as a group organize this information into categories such as those listed below.

1. What does my pet like to eat?
2. How does my pet play?
3. What kind of space (cage, yard, pet bed) does my pet require?
4. How much does it cost to have a pet like mine?
5. What kind of climate does my pet prefer?
6. To what diseases is my pet susceptible?
7. What are the advantages and disadvantages of owning a pet?

The Writing Assignment

Read aloud or hand out to students the following instructions:

> Using the information you gained in studying unusual animals and the categories we discussed about owning a pet, make a case to present to your parents for taking on one of these unusual creatures as your family pet. Since these are nontraditional pets, you must consider the animal's appearance, temperament, habits, and living environment as you create your argument. Although you might touch on some of the disadvantages to show your parents that you have an informed, realistic view, you should concentrate on advantages in order to convince them to own this unusual creature.

What Else

When students have completed their first drafts, they return to their small groups to read and discuss the papers. Some suggestions for peer response follow.

1. Put a star next to the part you liked best.
2. Tell the writer what you learned about this unusual creature from reading his or her paper.
3. What is the writer's most persuasive argument?
4. Where do you need more information?
5. Make a suggestion for improving the writing.

Based on suggestions made by their peers, students revise their drafts and prepare a final copy for a bulletin board display entitled It's So Nice to Have a Pet around the House, accompanied by pictures or drawings.

Carol McCoy, Westview Elementary School, Lee's Summit, Missouri

Observe a Bird: Science with Poetry

Why

1. To help students enjoy poetry
2. To help students learn to write poetry
3. To encourage students to observe, which is the heart of the scientific process

Who

Middle and upper elementary students

How

Display a copy of Emily Dickinson's poem "A Bird Came down the Walk" on the chalkboard or on posterboard so that all can read it. Bring in objects that represent the images in the poem and that will help students understand the lines of the poem. For example, cooked macaroni could represent the worm eaten raw; grass moist with dew and a glass of water could show the bird's drinking from grass; beads could show how rapidly a bird's eyes can move; a piece of velvet could let students feel the texture of the bird's head as Dickinson imagined it; an oar or a picture of a rower could represent the bird's motion; a picture of the ocean and a silver bowl could demonstrate that the ocean has no seam and show what the sky looked like; a picture of a butterfly could represent the butterfly that leaps off flowers but makes no sound, no splash ("plashless"); and a picture of a swimmer could show what the butterflies looked like to the poet.

Read the poem aloud, perhaps inviting students to read along. Subsequent class discussion centers on what Dickinson's words mean. Ask students whether she chose good comparisons to show the actions of a bird.

After the discussion, students go outside to observe a bird themselves. As they watch a bird, encourage children to note everything the bird does by asking questions such as the following:

What do the bird's feathers look like?

What does the bird's head look like?

What shape are its feet?

What shape is its beak?

What sound does the bird make?

If you could touch the bird, what do you think it would feel like?

Next, ask students to collect objects that represent what they saw when they observed their birds. For example, a red balloon might represent the stomach of a robin; toothpicks could stand for its tiny feet; silver beads might indicate the eyes; a blue pen could represent the color of a bluejay's feathers; a paper airplane could represent the lightness of feathers. Students paste their objects onto a piece of construction paper and label the objects according to what they represent, such as "The bird's head = round as a cotton ball."

Gather a selection of bird identification books from the school and local libraries and ask students to find a picture of their birds in one of the books. With a bird book open in front of them, students list the characteristics of their birds. Help by posing such questions as:

What is special about the bird?

Where does it live?

What does it eat?

Does it make a special sound, like "Teacher, Teacher"?

Next, students draw, color, and cut out a picture of their birds.

Finally, each student assembles on his or her desk the cutout drawing of the bird, the list of its char-

acteristics, and the paper containing the pasted-on and labeled objects representing the parts of the bird. With these materials as inspiration, invite students to write a poem about the bird. Encourage them to do what Emily Dickinson did: to describe the actions of the bird, its appearance, and their feelings as they watched the bird, creating their own comparisons of the bird's characteristics to other objects. Students' expressive language makes their poems a delight to read and helps them remember the characteristics of the birds they observed.

Two poems written by sixth graders are presented below.

The Wagtail I Watched

A wagtail bird
his stomach bright
as the sun
a piece of grass
mixed in with the yellow
his beak as sharp as a steak knife tip
and as brown as dead grass
his feathers sandpaper rough
but silk smooth
flew away silently
as a glider

Neil Wilkie

Fruit Pigeon

Colors like a rainbow
Sections of feathers
look like waves of the sea
Its eyes the shiniest silverball
It flies with the wind
like a thin feather
floating from the sky
The feathers feel
like soft, elegant fur
Its claw is as sharp
as a hook
After all, it is a Fruit Pigeon

Laron Moss

Margaret Queenan, Stamford Public Schools, Connecticut

Bees, Bees, Bees

Why

1. To extend students' oral language
2. To integrate writing with reading
3. To encourage class participation and involvement
4. To help students learn about bees

Who

Primary students

How

Day One

Initiate the activity by listing on chart paper questions that students have about bees. Read aloud an informative book about bees. Next, ask students to list new words or terms they heard, such as *honeycomb, drone, beekeeper, beeline, royal jelly, colony, queen, worker, cell, hive, proboscis,* or *tail-wagging dance.* Students then pair with a partner, choose a term from this list, and illustrate its meaning.

Keep a variety of books about bees, both factual and fictional, available for browsing, reading, and research. (A list of suggested titles appears at the end of the activity.) Some students might write and illustrate books about bees. The covers of the books can be made from black and yellow construction paper.

Day Two

Read aloud the poem "For the Love of Honey" by Sharen Scalena. Talk about the rhythm of this poem and ask students to name the rhyming words. Bring in a large loaf of bread and a jar of honey for students to spread on the bread. They'll need little encouragement to taste the honey. Make a language experience chart by asking students to list words that describe the honey, such as *sticky, sweet, yellow, gooey.*

Glue a "honey-shaped" piece of yellow construction paper to a larger piece of white or brown paper cut in the shape of a slice of bread. Invite students to write their impressions of honey on the yellow paper.

Day Three

Read aloud the poem "Wendy the Worker Bee" by Sharen Scalena. Read the poem several times so that students can enjoy the rhyme and rhythm of the words. Ask them to list the jobs Wendy disliked doing and what she would rather be doing instead of working. Then invite each student to complete the sentence "I am as busy as a bee when . . ." and to illustrate his or her response.

Day Four

Read aloud and enjoy "Claire the Bear" by Sharen Scalena, perhaps as a choral reading. Ask students to talk about why the bees were going to chase Claire home. Explain how most of us obtain our honey from a grocery store or a beekeeper, rather than collecting it from a beehive. Then have students, working in small groups, prepare Peanut Honey Candy from the following recipe: mix together 1 cup peanut butter, 1 cup honey, 1 cup powdered milk, ½ teaspoon vanilla, and ½ cup peanuts; shape into bite-sized balls.

Day Five

Read aloud *Fire! Fire! Said Mrs. McGuire* by Bill Martin, Jr. Ask students to write a group bee story patterned after the book. One class wrote the following story.

> "Bees, Bees!" said Mrs. Cheese.
> "Where, Where?" said Mr. Care.
> "In the beehive," said Mr. Brive.
> "In the cell," said Mr. Bell.
> "Underground," said Mr. Brown.
> "What a stinger!" said Mrs. Binger.
> "Help, Help!" said Mrs. Belp.
> "Beekeeper, Beekeeper!" yelled Mrs. Reepeeper.
> "Safe and sound!" said Mr. Bound.

Students then choose a phrase from the group story or the original story and illustrate it for a class book or wall mural.

Day Six

Invite a beekeeper to school to describe his or her job and to display the necessary clothing and equipment. Students then share their illustrations, charts, and books about bees, read aloud the bee poems, and serve the Peanut Honey Candy. Afterward, they write thank-you notes to the beekeeper for speaking to the class about bees.

Suggested Reading List

Barton, Byron. *Buzz, Buzz, Buzz.* Macmillan, 1973.

Goudey, Alice E. *Here Come the Bees.* Scribner, 1960.

Lecht, June. *Honey Bees.* National Geographic Society, 1973.

Neal, Charles. *What Is a Bee?* Benefic Press, 1961.

Scalena, Sharen. *Reading Experiences in Science Series: Bees.* Peguis Publishers, 1980.

Swenson, Valerie. *Bees and Wasps.* Maxton Publishing, n.d.

Teale, Edwin W. *The Bees.* Childrens Press, 1967.
Tibbets, Albert. *First Book of Bees.* Watts, 1952.

Mary A. Evans, Columbia Public Schools, Missouri

What's Happening Here?

Why

The abilities to observe and describe are prerequisite skills for making meaning of process-oriented learning experiences, including scientific processes and aesthetic experiences such as art, music, and literature studies. Effective problem-solving and decision-making abilities in the social, political, and economic worlds are grounded in accurate observation and description. It is important for students to distinguish among and accurately describe phenomena or events, inferences, and personal reactions or feelings. Through involvement in the activities in this unit, children will have the opportunity to:

1. demonstrate a variety of ways to observe (touch, taste, smell, hear, see)

2. demonstrate a variety of ways to describe (oral descriptions, written descriptions, bar and line graphs, charts, lists, drama, pantomime, models, drawings)

3. develop vocabulary for descriptions, observations, inferences, and feelings

4. distinguish among observations, inferences, and feelings

5. be able to describe events in terms of the sequence in which they occur

6. be able to make decisions based on observations

Who

All elementary students

How

1. Sensory Maze

Make a maze for students to walk through barefoot and blindfolded. Include such objects as ice, cooked noodles, wet mud, water, dry cereal, or other tactile objects. Have students walk through the maze one by one, using their hands or feet to feel their way through. Then ask the still-blindfolded students to infer or guess what they walked through and to name the properties that identified the objects, such as "It was ice because it was cold."

Explain to students that they are *inferring* what was there by how it felt and that they need to use other senses to be certain. Ask what other senses they could use. Ask students to go back through the maze, this time *observing* with their eyes also. Then they discuss properties of the objects that they saw with their eyes.

Next, ask children to *describe* what they saw by making a map of the maze on which they label each item they saw and felt. Students might also write about what they observed in the maze with their eyes, hands, and feet. The following questions might stimulate their writing:

What did we observe?

What did I first think it was?

How did it feel?

How did it look?

2. Do You Want It?

Fill a plastic gallon juice or milk container with water, red food coloring, and pure lemon juice; the liquid should look like red Kool-Aid. Blindfold children and ask them to sit in a circle. Tell them that you are holding a mystery object. Do they want it? Explain that you will give them clues to *observe* with their various senses so that they can infer what the object is and can decide if they want it.

1. Shake the jug. Ask children if they want it. Why? What properties does it have? List the properties on the chalkboard.

2. Walk around and let children feel the jug. Ask if they want it. Why? What properties does it have? Make a second list.

3. Children remove their blindfolds and see the jug. Ask if they want it. Why? What properties does it have? Make a third list and review the characteristics on the three lists.

4. Pass the jug around and let children smell the beverage. Ask if they want it. Why? What properties does it have? Make a fourth list, again reviewing the other lists.

5. Give everyone a taste of the beverage. Ask if they want it. Why? What properties does it

have? Make a fifth list and review the other lists.

Discuss what happened and why. Make a chart that lists all the ways they observed: *hearing, feeling, seeing, smelling, tasting.* Make a chart that lists the way they *inferred* (by *guessing,* by *thinking,* and so on). Make a chart that lists the words used to describe (*it smells like, it feels like, it looks like,* and so on). Make a chart that lists ways to describe. On all of these charts include columns so that you or students can check off daily when they use a particular sense and when they use a particular way of describing.

What Else

Continue to stimulate students' abilities at observation and description with the following activities.

1. Can You Guess What I See?

Demonstrate a guessing game by placing an object behind a barrier (perhaps in a box). Describe the object's properties and then ask the children to guess what the object is. After you've repeated the procedure with several objects, point out how important the students' descriptions are. They must describe all properties before they can make a guess.

Pair children with partners and ask them to describe an object, such as a cup, an ear of corn, a clock, or a ball. Emphasize that they cannot say what the object does — they are to describe the properties they observe. After students have described several objects, discuss the activity with them. Mark the charts for types of observing, inferring, and describing. Ask children to write about the activity in their observation books. Encourage their writing by asking questions about what they observed.

2. Object Tray

Fill a tray with a variety of unrelated objects. Divide the class into three teams. Tell each team that they will see the tray for one minute and then are to list all the objects they remember seeing. Students discuss their lists and learn how well they do at observing. Students then mark the charts and report the activity in their observation notebooks.

As an additional activity, ask each team in turn to classify the objects on the tray. They are to observe characteristics that are similar, such as all metal or all red objects. Students list and discuss their categories.

3. Mirrors

Pass out mirrors and ask children to observe themselves. Invite them to describe themselves by making a picture and a written description for their notebooks. Students mark on the charts the type of observations and description that they used.

4. Tasting Tray

Fill a tray with a variety of foods and invite students to taste the items. Graph on a bar graph their observations, such as *sweet, salty, sour, tasteless.* Make a separate graph for each child so that everyone can insert a graph in his or her observation notebook.

5. Celery Stalk

As children observe, place a celery stalk with leaves in a jar filled with water and food coloring. Discuss the procedure and ask students to report their observations as a separate chapter in their observation notebooks. They are to observe this plant daily and to record their observations. When the color starts moving upward, encourage children to measure it and record its progress. They make a line graph in their notebooks and fill it in daily. Encourage discussion throughout the experiment.

6. What Sound Is It?

Behind a barrier, make a sound and ask children to infer what the sound was. Then display the object. Discuss if they had enough information from the sound alone to observe what the object was. Students write up the activity in their observation notebooks.

7. Pantomime

Invite an older student, a parent, or another student to pantomime an activity, such as putting on a raincoat or planting a row of beans. Children observe and describe the pantomime, and then guess what activity was being demonstrated. In the discussion that follows, students may want to imitate the pantomime. They report on the activity in their notebooks and keep charts up-to-date.

8. Observation of Feelings

Arrange for another person to run into the room as if there were an emergency or as if something has angered or upset this person. Dramatize a series of events that would create a stressful situation.

When the crisis is over, tell children it was just a drama and ask for their reactions. List how they felt and what feelings they observed: fear, anger, humor, or another emotion. Encourage students to re-create the drama in sequence, explaining that this is a way to describe what happened. The class writes a group story of the event. Type and duplicate copies of the story so that students can add it to their notebooks.

Sandra Lee Smith, Phoenix Elementary School District #1, Arizona, and Willard Kniep, Global Perspectives in Education, New York, New York

Section B:
Reading and Writing Newspapers
Compiled by Peter Hasselriis,
University of Missouri–Columbia

Introduction

In a fully integrated language arts program, few resources are as adaptable or as flexible as newspapers. Offering information with relevance in virtually all content areas, they can provide numerous experiences that benefit instruction in all the language arts. In other words, if you are searching for materials that will enhance growth in the various language arts and provide subject-matter content, you need oftentimes look no further than the nearest available newspaper.

"Nearest available newspaper," moreover, should not necessarily be interpreted as meaning only newspapers that are written for children. On the contrary, adult daily or weekly newspapers should be given a place in your classroom. Use the style and format of that same newspaper as a model for at least some of the publications that your students produce as a regular part of their writing program.

Newspaper publishers are very aware of their readers, and therefore there is a trememdous range of reading levels reflected in newspapers. But because of the predictable structure of newspapers, a student possessing strong background information in a given area can overlook the vagaries of reading levels, readabilities, and the like.

If you organize a classroom in such a way that everyone must read the same material at the same time, and if you feel that when students read they must be able to define and pronounce each and every word they read correctly, then you probably will not be satisfied using newspapers. If, on the other hand, you are comfortable placing emphasis on topics that *students* choose as interesting and valuable, and if you are concerned that students read with understanding whether or not their reading is word perfect, you are likely to find that newspapers are a valuable addition to the classroom.

This section provides information to help you draw from typical daily or weekly newspapers a variety of exercises to enhance your current program in reading and writing and to start generating your own classroom or school newspaper.

Following Up a Newspaper Story

Why

1. To improve students' writing and critical thinking
2. To promote students' involvement in community events and affairs
3. To aid students in recognizing information change and understanding mass media

Who

Middle and upper elementary students

How

Ask students to read or listen to a particular story in a local newspaper, one that would be of interest to many students. Discuss the story, elaborating on points of interest. Develop a list of questions about the story and encourage children to speculate about possible answers. Explain that there may or may not be a follow-up story in the next day's or next week's newspaper and that the students will need to do some detective work on their own. Ask the class to examine the story for information about sources to contact for additional facts or developments. Students explore the approaches available for contacting persons who might provide follow-up information, such as by mail, telephone, or personal visit. Students work in pairs to contact their sources.

After a week or two, students bring to class the information they've gathered, even if the response was "No comment." Discuss any and all responses, and ask students to speculate about reasons for such responses as "No comment" or form letters. Students might write a follow-up to the original story based on the information they gathered.

What Else

1. If the local newspaper does not print a follow-up story, submit the student's follow-up story.
2. The class might write a letter to the editor if there are discrepancies between the newspaper story and information discovered by the class.
3. Expand the idea to include materials other than newspapers. Electronic media, books, magazines, and so forth can also provide stories that lend themselves to this treatment.

Joel Dean Brown, Ganado Intermediate School, Arizona

Lovelorn

Why

1. To provide students with opportunities to organize ideas
2. To give students an enjoyable way to practice reading for the purpose of discerning the gist of an author's writing

Who

Upper elementary students; with adaptation, younger students

How

Collect advice-to-the-lovelorn columns of particular interest to students. Separate each letter to the columnist from the reply, removing the columnist's salutation. Ask students to read the letters and replies and to match them appropriately.

What Else

1. Circulate only the letters asking for advice. Encourage students to write their own replies. Students work in small groups to compare their replies with those written by the columnists.
2. This activity can be adapted to involve a much wider variety of content. For example, clip the

headlines apart from the news stories or from articles in other parts of the newspaper and ask students to match the two. Additionally, students might read stories, write their own headlines, and then compare their headlines with the originals; or they might read the headlines, predict the content of the stories, read the stories, and compare their predictions with the printed stories.

Marjorie A. David, Bardwell Junior High, St. Charles, Missouri

Turning the Tables: The Students Ask the Questions

Why

To provide an opportunity for students to formulate questions for the teacher to answer about news stories, and to evaluate the teacher's answers

Who

Upper elementary students, particularly reluctant readers who have become passive rather than active participants in the process of reading

How

Prepare for the activity by reading all the news stories in one day's newspaper. Ask each student to select three news stories in the paper and to read them silently. Students formulate a question about the content of each article and write each question on one 3″ × 5″ index card.

Read aloud the questions one by one, explaining the type of question, such as recall of details or discernment of cause-effect relationships. Provide a suitable answer for each question.

What Else

1. Discuss different kinds of questions. Ask students to indicate which kinds of questions you usually ask on tests or to promote class discussion.
2. Students read other types of reading material (such as science or history books), formulate questions, and then answer the questions in small groups or pairs.
3. Students write a series of questions to be used during an interview.

Jessie M. Brooks, Southeastern Illinois College, Harrisburg, with help from Marion Carroll, Carterville, Illinois, and Pat Rigg, Tucson, Arizona

Student Newspapers: Each One Writes One

Why

1. To heighten students' knowledge of newspaper production as they create individual newspapers
2. To increase students' pride in their finished products

Who

Upper elementary students

How

Each student selects a career of personal interest and then obtains information by interviewing people who practice the chosen career, by writing letters to other authorities, and by locating and reading pamphlets, books, and articles. Explain that students will produce newspapers to convey the information they've gathered.

Students examine many different local newspapers and note their similarities and differences. Discuss the different sections of newspapers and appropriate terminology. A field trip might be taken to a local newspaper to observe the writing, editing, layout, and printing stages.

All student newspapers are to contain the following sections:

1. *Masthead*: contains a creative design related to the particular career and a title done in appropriate calligraphy.
2. *Articles*: relate the facts about the career, the details of educational requirements or other preparation, on-the-job tasks or responsibilities, and the stories of interesting incidents, people, and places related to the career; enough copy is needed to fill the first two newspaper pages.
3. *Sports stories*: report on physical contests and abilities somehow related to the career, including such creative accounts as secretaries' typing races and surgeons' sewing contests.

4. *Crossword puzzle*: contains at least ten vocabulary words important to the career.
5. *Classified ads*: advertise imaginary items for sale and imaginary positions available in the career.
6. *Editorial page*: presents an essay of opinion and at least two letters to the editor, all related to the career.
7. *Comic strip*: develops an incident that could occur in the career.
8. *Television schedule*: lists imaginary, humorous program titles (including wordplays on actual program titles) for one full day on various channels, all career related.
9. *Advertisements*: sell student-invented products that are crucial to the career.

Optional sections that students might include in their newspapers are listed below:

1. *Obituaries*: summarize the lives of famous persons who have actually practiced the career.
2. *Horoscope*: predicts good times and possible pitfalls in doing career tasks.
3. *Lovelorn column*: presents problems and advice about issues that arise in practicing the career.
4. *Weather box*: contains imaginary reports indicating weather events that relate to the career.
5. *Fashion column*: gives pointers on how to dress for the career.
6. *Food column*: presents inventive recipes related to the career.
7. *Political cartoon*: depicts some folly that might occur in the career.

Students write rough drafts of the various sections of their newspapers and then use ink to print the edited stories in column form on large sheets of butcher paper, folded so that the newspapers have four pages. (Butcher paper is sturdier than newsprint.)

The completed newspapers can be read aloud, described orally, or displayed in the class library or on the bulletin board. Encourage students to sample numerous newspapers and to discuss the different presentations of similar material.

What Else

Redesign the activity to highlight a curricular area other than career education, such as a historical event.

Greta Nagel, John Marshall Elementary School, Anaheim, California

Writing News Stories from Different Points of View

Why

1. To increase students' understanding of the concept of point of view in writing
2. To highlight the differences produced by writing from different viewpoints

Who

All elementary students, especially those who have difficulty distinguishing the storyteller from the other characters

How

Provide students with a newspaper article chosen for its human interest. (A story with a photograph might assist students who have some difficulties with reading or writing.) Students read and discuss the article in small groups.

Then divide the class into two groups. Ask the students in one group to pretend that the event described in the news article happened to them, and to write the story from that viewpoint. Ask the students in the other group to act as if they were "observers," and to write about what they saw in the third-person veiwpoint. Allow sufficient writing time and do the assignment yourself. Share the writings and compare the differences that can be attributed to the different points of view from which the students' (and your) writings were written.

What Else

Ask several students to dramatize a chosen event for the class. Students report the dramatized events from their own points of view and then compare the various accounts.

Linda R. Morrow, Oakland Junior High School, Columbia, Missouri

American Revolutionary War Newspaper

Why

1. To help students compose articles that show the views of the Patriots and the Loyalists toward the American Revolutionary War
2. To promote student discussion of the reasons for the occurrence of the Revolutionary War

Who

Upper elementary students in social studies classes

How

Read aloud Henry Wadsworth Longfellow's poem "Paul Revere's Ride." Present additional information on the American Revolutionary War in a variety of different forms: filmstrips, poems, textbooks, short stories, novels, and so on.

Help students brainstorm reasons for the war, covering the opposing viewpoints of the Patriots and Loyalists. After the class thoroughly discusses the information, suggest writing a Revolutionary War newspaper. Students are grouped according to topics of interest. Each group makes individual assignments, reads and edits the news stories, and submits its part of the newspaper in completed form.

What Else

1. Students could produce more than one newspaper, each consistent with a single view of the Revolutionary War. The papers could contain stories on the same events or people, but each paper would be advocating a particular viewpoint.
2. Students could produce newspapers focusing on other historical events.

Cecilia Holbrook, Southern Boone County R-1 School, Ashland, Missouri

Car for Sale

Why

1. To help students learn to observe what is known and to predict what is not known

2. To help students learn how to take notes and to organize the notes into a written advertisement
3. To provide experience with the persuasive mode

Who

Upper elementary students

How

To initiate or complement an advertising unit, share car ads from local newspapers. Ask students to notice what features are mentioned and what prices are assigned to different makes and years. Hand out the following information sheet.

Car for Sale

Name:_____
Make:_____
Model year (make a guess):_____
Color:_____
Condition:_____
Transmission
    Standard stick:_____
    Automatic:_____
Price:_____

Make notes below about special features of the car you are selling, such as space for a large family, number of doors, good gas mileage, appearance, radio or tape deck, and so forth.

Working in pairs, students select a specific car in the staff parking lot and complete the information sheet. Back in the classroom, the pairs write advertisements for the cars in the format of the newspaper ads. Organize the completed advertisements in booklet form and distribute them to the staff.

Two car advertisements follow.

We have a Plymouth Horizon in fantastic shape. It has 4 doors and gets 25 miles per gallon. It has AM-FM radio plus it comes with the daily newspaper. It has black seats and carpet. It has a terrific price — only $6,300.00. It has a 5 cylinder engine. It is a terrific car. Call Mike or Karen.

Buy this Volkswagen that is red, white, green, and a rusty brown and a hole by the windshield where the antenna was. In this car there is a diaper and a Rubeck's cube where a seat used to be but we will replace it. There is a bike and a ladder on top and lots of signs. The price is $1000.00. See Leslie or Bryan.

What Else

These advertisements might accompany interviews or biographies of the car owners.

Carol W. Devino, retired from Rock Bridge Elementary School, Columbia, Missouri

Organizing a School Newspaper

Why

A school newspaper is one of the most purposeful ongoing writing and reading activities that students can be offered. Its functions, form, and processes are identical to newspapers that students see outside of school, thus establishing realistic communication between writers and readers. During the process of creating a school newspaper, students become aware of the need to make writing interesting, clear, and concise. Deadlines become viewed as necessities, rather than as arbitrary standards set by teachers. Writing conventions become viewed as simple courtesies to readers as well as essential to obtaining and maintaining readership. Additionally, writing a school newspaper encourages students to look closely at school events and, by extension, other current events; and it often provides students with opportunities to discuss ethical issues that are faced by the news media.

Who

Upper elementary students

How

A school newspaper can be produced within a single classroom or as a school club. It can range from a class-composed monthly letter to parents to a professionally styled newspaper. It can be handwritten and posted, run off on ditto sheets, mimeographed, photocopied, or printed by offset. Thus, there is a wide range of options available to meet the needs of students and the practical limitations of a given situation.

It is essential that there be a working staff consisting of highly motivated students who write well. These students become the editors, feature writers, columnists, and publishers. Other students serve in such essential roles as staff writers and reporters.

Below is a six-week schedule followed by two teachers and students in the fifth through eighth grades who meet once a week for the last hour of the school day and one hour after school. The resulting paper is attractive, and it includes students in every part of the production process.

Week One: Assignments

On assignment day, teachers and students establish the schedule of deadlines and the publication date for the issue. All story ideas are listed under general categories such as news, features, and sports. Editors often come to the meetings with an assignment list. Students often request assignments — sometimes in conjunction with other students, sometimes on an ongoing "beat."

Week Two: Deadline for Rough Drafts

The rough-draft deadline is important for helping writers revise their work. This week's meeting becomes a workshop on writing and revising. Some writers will not have their assignments ready. The whole staff can discuss these delays on a case-by-case basis so that the group can share strategies for meeting deadlines. Some writers will need to improve the organization of their time; some must learn when to stop gathering information and to start writing.

During the first few issues, rough drafts are read aloud by the sponsoring teachers and critiqued by the group. The focus is on writing an interesting story clearly and concisely. At the end of the editing session, all stories are returned to the writers for revision. Eventually, page editors can read and critique the stories with the writers, and this session then consists of many simultaneous editing conferences.

Week Three: Final Deadline

Students must learn immediately that newspapers require a firm deadline. If writers do not turn in their assignments on this day, the stories will not be in the paper. Deadline day demands a teacher of steel nerves, one who is prepared to print a paper lacking a major story. This helps everyone remember that it is the experience and not the product that is important.

On this day each writer's final draft is edited for spelling, usage, punctuation, and so forth. Sometimes an editor may still suggest organizational changes (particularly if an article is lengthy) or suggest improvements in wording, but this draft is the writer's best, and every effort should be made to minimize tampering. Stress that the role of an editor in changing articles is a real issue among journalists, and it should be a frequent discussion at workshops and staff meetings.

In an effort to achieve some uniformity of style, many newspapers develop or adopt style manuals. Style guidelines or a style book might be developed by the sponsoring teachers and students to resolve such common issues as references to teachers or students.

Week Four: Layout

A list of stories is posted with the number of column inches needed for each story. Add one and a half inches per story for headlines. Other space holders such as the masthead, the staff box, and any photographs or drawings are also posted.

Use three columns on $8\frac{1}{2}" \times 11"$ sheets of paper. Three columns give students a chance to learn more about actual layout than two columns do. Layout guides for each page are drawn on the chalkboard. The staff discusses where to place stories, beginning with page one. Suggestions are discussed, and decisions are made by consensus or a vote. Students use the following guidelines in order to mark the page layout on the layout guide:

1. Place the most important story at the top of the page and then position other stories according to their importance.
2. Plan space for headlines.
3. Place every part of a story under its headline.
4. Try to make pages look pleasing and clear.

After the layout has been sketched on the board, it is copied on paper.

Week Five: Pasteup

Pasteup is the most time-consuming and intricate job in preparing the newspaper. It can be done by the sponsoring teachers at home, taking many days, or the pasteup can be completed by the student staff within two hours.

Supplies for pasteup include graph paper, scissors, one-sided razor blades, rubber cement, transparent rulers, hard cardboard sheets for cutting boards, correction fluid or tape, nonreproducing pencils, and masking tape. Provide press type for headlines and line tapes for lines and boxes. The finished stories are typed in columns 2¼ inches wide.

Teams of students tape a sheet of graph paper to a desk, and pencil in pasteup guidelines and layout plans with a nonreproducing pencil. Next, typed articles are cut and placed on the graph-paper layout sheets before pasting. Students use the razor blades to cut between lines of text. Emphasize that students make precise measurements of the articles before cutting between lines since single lines of text are hard to position. It often helps, when pasting, to start at the bottom and see how much space is left for other articles and headlines. To keep the copy even, transparent rulers are used with the graph-paper lines as guides.

Under close supervision, students use sheets of press type to place headlines on graph paper, working letter by letter. The headlines are then cut out and pasted to the pasteup sheets.

After the pasteup is complete, students add finishing touches, such as the date and page numbers. Special tapes are used to create lines and boxes to set off articles. The pages are now ready for printing.

Week Six: Collating

This is a triumphant week, as the staff collates and staples the printed pages. In the mornings staff members gather to distribute the newspapers. The first issue is given away to establish readership; subsequent issues are sold.

After the first issue, this week can also be the assignment week for the next issue so that the newspaper can be published every six weeks. Editors and other staff members can begin thinking about assignments during the layout and pasteup period, allowing more time for writing articles and features.

What Else

1. *Fluidity.* In a situation where space is available, a newspaper room or corner could have writing and publication going on simultaneously. As assignments are made, editors could begin to think of layout and could begin pasteup sheets with outlines of page headings and so forth.

2. *Critique.* After each contributor has read the printed issue, a staff meeting can be devoted to critiquing the writing, layout, and general quality of the newspaper. Especially well-written stories or attractive page layouts can be identified, and suggestions can be made for improvements in future issues. Expect students to work hard and to produce a paper that reflects everyone's best efforts. Also expect student-quality work that is moving toward professionalism. Express your own opinions of students' work during these critiques.

3. *Whole School Involvement.* Contributions from students other than those on the staff can appear on a literary page, as letters to the editor, in advice columns, as guest articles, or in personal advertisements. Younger students will enjoy reading the paper and contributing.

4. *Variety.* Focus initially on news and feature writing. As the year progresses, interested students can contribute photo spreads, advertisements, or special thematic material.

5. *Word Processing.* If computers and advisers are available, students can write, edit, and type their stories directly into columns for the newspaper. Special print options can also be used for type for headlines, italicized material, and so forth. Computers can help make the newspaper production process nearly identical to that of a professional newspaper.

6. *Guests and Field Trips.* Invite working journalists to talk to the student staff. Ask college journalism instructors to provide special student workshops. Visit a high school newspaper or the offices of local professional newspapers or newsletters.

Reference

News for You, Edition B, Index Cards. Cited in *Using the News* by Jessie M. Brooks, Marion Carroll, and Pat Rigg.

Debra Goodman, Detroit Public Schools, Michigan

PART 4

Chapter 8:
Kids Helping Other Kids:
The Collaborative Effort

The classroom is a community in which learning should occur constantly in warm and accepting social settings. When students are encouraged to work together and to be resources for one another, everyone benefits. The learner begins to understand a new concept when a friend helps. The child-teacher becomes truly engaged in his or her role and responsibility as resource and helper. Helping another person by demonstrating, beginning an answer and letting a friend finish it, or by asking leading questions (Vygotsky, Mind in Society, 1978) promotes the crystallization of knowledge and ownership of the learning process.

— Carol Gilles, special education teacher, Columbia, Missouri

It would be difficult to find an activity in this book that did not involve individuals interacting with other individuals (motivated by, used as sounding board, acting as audience, serving as editor or study partner, and so on), but in this chapter the special focus is on children enjoying and making each other look good. The strategies involve students talking, reading, writing, playing, and learning together — both inside and outside the classroom.

Section A:
Cooperative Learning

Listen to Learn

Why

Writers listen. In a school where writing is taught with an emphasis on the process, there are three main components in the writing program: *write, respond, read.* The teacher models and teaches the students how to listen in each of the three situations.

Who

All elementary students

How

Listen to Learn from the Text

Write. The students write every day, or almost every day. As they do so, they listen to their own words, following what Pulitzer Prize-winner Eudora Welty (1983, 12) advised:

> My own words, when I am at work on a story, I hear as they go, in the same voice I hear when I read books. When I write and the sound of it comes back to my ears, then I act to make my changes. I have always trusted this voice.

When young children write, the "sound of it" literally comes back to them because they reread out loud as they monitor their meaning. Gradually, writers listen more to their internal voices as they write. They let their words just flow, as when talking. Writers also let a few surprises pop in to catch their listeners off guard. Writers like to listen to themselves; otherwise they do not write.

Respond. Writers respond to each other's attempts during each writing session. They learn not to simply say, "Oh, I liked it" or "That sounded great," comments that could be made without listening. Demonstrate to students how to learn from each other's writing. Initially, respond to a student's writing by saying something like, "You felt pretty bad when your hamster died" or "You're sure lucky the pillow didn't go up in flames." Model a response about something you learned from the writing, explaining that you always listen to learn whenever someone is reading. When a student is ready to read aloud a draft or final version, invite other students to listen for what they can learn and to tell the writer what they've learned.

Read. Read to the class every day, selecting such different genres as poetry, magazine articles, fiction, nonfiction, writing written by children in the class, writing of other students in the school, your own writing, and writing of other teachers. Invite students to read aloud also. Writers must be immersed in the writing of other people so that they become familiar with good writing. As soon as you or the student reader finishes reading, invite students to respond to the selection. In response to *Alexander and the Terrible, Horrible, No Good, Very Bad Day* by Judith Viorst, one student might say, "The funniest part was when Alexander said he was going to Australia every time something went wrong." Someone else might offer, "A part I remember is when he hopes the top falls off his friend's ice cream cone. That was a good idea for the author. Alexander's friend would be so mad."

Listen to Learn beyond the Text

Write. Writers write to learn. People who don't write think writers write to tell. But when writers try to put their knowledge on paper, they are first clarifying this information for themselves. As they write, they are pulling together and organizing ideas that they've thought about, adding new insights that occur to them. By providing a supportive environment for your writers, teachers encourage students to explore and to follow their own surprises, and help students find the something that makes each one of them different.

Respond. Responders learn from writers because each writer knows things the others don't know. They have many different experiences to share, and they are experts on topics the others know little about. When they listen to each other's writing, they wonder what the writer will say. Once students learn to respond to what they hear, encourage them to ask the author for clarification or elaboration. After one student read aloud a paper on the flying squirrels she saw in the woods, one classmate asked what color they were, and another student said, "I never heard of flying squirrels. Do they fly in a V-shape like Canadian geese?"

Read. When students read aloud to the class, to a group, or to just one other student, the others should listen in the manner suggested by Virginia Woolf (1932, 282–83):

> Do not dictate to your author. Be his fellow-worker. If you criticise at first, you are preventing yourself from getting the fullest possible value from what you read. But if you open your mind, then hints of fineness will bring you into the presence of a human being unlike any other.

After the listeners have commented on the author's work, they expand upon the content. Sixth-grade students did so in their discussion of *Alexander and the Terrible, Horrible, No Good, Very Bad Day:* "I would never have thought of drawing an invisible castle," said one. "Let's make 'em when we go to art today" was the response.

Works Cited

Welty, Eudora. *One Writer's Beginnings.* Harvard University Press, 1984.

Woolf, Virginia. "How Should One Read a Book?" In *The Second Common Reader.* Harcourt, Brace and World, 1932.

References

Butler, Andrea, and Jan Turbill. *Toward a Reading/Writing Classroom.* Heinemann Educational Books, 1984.

Stebbins, A. M. "The Teacher's Chair." In *Children Who Write When They Read* (a collection of narratives from the Mast Way Research Project). Writing Process Lab, University of New Hampshire, 1984.

Jane Hansen, University of New Hampshire, Durham

Paired Classrooms: The Big Friend Program

Why

To promote written and oral communication between big and little friends

Who

Primary students paired with upper elementary students

How

Arrange to pair a class of younger students with a class of older students. Individually assign each young child to an older child (making several copies of the list since the pairings will remain intact all year). Plan a main project for the pairs at the beginning of the school year and watch for other occasions for the students to work on projects together. Host a get-acquainted session at which you explain the project and introduce the pairs of students.

The Big Friend Program has been in effect in our school for several years, and both the younger and older children enjoy their sessions together. The younger students save all of their gifts from their big friends and seem more at ease around older children as a result of these friendships. And they look forward to the time when they can be the big friends. Some of the activities that our big and little friends have enjoyed together are described below.

1. The older children composed a list of questions and interviewed their little friends. They used the information to write "biopoems" describing their young friends. Each biopoem was affixed to a silhouette drawing of the kindergarten student and displayed in the classroom. Then the younger students took their biopoems home to share with their families.

2. The younger students dictated their holiday wish lists to the older children. The lists were mailed to the local newspaper for publication.

3. The older students interviewed the younger students to gather information about each child's family, friends, and favorite activities, stories, or cartoon characters. They used the information to write an adventure story about each child. The stories were illustrated and bound with a tagboard cover. At a joint meeting of the two classes, the older students read the stories aloud, with the young children at their sides, and then presented the stories as gifts to their little friends.

4. The two classes worked together making puppets and banners as a service project. These were presented to local children's institutions.

5. As an extended literature activity, the older students contributed pages to class books for the younger students, which they titled The Important Book and The Happiness Book.

6. The two classes performed plays, songs, and choral readings for each other.

7. The older students found copies of their favorite books from their primary years and read them aloud to the younger children.

8. The younger children wrote thank-you cards and greeting cards to their big friends many times throughout the year.

9. After exchanging valentines, the friends shared the valentines they received from their classmates, with the older students helping the kindergartners read their cards.

10. Each of the older students created an activity, game, or puzzle, and dedicated it to his or her young friend. These were duplicated, collated, bound, and presented to the young children as gifts.

Beverly Odum, Columbia Catholic School, Missouri

The Big Cheeses

Why

As older students work with primary students, both groups improve their self-concepts and increase their interest in reading. The interaction can help the older students examine their own reading strategies and discover more efficient ones, and can help transform all the students into confident, competent readers.

Who

Upper elementary students (including reluctant and nonproficient readers) working with kindergartners

How

Once a week an older student reads aloud to a group of kindergartners. Use a rotating schedule so that each student has several opportunities to read throughout the school year. Students follow the general routine described below.

On Mondays the book to be read is selected from a collection of predictable books, such as those listed in the Bibliography. This selection is based on weekly activities planned for the kindergartners, the older student's own preference, and teacher input. (Having a cooperative kindergarten teacher makes the book selection fun and enjoyable for all.)

Once the book is chosen, the student begins by reading the book silently several times. On the following two days, the student practices reading the book aloud. There is no set structure for these practice readings. The book may be read to peers, parent volunteers, the teacher, a classroom mirror, or a tape recorder. Frequently, the student will take the book home to read to a parent or sibling.

On Thursdays the reader is responsible for going to the kindergarten class to collect a group of listeners and to bring them to the reading room. Often the student reads the story twice, so that two different groups of kindergartners can hear it.

What Else

The older students may make their own predictable books, complete with illustrations, to share with the younger students.

Kathleen Evans-Bates, Southside Elementary School, Cabot, Arkansas, and Virgilee Reed, Stillwater Public Schools, Oklahoma, with help from Pat Rigg, Tucson, Arizona

Partner Book Selection

Why

Some students often have difficulty choosing books for themselves to read, claiming that they have no interests and don't like to read anything. These same students, however, may be enthusiastic about selecting appropriate books for their classmates.

This strategy provides an opportunity for students to interview other students, so it is especially appropriate at the beginning of the school year as a way for students to learn more about their classmates.

Who

Upper elementary students, especially those who have difficulty choosing books for themselves

How

Encourage students to discuss what they need to know about a person before they can select a suitable book for that person to read. As students brainstorm, list their ideas on the chalkboard. They might suggest learning whether the student has any hobbies, if he or she likes to read, how often he or she reads, and what genres he or she prefers. Ask a scribe or a committee to jot down the ideas in a questionnaire form, and make copies of the completed questionnaire for all the students.

Ask students to choose a partner. Students then use the questionnaire to interview each other, recording the answers directly on the questionnaire. Students now go to the library with the completed questionnaires in hand and select one or two books that they feel are appropriate for their partners. Students also choose one book that they would enjoy reading themselves.

When students return to the classroom, ask them to compare their own selections with the partner-selected books. The partners might meet again to discuss their reasons for choosing the books. During the silent reading time that follows, students may read from either book, but encourage them at least to sample the partner-selected book.

What Else

1. Many students in one class enjoyed *Little House on the Prairie* and the other books in the series. They wrote to a community resource person who knew a lot about Laura Ingalls Wilder. She responded by volunteering to present a program about Wilder. The class took off with the new idea. Students wrote invitations to other people knowledgeable about Wilder, arranged for them to speak to the class about Wilder, and wrote thank-you notes after the presentation. The program was informative and interested other students in Wilder's books.
2. This strategy can be used in a particular content area, such as social studies. Students devise interview questions that pertain to the content area or narrow their questions to pertain to a certain subject, such as biographies of famous people. Students then find appropriate books for one another related to that subject. Or they might enjoy selecting books that take place within a certain time period, such as in

prehistoric times, in the era of medieval knights, or at some future time.

Carol Gilles and Paul Crowley, Jefferson Junior High School, Columbia, Missouri

Team Teaching and Team Learning — Across Age Levels

Why

To provide an opportunity for students of different grades to share their experiences, books, writing, and discussions

Who

Upper elementary students paired with primary students

How

Reading and Follow-up Activities

1. Both classes read and discuss *The Popcorn Book* by Tomie de Paola. Then the classes join together for a brainstorming session, answering such questions as "How does popcorn appeal to the senses? How does it look, smell, taste?" Next, the two classes form two groups, each containing both older and younger students. One group pops a large bowl of popcorn with a hot-air popper, while the other group makes popcorn with an electric popper that uses oil (or on a burner of the stove if you're comfortable with this method). Ask students to compare the two methods and to sample both batches of popcorn. Invite students to write popcorn stories or poems. Older students work with their young partners and serve as the scribes. The final copy is written on paper cut in the shape of a popped kernel of popcorn.
2. Read aloud to both classes *The Fall of Freddy the Leaf* by Leo Buscaglia, a book appropriate for all ages, and encourage students to discuss the story. Children may draw pictures to illustrate an event in the book.

Special Times Together

1. At Christmas time the younger students write letters to Santa. The older students serve as Santa's elves, answering the letters and being available to read the responses to their young friends.

2. Older students can write and present skits about Jewish and Moslem holidays and celebrations. They might teach songs to the younger students or prepare food from countries that they are studying.
3. The students exchange poems, books, and letters on Valentine's Day.

Special Interests

1. Talented parents or teachers might demonstrate a craft or special skill, such as spinning or quilting. Follow the demonstration with a writing activity in which children write factual stories of what they have seen or create imaginative tales.
2. Older students may help younger students with cooking projects, and then the partners write about the experience.
3. Older students can serve as tutors for the younger students. One or two students go to the younger students' classroom at the same time every week and work with the same individuals. They follow a set routine, so they know what is expected of them. Tutoring might include helping with academic problems, listening to a child read a book, reading to a child, or listening to a child's written piece and helping with the revising.
4. Students love to receive notes. A daily mailbox can be set up outside the two classrooms where students can leave notes for one another about topics that interest them, such as books, movies, school events, outside activities, questions, and invitations. Partners may also want to meet periodically to chat with each other.

Grace Vento-Zogby, Sauquoit Valley Central School, Sauquoit, New York; Cecilia Holbrook, Southern Boone County R-I Schools, Ashland, Missouri; and Linda Boothe, Montgomery County R-II, Bellflower Elementary School, Bellflower, Missouri

Writing Predictable Books for Younger Readers

Why

1. To raise aspects of the reading process, including patterns and predictability in print, to a conscious level
2. To view children's books as a model for writing
3. To create an authentic reason for writing

4. To help students learn to write for a specific audience

5. To enhance young authors' and readers' feelings of self-worth

Who

Upper elementary students

How

Older students "adopt" a class of younger students and are matched with partners. Frequent interactions are possible if the two classes are in the same building, but the activity will work with students in different buildings.

Bring in a variety of good children's literature, including highly predictable books. (See the Bibliography for a list of predictable books.) The older students read the books and discuss the ways authors use predictable language and events and how illustrations help readers make predictions.

Encourage students to think of three story ideas for predictable books and to discuss them with a classroom friend. Students choose the best idea for the story line and write first drafts. After the stories are completed, encourage students to use each other and published books as resources. Students can make suggestions regarding the dialogue, plot, predictable language, and so on and can help one another edit their books for mechanics such as spelling and capitalization. When the writing is complete, students choose the format for the text to their books — handwriting, typing, or word processing. Students prepare their own illustrations or collaborate with a partner. (If the text will appear on the same page as the illustration, the illustration might be created first so that the text does not need to be redone if the artist is not pleased with the illustration.) Completed books are bound with cloth, cardboard covers, or other materials selected by the students.

Once the books are completed, students practice reading their books aloud to a classmate or a small group of students, who make suggestions regarding each presentation. Then students read their books to their partners in the class of younger students. If the adopted classroom is far away, students record their stories on cassette tapes and send the tapes and the books to the other school. Each younger student can listen to the tape while reading his or her book.

What Else

When students work together and see the responses of their young partners, follow-up activities are often student motivated. Students may suggest writing more books, listening to their partners read aloud, writing plays based on published books or their own stories, or some other activity that the teacher never considered.

Carol Gilles, Jefferson Junior High School, Columbia, Missouri

The Way It Is

Why

When the audience that students write for is other students, the student authors have a clear understanding of the background and expectations of that audience. Purposes are understood and writing is meaningful. Similarly, reading a piece written by someone who understands the reader's perspective brings the reader and author closer together in the meaning-making process.

Who

Middle or upper elementary students who want to help younger students

How

This activity is most effective as a culmination of the entire school year. Ask students to think about what they have learned during the year, what they feel good about, what they would change. Jot down these feelings in a brainstorming session. Then students draft letters to specific children in the grade below them, or they can write an open letter. Remind students of the apprehension they may have felt on the first day of school in the fall, and explain that their letters may help the incoming students feel more at ease in their new classroom. The letters may contain pointers about what students will study in that grade, hints about homework, information about the physical setting and routines (such as when recess starts or when lunch is served), favorite books that are available in the room, or common activities and traditions.

What Else

At the beginning of the next school year, distribute the letters to the new students. Read and discuss the letters, and talk about classroom procedures. The letters might prepare students for forming a class government, beginning special projects, or initiating pen pal letters in which the incoming students write to former students to ask further questions.

At the end of the school year, bring out these letters to guide students in writing letters to their successors and to stimulate discussion about progress and change.

Carol Gilles, Jefferson Junior High School, Columbia, Missouri

Team Learning

Why

Team learning is an effective method for developing and strengthening language arts abilities. Experience shows that the more opportunities students have to discuss their ideas and to listen to those expressed by peers, to plan together, and to work out solutions to problems, the more proficient they become in all areas of the language arts. One of the greatest benefits of team learning is its versatility. It can be used to work out solutions to classroom problems, to study current events, and to conduct studies in content areas.

Team learning removes the risk-taking factor that discourages some children from participating fully in whole class activities. It is a vehicle for productive group interaction and allows less able students to benefit from sharing an assignment with more able peers. Completing a team task usually requires diverse talents and contributions; this cooperative effort enables every member of the group to contribute ideas.

Who

All elementary students

How

Children's literature, by its very nature, reflects various predicaments, problems, and alternative solutions that stimulate personal reactions. It covers a wide range of subject areas and is rich with human experience, thus supplying a wellspring of situations for team learning.

After a book has been read to or by the children, divide the class into teams of three to six students. Give each team a page containing an assignment. Team members select a recorder and then discuss the task to be completed, as the recorder makes note of the group's decision or solution. Teams choose a creative way in which to share their findings with the other students, such as a panel discussion, a debate, an interview, or role-playing. Students listen, ask questions when necessary, and participate in a discussion of each team's findings.

During the reading of *The Emperor's New Clothes* by Hans Christian Andersen, several students in one class expressed opinions about some of the characters and incidents in the story. During the team learning, they had an opportunity to discuss the story in depth, reacting to story situations and raising questions not fully covered in the brief class discussion. Students discussed the following questions, decided on their responses, and presented the information to their classmates.

1. Discuss some thoughts that the swindlers might have had as they explained the "fine stuffs" to the Emperor and worked late at night on the "magic cloth."
2. Do any thoughts (or words) of the minister indicate that he might have been afraid of becoming discredited? Explain.
3. What might the townspeople have said about the Emperor after the procession?
4. Why did the Emperor continue the procession after the people announced that he had no clothes on?
5. What reasons might the officials have had for pretending to see colors and designs in the cloth?
6. Why has this story lasted for centuries? Does this kind of thing happen today?

Jane M. Hornburger, Brooklyn College, City University of New York

Feelings

Why

1. To increase students' language appreciation
2. To provide an opportunity for students to practice their speaking skills

3. To encourage the use of facial expressions and body language to communicate

Who

All elementary students, especially those who need practice in communicating orally

How

On folded slips of paper, write some "feeling starters" that will help students express their emotions. Some examples are listed below.

> I feel so mad I could. . . .
>
> I'm so happy I could. . . .
>
> I'm so hungry I could. . . .
>
> I feel so blue today because. . . .
>
> I felt so stupid yesterday because. . . .
>
> I feel so excited I just. . . .
>
> I'm so tired I. . . .

Place the feeling starters in a hat or box and ask students to gather in a circle. Pull a feeling starter out of the hat and read it aloud, completing the expression. For example, you might say, "I'm so-o-o-o hungry I could eat three whole cans of spinach." You may want to model the activity a second time so that students understand what they're to do.

Proceed around the circle, inviting eight to ten students to take turns responding to the same feeling starter. One student might say, "I'm so-o-o-o hungry I could eat my basal reader," while another might offer, "I'm so-o-o-o hungry I could eat a dinosaur." Allow students to pass if they choose. Encourage all the students to chant, with expression, the first part of the feeling starter together, and then the student next in line completes the phrase. When the emotion in students' voices starts to sag, it's time to move on to a new feeling starter.

What Else

1. Students make a class book or individual books using a feeling starter as a theme, such as "I feel so intelligent I just. . . ."
2. Students make posters using a feeling starter as a topic.
3. Encourage interested students to write plays that involve several emotions and to act out their plays before the entire class.

Susan M. Chevalier, University of Missouri–Columbia

Mapping the Way to My Home

Why

1. To encourage students to use information they already know
2. To show students a practical use of their knowledge
3. To provide an opportunity for students to work individually and in small groups
4. To let students see their work used as part of the learning process
5. To give students an opportunity to work with another student's work
6. To provide an informal, nonthreatening way for students to get to know their classmates better

Who

Middle and upper elementary students

How

Divide the class into groups of four students, grouping together students who do not know each other well. Ask each student to use only symbols and lines to draw a map directing a newcomer to his or her home. The starting point for every map is the school. Students are to use a legend to show features they think are needed. For example, a *T* could stand for an intersection or a # could stand for a traffic light. Remind students to consider every choice that the newcomer would have to make in order to find the way.

When their maps are completed, ask students to use only the information on their maps to put the same directions in writing. They are to write the directions for a newcomer who will not be able to look at the map.

Each student exchanges maps with one other member of the group. Ask the students to study the maps and to clarify anything they don't understand. Then each student is to use only the map to write the directions to the other person's home.

Students exchange their newly written descriptions with one of the remaining two members of their group. Each student studies these directions and draws a map to his or her partner's house.

Then the two sets of directions and the two maps are returned to the first student for comparison. Students complete the activity by compiling a list of things they have learned about giving accurate directions.

Carol A. Roark, Simonsen Junior High, Jefferson City, Missouri

Don't Spill the Beans: Cooperative Conversations

Why

People of all ages talk together in order to solve problems. The use of discussion as a problem-solving technique is so common that we often take it for granted, but not everyone is equally good at it. Cooperative conversation — talk in which the conversants talk together to reach a common goal — can be learned, practiced, and improved. In the following strategy, students are encouraged to use language to persuade — through speaking, listening, responding, and reacting.

Who

All elementary students, especially those who need practice in working effectively as a member of a group and those who need practice in using persuasive language

How

Fill a large and unevenly shaped jar (such as an apple juice glass jug) with beans. Then announce a class contest: students are to guess how many beans are in the jar, without taking off the lid. Teams of three to five students are formed. Each team is to study the jar and to determine a method for estimating the number of beans. Make available smaller containers and several cups of beans so that students can develop a system of comparisons for estimating the beans in the large jar. When each team reaches a decision on the number of beans, it records its guess on a card, places the card in an envelope marked with the team's name, and seals the envelope. Each team is allowed to make only one guess.

As each team debates how to solve the problem, each team member contributes ideas and tries to persuade the others to use his or her solution. Only one guess can be recorded per team, so the group must reach a consensus.

Each member of the group writes a report on the process that the group went through in deciding the number of beans in the jar. Members share their reports and discuss each report and the process of reaching a consensus. Students might work together to prepare one group report.

When all the reports are written, open the jar and let the students count out all the beans and determine which team made the most accurate guess.

What Else

1. Students discuss the negotiation process that their teams went through. If they seem to recognize the forms of language that they used in persuading, they can examine written forms of persuasive language — such as advertisements, campaign speeches (perhaps the Gettysburg Address), editorials, and so on — and can try to identify the sorts of language they used in their groups in guessing the number of beans and writing up the report.
2. This process of reaching a consensus can be used in solving other problems, ranging from answering an assigned exercise to raising money for school trips.

Pat Rigg, Consultant, American Language and Literacy, Tucson, Arizona; with help from Jessie M. Brooks, Harrisburg, Illinois; Marion Carroll, Carterville, Illinois; and Susan Vaughn, Carbondale, Illinois

Fourth-Grade Students Have Stories to Tell and Experiences to Discuss

Fourth-grade students sit at a table, confiding in each other and the teacher.

"I'm afraid if I don't put the shades down at night, someone's gonna see in, maybe even come in," says one student.

Another student adds, "I have a spaceship I'm scared of — it's in my room at night."

Primary-grade curricula have always placed much emphasis on the development of oral language skills. However, it is unusual to find a fourth grade in which discussions are a priority. In many middle and upper elementary classrooms, the use of oral langue is considered to be less important than reading and writing. The importance of oral language skills as they relate to reading and writing goes unnoticed.

Students in Mrs. Kinzie's fourth-grade class at the Mast Way School in Lee, New Hampshire, regularly support their reading and writing by talking about their experiences. One discussion took place after four students and Kinzie had read *Blubber* by Judy Blume. They talked about hurting other classmates through senseless pranks.

Liz extended the story to her own life: "If we had a fat girl in our class, I wouldn't call her names or make fun of her 'cause she's fat. It *is* cruel. Just like I think it's cruel when we make fun of someone who gets out in softball."

In Kinzie's class, students talk with each other during the first fifteen minutes of every morning. As children enter the classroom, they immediately get together in informal groups, much like those on the playground, and discuss current events in their lives. Writing time in this classroom usually follows the morning conversation time. These early morning discussions may serve as springboards for topics students write about, and sometimes serve as a rehearsal for an author.

Tom met with some students in his class as soon as he entered the room. "No," he said, "I didn't win the swim meet Saturday, but that was okay. At least I beat my own best time. I was nine seconds better than the last time I was timed." That same morning he wrote the following:

Taking Off Time

As soon as I hit the water, I began doing the butterfly stroke, bringing my arms out over my head. When I hit the wall I turned over on my back and started doing the backstroke. I got my arms out of the water and kicked my legs as hard as I could . . . One of the swimmers was pretty far away, but the other was close by. I increased my speed and came alongside the person closest to me and passed him. I touched the wall and started doing the freestyle stroke. I was exhausted, but just then I hit the wall!

I got out of the water and asked the timer for my time.

"1:37:66," said the timer.

"1:37:66, talk about taking time off!" I said. I had just beaten my best time by nine seconds.

Oral language abounds in this classroom while children are in the process of writing. Brian read his draft about Dickie, his pet canary, to Tim and Kinzie. They commented on the draft and asked questions. The discussion helped Brian identify more information that he could add to his piece.

Discussions and storytelling are not only important in primary grades but in upper elementary as well. And as Kinzie's classroom demonstrates, fourth-grade students have stories to tell.

Ann Marie Klein, Clark School, Amherst, New Hampshire

Spotlighting the Value of Sharing

Why

1. To encourage students to learn as much as possible about sharing through the use of all the language arts and other media
2. To provide an opportunity for students to explore with one another the feelings, the values, and the problems that are involved in sharing

Who

Students in kindergarten and grade 1; with adaptation, all elementary students

How

Begin a unit on sharing by assembling a collection of books in which sharing takes place, such as those suggested at the end of the activity. Read the books aloud, stopping at appropriate intervals to articulate the problem, to encourage children to label the feelings of the characters, and to discuss how sharing resolves the problem and how it has a positive effect on the characters. Older students can read the books and other printed materials independently and then discuss their thoughts and feelings.

Situation pictures demonstrating sharing (teacher-made or cut from magazines) can serve as springboards for discussions about sharing. Using questioning techniques derived from the work of Hilda Taba, ask students to look at the photographs and to answer questions such as the following:

What do you see?

What's happening?

How can we label the problem?

What feelings are involved?

Why do you think this happened?

How can we account for it?

What could happen next and under what conditions?

What could have prevented this and under what conditions?

What seems important here, and why is it important?

These same questions can be used to stimulate discussions following the showing of a film or filmstrip or the reading of a book.

Accompany reading, listening, and viewing experiences with activities that help students solidify their knowledge, express their thoughts and feelings about sharing, and discuss their perceptions and conclusions with others. The following activities would be suitable for kindergartners and first graders.

1. Using any acceptable medium (paints, markers, crayons), students create a "before" (before the problem is resolved) and an "after" (after the problem is resolved) picture of one of the central characters in a story. Encourage them to capture the character's feelings and body gestures. Students dictate or write a statement to accompany each picture.

2. Students suggest entries for a word chart that lists in one column all the feelings the characters entertain before the problem or conflict is resolved and that lists in a second column the characters' feelings after sharing resolves the problem.

3. Create a class book in which each student completes the statement "Sharing means . . ." on a separate sheet of drawing paper and illustrates his or her idea. Tape-record students as they read their own statements, accompanied by suitable background music. During story time, play the recording while turning the pages of the class book for all to see.

4. Select one of the stories read in a previous session for a dramatic activity. Read the story again, stopping at a point where the problem has been well articulated. Ask students to assume the roles of the central characters and to act out the remainder of the story as they remember it. Encourage several students to repeat the ending in their own words. Simple props, such as character name cards suspended on yarn and worn around the neck, will suffice.

5. Write several short dilemmas involving people or animals in humanlike situations. Ask students to illustrate a solution to the dilemma. Students then write or dictate what they have illustrated.

6. Assemble a collection of photographs cut from magazines, newspapers, or old books. Ask students to select pictures in which a kindness is evident or in which sharing is central. Students discuss each picture before mounting it on baseboard or posterboard.

7. Photograph students as they demonstrate sharing situations. Students decide on the content of each picture and help pose the subjects. Each photograph can become a page in a class book or part of a bulletin board display. The class dictates appropriate stories or annotations to accompany the photographs.

What Else

The same procedures can be used to spotlight other subjects. Ample resource materials can be found on the following topics: handicapped persons, death and dying, divorce or separation, mental illness, aging, growing up, and parent/child relationships.

Suggested Reading List

Crosby N. Bonsall; *It's Mine*
Barbara Brenner; *Mr. Tall and Mr. Small*
William Cole; *Aunt Bella's Umbrella*
Ezra Jack Keats; *Peter's Chair*
Leo Lionni; *Frederick*
Ann H. Scott; *On Mother's Lap*
Shel Silverstein; *The Giving Tree*
William Steig; *Amos and Boris*
John Steptoe; *Stevie*
Charlotte Zolotow; *Do You Know What I'll Do?*

Jane A. Romatowski, University of Michigan–Dearborn

Listen to Me and Take Note

Why

Listening provides background information that makes reading or writing possible. This strategy demonstrates that listening is selective and that understanding comes from discussing with others what one has learned. It illustrates the utility of notetaking but also demonstrates that students need not get every detail from a single hearing or reading; subsequent discussion may provide further information. For students who are reluctant to read to others, the risk of reading aloud is reduced since the listeners, unable to see the text, are more concerned with understanding the meaning of what they are listening to than with the oral rendition of the reader. The fact that the oral reading is shared with another student also reduces the stress of reading aloud that a less fluent reader might have.

Who

Students in grades 4–6

How

Assemble the students in groups containing four to six members. Each group selects two students to be readers. The readers choose a selection from a collection of books and other reading materials that you have assembled, and quickly skim the selection together. They take turns reading the selection aloud to the group, perhaps alternating paragraphs or one student reading the first half, the other reading the second half.

Each listener makes notes as the selection is read. The selection is read only once, and then students take turns discussing whatever information they are able to recall from the reading by referring to their notes. If necessary, students may refer to the article during the discussion to clarify any points of confusion that arise.

After the discussion, everyone writes a brief summary of the selection. The completed summaries are read to the group and then discussed.

Mary Lynn Woods, Orchard Country Day School, Indianapolis, Indiana

---

Partner Editing: A Guide for Peer Review

Why

Students are often reluctant to alter and revise their initial writing attempts, but the comments and suggestions of peers may encourage students to review and revise their stories and other writings. Peer editors can help writers solve problems and provide evaluation in a give-and-take atmosphere.

Who

Upper elementary students

How

After completing the first draft of a writing assignment, students exchange papers with a partner. Each reads the partner's paper, using a guide sheet to evaluate the paper and to organize his or her comments. Then the two students discuss the papers and suggest revisions.

To develop a guide sheet for partner editing, solicit questions from the students themselves. Next, proceed with a trial run, following the process of first draft/rewrite/final draft, and revise the questions as needed. Guide sheets can be adapted to various forms of student writing across the curriculum. With experience, students internalize the basic criteria, reducing the necessity of the guide sheet. The following questionnaire is appropriate for both oral and written responses to stories that the children create.

1. Setting
   a. Does the reader know when the story takes place?
   b. Does the reader know where the story takes place?
   c. Does the reader know what the place looks like? feels like?
   d. Editor's advice.
2. Characterization
   a. Are the physical features of the characters described?
   b. Are the personalities clear?
   c. Are the characters real? interesting? convincing?
   d. What point of view is expressed in the story?
   e. Editor's advice.
3. Plot
   a. How and when is the problem in the story introduced?
   b. Is the problem believable? exciting? interesting?
   c. Does the reader want to find out? predict?
   d. How does the author resolve the problem or conflict?
   e. Are the events in order? Do they fit in the story?
   f. Is the ending satisfying?
   g. Editor's advice.

What Else

After the peer conferences, teacher-student conferences take place and provide further support and encouragement for the student writers. Negative comments and personality problems will sometimes occur in the peer conferences, but if students remain open to peer review, growth in writing and rewriting will prevail.

Lois Monaghan, Jones Middle School, Columbus, Ohio

Section B: Games and Holiday Activities

Language through Pantomime

Why

To assist students in communicating meaning through forms other than written or spoken language

Who

Upper elementary students

How

Distribute a blank 3″ × 5″ card to each student. Ask students to write down the name of three movies, books, or songs that could be acted out in a game of charades; then collect and shuffle the cards. Organize the students in groups of three or four and redistribute the cards. After time for practice, the groups present their charades to the class, and the others try to guess each title.

Next, the students choose partners who were not in their original groups. This time distribute to each student a card listing three or four emotions or attitudes, such as surprise, weariness, agitation, elation, sadness, confusion, fear, doubt, and anger. Students practice acting out the emotions with a partner, concentrating on facial expressions, and then demonstrate the emotions to the class.

Ask for volunteers to pantomime a situation of their own choosing, or they might act out a scene that you select, such as one of the following:

> being a bank teller during a robbery
>
> arriving at their first baby-sitting job
>
> doing laundry in a crowded laundromat
>
> trying to avoid an angry bumblebee
>
> being trapped in an elevator

The class tries to determine what the situation is. Students then discuss the difficulties and the challenges in doing mime, and talk about its power for communication.

What Else

Try the reverse of mime. Ask students to describe objects without using their hands or other body language. Some possible objects to describe are a spiral staircase, a goatee, a hammer, an egg beater, and a lawn mower.

Beverly Reed, Maplewood–Richmond Heights School District, St. Louis, Missouri, with help from Mary Bixby, Columbia, Missouri

One More Question: A Literature Game

Why

Literature contains settings that can take a young reader to another place or another time, characters who can act as role models, plot structures that can be credibly and uniquely structured to create intriguing stories, styles of writing and expression that can increase syntactic maturity, and themes that can provide provocative and challenging dilemmas for problem solving. As an alternative to teacher-led discussions of teacher-prepared questions regarding those elements, students write the questions and act as arbitrators during the discussion of several works of literature. The literature game encourages students to review and analyze literary content, and it allows students to practice skills needed to answer questions focused on literal recognition, inference, evaluation, and appreciation.

Who

Middle and upper elementary students

How

Students first need to become familiar with the content and purpose of four questioning strategies (literal recognition, inference, evaluation, appreciation) and with the literary elements (setting, characters, plot structure, style, theme). An additional element is added to this list — trivia. The trivia category helps youngsters with the game, and they enjoy searching out trivial items in the literature that other readers may miss.

As they read the literature, students decide what questions they want to pose to other readers. For each work of literature, each student puts together a game card with one question for each literary element plus a trivia question. The questions on each card should represent at least three of the four questioning strategies. The following questions were devised by a student reader for *Dragonwings* by Laurence Yep.

> *Setting*: What was the name of the area in San Francisco in which Windrider and the other Tang people lived? (literal recognition)
>
> *Characters*: Why do you think Mrs. Whitlaw befriended Moon Shadow and Windrider? (inference)
>
> *Plot*: Why couldn't Moon Shadow and his mother go live with Windrider in the Land of the Golden Mountain? (literal recognition)
>
> *Theme*: Bright Star talks many times about superior men. Who might be superior men in this story? Why? (evaluation)
>
> *Style*: Robin tells Moon Shadow that her auntie would "have kittens if she found out." What does this mean? What other figure of speech is used in the story? (literal recognition/evaluation/appreciation)
>
> *Trivia*: What was the title of the book that Robin gave to Moon Shadow? (literal recognition)

Students write the answers and acceptable alternative answers on the back of their game cards. Page numbers where answers can be found are included in case a question is challenged or if no one can answer the question. One class of students could generate approximately thirty game cards for each group of players.

Students form groups of five players, and each group is given a set of game cards. A tally sheet lists the names of the players on the left and the names of the categories of literary elements across the top. One player is selected to keep the tally, and a plus mark (+) is given to players when they successfully answer a question in a given category.

One player picks the top game card from the set of cards and begins the game by asking the person to his or her right any question on the game card. If the player answers correctly, a plus mark is placed next to his or her name under the correctly answered category, and the same student is asked another question. If the player cannot answer the question, he or she must pass the question to the player on his or her right. If all four players cannot answer the question, the tally keeper reads the answer, and a discussion, if necessary, takes place. That game card is then returned to the bottom of the set, and the next person in the round picks a new card from the top of the set. In this way, all players have a chance to either ask or be asked a question.

The questioning proceeds, with the students being asked questions in those categories in which they've not successfully answered a question. The winner is the player who first answers one question correctly in each category and who is able to answer a game-winning question. This question is selected by the next highest scorer and can be any question from a new card taken from the set (most often the trivia question). If the player answers incorrectly, the game continues until an eligible player correctly answers a game-winning question.

What Else

To encourage group participation and cooperation, establish teams of players rather than playing the game with individual players.

Teri Platek, State University of New York College at Buffalo

Games Based on Children's Literature

Why

1. To encourage students to use predicting strategies
2. To broaden students' vocabulary
3. To expand students' knowledge of sentence structure
4. To emphasize literature in the reading program

Who

With adaptation, all elementary students

How

Game Board

Invite students to select a favorite book or story. Make a game board out of posterboard, mat board, oaktag, or cardboard, and design a pattern of spaces for playing pieces to occupy. The book or story might determine the shape of the spaces, such as foot shapes for a game based on Tomie de Paola's *Now One Foot, Now the Other.* For the spaces, include three alternating colors that will be color-coded to the activities that accompany the game. Not all spaces need to be color-coded — some can be "free" spaces where no activity occurs. Spaces can be colored, painted, or made from colored paper pasted to the board. Be sure to consider storage, cost, durability, and attractiveness when choosing materials for your games.

Cloze Cards

These cards encourage students to predict language. Choose one of the colors used on the game board, and cut the cloze cards in any uniform size and shape. These cards will become one of the decks for playing the game. Select a sentence or short passage from the book. Print or type the selection on a card, omitting one key word and leaving a blank space in its place. Make all the blanks the same length so that readers will use meaning as their strategy in determining the missing word rather than counting letters. Two sample cloze sentences are shown below.

> "Now, tell me the story about how you ———— me to walk," Bobby said.

> Bobby was named after his best ————, his grandfather, Bob.

Make several more cloze cards than the number of spaces your game board has in that color. During the game, players landing on a space of that color will draw a cloze card, read the card aloud, and fill in the blank with the word from the book or a word that makes just as much sense. The other players decide if substitutions are acceptable, meaningful language. The player will advance a predetermined number of spaces if the other players agree on the appropriateness of the response.

Meaning Cards

Prepare a second deck of cards, selecting another color on the game board. Cut the cards in any desirable size or shape. Again, select phrases or sentences from the text of the book or story. Print or type each selection from the book onto a card, underlining one word or phrase significant to the meaning of the story. Sentences from two sample meaning cards are shown below.

> Sometimes the <u>tower</u> would be almost finished.

> And they would <u>carefully</u> put the elephant block on the very top.

Players landing on a space of that color will draw a meaning card from this color deck, read the card aloud, and explain what the underlined word means in relation to the rest of the text. Responses must meet with the satisfaction of the players.

Language Strips

Cut strips of paper to match the remaining color on the game board. Select sentences or paragraphs from the book and print or type one selection on each strip. Cut each sentence or paragraph strip into two, three, four, or five segments, depending on its length and on the sophistication of the children (longer segments for younger children), and clip the segments together. When students land on a space of this color, their task is to reconstruct a meaningful text to the satisfaction of all the players. For example, a student would need to rearrange the following segments

> the fireworks.

> And when it got

> dark, they watched

into this sentence

> And when it got dark, they watched the fireworks.

General Procedure

To regulate movement in the game, use a game spinner or die from another game, or make a game die from a sponge cube. Decide on the maximum number of players for the game and provide that many different playing pieces to move around the game board, using buttons, corks, small toy cars, or other toy pieces. Taking turns, players move their playing pieces around the board according to the spinner or die and then must answer a question from the deck of cards that matches the space their playing piece is occupying. The winner is the player who completes the game-board circuit first or who answers the most questions correctly.

Write an instruction sheet or card that can be read and understood clearly by students. Make this and all game pieces more permanent by laminating them or covering them with clear adhesive-backed paper.

What Else

Invite children to construct games for their own class as well as for younger children.

Wendy C. Kasten, University of South Florida at Sarasota

The Wish Book: Reading and Writing Descriptions

Why

The written descriptions of items in mail-order catalogs can serve as a good example of functional written language. The descriptions of the merchandise match the pictures, and students must read the text to see if the items really are what they appear to be.

Who

All elementary students who need a greater appreciation of the function of written language and who have trouble reading

How

Begin by bringing in several mail-order catalogs. Open one catalog to a page of items that the students would probably like. Read the description of one item and ask a volunteer to name the item. Continue reading, asking students to guess the item as soon as they recognize it. Then pair students with partners and hand out a catalog or two to each pair. Ask them to find their own page of interest and to take turns reading and guessing.

What Else

1. Invite the students to cut out items from the catalogs and to write their own descriptions. Make a class catalog of favorite items. Duplicate the order forms and ask children to pretend they have a certain amount of money to spend on items. They are to figure the total cost of their orders, including tax and shipping.
2. On each child's birthday, invite him or her to make a page of pictures of desired objects and written descriptions for the class Wish Book.

Stephanie Elletson, West Boulevard Elementary School, Columbia, Missouri

The Great Literature Trivia Contest

Why

1. To encourage students to read a variety of novels, poems, plays, and short stories
2. To promote the sharing and excitement of favorite books, characters, settings, and plots
3. To provide students with an opportunity to discuss their reading

Who

Middle and upper elementary students

How

This activity builds on students' interest in answering little-known facts about a variety of topics — better known as *trivia*. Students begin by selecting and reading a variety of novels, poems, plays, and short stories. They discuss how to write an appropriate trivia question and practice writing together questions that are not too difficult or too obvious. Then each student submits several questions and answers based on the literature the class has read. Select a variety of questions and type them on a sheet of paper labeled "The Great Literature Trivia Contest Sheet."

Each member of the class receives a copy of the trivia contest sheet and tries to answer the questions based on his or her knowledge of the familiar literature. After a reasonable period of time, stop the contest and ask students to exchange their contest sheets with a classmate for marking.

To obtain answers to the questions, each author reads his or her question aloud and selects a classmate to answer it. Often this leads to a discussion of the question and the appropriate answer. Students mark each other's contest sheets after each answer is finalized. This procedure continues until all of the questions are answered.

What Else

Drama is another medium to use for this activity. One student can become a character from literature and provide clues to his or her identity. Or a group of students can act out a scene from a short story or novel.

Richard E. Coles, Givins-Shaw Public School, Board of Education, Toronto, Ontario, Canada

Find It, If You Can (But Follow My Directions)

Why

To provide practice in giving directions

Who

Middle and upper elementary students

How

Privately assign a number to each member of the class and make a list, matching students' names with their numbers. Keep the list handy for those students who forget their numbers, but remind students not to announce their numbers.

Give students a half sheet of paper and invite them to write down a favorite quote, riddle, or joke. Students fold the sheet twice, writing their numbers on the outside of their sheets. Designate an area of the room or a specified length of hallway as the hiding spot. Ask students to hide their papers, leaving at least a corner visible, and to return to their desks.

Give students a second half sheet of paper and ask them to write their numbers on one side of the paper. Students then turn the paper over and write directions for locating the sheets of paper that they have hidden. Collect the directions, mix them up, and have each student randomly select a set of directions. Each student then follows his or her set of directions and finds the hidden quote, riddle, or joke.

Invite students to respond to the hidden messages in a positive way and to critique the directions — either orally or (if the authors' identities are revealed) in a written response addressed to the student who wrote the original material.

Pansy Collins, Evangel College, Springfield, Missouri

Hangman: A Predicting Game

Why

1. To review content-area concepts
2. To help students understand that it is effective

and efficient to use global predicting strategies based on the semantic constraints of a passage and their own knowledge

Who

Middle and upper elementary students

How

Select a topic that is well known to the students and locate a passage about that topic written at the students' level of comprehension. Avoid choosing a passage that introduces concepts not likely to be known, even though the topic is familiar.

Prepare five or six short-answer questions about the passage and write them on the chalkboard. The answers should be somewhat difficult but not impossible to guess. Prepare and distribute a sheet containing just the title of the passage, blanks for each letter in the passage itself, and spaces between each word. For example, the sentence

An important source of light is the sun.

would appear on the sheet as

__ _____ _____ __ _____ __ ___ ___.

Prepare a transparency of the sheet containing the blanks.

Draw a gallows on the chalkboard. Inform the students that their goal is to answer all the questions before their little stick person is hanged. Children can take turns or volunteer to guess letters, words, phrases, or answers to questions. For each wrong guess, a part of their person will be drawn on the gallows. By using the head, trunk, arms, hands, legs, and feet as the body components, students will get ten wrong guesses before the little person is hanged. Students will have more chances if the person's eyes, nose, mouth, ears, hair, and clothes are used. As each right guess is made, fill in all the appropriate blanks for that letter, word, or phrase. Encourage students to fill in this information on their own sheets as well. As the game is played and a correct answer is given for one of the questions on the chalkboard, check off that question and write the answer on the board.

Evaluate the lesson when the game is completed. If this strategy lesson is successful, students will learn that focusing on individual letters is not effective in arriving at the goal of answering questions, and that taking risks by guessing larger chunks of information such as words, phrases, or answers to questions pays off in the long run. The lesson can be considered successful if students use their background knowledge and the semantic constraints provided by the title to make reasonable guesses rather than guessing unrelated words or function words that carry no information.

What Else

Students can play this game in small groups or teams, taking turns selecting a passage and preparing a hangman sheet and questions.

Carolyn K. Ewoldt, York University, North York, Ontario, Canada

Comprehendos — A Comprehension Game

Why

To provide students with an enjoyable way to begin analyzing and categorizing information available in a text

Who

All elementary students who exhibit word-calling tendencies or who have difficulty organizing and remembering information

How

Prepare for the game by cutting thirty-five to fifty 6″ × 12″ cards from any stiff paper such as posterboard. Draw a line down the center of each card with a dark colored marker. Alternately print on about 80 percent of the cards one of the following words: *Who, What, When, Where, Why,* and *How*. Put two words on several cards. Leave the remaining cards completely blank. When you are satisfied that there are enough cards and options for two to four players, laminate the cards or cover them with adhesive-backed paper.

Ask students to read a narrative story or expository text. Discuss the reading with them, extending and elaborating their background of knowledge, the visual images, their vocabularies, and so on.

Provide students with felt-tip markers or grease pencils that will erase from laminated surfaces with a tissue. Shuffle the cards and deal them face down, dividing them evenly among the players.

As in dominoes, the first play is a double card containing two words. The first player writes on the blank half of one of his or her cards an answer from the story or text selection that answers the question posed by one of the two original words, such as "Grandma's house" in response to *Where*. This card is positioned next to the original card. The game proceeds with players matching their cards with those already played, supplying the necessary information where blanks occur.

The children moderate the answers. Challenges can be referred to the text, the teacher, or another child who is familiar with the material but who is not playing the game.

The floor might work best for the game since the cards are spread over a large area as the game proceeds. Displays of the complete Comprehendos game design make interesting reading for the other students before the pieces are dismantled.

I do not include a scoring or points system since I encourage children to play for fun and to help each other. However, if they prefer competitive games, a point system can easily be worked out.

What Else

1. Students may wish to draw pictures on the cards rather than write an answer. A combination of words and pictures is also interesting.
2. Semantic mapping and story wheels are a logical extension of this experience. Children who have played Comprehendos seem to catch on to mapping strategies quickly.
3. Rewriting the material into a newspaper article or a news release is a logical follow-up since the cards call for answers to the five *W* questions.
4. A cartoon strip of the story works well following a game of Comprehendos. After students have broken down the story into its elements, it's a good idea to return to the whole story.

Carole F. Stice, Tennessee State University, Nashville

Holiday Delights

Why

To use greeting cards to extend or initiate oral and written language expression

Who

Kindergartners, primary and middle elementary students

How

Encourage students to collect December holiday greeting cards. Discuss with them the approaching holidays and the purposes for sending holiday greeting cards. Students then choose a person or persons to whom they wish to send a greeting card. They make their own greeting cards from construction paper, gluing the front page from the cards they've collected onto the front of the construction paper. On the inside they write their own messages.

What Else

1. Students make writing booklets in the shape of a Christmas tree, bell, holiday wreath, or dreidel.
2. Students write individual letters to Santa. Arrange for an older student, a parent, or another adult to serve as Santa and to answer the letters.
3. Read aloud several holiday stories and poems, such as *Rudolph the Red-Nosed Reindeer*. Ask the children to act out the story. Discuss how Rudolph felt and how the chosen reindeer felt. Or introduce and discuss a book like *A Picture Book of Hanukkah* by David A. Adler or *I Love Hanukkah* by Marilyn Hirsh to familiarize children with holidays other than Christmas.
4. Write the words to favorite holiday songs on the chalkboard or on chart paper. Let children take turns being the song leader, perhaps pointing to the words as the class sings.
5. Ask children to write lists of their holiday "wants." Use these to make graphs, to classify, or to count.
6. Pick a favorite holiday treat to cook with the class. Write the recipe with the children as a language experience activity. Cook, talk, and enjoy.
7. After the holiday season is over, children write thank-you letters to Santa, Mom and Dad, Grandma and Grandpa, and other relatives.

Jill Janes, Hannibal Public Schools, Missouri

March Is for Leprechauns

Why

To expand students' language development through experiences in concept building

Who

All elementary students

How

With the children's help, draw and color a large rainbow with a pot of gold at the end. Include some leprechauns in the picture. Before March 17th, tell or read some of the stories in Virginia de Haviland's *Tales Told in Ireland* or *Leprechauns Never Lie* by Lorna Balian.

On the morning of St. Patrick's Day, make it appear to younger children as if a leprechaun has been there. Leave on each child's desk a letter from the leprechaun and something green, such as green gum or a green balloon. Make footprints on the chalkboard with fingers first rubbed on the chalk tray, and leave some toys out. Sprinkle a little "magic dust" (gold glitter) around the room.

Meet the students outside the classroom and explain that you think leprechauns have visited the room. As the class begins to hunt for the leprechauns, pretend to catch one in a paper bag in which you previously punched a small hole and placed a note saying something like "Ha, ha. See ya next year! Love, Lenny." Fasten the bag with a rubber band and place it on your desk. A little later in the day, open the bag, discover the note, and read it aloud. Talk about how the leprechaun might have entered and left the classroom.

Numerous writing assignments can follow the leprechaun episode. Ask younger children to:

> write or dictate a story about what happened that day
>
> draw and write about where they think the leprechaun is now
>
> dictate or write how they plan to catch a leprechaun next time
>
> write a letter inviting their leprechaun to return to the classroom

Older children might be asked to:

> write the letters left by leprechauns on the desks of younger children, perhaps including pictures of the leprechauns
>
> write their own leprechaun stories, songs, poems, and plays to read aloud to a young friend
>
> write a story from the point of view of a leprechaun

explain what they would do if they found the leprechaun's pot of gold

describe where a leprechaun would live and how it would spend a typical day

describe how they would catch a leprechaun

make up their own characters for a particular holiday and write stories involving those characters

Pamela Shriver, Cedar Rapids Schools, Cedar Rapids, and Linn-Mar Schools, Marron, Iowa

Chapter 9:
Home Is Where the Start Is

Within the context of the family, the transmission of literary styles and values is a diffuse experience, often occurring at the margins of awareness. Even when parents quite consciously introduced their children to print, the words were locked into the context of the situation. The label on the shampoo bottle, the recipe for carrot bread, and the neon signs in the street were not constructed to specifically teach reading; they were part of the child's world, and the child learned of their purpose as well as of their meaning. . . .

Leo and Jill Langdon had not consciously tried to teach their children to read, but in the middle of Ken's first-grade year, it became clear that he was learning to read without difficulty. He was interested in words; he was inquisitive about the words in his own home. At that time Leo and Jill began to participate in his reading activities. He explained, "A couple of months ago I went over to see his teacher and I had spoken to her and told her how well he was doing, how we felt. I asked her if he could bring books home so that we could help him and he could read and she said 'sure.'"

— Denny Taylor, *Family Literacy: Young Children Learning to Read and Write* (Heinemann Educational Books, 1983), 20

The strategies in this chapter encourage teachers to respond as Ken's teacher did and then to do more — to take the initiative for home-school communication. The strategies involve suggestions, information, and invitations to parents.

Parent Reviewer

Why

1. To involve parents in their children's literary efforts
2. To encourage children to read by seeing their parents reading and writing

Who

All elementary students

How

After the children have completed written projects, stories, books, and so on, invite the parents to review the literature by sending home a note similar to the following:

> Dear Parents,
>   Your young author has just finished writing an important piece of literature called "I Just Love. . . ." Please ask him or her to read it with you. Then play Book Reviewer and write a short commentary on the strengths of your author's writing. Send your comments back tomorrow, along with your child's writing. We'll share all the parents' comments in class.

The children return the next day with reviews similar to those shown below.

> I think Jill is progressing very nicely. I like the way her book goes from jack-o-lanterns to mommy

and daddy!! At least her picture of me doesn't look like the jack-o-lantern!!

Love,
Daddy

I love it when Jill brings home her writings. I especially enjoyed the pictures! I wish I had such artistic talent. I thought it was interesting that the author loved sad as well as happy faces.

I could really relate to the subject of this book because I also love Buffy, Daddy, Jennifer, BJ & Christopher but I also love Jill and her wonderful book!

Mom

I just love Rebecca's I Just Love Book. From its neat heart shape to the pretty colors in the pictures. Most of all I just love that Rebecca is writing her own books with words she can read and understand! This book is very special and I am very proud of Rebecca.

Mary L.

The children share their own writings and their parents' reviews with the class.

What Else

Children ask an adult who is not a relative to review the book or story. They might ask the principal, other teachers, or a neighbor to do so. Or children could review their own writings, which would encourage revision.

On the back of each book write, "I read this book to ———" at the top and "My book was read by ———" in the middle. Ask children and adults to provide a record of the book review by signing the back of the book as they complete their tasks.

Deborah Schilb Lacy, Our Lady of the Snows, Mary's Home, Missouri

New-Baby Books

Why

Children in elementary school often are members of expanding families. Frequently, getting ready for a new baby is a time of crisis for the older child. The following strategy focuses on the event with a sharing of experience, information, and imagination.

Who

Any elementary student whose parents are expecting another child

How

Encourage the class or a group of students to discuss the following questions:

1. Have you ever had a new baby at your house, or do you know anyone who has?
2. Before the new baby arrived, what did you think it would be like?
3. How did you react when the new baby arrived?

After the discussion, invite each student to draw or make a collage picture indicating something a new baby does, and to write a caption or story for the picture. Invite children to write letters to the new baby.

What Else

1. Make a book of the students' new-baby collages for the classroom library.
2. Assemble a collection of new-baby books and encourage students to read them.

Pansy Collins, Evangel College, Springfield, Missouri

Travel Log

Why

A family vacation that comes in the middle of a school year can be an educational and enjoyable experience for all. This strategy can be used as an alternative to the in-class assignments missed during the trip, while ensuring continued, constructive use of all the language arts. This strategy can also be used to take an imaginary trip.

Who

All elementary students

How

Careful planning, communication, and cooperation between teacher, parent, and student are required. Encourage parents to notify you of midyear trips well in advance. If time permits, work with the student to assemble the following:

1. a pocket folder with bindings to hold notebook paper

2. lined and unlined notebook paper

3. pencils, pens, and colored markers

4. a map of the states, regions, or countries in which the family will travel (obtained from an auto club, chamber of commerce, convention bureau, and so on)

5. a suggestion sheet of activities, proposed by the student or the entire class

Discuss the project with the entire class. Study the maps together and ask the other students to trace the traveling student's itinerary. The class might calculate the total number of miles in the trip or determine the quickest route or the most scenic route. Students might use travel literature, library books, or firsthand experience to prepare a list of landmarks or historic sites for the traveler to visit.

The traveling student can use his or her travel log for keeping track of the following information. The activities are varied and involve across-the-curriculum projects.

1. Students note their departure time and the starting mileage if traveling by car. They calculate the mileage to various points along the route, estimate the arrival time at these places, and note the actual time and mileage.

2. Students help keep track of travel expenses, such as gasoline purchases (older children can calculate miles per gallon between fill-ups), tickets, meals, lodging, and recreation, and could be involved in staying within the budget.

3. Students record their feelings and impressions of cities and towns they visit. They might ask themselves the following questions:
   a. Does the town make a good impression — clean or dirty?
   b. Do the people look friendly?
   c. Would I like to live here?

4. Students record visits to historic sites, landmarks, and other places of interest. Encourage them to collect and read all available free brochures, and to save the materials to share with classmates on their return. If possible, students purchase picture postcards, take pictures, or make drawings and sketches. Those interested in physical fitness might look for a stadium, fieldhouse, or other place where sporting events are held. They might count the joggers they spot and check whether their motels have facilities for physical fitness. Students with an interest in art might visit art galleries and record their impressions of the artwork they view. Or they might comment on the various architectural styles and features that they see.

5. Other things that students might look for along the way are listed below.
   a. different climates or changes in weather
   b. geographical features
   c. types of music heard on the radio or in stores
   d. environmental print, such as billboards, bumper stickers, license plates, graffiti, T-shirts
   e. time zone changes

What Else

1. Invite students to prepare any of the following:
   a. a travel log of a field trip
   b. a travel log of a trip around town
   c. a travel log of a trip around school
   d. a travel log of a trip through a book
   e. an imaginary captain's log aboard a ship — perhaps Christopher Columbus's
   f. a proposed itinerary for a "dream summer"

2. Read aloud to older students *Beyond the Divide* by Kathryn Lasky, a work of historical fiction written as a travel log.

Linda M. Hope, Glen Springs Elementary School, Alachua County Schools, Gainesville, Florida

Special Days

Why

1. To highlight what is special about each child in the classroom

2. To help students learn more about each other and focus on everyone's positive attributes

3. To give each child something to look forward to in school, thus developing positive attitudes toward school

4. To draw the home and school more closely together by encouraging parents to attend school

5. To promote variety in the curriculum and communication in the classroom

Who

All elementary students

How

At the beginning of the year, ask parents to select a day during the school year that will be their child's special day, perhaps the child's birthday or another day that has significance for the family. Explain that their child will be celebrating his or her uniqueness and sharing with classmates some special things about himself or herself. Encourage the parents to plan to attend and to invite other family members, too.

On the child's special day, the parents and other relatives or special friends visit the classroom. Classmates meet baby sisters and brothers and perhaps grandparents, aunts and uncles, and cousins. Sometimes the family shows home movies or photo albums featuring the child. If the child takes music or dance lessons, he or she is invited to perform for the class. Or the child might tell the class about a pet, a favorite activity, or a special event in his or her life.

Many language activities emerge on special days. This is an opportunity for the special child to speak in front of the class about a topic he or she knows well. Discussions of hobbies introduce new vocabulary and concepts. The special child might share his or her favorite book with the class. A younger child might bring to school a favorite stuffed animal and tell about its origin and why it is so special.

The rest of the class celebrates by letting the special child know how special he or she really is. One kindergarten teacher has the children make a long experience chart that says, "I like ——— because. . . ." Each child contributes a unique reason for liking the special child, and the teacher supplies the last line. The students gather in a circle and read aloud to the special child what they have written. The chart is rolled up for the special child to take home at the end of the day.

A first-grade teacher asks each child to write a card for the special child; then several students make wrapping paper by painting or drawing on newsprint. The cards are placed in a box and wrapped as a gift for the special child to open at a special sharing time at the end of the day or while the child's parents are there. The students help the special child read their cards, and then the special child takes the cards home.

A second-grade teacher asks each child to write a letter to the special child. The letters are bound together into a book for the child to take home and enjoy.

One teacher asks the special child to fill out a form called "All about Me," listing all his or her favorite items. A picture of the child is added to the poster, which is displayed on a bulletin board for all the children to read. The students enjoy comparing such favorites as foods, colors, and activities.

Sometimes special children make the day special for the other children as well. Their parents may supply refreshments. Some parents or friends bring in unusual activities for the class to participate in or help lead the children on field trips. One parent helped a class make a piñata. Sometimes the parents talk about their occupations. One parent who was a hairdresser talked about good grooming and then gave each child a shampoo sample to take home. Sometimes students' pets make visits to the classroom on special days.

What Else

If children enjoy celebrating their own special days, they might also celebrate the birthdays of historic figures or the anniversary dates of special events in history.

Linda Leonard Lamme, University of Florida, Gainesville

Mailboxes at Home

Why

Written communication between parent and child provides opportunities for the child to interact with text. Such communication is highly motivating in that it requires the child to understand meaning both as reader and as author.

Who

All elementary children and their parents

How

Send home to parents a letter similar to the following:

Dear Parents,
    Your child has been enjoying a variety of reading and writing experiences at school. [Here I might describe those activities.] In an effort to involve you in this exciting period of your child's written language development, I would like to suggest the following *ongoing* activity.

1. Place one mailbox by your child's bedroom door and a second one by yours. A shoebox

or other small box works well. Encourage your child to decorate the boxes.

2. Provide your child with notepaper and pencil, and keep a set handy for yourself.
3. Leave a note in your child's box. Start out writing things your child might expect you to say. Comment on familiar things or events. Encourage your youngster to read the note unassisted. He or she will ask for assistance when needed.
4. Encourage your child to write back, responding to your note.
5. Continue this exchange of notes through the coming months.

This continued involvement with print will be an enriching experience for your youngster. Some of the notes you receive will no doubt be priceless. Try to be accepting of what your child writes. Place value on *what* he or she is saying rather than on *how* it is being said. Expect invented spellings and unusual punctuation. We will talk more about this at our next parent meeting, and feel free to contact me throughout the year to share your ideas and concerns.

What Else

1. Encourage students to share notes that have been received and written. Special items or notes can be made at school for children to put in their parents' mailboxes.
2. Older children might enjoy keeping a notebook with their parents. The parent enters a dated message to the child, who, in turn, makes an entry in response. The notebook could become a treasured keepsake.

Dee White, Chapter One Reading Teacher, Columbia, Missouri

"When You Care Enough to Send the Very Best"

Why

1. To keep parents involved with their child's language development through a simple and fun family activity
2. To encourage parents and child to write messages to one another

Who

Families of all elementary children, especially those with a hearing-impaired child

How

Parents make a collection of several Christmas cards or cards for other holidays. They replace the "greeting" page or cover the message by taping blank construction paper over it. Each family member writes a holiday message on a card to each of the other family members. At a set time (perhaps after dinner), the family members pass out their cards, open them, and take turns reading them aloud.

What Else

This activity can be done in the classroom with partners or groups.

John W. Balk, Multi-District Hearing-Impaired Program, Blue Springs R-IV Schools, Missouri

Primary Camping Trip

Why

1. To help students bring their knowledge and experiences to their reading
2. To stimulate practical reading and writing
3. To help students understand their interdependence with nature and to enjoy outdoor activities

Who

With adaptation, all elementary students

How

Three second grades received permission from the school district to go camping in a Wisconsin state park located fifty miles from the school. The group included twenty parents, five teachers, one principal, and fifty-six children.

The children worked in small groups, discussing and listing the items each would need for the trip. The groups shared their lists, and together the students decided on a master list of supplies. This list and permission slips were sent home with each child.

The teachers met to divide the fifty-six children into groups of four, assigning each group a parent counselor. Each group met and decided upon a group name. The children then designed their own name tags. They wrote their names with felt-tip pens on pieces of leather, drew a symbol for their group name, and wore the name tags around their necks.

Much preparation was involved before the day of departure. Some children were interested in planning the menus. After many meetings, the children decided on three menus, which they presented to the head cook, a parent volunteer. Other parents and children brought the food.

The state recreation agency furnished a list of camp rules. During class discussion, children had a chance to add their own rules to the list. The Outdoor Manners Coloring Book resulted, with illustrations and text by the children. Children took their books home to share and discuss with their families.

One student group decided to become familiar with songs that could be sung in the evening. These children took the role of teacher and taught the other children. "Down by the Creek" (which contains repetition and predictable language) was a favorite. On the camping trip, the children enjoyed singing to the accompaniment of a guitar that a father had brought along, and they made up some verses of their own.

The first full day at camp, the children were assigned to numerous outdoor activities on a rotation basis. Teachers led the following groups:

Adopt a Tree

Sounds around Us

Animal Tracking and Plaster Molds

Forest Concentration Game

The Fallen Log

Walking a Stream

My Plot of Soil

Trailmaking

Fishing with the Principal

Teachers brought along appropriate supplies and books. The activities were planned to promote reading and writing and to increase children's knowledge of nature and the outdoors. Children in the Adopt a Tree group were encouraged to select a particular tree and then to respond orally and in writing to the following questions:

What is it like under your tree?

Can you hug your tree?

How does the bark look and feel?

What kinds of things have hurt your tree?

Has the tree cast seeds?

Have any seeds developed into seedlings?

Is your tree crowded by other trees?

Where is its shadow?

What insects and animals visit your tree when you are there?

What animals make this tree their home?

How would you describe your tree to a friend?

On their return, the children shared the events and their impressions of the camping trip with each other and their parents. Some wrote to thank the park ranger for his help. Some children wrote about and illustrated their experiences in the form of a book. Parent volunteers typed the text for each page.

What Else

Further follow-up activities included weekly visits to a wooded area near the school. Children adopted their own trees and made journal entries about each visit. Some took their trees to lunch by eating a picnic lunch under the tree. Others wrote cinquains about their trees, such as the following:

Trees
Shady, bare
Branching, blooming, stretching
Provide a home
Trees

Donna Hahn, Tonawanda School, Elmbrook District, Elm Grove, Wisconsin

Friday Sharing Time

Why

1. To encourage students to participate in a special activity each Friday during the school year
2. To encourage parent-child interaction

Who

Primary and middle elementary students

How

Each Monday send home a bulletin announcing the activity for that week and encouraging the parents and children to work together to prepare for the Friday sharing time. The following suggestions for the school year will give you a start on preparing your own list of activities that are appropriate for parent-child interaction and Friday sharing time:

September

1. Students bring a family photograph or drawing to class.
2. National Play-Doh Day — students bring a Play-Doh sculpture.
3. Birthday of the ice cream cone — students draw a picture of their favorite flavor of ice cream in a cone.
4. Students create a leaf picture.

October

1. Students make or draw a ship for Columbus.
2. Birthday of Theodore Roosevelt — students bring in a favorite teddy bear.
3. Students create a Halloween mask from whatever materials are available at home.

November

1. Apple Festival Weekend — students bring in a fresh apple; you furnish the cider.
2. Mickey Mouse was born November 18, 1928 — students make birthday cards for Mickey, which are shared with the class and then mailed (1313 Harbor Boulevard, P.O. Box 3232, Anaheim, CA 92803).
3. Students make a Thanksgiving decoration from materials available at home.

December

1. Students write a letter to Santa — the letters are shared with the others and then mailed to the North Pole.
2. Students make an ornament for the Christmas tree/Hanukkah bush.
3. Students make a greeting card for a special person in the school.

January

1. Students make a snowman out of a paper plate, old fabric scraps, and other available materials at home.
2. Wolfgang Mozart Day — students bring a favorite record or tape to class, or they choose a favorite song to sing to the class.

February

1. Students make a valentine card for a special person in the school.

2. Dental Health Month: "A healthy smile brightens everyone's day" — students write and illustrate five things that make them smile.
3. American Music Month — students make a musical instrument for a class band.

March

1. National Physical Education and Sport Month — students draw a picture of a favorite sport.
2. St. Patrick's Day — students bring in something green to share with the class.
3. Celebrate spring — students cut spring pictures out of magazines or draw pictures of birds, flowers, bees, grass, a sunny day, ladybugs, or butterflies. They paste the pictures on paper, perhaps adding real spring objects.
4. National Goof-Off Day — students draw a comic strip with five boxes showing their favorite ways to goof-off.

April

1. Wilbur Wright Day — students make a paper airplane to fly on the playground.
2. Career Day — students decide what they want to do when grown and come to school dressed like a person in that occupation.

May

1. May Day baskets — students make a basket from available materials at home; at school they make paper flowers to put in their baskets.
2. T-Shirt Day — students wear a favorite T-shirt containing writing or a picture.
3. Students bring in a picture of Mom and write a few sentences about her to read aloud to the class.
4. Field trip to the zoo — students read a book about an animal that they might see at the zoo.

June

1. June Bug Day — students create an insect from materials available at home and explain to the class where the bug lives, what it eats, and whether it is dangerous to humans.
2. Students draw or make a picture showing some of their summer vacation plans.

Susan Myers Cotten, A. V. Baucom School, Wake County Public Schools, Apex, North Carolina, and Susan M. Brewer, Northwood Elementary School, High Point City Schools, North Carolina

Calendar: Parent and Child Activities

Why

1. To encourage the parent and child to work together
2. To give the parent insight into the development of the child's reading, thinking, and writing abilities

Who

Primary students; with adaptation, older students

How

Send parents a letter informing them of the reading and writing activities the children are engaged in at school. Attach to the letter a calendar of activities the children may want to do at home, including activities that involve parent and child interaction. A sample calendar appears in Figure 9-1.

Parents and children keep the calendar at home and are responsible for developing each activity together. Encourage parents to give assistance when needed or when requested by the child.

What Else

Students might bring in completed projects to share with the teacher and, if the child wishes, with the class.

Sunday	Monday	Tuesday	Wednesday	Thursday	Friday	Saturday
FEBRUARY	1 Put crumbs out for the birds	2 Watch for news about Mr. Groundhog	3 Say hello to your music teacher	4 Mark on your calendar all the birthdays you know	5 Write a letter to a relative	6 Help put away the groceries
7 Telephone a special person	8 Write a story about hearts	9 Guess how many hearts are in the jar at school	10 Make a list of things that make you happy	11 How many times does your heart beat a minute?	12 Look at a penny and draw a picture of Abe Lincoln	13 Make a valentine for someone
14 Wear a red heart today	15 How many red foods can you find?	16 Thank the cafeteria workers for a nice lunch	17 Act out a story	18 Do something kind for your family	19 Where is it snowing? Watch the TV weather	20 Look at the family photo album with a family member
21 Make a cherry tree	22 Draw a picture of George Washington	23 Make a red jam sandwich	24 Sing a song	25 Help make popcorn	26 Smile at someone and see what happens	27 Make an address and phone number book
28 Help make breakfast	29 An extra day — do an extra chore at home					

Figure 9–1. A sample calendar of at-home activities

*Sister Linda Burkitt, Seton Catholic School,
Moline, Illinois*

Letters to Parents

Why

To give parents insight into the development of their child's reading, thinking, and writing abilities

Who

With adaptation, all elementary students

How

Each month I send a letter to parents to keep them current with their child's language development. Below is a set of letters that I sent out one school year.

September

Dear Parents,

Isn't it amazing how much your child has learned over the past few years? Do you remember when your child said his or her first word? The word probably wasn't pronounced correctly, but you knew what was meant. Your child was experi-menting with language. Remember how you smiled and praised, and probably even bragged about this first word?

Your child will be experimenting with written language this year, just as he or she experimented with talking. By written language, I don't mean handwriting, but rather, whatever children choose to say to us on paper. You'll see some amazing changes over the year, and I hope that you'll be just as excited with your child's early writing attempts as you were with his or her first speech attempts.

Praise your child for the pictures, scribbles, upside-down letters, and crazy spellings; these are normal phases of writing development.

Your encouragement will give your child the confidence needed to take risks with writing development.

Your encouragement will give your child the confidence needed to take risks with writing. Risk taking teaches more than corrections ever can!

October

Dear Parents,

Children's spelling goes through natural phases over an extended period of time. Attached to this note you find some writing samples from a kindergartner who was in my class last year. You will also find my comments and translation into standard spelling to help you read the samples. [See Figure 9-2.]

1. This kindergartner knows several letters and that print should appear in lines. She can write part of her name.

2. She copies the words *school box* and then tries to write *spaghetti.* At the bottom she has written, "I like spaghetti."

3. Later in the year she is able to write, "Can I go to town? When I go to town I get paid."

Figure 9–2. A kindergartner's writing samples.

Notice how the child's spelling changes over the months, as she becomes a more fluent reader and writer. Try to figure out why she spells the way she does. She depends a great deal on the way the letter sounds when she says the word. Notice how the length of her work increases as she becomes more confident as an author who is making decisions and taking chances with spelling.

Be sure to read over your own child's writing samples and give lots of praise! Feel free to write to your child or to me on the back of this month's folder.

November

Dear Parents,

Have you noticed the group books we've made? Each child is responsible for the illustrations and for dictating, or writing, the captions. These books are a great way to get children interested in reading and attending to print. Feel free either to take dictation from your child at home or to encourage your child to write using invented spelling.

Many of the books we read in class are predictable books. That means the stories have repetitions or cumulative lines, rhyming words, and familiar concepts. On the whole, they are well written. Predictable books encourage children to trust print and to read.

When your child brings home something to read to you, don't be alarmed if what he or she reads doesn't match the words on the page. At this point we're concerned that the children are catching the meaning and enjoying the story.

By the way, as you read aloud to your child, let your fingers skim along the words. In a study done with young children, it was found that many of them thought that the parent was reading the picture, not the print.

December

Dear Parents,

Here are four types of spelling that children will use if they're given the chance to experiment.

Phase 1: Pre-phonemic Spelling. These young children string letters together without trying to represent specific sounds. For example,

JFHLO = I love dogs.

Phase 2: Early Phonemic. These spellers are conscious of different sounds or syllables and try to represent them with letters. For example,

ILDS = I love dogs.

Phase 3: Letter Name Spelling. Children at this stage are more conscious of sounds and use more than one letter for a word. For example,

I LV DGS = I love dogs.

Phase 4: Transitional Spelling. When children have had lots of exposure to print and are reading, they try to gain control of standard spelling. They may have misspelled words, but these misspellings

will decrease in number as the children become more fluent readers. For example,

I lov dogs = I love dogs.

You may want to refer to this list as the year goes on and as your child's perception of written language changes.

January

Dear Parents,

Here are five features common to early children's writings. See if you can find any of them in your own child's writings.

Recurring Principle. Children discover for themselves through observation of print that writers use the same shapes again and again. For example,

Generative Principle. Children eventually notice that writing is made of a limited number of characters, mixed in a variety of combinations. For example,

CAFL
LFA

Inventory Principle. Have you ever noticed your child making a list of words that he or she knows, or a list of people in your family? For example,

MOM	T.V.
DAD	NO
E.T.	YES

Contrastive Principle. Children use writing to express size, such as in the example below:

If CAT = cat, then CAT = kitten

Space Concept. Do you speak with a distinct pause between words? Of course not! Children have to learn from print that there are spaces between words. This can be a tricky concept to grasp. For example,

Mi brdas tda = My birthday is today.

If you'd like more information on what to look for in children's early writing, ask to borrow my copy of *What Did I Write?* by Marie Clay. It's short and very interesting.

February

Dear Parents,

Some of you may be wondering why your child's writings are so brief. Have you ever considered what children go through in order to spell a word? It's a very complicated thought process. Your child must go through the following steps:

1. Say the word silently.

2. Break off the first sound from the rest of the word.

3. Mentally sort through the alphabet to find a letter to match the sound. Some sounds do not have one corresponding letter, such as the *ch* sound in *chair.*

4. Write down the chosen letter.

5. Recite the word silently again.

6. Recall the first sound, subtract it from the word, and figure out the next sound to be spelled, following the above process.

That's a lot of work. But your child is doing it for a purpose — to write about what he or she thinks is important, whether it be about the family cat or the Care Bears. There's an immense satisfaction in successfully communicating to an audience. It will influence everything from the decisions your child makes about writing topics to the care that he or she will eventually use with punctuation and spelling. It will all come a step at a time — in your child's own time.

March

Dear Parents,

You can make a big difference in your child's success as a reader. The best thing you can do at home to encourage reading is to make reading as enjoyable as possible. If reading becomes a chore or unpleasant for either you or your child, stop. Then begin again when you're both ready.

As you and your child read, encourage your child's questions and ask a few of your own. Beginning a question with "I wonder . . ." is a good way to check your child's comprehension and to expand his or her thinking.

Reading to or with your child does not always have to be a formal occasion. Reading cereal boxes is a great way to begin the day. I have a list of ideas for making reading an important part of your child's day and would be pleased to share it with you.

April

Dear Parents,

As you've probably noticed by now, we try to do a lot of writing in class. Writing is an excellent way to develop reading skills and thinking skills.

Perhaps you've found yourselves writing less and less as time goes by. There are a variety of reasons why people don't like to write. Some believe they have nothing of value to say. Some feel incompetent at conveying information. Some are overly concerned with avoiding mistakes in writing rather than thinking about communicating effectively.

Here are just a few reasons why we write each day. If you would like more information about any of these reasons, ask to borrow an article by Donald Graves entitled "Balance the Basics: Let Them Write."

1. Writing contributes to intelligence.
2. Writing develops initiative.
3. Writing develops courage.
4. Writing contributes to better reading.
5. Writing contributes to learning math.
6. Writing contributes to reading comprehension.
7. Writing increases spelling power.
8. Writing develops creativity.
9. Writing gives a heightened experience.
10. Writing helps children master the conventions of language (such as grammar, punctuation, spelling).

May

Dear Parents,

I have listed below the authors and titles of books that I can practically guarantee *you* will love to read to your child, and that I know your child will love.

Harry Allard; *Miss Nelson Is Missing; The Stupids Die*

Judi Barrett; *Cloudy with a Chance of Meatballs*

Eric Carle; *The Very Hungry Caterpillar*

Paul Galdone; *Wriggles the Little Wishing Pig*

Jerome Harste; *It Didn't Frighten Me!*

Dubose Heyward; *The Country Bunny and the Little Gold Shoes*

Russell Hoban; *Bedtime for Frances*

Stephen Kellogg; *Can I Keep Him?*

Mercer Mayer; *What Do You Do with a Kangaroo?*

Robert McCloskey; *One Morning in Maine*

Maurice Sendak; *Where the Wild Things Are*

Shel Silverstein; *Where the Sidewalk Ends*

William Steig; *Sylvester and the Magic Pebble*

Mary Stoltz; *Emmet's Pig*

Remember while you're reading that the number one problem with reading aloud to children is: *Adults read aloud too fast.* If you're interested in reading *The Read Aloud Handbook* by Jim Trelease, ask to borrow my copy.

Carmen Kennedy, Saints Peter and Paul Elementary School, Boonville, Missouri

Take-Home Books

Why

1. To make learning to read easier by providing highly predictable books and other good literature

for students to enjoy independently and to share with their parents and others in the home

2. To establish the habit of reading at home as early as possible

3. To involve parents in their children's reading development

Who

All primary students, especially beginning readers, students considered remedial readers, and students who may have difficulty finding books in the library that they can read successfully

How

Acquire for your classroom or remedial program a collection of paperback books selected from lists of predictable books (such as those listed in the Bibliography) or other recommended books. Students might help raise money to add books to the collection during the school year.

Fill out a library card for each book, and place each book and card in a sturdy, reclosable plastic bag. When a student chooses a book to take home, he or she signs the card and fills in his or her name and the title on the following form.

For a Read-Aloud Book

My name is _____.
My book is _____
_____.
I shared my book with _____
                              (signature)
and with _____.
                    (signature)

For a Read-It-to-Me Book

My name is _____.
My book is _____
_____.
_____ read my book to me.
       (signature)

This form is placed in the bag with the book to aid in the distribution of the books just before school is dismissed for the day.

A box for the returned books is placed in a convenient location. Check in the books, return them to the classroom library, and date the signed forms. Staple together each student's forms and send them home at the end of the quarter as a record of the student's outside reading.

For first graders, introduce books through shared print or assisted reading procedures beginning on the first day of school, and encourage the children to take home books. Students come to school expecting to learn to read, so satisfy this desire and begin to build their confidence immediately.

Plan a conference with parents early in the school year, or send a letter home explaining the importance of being a good listener and how to be one. If a child chooses to read a book aloud, parents are asked not to demand word-for-word accuracy and are told why. Share with them the strategies that you encourage students to use in order to unlock new words, and ask parents to help students use these same strategies. If possible, demonstrate how and why these strategies work. Suggest to parents several ways that a book may be shared, such as letting the child retell the story, or at least the best part. Many students like to read to younger brothers and sisters, and those listeners should also sign their names to the forms.

What Else

Also make available for checkout concept books and storybooks that are too difficult for a specific child to read but that are good for listening and discussion activities. A different form printed on colored paper will alert parents that these books should be read *to* their children.

Jane L. Decker, Columbia Public Schools, Missouri

Take-Home Tape Recorders

Why

1. To provide books and cassette tapes for children who are not consistently read to at home

2. To provide children with good oral readers for models

3. To provide children with the materials for assisted-reading activities at home

4. To expose children to the sound of written language, which *is* different from the sound of the spoken language they are used to hearing in their home environments

Who

Primary students, especially those considered remedial readers, and younger brothers and sisters at home; with adaptation, older students

How

After funds were raised by holding a schoolwide book fair, five tape recorders were purchased through a mail-order catalog. These were chosen because of their sturdy construction, simple operation, and safety features — they operate only on battery power. Sturdy bags with shoulder straps were donated to make it easier to carry the tape recorders, books, and cassette tapes.

When a student checks out a tape recorder for overnight use, he or she also chooses a book "package" — a sturdy, reclosable plastic bag containing a book, the accompanying cassette tape, and laminated directions for the use of the tape recorder (for parents). If the tape is recorded on both sides, a blank tape is included so that the child can record himself or herself reading the story if desired. A library card for each tape recorder and book package makes record keeping easy. Tape recorders and accompanying materials are checked out overnight or until the next school day. A penalty, loss of the next "turn," helps to get materials returned promptly.

While some commercial tapes are used, students prefer teacher-made tapes because of pacing. Look for thirty-minute tapes (fifteen minutes on each side) to save time and batteries winding and rewinding the unused length. When making your own tapes, tape on only one side, protect it by removing the appropriate tab, and let the children tape on the reverse side. (I have found it is better not to explain to the students how I protected the recorded side of the tape. I edit the directions that come with the tape recorder so that this information does not go home.)

What Else

Older students enjoy making tapes for younger students.

Jane L. Decker, Columbia Public Schools, Missouri

Thinking Games for Parents and Children

Why

1. To increase parent-child verbal interaction
2. To encourage children's creative thinking and playing with language

Who

Primary students and their parents

How

In a letter to parents, suggest that they play one of the following games with their children. The games are appropriate for odd moments during the day, such as while riding in the car, waiting for a doctor's appointment, in the driveup lane at a fast-food restaurant, during dinner, at bath time, or at bedtime. Encourage the whole family to take part.

1. Initiate a game of categorizing by asking a brainstorming question such as those below. Children brainstorm all the words they can think of to answer the question, and they are to be prepared to explain or demonstrate any answer.
   a. What can be worn on your feet? (Possible answers include skates, shoes, skis, stilts, sandals, socks, running shoes, hiking boots, slippers, nylons, clogs, oxfords, loafers, rubbers, thongs.)
   b. What can you do with your fingers? (Possible answers include pinch, grab, poke, squeeze, point, touch, scratch, feel, lift, wiggle, write, pat, slap, rub, wave, slap, tap, pound, snap, shake, pull, push, bend.)
   c. Name things you can look through.
   d. What can you do with your feet?
   e. How many flavors of ice cream can you name?
   f. What things taste sweet?
   g. What noises do animals make?
2. Initiate the Backwards Game. Parents provide the answers; children make up the questions. Key words in this game are *who, what, where, when,* and *how.* For example, for the answer "at night," children might ask: "When do you sleep?" "When do ghosts come out?" "When does it get dark?" "When can you see the moon?" or "When do cars use headlights?" Some possible answers for parents to give are listed below:

kick it
around your waist
fingerprints
a hearing aid
sour
cry a lot
eyelashes
to help them see better

in the sink
a fireplace
in a haunted house
after school
the principal
with my family
hopscotch
a castle
three strikes
black and white
with its trunk
in a barn
eats bananas
king of the jungle
at a party
Bugs Bunny
in summer

3. Initiate the game Alike and Different to help children look for details and learn to compare and contrast. Children select a pair of items and explain all the ways in which the two objects are alike and different. Children might focus on the following aspects of each object: size, location, color, texture, action, category, shape, use, parts, sound, and feeling. Some possible objects to compare and contrast are listed below:

apple–orange
house–school

shirt–coat
boy–man
girl–woman
stare–peek
radio–TV
flower–tree
dog–cat
truck–car
slide–swing

These games might be demonstrated to parents in small groups. Parents need to know that games such as these help build and expand children's language and set the stage for them to become eager readers and writers. Parent volunteers might assemble the games into booklets.

What Else

Teachers might use the games at school while children are waiting for the school bus, getting ready for recess or lunch, turning in papers, or during those numerous other times when there are a few minutes in between planned activities. Once the format of the game is learned, both teachers and parents will think of additional ideas. Any one item in one of the games might be sent home for "homework."

Janet Maschoff, Grannemann Elementary School, St. Louis, Missouri

PART 5

September 1

I & Dear Ms Copeland

I Dear Ms. Copeland

September 10

AGFA ODR HP Y.

A girl found her puppy.

October 1

Russell. The M~H—s B—s
the m—n is 6—n FeB—s too
t de B—c T de B—o FK I—.

The man has balloons. The man is giving the
balloons to the boy. The boy took off.

November 30

The girl MOM is LON The Cds
the girl is B Yen The Cos Aot
Th P Q r L is eTen The C KC.

The girl's mom is lighting the candles.
The girl is blowing the candles out. The
girl is eating the cake.

February 1

Dear MS Copeland.

I am goona in A vaKCNtSSumr.

We ate fis Two Day.

I am hwppe.

Please guv me A lagrrss.

Dear Ms. Copeland,
  I am going on a vacation. We ate
fish today. I am happy. Please give
me a long recess.

December 10

Q by Monkey Sw ð A
ð/g A MMI ðt hð
A Lun
nos
iStut
wt I
LQK LQK
HOSDHs
m the
You ure
BUBB Monkey
AND You Ore
Vrre BUDFFL

Baby Monkey saw a big animal. It had a
long nose. "Is that what I look like?"
"No," said his mother, "you are Baby
Monkey and you are very beautiful."

March 26

MARCH The 26
    From Russell

No Yes
I like You

Dear Robyn EStE is ALL MOSTE Herr.
I HO PE I GET A BABY Rabbit. MY
Brt DAY is ALL MoSiE Herr. I
CAN READ A 61 PAGD BOOK OF
GArreh E66S AnD HAM.

         No Yes X
           I like you
Dear Robin,
  Easter is almost here. I hope I get a baby
rabbit. My birthday is almost here. I can
read a 61 page book of Green Eggs and Ham.

Chapter 10:
Valuing and Evaluating the Learners and Their Language

My grading system has to reflect the expectations I communicate to my students in each day's writing class. If evaluation is to be valid, I can't turn around at the end of nine weeks and impose objective standards for "good" writing, grading accordingly. When a student tries her hand at a letter to the editor, attempting to persuade readers of the local paper to vote to close a nuclear power plant, it's the attempt I value first. The writer is trying a new mode — persuasion — and risking a wide, critical audience. I'll help her find and get down her feelings and reasons. I'll ask her to consider the attitudes and needs of her readers. But, when the letter is not particularly well-argued, I won't punish the attempt in my grade book or view it as a failure. My students have each taught me that writing growth is seldom a linear progress, each piece representing an improvement over the last.

— Nancie Atwell, *Understanding Writing: Ways of Observing, Learning and Teaching* (Northeast Regional Exchange, 1982)

Keeping samples of student language and maintaining records over time will provide a much better indication of growth than will end-of-level or end-of-book test scores or standardized test scores, for the learner is at the heart of assessment. The teacher considers what is known about language, learning, and the student as an individual, while making observations in authentic oral and language experiences. The results of informed assessment point the way to future opportunities for language use that builds on learners' natural meaning-making attempts. The chapter provides suggestions for several formats to help teachers observe students as developing language users. The most productive forms of evaluating — documenting, sharing, responding, and valuing — may not involve letter grades at all.

Assessment Suggestions for Literature Discussion Groups

Why

The assessment of children's work in literature discussion groups must help both children and teacher move forward in their eager pursuit of intensive and extensive reading, and in their understanding and creating of new knowledge; that is, assessment must help create curriculum. Additionally, evaluation must be in keeping with the model of reading on which the literature discussion groups themselves are built.

Who

With adaptation, all elementary students

How

Twice during the school year, the literature discussion groups are videotaped. The students and teacher view the tapes and then carefully consider their own roles and contributions to the group. A written evaluation sheet can help direct students' thinking. The teacher and students should work together to create an instrument that the students consider helpful in evaluating themselves. Students need to understand, approve, and suggest items. The form might include the following items:

Reading and Dialogue

1. As I read the story, I make it make sense.
2. I prepare for the discussion by:
   a. reading the assigned pages
   b. writing in my log
   c. drawing in my log
   d. doing some research
   e. thinking about what I want to say in the group
   f. picking out something in the story or poem to share
3. I relate the story to things that have happened to me.
4. I relate the story to other stories or poems I have read, in terms of the following elements: setting, plot, theme, characters, style, mood, illustrations.
5. I look for patterns in the story and pictures.
6. I connect my ideas with those of other members of the group.
7. I help keep the discussion going by:
   a. staying on the subject
   b. contributing appropriate information
   c. encouraging others

Participation

1. I listen to other members of the group.
2. I show my attention by looking at the speaker and by responding.
3. I encourage others to speak.
4. I am willing to listen to opposing opinions.
5. I ask for clarification when I don't understand.
6. I speak clearly and loudly enough to be heard by all group members.
7. I speak to all members, not just the teacher.
8. I contribute my fair share to the discussion — not too much, not too little.
9. I am not easily distracted.

If I am to be graded on the reading and discussion of this book, I would give myself a ———.

Give reasons for your answers if you want.

What Else

The teacher and students compose questions to be answered either in a short discussion or in written form once a week. Consider some of the following items:

1. The discussions this week were good because. . . .
2. Since the beginning of the year the discussions have improved in these ways:
3. The discussions help me understand. . . .
4. I have become a better discussion member in these ways:
5. To improve our discussions we should work on. . . .
6. I personally need to work on. . . .

Dorothy J. Watson, University of Missouri–Columbia

Evaluating Literature Groups

Why

Evaluation is necessary in literature groups, not only to comply with district guidelines for student grades, but also to monitor and record the progress of students and the effectiveness of the program. Rigorous evaluation and documentation also legitimizes literature groups as a viable part of the curriculum, not a frill. In addition, the written evidence in the journal entries and follow-up activities can be used to document children's growth and can be presented to parents in parent-teacher conferences.

Who

All elementary students

How

Teachers can use the following methods to evaluate students' reading, writing, and talking about books.

1. List all available sources of acquiring data that help evaluate students' growth. For example, data may be collected by examining students' reading behaviors as they read a book, their journal entries, their book-extension activities, and their group discussions, and by administering various self-evaluation and peer-evaluation instruments.
2. Keep a representative sample of materials in a folder for each student, including the following:

list of titles and authors of books read in literature groups

response logs for the entire year

at least one extension activity each month

writing samples, in order to see connections between the types of books read and the growth in writing

list of titles and authors of books read for leisure reading at school and at home

3. Construct your own self-evaluation, peer-evaluation, and program-evaluation instruments based on criteria that you and students think are important, as shown in the following examples. The instruments will change as you, the students, and the program change.

4. Use each student's folder, as well as the various evaluation instruments, as a measurement of growth at parent-teacher conferences and as a basis for determining grades. Let students read through their folders occasionally and write about the progress they see themselves making.

Examples

1. *Self-evaluation at the beginning of the year.* These items reflect the students' need for a routine.

5 = always, 4 = almost all the time, 3 = sometimes, 2 = occasionally, 1 = never

_____ 1. I get my learning log and book at the beginning of the hour.

_____ 2. I get quiet during the tardy bell and only whisper to someone close to me.

_____ 3. I listen when directions are given.

_____ 4. I write thoughtfully in my learning log.

_____ 5. I date my entries.

_____ 6. I remember to write down the page number I stopped on.

_____ 7. I stay on task when reading.

_____ 8. I discuss the book in my group and listen when others talk.

The grade I deserve: _____. Why?

2. *Self-evaluation during the middle of the year.* Notice the emphasis has shifted from routine to more thoughtful questions.

5 = always, 4 = almost all the time, 3 = sometimes, 2 = occasionally, 1 = never

_____ 1. I finish the book.

_____ 2. I read carefully and try to make connections between my reading and my life.

_____ 3. I write thoughtfully in my learning log.

_____ 4. I look at the people in my group.

_____ 5. I listen to others talk in my group and show respect for their opinions.

The grade I deserve: _____. Why?

3. *Peer evaluation.* This is a freewriting opportunity for students to note what happens in their literature discussion groups. It helps both the students and teacher focus on individuals that help the discussion.

Think about the discussion group. Did the group discussion help you with the book? Discuss things you liked and things you didn't like about the group. What would you change in the future? *Who* or *what* made the group more interesting?

4. *Program evaluation.* This writing gives students a chance to evaluate the program and gives them an audience — other students their age. Their responses indicate how they feel about the experience, and it is hoped that students will be honest and serious in writing to their peers.

Literature groups are being considered as a choice for reading instruction in many other school districts. Kids in other towns want to know what it is really like to read books and then to meet and talk about them. What would you tell these other students about literature groups? How do you feel about them?

Carol Gilles, Jefferson Junior High School, Columbia, Missouri, with help from Shirley Johnsen, Columbia, Missouri

Teachers Writing to Learn in Journals

Why

To provide teachers with an opportunity to reflect on their teaching and on their students

Who

All elementary teachers

How

Write in your journal during student journal-writing time, during sustained silent writing time, during planning time, or at home. If this activity adds too much to your workload, evaluate how time is spent and revalue time set aside for professional growth. Perhaps you have other responsibilities that can be shifted to the students, freeing up additional time in your schedule.

There is no specific set of procedures for keeping a journal, but there are a number of purposes it can serve:

Recording student and teacher behavior. Teachers keep anecdotal records of classroom events, language stories, and special interests.

Assessing student growth. Teachers discuss students' growth over time and analyze what the behaviors mean.

Assessing teacher growth. Because of the intense demands of teaching and concerns with student growth, teachers often neglect their own growth. A journal provides you with the opportunity to be reflexive: to question assumptions, to consider theoretical issues, and to plan for the future.

Problem solving. When something is happening in the classroom that is troublesome or confusing, teachers can often clarify their thinking by writing about the problem. It could be that a student doesn't seem to be learning, that the class is losing interest in an activity, that there is a problem with behavior, or that you are frustrated. By reflecting on and writing why a child is not learning or a class is losing interest, you can more easily identify the factors contributing to the problem.

Catching a fleeting moment. There are many exciting moments in a classroom that are easily lost with time: an insight, a joke, a thoughtful question, a lively discussion. It is valuable to jot down these descriptions and quotes so that you might consider and expand on them at a later time.

What Else

1. Share selections from your journal with your students and invite them to respond to your perceptions.
2. During parent-teacher conferences, share language stories and your assessment of the child's progress.
3. Compare the classroom data collected in the journal and through other informal means with the results of mandated standardized tests or skills checklists. This comparison clearly demonstrates that reductionist measures reveal very little information about learners and can be inaccurate and misleading. It is often easy to demonstrate by observation of students in the processes of reading and writing that certain skills are mastered — worksheets and end-of-level tests are unnecessary when the teacher provides students with authentic experiences and is an informed observer. It is important for teachers to assert their professional expertise to administrators and parents.

Paul Crowley, Jefferson Junior High School, Columbia, Missouri

---

Kid-Watching Guides

Why

According to Yetta Goodman (1978), teachers should generate questions based on their own knowledge about language development and their knowledge of their students. The data can be used to focus the teacher's analysis of students' language development and to provide documentation of language learning. In addition, the data can inventory and describe opportunities students have for language learning.

Based on Goodman's ideas, the kid-watching guide in Figure 10-1 was developed as a starting point for observing a particular student at a particular time in a specific classroom. It served as one way for the teacher to become consciously aware of and to document a student's language development. It is offered here as a suggestion.

Who

All elementary students

How

Questions about language use in the classroom and in the student's environment, along with questions about the student's language development, suggest categories to be considered. Goodman states that teacher comments should include the quantity and quality of the student's oral and visual language, the student's interests, responses, and strategies, and the student's interactions in a variety of language-using settings.

Other categories spring from the kinds of language opportunities available to the student. Questions should be considered in light of current knowledge concerning language development; for example, Goodman's article is a contribution to current understanding, and it is strongly recommended reading for teachers who wish to use kid-watching strategies.

Kid-Watching Guide

Student's Name_____ Age_____

Grade_____ School_____

Teacher_____ Date_____

	Degree of Participation	Comments
	High _____ Low	

Oral Language

One-to-one
interactions

Small group
discussions

Listening

One-to-one
interactions

Small group
discussions

Large group
discussions

Reading

Sustained
silent
reading

Silent reading,
assigned

Silent reading,
self-selected

Oral reading

Oral reading,
rereading aloud
for a purpose

Functional reading
in the classroom
(directions, etc.)

Reading at home

Writing

Functional
writing

Journal writing

Writing in
answer to
invitations

Spelling

(Invented, functional,
standard)

Other Comments:

Figure 10–1. Sample kid-watching guide.

What Else

Goodman notes that teachers' questions should change as knowledge of language and students develops. Hence the kid-watching guides should change. Continued redevelopment of questions can finely adjust the focus of observation, facilitate personalization of language opportunities, suggest instructional changes, and provide ongoing documentation of change.

From time to time, the data recorded on the guide should be written in narrative form. The process of writing the narration involves the teacher in analyzing and evaluating the student's language development and learning opportunities. It thus generates a descriptive view of the student, the environment, and the teacher's current beliefs about language and how it is learned.

Work Cited

Goodman, Yetta. "Kid Watching: An Alternative to Testing." *National Elementary School Principals* 57, no. 4 (1978): 41–45.

Carole Sue Gile, University of Missouri–Columbia

Criteria for Measuring Growth in the Writing of Children

Why

To measure growth and development in students' writing

Who

All elementary students

How

The following criteria, adapted from Cramer (1978), can be used in evaluating students' writing:

1. *Thought.* Note the quality of thinking that underlies the ideas: How rich are the ideas? Are any unique? Do the ideas show any critical thinking? any logical thinking?
2. *Authenticity.* Is the writing sincere? Does it represent a genuine (or convincing) personal experience? Is it honest? Do you hear the "voice" of the writer? Is the reader able to participate in the writing and become involved? (Remember: writing is to be read. Children seldom relate their experiences to a reader insincerely, unless the circumstances of the teaching encourage it.)
3. *Power.* Is the language use effective, within the constraints of the child's current abilities and development? What are the evidences of language power — knowledge of reading a lot? irony? vocabulary development? use of invented spellings? (Remember: new language elements may be incorporated into students' oral language long before the elements will show up in their written work.)
4. *Growth.* Has the child improved? Is the child taking any risks? Is the child trying out any new language forms? (Remember: errors are by-products of growth.)
5. *Conventions.* Does the writer adhere to courtesies for the reader? Consider *effective* use of grammar, standards of usage, spelling, and other writing conventions. (Remember: sometimes fragments are more effective in contributing to the effect or mood of the writing than are complete sentences.)

Work Cited

Cramer, Ronald. "Evaluating Children's Writing." In *Writing, Reading, and Language Growth*, 82–103. Charles Merrill, 1978.

Ronald L. Cramer, Oakland University, Rochester, Michigan

Evaluation

Why

To promote steady growth in writing at each student's individual level

Who

Primary students; with adaptation, older students

How

An anecdotal record sheet can be made by dividing a sheet of paper into blocks and by labeling one block for each student. Keep the sheet handy throughout the day or week so that pertinent comments can be made when the occasion arises. A portion of one teacher's anecdotal record sheet is shown in Figure 10-2.

Jan	Ron	Kigi	Donna	Isaac	Annie
Spells with consonants	Spelled 10 words correctly today	Uses combinations of scribble, consonants, and invented spellings	Has just begun to word scribble	Scribbles with no communication	Published her first book today

Figure 10–2. Sample entries from one teacher's anecdotal record sheet.

Keep a manila work folder for each student, in which the student keeps pieces of writing currently being worked on and the daily diary. The front and back covers and the inside of the folders can be used for teacher and student comments on the student's writing growth. Students might want to record what they already know, what they want to write about, and what language skills they are working on, such as using letters in spelling. Teacher comments might pertain to general abilities, such as the student has directionality, the student has a concept of spaces, the student uses initial consonants. The comments boost students' morale and provide a measurement of writing progress to share with parents at parent-teacher conferences.

A more detailed evaluation of writing accomplishment is made in the Natural Writing Behavior Inventory shown in Figure 10-3. A similar form is kept for each child as a checklist of his or her progress in writing.

Gail Heald-Taylor, Waterloo Board of Education, Ontario, Canada

Setting Personal Goals for School and Home: Basis for Evaluation

Why

To provide an opportunity for students to set goals for improvements to be made at home and at school

Who

Middle and upper elementary students

How

At six-week intervals, the students and I list two or three school and home goals. I encourage them to begin affirmatively with a statement like "I will . . . ," and to stress specificity over generality by making a statement such as "I will write in my journal for at least fifteen minutes every day" rather than the more vague goal that "I will improve in writing."

Students read their goals aloud and make suggestions for writing more specific, attainable, and practical goals, such as the following:

1. I will improve in spelling by attempting to spell every word by myself before asking for help.
2. I will improve in writing by spending more time on revision.
3. I will make my bed every morning without being told.
4. I will improve my handwriting by rereading my written work to see that it is legible.

The class suggests helpful hints that might aid students in attaining their goals. (One student was reminded to floss by a happy-face sticker on the bathroom mirror.)

What Else

To pinpoint the necessary actions to take, older children could write out a plan or procedure for accomplishing their goals. Recording these goals in spiral notebooks gives students ready access so that they can read the goals periodically during the six-week period and can write about their progress in attaining the goals.

Natural Writing Behavior Inventory

Name: _____

	Date	Comments
Scribble Behavior The child: • Scribbles with no intended message. • Scribbles using vertical and horizontal movements. • Scribbles to communicate ("reads" the scribble). • Scribbles from left to right across the page. • Consistently scribbles horizontally. • Scribbles uniformly. • Uses a line of scribble to represent a thought (sentence). • Uses a scribble to represent each word, leaving spaces between scribbles. • Makes the scribble match the length of word. • "Reads" the scribble story by rote, maintaining a consistent oral text.		
Consonant Spelling The child: • Uses random letters in writing (no intended communication). • Uses letters and scribble to communicate (no sound-symbol correspondence). • Uses letters to communicate (no sound-symbol correspondence). • Uses letters and sound-symbol correspondence (initial consonant spelling). • Uses letter name spelling. • Uses initial consonant spelling and scribble. • Uses initial and final consonant spelling. • Uses combinations of scribble and consonant spellings.		
Invented Spellings The child: • Uses invented spellings with initial and final consonants and vowels. • Uses known words in stories. • Begins to make transition from invented spelling to standard spelling. • Begins to use punctuation at end of lines (not necessarily at end of a sentence). • Writes stories up to three sentences long on one topic. • Develops an awareness of capital letters for the word *I* and children's names.		
Early Transitional Behaviors The child: • Uses more invented spellings than standard spellings. • Uses many vowels in invented spellings. • Writes stories consisting of five or more sentences on one topic. • Sequences two or more events in stories. • Uses punctuation at end of lines. • Occasionally uses punctuation at end of sentence. • Uses capital letters for the word *I* and names.		

	Date	Comments
Later Transitional Spelling The child: • Begins to make transition from invented spellings to standard spellings. • Uses equal number of invented spellings as standard spellings. • Writes stories longer than five sentences on one topic. • Uses punctuation at end of sentences with consistency.		
Stabilization of Standard Spelling The child: • Uses more correct spellings than invented spellings. • Writes stories longer than five sentences. • Writes stories longer than five sentences, and the sentences are on one topic. • Can sequence three or more events. • Begins to use capital letters at beginning of sentences.		
Growth in Mechanics The child: • Uses more correct spellings than invented spellings. • Uses capital letters at beginning of sentences consistently. • Uses punctuation in addition to the period (? ! " "). • Uses periods consistently. • Uses quotations in stories, but doesn't use marks accurately. • Begins to use quotation marks with some accuracy.		
Imaginative and Fantasy Stage The child: • Begins to use imagination in story writing. • Begins to use quotation marks appropriately. • Develops an awareness of a variety of purposes for writing (posters, labels, lists, letters, research, poetry).		
Writes for a Variety of Purposes The child: • Writes interesting stories. • Consistently uses punctuation accurately. • Consistently uses capitals accurately. • Writes for a variety of purposes (poetry, research, invitations, etc.).		

Figure 10–3. Natural Writing Behavior Inventory.

At the end of the six weeks, students evaluate their goals, writing whether or not they reached their goals and why or why not. I begin the group discussion by discussing my accomplished or unaccomplished goals. I collect the written goals and evaluations and write a positive note to each child. Feelings of accomplishment when goals are attained enhance children's self-worth.

A list of each student's goals goes home in the envelope with the report card so that parents know what priorities their children have set for school and for home. Setting and reaching goals gives children a tangible lesson dealing with responsibility, discipline, and self-worth.

Jo Beth Bellamy, Conroe ISD, Sally K. Ride Elementary, Woodlands, Texas

Reader-Selected Miscues

Why

1. To put the reader in control of the reading task, so that the reader and the author are allowed their own transaction without interruptions from outsiders
2. To show students that everyone, even proficient readers, makes miscues
3. To demonstrate to students that some miscues move the reader right along in the text while others disrupt meaning
4. To provide the teacher with trustworthy information about a student's reading

Who

Middle and upper elementary students who need to realize that the flow of reading should not be stopped in order to "get every word," but rather, that efficient reading involves constructing meaning by using background information provided by the reader and on-the-page information provided by the author

How

Before silent reading time, give each student several 2″ × 8″ bookmarks. Ask the students to read as usual but to stop momentarily when they encounter any difficulty in reading. They are to place a bookmark at the trouble spot and then to continue reading.

A few minutes before the end of the reading time, ask the students to examine their miscues and to select three that caused problems in the long run of the reading; that is, miscues that caused them to lose the meaning of the text or to be distracted from the reading. Ask the students to write on each bookmark one of the sentences that contained a miscue and to underline the problem. They add their names to the bookmarks as well.

Collect the bookmarks and categorize the miscues. Study the miscues carefully to determine the cause of the problem, such as overuse of phonics, lack of concepts, failure to attend to grammatical information, failure to make inferences, or meager background information.

Group together children who are making similar miscues, and briefly discuss the problems they have encountered. Children actually enjoy these short talks about the reading process, and with the teacher's help, they begin to develop more proficient and efficient strategies for constructing meaning.

What Else

Older readers may want to keep a log of their miscues and to discuss the logs periodically with the teacher or in small groups.

Dorothy J. Watson, University of Missouri–Columbia

Shared Evaluation

Why

To create an opportunity for students to share the valuable responsibility of evaluating their work

Who

With adaptation, all elementary students

How

Conduct a survey with students to determine their attitudes concerning grade reports. This can be in the form of a written questionnaire, individual interviews, or general class discussion. Some of the following questions may be asked:

What are your feelings about grade reports?

Are you satisfied with the grades you receive?

Is there anything you would like to change?

What do you think should be included in deciding your grades?

After discussing students' initial responses, focus on the last question and ask students to brainstorm ideas about determining their grades. Explain that you would like them to help you design a self-evaluation form that they could use in monitoring their own progress.

Next, divide students into groups of three. One student is to be the leader or organizer, the second is to be the recorder, and the third is to be the reporter. Each group meets to discuss students' ideas for the self-evaluation form, announces its recommendations to the entire class, and prepares a written report. In a class of older students, a student editorial committee might help you select the items for the self-evaluation form.

Students use the form to assess their progress in reading and writing, to grade particular assignments, and to record what they have learned. After a trial period, students might suggest some revisions in the evaluation form.

The weekly evaluation form in Figure 10–4 was developed by students in my reading classes. They decided to include room on the form for assessing work attempted but not yet completed after one student suggested that he should be able to evaluate unfinished projects as well as finished ones.

What Else

The evaluation form may be changed to fit specific needs. In a primary classroom, the form can include

Self-Evaluation

Name _____ Grade

Sustained Silent Reading _____

Writing Activities _____

Content-Area Reading _____

Special Assignments _____

Work Attempted _____

Work Completed _____

This week I learned:

Figure 10–4. Sample self-evaluation form.

specific curricula components or very general evaluation information. Young children can respond by illustrating something they learned that was important to them. The form is not as important as the concept that we *share* in evaluation. Students have a sense of what they know about their successes and challenges. The shared experience can be valuable.

Shirley R. Crenshaw, Webster University, St. Louis, Missouri

BIBLIOGRAPHY

wans a pond tym ther
was a prensas wan bay
she got last ni the wods

Andrew

Bibliography

Introduction

Why

To provide a resource for those interested in implementing or expanding a literature-based whole language program

Who

Teachers, administrators, curriculum planners, parents, or anyone interested in locating reading materials that appeal to young readers

How

This bibliography is divided into several categories, according to the type of book and the age of reader. Each section contains an alphabetical listing of recommended authors and their works. Some of the books have been recommended in particular activities, while others would be appropriate alternatives. The rationales and methods for using these materials have been discussed previously in corresponding sections. Whenever possible, the most recent version of a book is listed. If numerous editions are available, no publisher is indicated. When two publishers are listed, the first name is the original publisher, the second is the current distributor.

There are several considerations we wish to note. The category titles were chosen to guide the teacher in selecting books for a particular activity or books in a particular genre. Books, like children, often defy specific categorization. A sing-along book might also be used for a read-aloud activity, while a wordless book may inspire language play. Feel free to pick and choose. Secondly, while award-winning books have been included within the categories, we have not placed them in a special section nor identified the awards. Local libraries can furnish this information. Lastly, booklists are not set in stone. New authors and new books by old authors arrive on the scene every day. Each person must have a plan for "keeping in touch" with new literature. Publishers' lists, bookstores, professional journals, libraries, other teachers, and students themselves are valuable sources of this information.

We welcome you to sample the books listed on the pages to come and to share your favorites with your students.

Kay Clapp, Northeast Missouri State University, Kirksville, and Donna L. Fisher, Columbia, Missouri

Read-Aloud Books

Primary Students

Aardema, Verna. *Why Mosquitoes Buzz in People's Ears: A West African Tale.* Dial Books, 1978.

Alexander, Martha. *Three Magic Flip Books (The Magic Hat; The Magic Picture; The Magic Box).* Dial Books, 1984.

Allard, Harry. *Miss Nelson Is Missing.* Scholastic, 1978.

———. *The Stupids Step Out.* Houghton Mifflin, 1974.

Barrett, Ron. *Hi-Yo Fido!* Crown, 1984.

Birrer, Cynthia, and William Birrer. *The Shoemaker and the Elves.* Lothrop, Lee and Shepard, 1983.

Collodi, Carlo. *The Adventures of Pinocchio: Tale of a Puppet.* Trans. by M. L. Rosenthal. Lothrop, Lee and Shepard, 1983.

de Paola, Tomie. *Strega Nona.* Prentice-Hall, 1975.

Domanska, Janina. *If All the Seas Were One Sea.* Macmillan. 1971.

Fisher, Robert, ed. *Ghosts Galore: Haunting Verse.* Faber and Faber, 1986.

Gág, Wanda. *Millions of Cats.* Coward, McCann and Geoghegan/Putnam, 1977.

Heide, Florence Parry. *The Shrinking of Treehorn.* Holiday House, 1971.

Hoban, Russell. *Bedtime for Frances.* Harper and Row, 1976.

Hogrogian, Nonny. *One Fine Day.* Macmillan, 1971.

Kellogg, Steven. *The Island of the Skog.* Dial Books, 1976.

———. *Pinkerton, Behave!* Dial Books, 1982.

———. *A Rose for Pinkerton.* Dial Books, 1984.

Kennedy, Richard. *The Contests at Cowlick.* Little, Brown, 1975.

Larrick, Nancy, comp. *When the Dark Comes Dancing: A Bedtime Poetry Book.* Philomel/Putnam, 1983.

Lobel, Arnold. *Frog and Toad Are Friends.* Harper and Row, 1985. (Also see other books in the series)

Lowry, Lois. *The One Hundredth Thing about Caroline.* Dell, 1985.

Lunn, Janet. *The Root Cellar.* Penguin, 1985.

McCloskey, Robert. *Make Way For Ducklings.* Penguin, 1976.

Michels, Barbara, and Bettye White. *Apples on a Stick: The Folklore of Black Children.* Coward, McCann and Geoghegan/Putnam, 1983. (Poetry)

Mosel, Arlene. *The Funny Little Woman.* Dutton, 1972.

———. *Tikki Tikki Tembo.* Scholastic, 1984.

Ness, Evaline. *Sam, Bangs, and Moonshine.* Henry Holt, 1966.

Parish, Peggy. *Amelia Bedelia.* Harper and Row, 1983. (Also see other books in the series)

Pinkwater, Jill. *The Cloud Horse.* Lothrop, Lee and Shepard, 1983.

Potter, Beatrix. *The Tale of Peter Rabbit.*

Robison, Deborah. *Bye-Bye, Old Buddy.* Houghton Mifflin, 1983.

Ross, Tony. *I'm Coming to Get You!* Dial Books, 1984.

Sadler, Marilyn. *Alistair in Outer Space.* Prentice-Hall, 1984.

Sendak, Maurice. *Where the Wild Things Are.* Harper and Row, 1984.

Steig, William. *Amos and Boris.* Penguin, 1977.

———. *Doctor De Soto.* Scholastic, 1984.

———. *Sylvester and the Magic Pebble.* Simon and Schuster, 1969.

Thomson, Pat. *Rhymes around the Day.* Lothrop, Lee and Shepard, 1983.

Viorst, Judith. *Alexander and the Terrible, Horrible, No Good, Very Bad Day.* Atheneum/Macmillan, 1976.

———. *Alexander Who Used to Be Rich Last Sunday.* Atheneum/Macmillan, 1980.

———. *The Tenth Good Thing about Barney.* Atheneum/Macmillan, 1975.

Waber, Bernard. *The House on East 88th Street.* Houghton Mifflin, 1975.

———. *Ira Sleeps Over.* Houghton Mifflin, 1975.

Williams, Margery. *The Velveteen Rabbit.*

Zemach, Harve. *The Judge: An Untrue Tale.* Farrar, Straus and Giroux, 1969.

Zemach, Margot. *The Little Red Hen: An Old Story.* Farrar, Straus and Giroux, 1983.

Middle Elementary Students

Babbit, Natalie. *The Devil's Storybook.* Farrar, Straus and Giroux, 1974.

Blume, Judy. *Freckle Juice.* Dell, 1986.

Bulla, Clyde Robert. *Dexter.* Crowell, 1973.

Cleary, Beverly. *Ramona the Pest.* Dell, 1982.

Dahl, Roald. *Danny: The Champion of the World.* Bantam, 1978.

———. *The Magic Finger.* Harper and Row, 1966.

Erickson, Russell. *A Toad for Tuesday.* Lothrop, Lee and Shepard, 1974. (Also see other books in the series)

Fleischman, Paul. *The Half-a-Moon Inn.* Harper and Row, 1980.

Grahame, Kenneth. *The Reluctant Dragon.* Henry Holt, 1983.

Hicks, Clifford. *Peter Potts.* Avon, 1979.

Kennedy, Richard. *Inside my Feet: The Story of a Giant.* Harper and Row, 1979.

Miles, Miska. *Annie and the Old One.* Little, Brown, 1971.

Peterson, John. *The Littles.* Scholastic, 1986. (Also see other books in the series)

Richler, Mordecai. *Jacob Two-Two Meets the Hooded Fang.* Bantam, 1977.

Robinson, Barbara. *The Best Christmas Pageant Ever.* Avon, 1986.

Smith, Doris B. *A Taste of Blackberries.* Scholastic, 1976.

Smith, Robert Kimmel. *Chocolate Fever.* Dell, 1978.

Van Allsburg, Chris. *Jumanji.* Houghton Mifflin, 1981.

Upper Elementary Students

Aesop. *Aesop's Fables.*

Alcott, Louisa May. *Little Women.*

Andersen, Hans Christian. *The Fir Tree.*

Arbuthnot, May Hill, ed. *Time for Fairy Tales, Old and New.* Scott, Foresman, 1952.

Armstrong, William H. *Sounder.* Harper and Row, 1972.

Babbit, Natalie. *The Search for Delicious.* Avon, 1974.

———. *Tuck Everlasting.* Farrar, Straus and Giroux, 1975.

Bellairs, John. *The House with a Clock in Its Walls.* Dell, 1974.

Brink, Carol Ryrie. *Caddie Woodlawn,* rev. ed. Macmillan, 1970.

Burnett, Frances Hodgson. *The Secret Garden.*

Burnford, Sheila. *The Incredible Journey.* Bantam, 1967.

Byars, Betsy. *The 18th Emergency.* Penguin, 1981.

———. *The Midnight Fox.* Penguin, 1981.

Carroll, Lewis. *Alice's Adventures in Wonderland.*

———. *Through the Looking Glass.*

Cleary, Beverly. *Dear Mr. Henshaw.* Dell, 1984.

Dahl, Roald. *Charlie and the Chocolate Factory.* Bantam, 1986.

———. *Charlie and the Great Glass Elevator.* Bantam, 1977.

———. *James and the Giant Peach.* Penguin, 1983.

Dickens, Charles. *A Christmas Carol.*

Dodge, Mary Mapes. *Hans Brinker; Or, The Silver Skates.*

Faber, Doris. *Robert Frost, America's Poet.* Prentice-Hall, 1964.

Fitzgerald, John D. *The Great Brain.* Dell, 1971.

Gates, Doris. *Blue Willow.* Penguin, 1976.

George, Jean. *My Side of the Mountain.* Dutton, 1975.

Gipson, Fred. *Old Yeller.* Harper and Row, 1956.

Grahame, Kenneth. *The Wind in the Willows.*

Hague, Kathleen, and Michael Hague, retold by. *East of the Sun and West of the Moon.* Harper and Row, 1980.

Holling, Holling C. *Paddle-to-the-Sea.* Houghton Mifflin, 1941.

Hunt, Irene. *Across Five Aprils.* Ace, 1984.

Juster, Norton. *The Phantom Tollbooth.* Random House, 1961.

Knight, Eric. *Lassie, Come Home.*

Konigsburg, E. L. *Jennifer, Hecate, Macbeth, William McKinley and Me, Elizabeth.* Dell, 1986.

Langton, Jane. *The Fledgling.* Harper and Row, 1981.

Lawson, Robert. *Ben and Me.* Dell, 1973.

———. *Rabbit Hill.* Penguin, 1977.

L'Engle, Madeline. *A Wrinkle in Time.* Dell, 1986.

Lewis, C. S. *The Lion, the Witch, and the Wardrobe.* Macmillan, 1986.

Lindgren, Astrid. *Pippi Longstocking.*

Martin, Bill, Jr. *Sounds Jubilee.* N.d.

———. *Sounds of a Distant Drummer.* N.d.

———. *Sounds of a Hunter.* N.d.

———. *Sounds of Mystery.* N.d.

Norton, Mary. *The Borrowers.* Harcourt Brace Jovanovich, 1986.

O'Brien, Robert C. *Mrs. Frisby and the Rats of Nimh.* Macmillan, 1986.

O'Dell, Scott. *Island of the Blue Dolphins.* Dell, 1987.

———. *Sing Down the Moon.* Houghton Mifflin, 1970.

Paterson, Katherine. *Bridge to Terabithia.* Avon, 1979.

Peck, Robert Newton. *Soup in the Saddle.* Knopf, 1983.

Pene du Bois, William. *The Twenty-One Balloons.* Viking, 1947.

Rawls, Wilson. *Summer of the Monkeys.* Doubleday, 1977.

———. *Where the Red Fern Grows.* Doubleday, 1961.

Saint-Exupery, Antoine de. *The Little Prince.* Harcourt Brace Jovanovich, 1982.

Selden, George. *The Cricket in Times Square.* Dell, 1970.

Silverstein, Shel. *The Giving Tree.* Harper and Row, 1964.

———. *Lafcadio: The Lion Who Shot Back.* Harper and Row, 1963.

———. *A Light in the Attic.* Harper and Row, 1981.

———. *Where the Sidewalk Ends.* Harper and Row, 1974.

Singer, Isaac Bashevis. *Zlateh the Goat and Other Stories.* Harper and Row, 1984.

Spyri, Johanna. *Heidi.*

Steig, William. *Abel's Island.* Farrar, Straus and Giroux, 1976.

Stevenson, Robert Lewis. *Treasure Island.*

Taylor, Theodore. *The Trouble with Tuck.* Avon, 1983.

Twain, Mark. *The Adventures of Tom Sawyer.*

Voight, Cynthia. *The Callender Papers.* Atheneum/Macmillan, 1983.

———. *Dicey's Song.* Atheneum/Macmillan, 1982.

White, E. B. *Charlotte's Web.* Harper and Row, 1952.

———. *Stuart Little.* Harper and Row, 1945.

Wilder, Laura Ingalls. *Little House on the Prairie.* (Also see other books in the series)

Poetry

Cassedy, Sylvia. *Behind the Attic Wall.* Avon, 1985.

Cole, William, ed. *Beastly Boys and Ghastly Girls.* Collins-World, 1964.

Covernton, Jane, and Craig Smith. *Putrid Poems.* Omnibus Books, n.d.

de Regniers, Beatrice Schenk. *Poems Children Will Sit Still For.* Scholastic, 1979.

Downie, Mary Alice, and Barbara Robertson. *The New Wind Has Wings: Poems from Canada.* Oxford University Press, 1984.

Fleischman, Paul. *Path of the Pale Horse.* Harper and Row, 1983.

Hoban, Russell. *Egg Thoughts and Other Frances Songs.* Harper and Row, 1972.

Hopkins, Lee Bennett, ed. *Moments: Poems about the Seasons.* Harcourt Brace Jovanovich, 1980.

————. *Potato Chips and a Slice of Moon.* Scholastic, 1976.

————. *Time to Shout: Poems for You.* Scholastic, 1973.

Hopkins, Lee Bennett, and Misha Arenstein. *Faces and Places: Poems for You.* Scholastic, 1971.

Hughes, Monica. *The Isis Pedlar.* Atheneum/Macmillan, 1983.

Kuskin, Karla. *Dogs and Dragons, Trees and Dreams: A Collection of Poems.* Harper and Row, 1980.

Lee, Dennis. *Alligator Pie.* Houghton Mifflin, 1975.

————. *Garbage Delight.* Houghton Mifflin, 1978.

McGovern, Ann. *The Arrow Book of Poetry.* Scholastic, 1965.

Mason, Anne. *The Dancing Meteorite.* Harper and Row, 1984.

Merriam, Eve. *Out Loud.* Atheneum, 1973.

O'Neill, Mary. *Hailstones and Halibut Bones.* Doubleday, 1961.

Payne, Bernal C., Jr. *It's about Time.* Macmillan, 1984.

Prelutsky, Jack. *Nightmares: Poems to Trouble Your Sleep.* Greenwillow, 1976.

————. *Rainy Rainy Saturday.* Greenwillow, 1980.

————. *Rolling Harvey down the Hill.* Greenwillow, 1980.

Silverstein, Shel. *A Light in the Attic.* Harper and Row, 1981.

————. *Where the Sidewalk Ends.* Harper and Row, 1974.

Sleator, William. *Interstellar Pig.* Bantam, 1986.

Spinelli, Jerry. *Who Put That Hair in My Toothbrush?* Dell, 1986.

Viorst, Judith. *If I Were in Charge of the World and Other Worries.* Atheneum/Macmillan, 1981.

Wilner, Isabel. *The Poetry Troupe: Poems to Read Aloud.* Scribner, 1977.

Kay Clapp, Northeast Missouri State University, Kirksville, and Donna L. Fisher, Columbia, Missouri

Wordless Books

Alexander, Martha. *Bobo's Dream.* Dial Books, 1970.

————. *Out, Out, Out.* Dial Books, 1968.

Amoss, Berthe. *By the Sea.* Parents Magazine Press, 1969.

Anderson, Laurie. *The Package.* Bobbs-Merrill, 1971.

Angel, Marie. *The Ark.* Harper and Row, 1973.

Anno, Mitsumasa. *Anno's Animals.* Philomel, 1979.

————. *Anno's Britain.* Philomel, 1982.

————. *Anno's Counting Book.* Harper and Row, 1986.

————. *Anno's Italy.* Philomel, 1984.

————. *Anno's Journey.* Philomel, 1981.

————. *Dr. Anno's Magical Midnight Circus.* Weatherhill, 1972.

————. *Topsy-Turvies: Pictures to Stretch the Imagination.* Weatherhill, 1970.

Ardizzone, Edward. *The Wrong Side of the Bed.* Doubleday, 1970.

Arnosky, Jim. *Mouse Numbers and Letters.* Harcourt Brace Jovanovich, 1982.

————. *Mudtime and More: Nathaniel Stories.* Addison-Wesley, 1979.

Aruego, Jose. *Look What I Can Do.* Scribner, 1971.

Asch, Frank. *The Blue Balloon.* McGraw-Hill, 1971.

————. *In the Eye of the Teddy.* Harper and Row, 1973.

Bakken, Harald. *The Special String.* Prentice-Hall, 1982.

Bang, Molly. *The Grey Lady and the Strawberry Snatcher.* Four Winds/Macmillan, 1980.

Barner, Bob. *The Elephant's Visit.* Atlantic Monthly/Little, Brown, 1975.

Barton, Byron. *Elephant.* Houghton Mifflin, 1971.

————. *Where's Al?* Houghton Mifflin, 1972.

Baum, Willi. *Birds of a Feather.* Addison-Wesley, 1969.

Bollinger-Savelli, Antonella. *The Knitted Cat.* Macmillan, 1972.

Briggs, Raymond. *The Snowman.* Random House, 1986.

Brinckloe, Julie. *The Spider Web.* Doubleday, 1974.

Bruna, Dick. *Miffy's Dream.* Price, Stern, Sloan, 1984.

Burton, Marilee R. *The Elephant's Nest: Four Wordless Stories.* Harper and Row, 1979.

Carle, Eric. *Do You Want to Be My Friend?* Harper and Row, 1987.

————. *I See a Song.* Crowell, 1973.

————. *My Very First Book of Colors.* Crowell, 1985.

————. *My Very First Book of Shapes.* Crowell, 1985.

————. *1 2 3 to the Zoo.* World, 1968.

————. *A Very Long Tail: A Folding Book.* Crowell, 1972.

————. *A Very Long Train: A Folding Book.* Crowell, 1977.

Carrick, Donald. *Drip Drop.* Macmillan, 1973.

Carroll, Ruth. *The Chimp and the Clown.* Walck, 1968.

————. *The Dolphin and the Mermaid.* Walck, 1974.

————. *Rolling Downhill.* Walck, 1973.

————. *What Whiskers Did.* Walck, 1965.

————. *The Witch Kitten.* Walck, 1973.

Carroll, Ruth, and Latrobe Carroll. *The Christmas Kitten.* Walck, 1973.

Charlip, Remy, and Jerry Joyner. *Thirteen.* Four Winds, 1985.

Crews, Donald. *Truck.* Penguin, 1985.

Cristini, Ermanno, and Luigi Puricelli. *In My Garden.* Picture Book Studio USA, 1985.

de Groat, Diane. *Alligator's Toothache.* Crown, 1977.

de Paola, Tomie. *Flicks.* Harcourt Brace Jovanovich, 1979.

———. *The Hunter and the Animals.* Holiday House, 1981.

———. *Pancakes for Breakfast.* Harcourt Brace Jovanovich, 1978.

Eastman, Philip D. *Go, Dog, Go.* Beginner Books, 1961.

Elzbieta. *Little Mops and the Butterfly.* Doubleday, 1974.

———. *Little Mops and the Moon.* Doubleday, 1974.

———. *Little Mops at the Seashore.* Doubleday, 1974.

Emberley, Ed. *A Birthday Wish.* Little, Brown, 1977.

Ets, Marie Hall. *Talking without Words.* Viking, 1968.

Fromm, Lilo. *Muffel and Plums.* Macmillan, 1973.

Fuchs, Erich. *Journey to the Moon.* Delacorte, 1970.

Gilbert, Elliott. *A Cat Story, Told in Pictures.* Henry Holt, 1963.

Goodall, John S. *The Adventures of Paddy Pork.* Harcourt Brace Jovanovich, 1968.

———. *The Ballooning Adventures of Paddy Pork.* Harcourt Brace Jovanovich, 1969.

———. *Creepy Castle.* Atheneum, 1975.

———. *An Edwardian Christmas.* Atheneum/Macmillan, 1978.

———. *An Edwardian Summer.* Atheneum, 1976.

———. *Jacko.* Harcourt Brace Jovanovich, 1984.

———. *The Midnight Adventures of Kelly, Dot, and Esmeralda.* Atheneum/Macmillan, 1973.

———. *Naughty Nancy.* Atheneum/Macmillan, 1975.

———. *Paddy Pork — Odd Jobs.* Atheneum/Macmillan, 1983.

———. *Paddy Pork's Holiday.* Atheneum/Macmillan, 1976.

———. *Paddy's Evening Out.* Atheneum/Macmillan, 1973.

———. *Paddy's New Hat.* Atheneum, 1980.

———. *Shrewbettina's Birthday.* Harcourt Brace Jovanovich, 1983.

———. *The Story of an English Village.* Atheneum/Macmillan, 1979.

———. *The Surprise Picnic.* Atheneum, 1977.

Hamberger, John. *The Lazy Dog.* Scholastic, 1973.

Hartelius, Margaret A. *A Sleepless Day.* Scholastic, 1975.

———. *The Birthday Trombone.* Doubleday, 1977.

———. *The Chicken's Child.* Scholastic, 1977.

Heller, Linda. *Lily at the Table.* Macmillan, 1979.

Hoban, Tana. *Big Ones, Little Ones.* Greenwillow, 1976.

———. *Circles, Triangles and Squares.* Macmillan, 1974.

———. *Count and See.* Macmillan, 1972.

———. *Dig, Drill, Dump, Fill.* Greenwillow, 1975.

———. *Look Again!* Macmillan, 1971.

———. *Over, Under and Through and Other Spatial Concepts.* Macmillan, 1973.

———. *Push Pull, Empty Full: A Book of Opposites.* Macmillan, 1972.

———. *Shapes and Things.* Macmillan, 1970.

Hoest, William. *A Taste of Carrot.* Atheneum, 1974.

Hogrogian, Nonny. *Apples.* Macmillan, 1972.

Hughes, Shirley. *Up and Up.* Lothrop, Lee and Shepard, 1986.

Hutchins, Pat. *Changes, Changes.* Macmillan, 1971.

———. *Rosie's Walk.* Macmillan, 1968.

Keats, Ezra Jack. *Kitten for a Day.* Four Winds/Macmillan, 1974.

———. *Pssst! Doggie.* Watts, 1973.

———. *Skates.* Watts, 1973.

Kent, Jack. *The Egg Book.* Macmillan, 1975.

Kilbourne, Frances. *Overnight Adventure.* Women's Writing Press, 1977.

Knobler, Susan. *The Tadpole and the Frog.* Harvey House, 1974.

Kojima, Naomi. *The Flying Grandmother.* Harper and Row, 1981.

Krahn, Fernando. *April Fools.* Dutton, 1974.

———. *Arthur's Adventure in the Abandoned House.* Dutton, 1981.

———. *The Biggest Christmas Tree on Earth.* Atlantic Monthly, 1978.

———. *Catch the Cat!* Dutton, 1978.

———. *The Creepy Thing.* Paradox, 1982.

———. *A Flying Saucer Full of Spaghetti.* Dutton, 1970.

———. *A Funny Friend from Heaven.* Lippincott, 1977.

———. *The Great Ape.* Viking, 1978.

———. *Here Comes Alex Pumpernickel.* Atlantic Monthly/Little, Brown, 1981.

———. *How Santa Claus Had a Long and Difficult Journey Delivering His Presents.* Delacorte 1977.

———. *Little Love Story.* Lippincott, 1976.

———. *The Mystery of the Giant's Footprints.* Dutton, 1977.

———. *Robot-Bot-Bot.* Dutton, 1979.

———. *Sebastian and the Mushroom.* Delacorte, 1976.

———. *The Secret in the Dungeon.* Houghton Mifflin, 1983.

———. *The Self-Made Snowman.* Lippincott, 1974.

———. *Sleep Tight, Alex Pumpernickel.* Atlantic Monthly/Little, Brown, 1982.

———. *Who's Seen the Scissors?* Dutton, 1975.

Lisker, Sonia O. *The Attic Witch.* Four Winds, 1973.

———. *Lost.* Harcourt Brace Jovanovich, 1975.

Lustig, Loretta. *The Pop-Up Book of Trucks.* Random House, 1974.

McCully, Emily Arnold. *Picnic.* Harper and Row, 1984.

McPhail, David M. *Oh No Go.* Atlantic Monthly/Little, Brown, 1973.

McTrusty, Ron. *Dandelion Year.* Harvey House, 1974.

Mari, Iela. *Eat and Be Eaten.* Barrons, n.d.

Mari, Iela, and Enzo Mari. *The Apple and the Moth.* Pantheon, 1970.

———. *The Chicken and the Egg.* Pantheon, 1970.

Mayer, Mercer. *A Boy, a Dog, and a Frog.* Dial Books, 1967.

———. *Ah-Choo.* Dial Books, 1976.

———. *Bubble Bubble.* Four Winds/Macmillan, 1980.

———. *Frog Goes to Dinner.* Dial Books, 1977.

———. *Frog on His Own.* Dial Books, 1980.

———. *Frog, Where Are You?* Dial Books, 1980.

———. *The Great Cat Chase.* Four Winds/Scholastic, 1974.

———. *Hiccup.* Dial Books, 1978.

———. *Oops.* Dial Books, 1978.

———. *Two Moral Tales.* Four Winds/Scholastic, 1974.

———. *Two More Moral Tales.* Four Winds/Scholastic, 1974.

Meyer, Renate. *Hide-and-Seek.* Bradbury, 1972.

Mordillo, Guillermo. *The Damp and Daffy Doings of a Daring Pirate Ship.* Quist, 1971.

Morris, Terry Neil. *Good Night, Dear Monster!* Knopf, 1980.

———. *Lucky Puppy, Lucky Boy.* Knopf, 1980.

Oakley, Graham. *Graham Oakley's Magical Changes.* Atheneum/Macmillan, 1980.

Olschewski, Alfred. *Winterbird.* Houghton Mifflin, 1969.

Ormerod, Jan. *Moonlight.* Penguin, 1984.

———. *Sunshine.* Penguin, 1984.

Remington, Barbara. *Boat.* Doubleday, 1975.

Richter, Mischa. *Quack?* Harper and Row, 1978.

Ringi, Kjell. *The Magic Stick.* Harper and Row, 1968.

———. *The Winner.* Harper and Row, 1969.

Rockwell, Anne F. *Albert B. Cub and Zebra: An Alphabet Storybook.* Crowell, 1977.

Ross, Pat. *Hi Fly.* Crown, 1974.

Schneider, Herman, and Nina Schneider. *Science Fun for You in a Minute or Two: Quick Science Experiments You Can Do.* McGraw-Hill, 1975.

Scott, Foresman Reading Systems. *The Baby Monkey.* Scott, Foresman, n.d. (Reading Unlimited Program, Level Three)

———. *The Man and the Donkey.* Scott, Foresman, n.d. (Reading Unlimited Program, Level Five)

Shimin, Symeon. *A Special Birthday.* McGraw-Hill, 1976.

Simmons, Ellie. *Family.* McKay, 1970.

Spier, Peter. *Noah's Ark.* Doubleday, 1981.

———. *Peter Spier's Rain.* Doubleday, 1982.

Turkle, Brinton. *Deep in the Forest.* Dutton, 1976.

Ueno, Noriko. *Elephant Buttons.* Harper and Row, 1973.

Wagner, Justin. *The Bus Ride.* Scott, Foresman, 1976. (Reading Unlimited Program, Level Two)

Ward, Lynd Kendall. *The Silver Pony: A Story in Pictures.* Houghton Mifflin, 1973.

Wezel, Peter. *The Good Bird.* Harper and Row, 1966.

Winter, Paula. *The Bear and the Fly.* Crown, 1976.

———. *Sir Andrew.* Crown, 1980.

Kay Clapp, Northeast Missouri State University, Kirksville, and Donna L. Fisher, Columbia, Missouri

Extending Literature: Reading Leading to Writing

Alain. *One, Two, Three, Going to Sea.* Scholastic, 1969.

Alexander, Martha. *Nobody Asked Me If I Wanted a Baby Sister.* Dial Books, 1977.

———. *When the New Baby Comes, I'm Moving Out.* Dial Books, 1981.

Aliki. *Go Tell Aunt Rhody.* Macmillan, 1986.

———. *Hush Little Baby.* Prentice-Hall, 1968.

———. *My Five Senses.* Crowell, 1962.

Allinson, Beverly. *Mitzi's Magic Garden.* Garrard, 1971.

Asbjornsen, Peter C., and Jorgen Moe; ed. by Marcia Brown. *The Three Billy Goats Gruff.* Harcourt, Brace and World, 1957.

Asch, Frank. *Monkey Face.* Parents Magazine Press, 1977.

———. *Turtle Tale.* Dial Books, 1980.

Balian, Lorna. *The Aminal.* Abingdon, 1972.

———. *Where in the World Is Henry?* Bradbury, 1972.

Banchek, Linda. *Snake In, Snake Out.* Crowell, 1978.

Barchas, Sarah. *I Was Walking down the Road.* Scholastic, 1976.

———. *Janie and the Giant.* Scholastic, 1978.

Barrett, Judith. *Animals Should Definitely Not Wear Clothing.* Atheneum/Macmillan, 1980.

Barton, Byron. *Buzz, Buzz, Buzz.* Penguin, 1979.

Baum, Arline, and Joseph Baum. *One Bright Monday Morning.* Random House, 1962.

Becker, John. *Seven Little Rabbits.* Scholastic, 1985.

Beckman, Per, and Kaj Beckman. *Lisa Cannot Sleep.* Watts, 1969.

Bellah, Melanie. *A First Book of Sounds.* Golden Press, 1963.

Benchley, Nathaniel. *The Strange Disappearance of Arthur Cluck.* Harper and Row, 1979.

———. *Red Fox and His Canoe.* Harper and Row, 1985.

Berenstain, Stan, and Jan Berenstain. *The Berenstain Bears and the Spooky Old Tree.* Random House, 1978.

Bishop, Claire H. *The Five Chinese Brothers.* Coward/Putnam, 1938.

———. *Twenty-Two Bears.* Viking, 1964.

Blance, Ellen, et al. *Monster Books,* Sets I and II. Bowmar, Noble, 1973.

Blegvad, Eric. *The Three Little Pigs.* Atheneum, 1980.

Brand, Oscar. *When I First Came to This Land.* Putnam, 1974.

Brandenberg, Franz. *I Once Knew a Man.* Macmillan, 1970.

———. *Nice New Neighbors.* Greenwillow, 1977.

———. *What Can You Make of It?* Greenwillow, 1977.

Bridwell, Norman. *Clifford, The Big Red Dog.* Scholastic, 1985. (Also see other books in the series)

———. *Crazy Zoo.* Scholastic, 1972.

———. *Kangaroo Stew.* Scholastic, 1979.

———. *A Tiny Family.* Scholastic, 1968.

Brooke, Leslie. *Johnny Crow's Garden.* Warne, 1986.

Brown, Margaret Wise. *The Dead Bird.* Addison-Wesley, 1958.

———. *Four Fur Feet.* Addison-Wesley, 1961.

———. *Goodnight, Moon.* Harper and Row, 1977.

———. *Home for a Bunny.* Western, 1983.

———. *The Important Book.* Harper and Row, 1949.

———. *The Runaway Bunny.* Harper and Row, 1977.

———. *Where Have You Been?* Hastings, 1963.

Burningham, John. *Avocado Baby.* Crowell, 1982.

———. *Mr. Gumpy's Motor Car.* Penguin, 1983.

Byars, Betsy. *Go and Hush the Baby.* Penguin, 1982.

Carle, Eric. *The Grouchy Ladybug.* Harper and Row, 1986.

———. *The Mixed-Up Chameleon.* Crowell, 1984.

———. *The Very Hungry Caterpillar.* Philomel/Putnam, 1981.

Cauley, Lorinda B., illus. *The Story of the Three Little Pigs.* Putnam, 1980. (Words by Joseph Jacobs)

Charlip, Remy. *Fortunately.* Four Winds/Macmillan, 1985.

———. *What Good Luck, What Bad Luck.* Scholastic, 1964.

Cohen, Miriam. *Will I Have a Friend?* Macmillan, 1971.

Cook, Ann, and Herb Mack. *Robot and the Flea Market.* Dell, 1982. (Also see other books in the series)

Cook, Bernadine. *The Little Fish That Got Away.* Scholastic, 1962.

de Paola, Tomie. *Bill and Pete.* Putnam, 1978.

———. *Oliver Button Is a Sissy.* Harcourt Brace Jovanovich, 1979.

de Regniers, Beatrice. *Catch a Little Fox.* Seabury, 1970.

———. *How Joe the Bear and Sam the Mouse Got Together.* Scholastic, 1983.

———. *The Little Book.* Walck, 1961.

———. *May I Bring a Friend?* Atheneum/Macmillan, 1974.

———. *Willy O'Dwyer Jumped in the Fire.* Atheneum, 1968.

de Regniers, Beatrice S., and Nonny Hogrogian. *The Day Everybody Cried.* Viking, 1967.

De Rico, Ul. *The Rainbow Goblins.* Thames and Hudson, 1978.

Domanska, Janina. *If All the Seas Were One Sea.* Macmillan, 1971.

Domjan, Joseph. *I Went to the Market.* Holt, Rinehart and Winston, 1970.

Duff, Maggie. *Jonny and His Drum.* Walck, 1972.

———. *Rum Pum Pum.* Macmillan, 1978.

Elkin, Benjamin. *Six Foolish Fishermen.* Scholastic, n.d.

Elting, Mary, and Michael Folsom. *Q Is for Duck.* Houghton Mifflin, 1980.

Emberley, Barbara. *Drummer Hoff.* Prentice-Hall, 1967.

———. *Simon's Song.* Prentice-Hall, 1969.

Emberly, Ed. *Klippity Klop.* Little, Brown, 1974.

Ernst, Kathryn F. *Danny and His Thumb.* Prentice-Hall, 1975.

Ets, Marie Hall. *Elephant in a Well.* Viking, 1972.

———. *Play with Me.* Penguin, 1976.

Flack, Marjorie. *Ask Mr. Bear.* Macmillan, 1986.

Freeman, Don. *Corduroy.* Penguin, 1976.

———. *Dandelion.* Penguin, 1977.

Friskey, Margaret. *Indian Two Feet and His Horse.* Childrens Press, 1959.

Gage, Wilson. *Squash Pie.* Dell, 1980.

Galdone, Paul. *The House That Jack Built.* McGraw-Hill, 1961.

———. *The Little Red Hen.* Houghton Mifflin, 1985.

———. *The Three Billy Goats Gruff.* Houghton Mifflin, 1981.

———. *The Three Little Pigs.* Houghton Mifflin, 1984.

Ginsburg, Mirra. *The Chick and the Duckling.* Macmillan, 1972.

Graham, John. *I Love You, Mouse.* Harcourt Brace Jovanovich, 1978.

Greenberg, Polly. *Oh Lord, I Wish I Was a Buzzard.* Macmillan, 1968.

Hargreaves, Roger. *Mr. Men Mealtime.* Price, Stern, Sloan, 1983. (Also see other books in the series)

Hazen, Barbara Shook. *The Gorilla Did It.* Atheneum/Macmillan, 1978.

———. *Tight Times.* Penguin, 1983.

Heilbroner, Joan. *This Is The House Where Jack Lives.* Harper and Row, 1962.

Hoban, Lillian. *Arthur's Honey Bear.* Harper and Row, 1982.

Hoban, Russell. *A Baby Sister for Frances.* Harper and Row, 1976.

———. *Bedtime for Frances.* Harper and Row, 1976.

Hoff, Syd. *Danny and the Dinosaur.* Harper and Row, 1978.

Hoffman, Hilde. *The Green Grass Grows All Around.* Macmillan, 1968.

Hogrogian, Nonny. *One Fine Day.* Macmillan, 1971.

Hunt, Bernice Kohn. *Your Aunt Is a Which: Fun with Homophones.* Harcourt Brace Jovanovich, 1976.

Hurd, Edith Thacher. *Come and Have Fun.* Harper and Row, 1962.

Hutchins, Pat. *Don't Forget the Bacon!* Greenwillow, 1976.

———. *Good-Night Owl.* Macmillan, 1972.

———. *Rosie's Walk.* Macmillan, 1971.

———. *Titch.* Macmillan, 1971.

Johnson, Crockett. *Harold and the Purple Crayon.* Harper and Row, 1981. (Also see other books in the series)

Keats, Ezra Jack. *Louie.* Greenwillow, 1983.

———. *The Snowy Day.* Penguin, 1976.

———. *Whistle for Willie.* Penguin, 1977.

———, illus. *Over in the Meadow.* Scholastic, 1985. (Words by Olive A. Wadsworth)

Kellogg, Steven. *Can I Keep Him?* Dial Books, 1976.

Kent, Jack. *The Fat Cat.* Scholastic, 1972.

———. *There's No Such Thing as a Dragon.* Western, 1975.

Klein, Leonore. *Brave Daniel.* Scholastic, 1969.

———. *Silly Sam.* Scholastic, 1971.

Krasilovsky, Phyllis. *The Man Who Didn't Wash His Dishes.* Doubleday, 1950.

Kraus, Robert. *Leo the Late Bloomer.* Crowell, 1971.

———. *Whose Mouse Are You?* Macmillan, 1972.

Krauss, Ruth. *The Carrot Seed.* Harper and Row, 1945.

Kroll, Steven. *The Tyrannosaurus Game.* Holiday, 1976.

Langstaff, John. *Frog Went A-Courtin'.* Harcourt Brace Jovanovich, 1972.

———. *Gather My Gold Together: Accumulative Songs for Four Seasons.* Doubleday, 1971.

———. *Oh, A-Hunting We Will Go.* Atheneum, 1974.

———. *Over in the Meadow.* Harcourt Brace Jovanovich, 1973.

Laurence, Ester H. *We're Off to Catch a Dragon.* Abingdon, 1969.

Lear, Edward. *The Jumblies.* Silver Burdett, 1986.

Lexau, Joan M. *Crocodile and Hen.* Harper and Row, 1969.

———. *That's Good, That's Bad.* Dial Press, 1963.

Littledale, Freya. *The Boy Who Cried Wolf.* Scholastic, 1977.

Lobel, Anita. *King Rooster, Queen Hen.* Greenwillow, 1975.

Lobel, Arnold. *Frog and Toad Are Friends.* Harper and Row, 1985. (Also see other books in the series)

———. *Mouse Soup.* Harper and Row, 1983.

———. *Mouse Tales.* Harper and Row, 1978.

———. *Owl at Home.* Harper and Row, 1982.

———. *A Treeful of Pigs.* Greenwillow, 1979.

Logan, Dick. *Thunder Goes for a Walk.* Creative Education, 1977.

Lopshire, Robert. *Put Me in the Zoo.* Beginner Books, 1960.

McGovern, Ann. *Too Much Noise.* Houghton Mifflin, 1967.

Mack, Stan. *10 Bears in My Bed: A Goodnight Countdown.* Pantheon Books, 1974.

Margolis, Richard J. *Big Bear, Spare That Tree.* Greenwillow, 1980.

Marshall, James. *George and Martha.* Houghton Mifflin, 1972. (Also see other books in the series)

Martin, Bill. *Brown Bear, Brown Bear, What Do You See?* Holt, Rinehart and Winston, 1983.

———. *Fire! Fire! Said Mrs. McGuire.* Holt, Rinehart and Winston, 1982.

———. *The Haunted House.* Holt, Rinehart and Winston, n.d.

———. *Monday, Monday, I Like Monday.* Holt, Rinehart and Winston, 1983.

———. *My Days Are Made of Butterflies.* Holt, Rinehart and Winston, n.d.

———. *A Spooky Story.* Holt, Rinehart and Winston, n.d.

———. *Tatty Mae and Catty Mae.* Holt, Rinehart and Winston, n.d.

———. *When It Rains, It Rains.* Holt, Rinehart and Winston, n.d.

———. *Whistle, Mary, Whistle.* Holt, Rinehart and Winston, n.d.

Mayer, Mercer. *If I Had . . . .* Dial Books, 1977.

———. *Just for You.* Western, 1975.

———. *Just Me and My Dad.* Western, 1977.

———. *There's a Nightmare in My Closet.* Dial Books, 1976.

Memling, Carl. *Ten Little Animals.* Western, 1961.

Mendoza, George. *A Wart Snake in a Fig Tree.* Dial Press, 1976.

Mills, Alan, and Rose Bonne. *I Know an Old Lady.* Rand McNally, 1961.

Minarik, Else Holmelund. *Father Bear Comes Home.* Harper and Row, 1978.

———. *Little Bear's Visit.* Harper and Row, 1984.

Moffett, Martha. *A Flower Pot Is Not a Hat.* Dutton, 1972.

Mosel, Arlene. *Tikki Tikki Tembo.* Scholastic, 1984.

Noodles. *How to Catch a Ghost.* Holt, Rinehart and Winston, 1983.

Palmer, Helen. *Why I Built the Boogle House.* Beginner Books, 1964.

Parish, Peggy. *Too Many Rabbits.* Scholastic, 1976.

Peppe, Rodney. *The House That Jack Built.* Delacorte, 1985.

———. *Odd One Out.* Penguin, 1975.

Pinkwater, D. Manus. *The Hoboken Chicken Emergency.* Prentice-Hall, 1984.

Piper, Watty. *The Little Engine That Could.*

Polushkin, Maria. *Mother, Mother, I Want Another.* Crown, 1986.

Preston, Edna Mitchell. *The Sad Story of the Little Bluebird and the Hungry Cat.* Scholastic, 1975.

———. *Where Did My Mother Go?* Scholastic, 1978.

Quackenbush, Robert. *She'll Be Comin' 'Round the Mountain.* Lippincott, 1973.

———. *Skip to My Lou.* Harper and Row, 1975.

———. *Too Many Lollipops.* Parents Magazine Press, 1975.

Raskin, Ellen. *Who, Said Sue, Said Whoo?* Atheneum, 1976.

Rey, Margaret. *Pretzel.* Harper and Row, 1984.

Rice, Eve. *Ebbie.* Greenwillow, 1975.

———. *Goodnight, Goodnight.* Penguin, 1983.

———. *New Blue Shoes.* Penguin, 1979.

———. *Oh, Lewis!* Penguin, 1979.

———. *Sam Who Never Forgets.* Penguin, 1980.

Robison, Deborah. *Anthony's Hat.* Scholastic, 1977.

———. *No Elephants Allowed.* Houghton Mifflin, 1981.

Rockwell, Anne. *Poor Goose.* Crowell, 1976.

Rockwell, Harlow. *My Kitchen.* Greenwillow, 1980.

Rokoff, Sandra. *Here Is a Cat.* Hallmark Children's Editions, n.d.

Rose, Gerald. *Trouble in the Ark.* Merrimack Publishers Circle, 1985.

Scheer, Jullian. *Rain Makes Applesauce.* Holiday House, 1964.

Sendak, Maurice. *Alligators All Around.* Harper and Row, 1962.

———. *Chicken Soup with Rice.* Scholastic, 1986.

———. *One Was Johnny.* Harper and Row, 1962.

———. *Pierre.* Harper and Row, 1962.

———. *Where the Wild Things Are.* Harper and Row, 1984.

Seuss, Dr. *Green Eggs and Ham.* Beginner Books, 1960.

———. *Hop on Pop.* Beginner Books, 1963.

———. *One Fish Two Fish Red Fish Blue Fish.* Beginner Books, 1960.

Sharmat, Marjorie Weinman. *I Don't Care.* Macmillan, 1977.

Shaw, Charles G. *It Looked like Spilt Milk.* Harper and Row, 1947.

Shulevitz, Uri. *One Monday Morning.* Scribner, 1967.

Sivulich, Sandra Stroner. *I'm Going on a Bear Hunt.* Dutton, 1973.

Skaar, Grace. *What Do the Animals Say?* Scholastic, 1973.

Sonneborn, Ruth A. *Someone Is Eating the Sun.* Random House, 1974.

Spier, Peter. *The Fox Went Out on a Chilly Night.* Doubleday, 1961.

Stevens, Carla. *Hooray for Pig.* Houghton Mifflin, 1974.

Stevenson, James. *Could Be Worse!* Penguin, 1979.

Stover, Jo Ann. *If Everybody Did.* McKay, 1960.

Sullivan, Joan. *Round Is a Pancake.* Holt, Rinehart and Winston, 1963.

Sutton, Eve. *My Cat Likes to Hide in Boxes.* Parents Magazine Press, 1974.

Testa, Fulvio, and Anthony Burgess. *The Land Where the Ice Cream Grows.* N.d.

Thaler, Mike. *A Hippopotamus Ate the Teacher.* Avon, 1981.

———. *There's a Hippopotamus under My Bed.* Avon, 1978.

Tolstoy, Alexei. *The Great Big Enormous Turnip.* Watts, 1969.

Ungerer, Tomi. *Crictor.* Harper and Row, 1983.

Van Leeuwen, Jean. *Tales of Oliver Pig.* Dial Books, 1979.

Viorst, Judith. *Alexander and the Terrible, Horrible, No Good, Very Bad Day.* Atheneum/Macmillan, 1976.

———. *I'll Fix Anthony.* Atheneum/Macmillan, 1983.

———. *The Little Boy Who Loved Dirt and Almost Became a Superslob.* Atheneum, 1975.

———. *My Mama Says There Aren't Any Zombies, Ghosts, Vampires, Creatures, Demons, Monsters, Fiends, Goblins, or Things.* Atheneum/Macmillan, 1977.

Vogel, Ilse-Margret. *The Don't Be Scared Book: Scares, Remedies, and Pictures:* Atheneum/Macmillan, 1972.

Waber, Bernard. *A Firefly Named Torchy.* Houghton Mifflin, 1970.

———. *Ira Sleeps Over.* Houghton Mifflin, 1975.

Wahl, Jan. *Grandmother Told Me.* Little, Brown, 1972.

Watson, Clyde. *Catch Me and Kiss Me and Say It Again.* Philomel/Putnam, 1983.

Weiss, Leatie. *Heather's Feathers.* Avon, 1978.

Welber, Robert. *Goodbye, Hello.* Pantheon Books, 1974.

Wildsmith, Brian. *Brian Wildsmith's "The Twelve Days of Christmas."* Watts, 1972.

Williams, Barbara. *Someday, Said Mitchell.* Dutton, 1976.

Williams, Jay. *Everybody Knows What a Dragon Looks Like.* Four Winds/Macmillan, 1976.

Wolkstein, Diane. *The Visit.* Knopf, 1977.

Wondriska, William. *All the Animals Were Angry.* Holt, Rinehart and Winston, 1970.

Wright, H. R. *A Maker of Boxes.* Holt, Rinehart and Winston, 1964.

Yolen, Jane. *An Invitation to the Butterfly Ball: A Counting Rhyme.* Philomel/Putnam, 1983.

Zaid, Barry. *Chicken Little.* Random House, n.d.

Zemach, Harve. *The Judge: An Untrue Tale.* Farrar, Straus and Giroux, 1969.

Zemach, Margot. *Hush, Little Baby.* Dutton, 1975.

———. *The Little, Tiny Woman.* Bobbs-Merrill, 1965.

Zion, Gene. *Harry the Dirty Dog.* Harper and Row, 1976.

Zolotow, Charlotte. *Do You Know What I'll Do?* Harper and Row, 1958.

———. *If It Weren't for You.* Harper and Row, 1966.

———. *Mr. Rabbit and the Lovely Present.* Harper and Row, 1977.

———. *Some Things Go Together.* Harper and Row, 1987.

———. *Summer Is . . . .* Crowell, 1983.

Barbara Flores, Phoenix, Arizona; Susan Lehr, Skidmore College, Saratoga Springs, New York; Lynn K. Rhodes, University of Colorado at Denver; Regie Routman, Shaker Heights City School District, Ohio

Predictable Language

Repetition

Aliki. *Use Your Head, Dear.* Greenwillow, 1983.

Argent, Kerry, and Rod Trinca. *One Woolly Wombat.* Kane-Miller, 1985.

Arno, Ed. *The Gingerbread Man.* Scholastic, 1973.

Asch, Frank. *Just Like Daddy.* Prentice-Hall, 1984.

Baum, Arline, and Joseph Baum. *One Bright Monday Morning.* Random House, 1962.

Bayer, Jane. *A My Name is Alice.* Dial Books, 1984.

Becker, John. *Seven Little Rabbits.* Scholastic, 1985.

Bond, Felicia. *Four Valentines in a Rainstorm.* Crowell, 1983.

Brandenberg, Franz. *I Wish I Was Sick, Too!* Penguin, 1978.

Brown, Margaret Wise. *The Runaway Bunny.* Harper and Row, 1977.

———. *Where Have You Been?* Hastings, 1963.

Carle, Eric. *The Very Hungry Caterpillar.* Philomel/Putnam, 1981.

Cowley, Joy. *Meanies.* Auckland, N.Z.: Shorthand Publications, 1983. (Distributed by the Wright Group)

de Regniers, Beatrice Schenk. *Going for a Walk.* Harper and Row, 1982.

Ets, Marie Hall. *Just Me.* Penguin, 1978.

Flack, Marjorie. *Ask Mr. Bear.* Macmillan, 1986.

Gág, Wanda. *Millions of Cats.* Coward, McCann and Geoghegan/Putnam, 1977.

Galdone, Paul. *Henny Penny.* Houghton Mifflin, 1984.

———. *The House That Jack Built.* McGraw-Hill, 1961.

———. *The Little Red Hen.* Houghton Mifflin, 1985.

———. *The Three Bears.* Ticknor and Fields, 1985.

———. *The Three Billy Goats Gruff.* Houghton Mifflin, 1981.

Graboff, Abner. *Old MacDonald Had a Farm.* Scholastic, 1970.

Guilfoile, Elizabeth. *Nobody Listens to Andrew.* Modern Curriculum Press, 1957.

Heide, Florence Parry, and Sylvia Van Clief. *That's What Friends Are For.* Scholastic, 1971.

Hutchins, Pat. *Don't Forget the Bacon.* Greenwillow, 1976.

Kesselman, Wendy. *There's a Train Going by My Window.* Doubleday, 1982.

Klein, Leonore. *Silly Sam.* Scholastic, 1971.

Koide, Tan. *May We Sleep Here Tonight?* Atheneum/Macmillan, 1983.

Krauss, Ruth. *The Carrot Seed.* Harper and Row, 1945.

———. *The Happy Egg.* Scholastic, 1972.

Kwitz, Mary DeBall. *Little Chick's Story.* Harper and Row, 1978.

Langstaff, John. *Oh, A-Hunting We Will Go.* Atheneum, 1974.

Lexau, Joan. *That's Good, That's Bad.* Dial Press, 1963.

Littledale, Freya. *The Magic Fish: Easy to Read Folktales.* Scholastic, 1986.

Lobel, Arnold. *A Treeful of Pigs.* Greenwillow, 1979.

McGovern, Ann. *Stone Soup.* Scholastic, 1986.

———. *Too Much Noise.* Houghton Mifflin, 1967.

Martin, Bill, Jr. *Brown Bear, Brown Bear, What Do You See?* Holt, Rinehart and Winston, 1983.

———. *Fire! Fire! Said Mrs. McGuire.* Holt, Rinehart and Winston, 1982.

———. *Monday, Monday, I Like Monday.* Holt, Rinehart and Winston, 1983.

Mayer, Mercer. *If I Had . . . .* Dial Books, 1977.

Melser, June, and Joy Cowley. *The Big Toe.* Auckland, N.Z.: Shorthand Publications, 1982. (Distributed by the Wright Group)

———. *In a Dark Dark Wood.* Auckland, N.Z.: Shorthand Publications, 1982. (Distributed by the Wright Group)

———. *Lazy Mary.* Auckland, N.Z.: Shorthand Publications, 1982. (Distributed by the Wright Group)

———. *One Cold Wet Night.* Auckland, N.Z.: Shorthand Publications, 1982. (Distributed by the Wright Group)

———. *Sing a Song.* Auckland, N.Z.: Shorthand Publications, 1982. (Distributed by the Wright Group)

———. *Yes Ma'am.* Auckland, N.Z.: Shorthand Publications, 1981. (Distributed by the Wright Group)

Mills, Alan, and Rose Bonne. *I Know an Old Lady.* Rand McNally, 1961.

Minarik, Else Holmelund. *Little Bear.* Harper and Row, 1978.

Morris, William Barrett. *The Longest Journey in the World.* Holt, Rinehart and Winston, 1982.

Peppe, Rodney. *The Kettleship Pirates.* Lothrop, Lee and Shepard, 1983.

Pienkowski, Jan. *Dinnertime.* Price, Stern, Sloan, 1981.

Pomerantz, Charlotte. *One Duck, Another Duck.* Greenwillow, 1984.

Preston, Edna M., and Rainey Bennett. *The Temper Tantrum Book.* Penguin, 1976.

Rose, Anne. *Akimba and the Magic Cow.* Four Winds/Scholastic, 1979.

Ruwe, Mike. *Ten Little Bears.* Scott, Foresman, 1976. (Reading Unlimited Program)

Seuling, Barbara. *The Teeny Tiny Woman: An Old English Ghost Tale.* Penguin, 1978.

Shulevitz, Uri. *One Monday Morning.* Atheneum/Macmillan, 1986.

Slobodkina, Esphyr. *Caps for Sale*. Scholastic, 1984.

Sonneborn, Ruth A. *Someone Is Eating the Sun*. Random House, 1974.

Stevenson, James. *Grandpa's Great City Tour: An Alphabet Book*. Greenwillow, 1983.

Szeghy, Joe. *The Lion's Tail*. Scott, Foresman, 1976. (Reading Unlimited Program)

Vigna, Judith. *Gregory's Stitches*. Whitman, 1974.

Viorst, Judith. *Alexander and the Terrible, Horrible, No Good, Very Bad Day*. Atheneum/Macmillan, 1976.

———. *The Little Boy Who Loved Dirt and Almost Became a Superslob*. Atheneum, 1975.

———. *The Tenth Good Thing about Barney*. Atheneum/Macmillan, 1975.

Wagner, Justin. *The Bus Ride*. Scott, Foresman, 1976. (Reading Unlimited Program, Level Two)

Williams, Barbara. *Someday, Said Mitchell*. Dutton, 1976.

Wood, Audrey. *The Napping House*. Harcourt Brace Jovanovich, 1984.

———. *Quick as a Cricket*. Child's Play/Playspaces, 1982.

Zemach, Margot. *Hush, Little Baby*. Dutton, 1975.

Zolotow, Charlotte. *Some Things Go Together*. Harper and Row, 1987.

Rhyme

Aardema, Verna. *Bringing the Rain to Kapiti Plain*. Dial Books, 1983.

Aliki. *Hush Little Baby*. Prentice-Hall, 1968.

Ahlberg, Allan. *Cops and Robbers*. Greenwillow, 1979.

Ahlberg, Janet, and Allan Ahlberg. *Each Peach Pear Plum*. Scholastic, 1985.

Baer, Edith. *Words Are Like Faces*. Pantheon, 1980.

Barchas, Sarah. *I Was Walking down the Road*. Scholastic, 1976.

Berenstain, Stan, and Janice Berenstain. *Bear Detectives*. Beginner Books, 1975.

———. *The Berenstain Bears and the Missing Dinosaur Bone*. Beginner Books, 1980.

Boynton, Sandra. *Hippos Go Berserk*. Little, Brown, 1986.

Brown, Marc. *Witches Four*. Parents Magazine Press, 1980.

Brown, Margaret Wise. *Goodnight, Moon*. Harper and Row, 1977.

———. *Yesterday I Climbed a Mountain*. Putnam, 1977.

Cameron, Polly. *I Can't Said the Ant*. Coward/Putnam, 1961.

Charles, Donald. *Time to Rhyme with Calico Cat*. Childrens Press, 1978.

Clifton, Lucille. *Everett Anderson's 1-2-3*. Holt, Rinehart and Winston, 1977.

———. *Everett Anderson's Nine Month Long*. Holt, Rinehart and Winston, 1978.

Cole, William. *What's Good for a 5-Year-Old?* Holt, Rinehart and Winston, 1971.

Cowley, Joy. *Mrs. Wishy-Washy*. Auckland, N. Z.: Shorthand Publications, 1982. (Distributed by the Wright Group)

Craft, Ruth. *Carrie Hepple's Garden*. Atheneum/Macmillan, 1979.

———. *The Winter Bear*. Atheneum/Macmillan, 1979.

Crowley, Arthur. *The Boogey Man*. Houghton Mifflin, 1978.

de Regniers, Beatrice Schenk. *May I Bring a Friend?* Atheneum/Macmillan, 1974.

———. *Red Riding Hood*. Atheneum/Macmillan, 1977.

Edelman, Elaine. *Boom-De-Boom*. Pantheon, 1980.

Eichenberg, Fritz. *Ape in a Cape: An Alphabet of Odd Animals*. Harcourt Brace Jovanovich, 1973.

Elkin, Benjamin. *The King Who Could Not Sleep*. Parents Magazine Press, 1975.

Farber, Norma. *There Once Was a Woman Who Married a Man*. Addison-Wesley, 1978.

Farber, Norma, and Arnold Lobel. *As I Was Crossing Boston Common*. Creative Arts, 1982.

Fisher, Aileen. *Anybody Home?* Crowell, 1980.

———. *Once We Went on a Picnic*. Harper and Row, 1975.

Gág, Wanda. *The ABC Bunny*. Coward, McCann, and Geoghegan/Putnam, 1978.

Gage, Wilson. *Down in the Boondocks*. Greenwillow, 1977.

Gelman, Rita Golden. *The Biggest Sandwich Ever*. Scholastic, 1980.

———. *Hey Kid!* Avon, 1978.

———. *More Spaghetti I Say*. Scholastic, 1977.

———. *Mortimer K. Saves the Day*. Scholastic, 1982.

———. *Why Can't I Fly?* Scholastic, 1977.

Ginsburg, Mirra. *The Sun's Asleep behind the Hill*. Greenwillow, 1982.

Hall, Katy. *Nothing But Soup*. Follett, 1976.

Harrison, David L. *Detective Bob and the Great Ape Escape*. Parents Magazine Press, 1981.

Hillert, Margaret. *What Is It?* Modern Curriculum Press, 1978.

Hoban, Tana. *One Little Kitten*. Greenwillow, 1979.

Hoberman, Mary Ann. *A House Is a House for Me*. Penguin, 1982.

Holl, Adelaide. *The Parade*. Watts, 1975.

Hutchins, Pat. *Don't Forget the Bacon*. Greenwillow, 1976.

Ipcar, Dahlov. *Hard Scrabble Harvest*. Doubleday, 1976.

Jensen, Virginia A. *Sara and the Door*. Addison-Wesley, 1977.

Kahl, Virginia. *Gunhilde and the Halloween Spell*. Scribner, 1975.

———. *How Many Dragons Are behind the Door?* Scribner, 1977.

Kalan, Robert. *Jump, Frog, Jump!* Greenwillow, 1981.

Knab, Linda Z. *The Day Is Waiting*. Viking, 1980.

Kraus, Robert. *Ladybug, Ladybug!* Dutton, 1977.

———. *Whose Mouse Are You?* Macmillan, 1972.

Kuskin, Karla. *A Boy Had a Mother Who Bought Him a Hat.* Houghton Mifflin, 1976.

———. *Herbert Hated Being Small.* Houghton Mifflin, 1979.

Langstaff, John. *Over in the Meadow.* Harcourt Brace Jovanovich, 1973.

Livermore, Elaine. *Three Little Kittens.* Houghton Mifflin, 1979.

Lobel, Arnold. *On Market Street.* Scholastic, 1985.

Martin, Bill, Jr. *Fire! Fire! Said Mrs. McGuire.* Holt, Rinehart and Winston, 1982.

———. *The Happy Hippopotami.* Holt, Rinehart and Winston, 1983.

Marzollo, Jean. *Uproar on Hollercat Hill.* Dial Press, 1982.

Melser, June, and Joy Cowley. *Boo-Hoo.* Auckland, N.Z.: Shorthand Publications, 1982. (Distributed by the Wright Group)

———. *Grandpa Grandpa.* Auckland, N.Z.: Shorthand Publications, 1983. (Distributed by the Wright Group)

———. *Hairy Bear.* Auckland, N.Z.: Shorthand Publications, 1981. (Distributed by the Wright Group)

———. *Obadiah.* Auckland, N.Z.: Shorthand Publications, 1982. (Distributed by the Wright Group)

———. *Poor Old Polly.* Auckland, N.Z.: Shorthand Publications, 1982. (Distributed by the Wright Group)

———. *Woosh!* Auckland, N.Z.: Shorthand Publications, 1982. (Distributed by the Wright Group)

Moncure, Jane B. *About Me.* Child's World, 1976.

———. *Magic Monsters Count to Ten.* Child's World, 1979.

Noodles. *Super Midnight Menu.* Holt, Rinehart and Winston, n.d.

Orbach, Ruth. *Apple Pigs.* Philomel/Putnam, 1981.

Paterson, A. B. *Mulga Bill's Bicycle.* Parents Magazine Press, 1975.

Patrick, Gloria. *A Bug in a Jug and Other Funny Poems.* Scholastic, 1973.

Pavey, Peter, illus. *One Dragon's Dream.* Bradbury, 1979.

Peck, Robert N. *Hamilton.* Little, Brown, 1976.

Peet, Bill. *The Luckiest One of All.* Houghton Mifflin, 1985.

Peterson, Jeanne W. *While the Moon Shines Bright: A Bedtime Chant.* Harper and Row, 1981.

Petie, Haris. *The Seed the Squirrel Dropped.* Prentice-Hall, 1976.

Polhamus, Jean B. *Doctor Dinosaur.* Prentice-Hall, 1975.

Pomerantz, Charlotte. *Ballad of the Long-Tailed Rat.* Macmillan, 1975.

Prelutsky, Jack. *The Mean Old Mean Hyena.* Greenwillow, 1978.

Rand, Paul, and Ann Rand. *I Know a Lot of Things.* Harcourt Brace Jovanovich, 1973.

Schwartz, Stephen. *The Perfect Peach.* Little, Brown, 1977.

Sendak, Maurice. *Chicken Soup with Rice.* Scholastic, 1986.

———. *Seven Little Monsters.* Harper and Row, 1977.

Seuss, Dr. *I Can Read with My Eyes Shut!* Beginner Books, 1978.

———. *In a People House.* Random House, 1972.

———. *Tooth Book.* Random House, 1981.

Shore, Wilma. *Who in the Zoo?* Lippincott, 1976.

Silverstein, Shel. *Giraffe and a Half.* Harper and Row, 1964.

Skorpen, Liesel M. *Plenty for Three.* Coward, 1971.

Slepian, Jan, and Ann Seidler. *The Hungry Thing.* Scholastic, 1972.

Sundgaard, Arnold. *Jethro's Difficult Dinosaur.* Pantheon, 1977.

Thomas, Patricia. *There Are Rocks in My Socks! Said the Ox to the Fox.* Lothrop, Lee and Shepard, 1979.

Watson, Clyde. *Midnight Moon.* Philomel, 1979.

Wells, Rosemary. *Don't Spill It Again, James.* Dial Books, 1977

———. *Noisy Nora.* Dial Books, 1980.

Willard, Nancy. *All on a May Morning.* Putnam, 1975.

Yolen, Jane. *All in the Woodland Early: An ABC Book.* Philomel/Putnam, 1983.

Zolotow, Charlotte. *The Hating Book.* Harper and Row, 1969.

Lynn K. Rhodes, University of Colorado at Denver, and Regie Routman, Shaker Heights City School District, Ohio

Predictable Life Experience Books for Upper Elementary Children

Alternate Forms

Armstrong, William H. *Sounder.* Harper and Row, 1972.

Cebulash, Mel. *Herbie Rides Again.* Scholastic, 1974.

Claro, Joe. *Herbie Goes Bananas.* Scholastic, 1980.

Crume, Vic. *The Billion Dollar Hobo.* Scholastic, 1979.

Farley, Walter. *The Black Stallion.* Random House, 1982.

Gelman, Rita G. *Benji at Work.* Scholastic, 1980.

Gipson, Fred. *Old Yeller.* Harper and Row, 1956.

Hamner, Earl. *Spenser's Mountain.* Dell, 1973.

Head, Ann. *Mr. and Mrs. Bo Jo Jones.* New American Library, 1973.

Herz, Peggy. *The Mork and Mindy Story.* Scholastic, 1979.

———. *Nancy Drew and the Hardy Boys.* Scholastic, 1978.

———. *The Truth about Fonzie.* Scholastic, 1977.

Kipling, Rudyard. *The Jungle Book.*

Lely, James A. *Star Wars.* Creative Education, 1979.

Schulz, Charles. *You're the Greatest, Charlie Brown.* Scholastic, 1980.

Wilder, Laura Ingalls. *Little House on the Prairie.* Harper and Row, 1975.

Books in a Series

Alexander, Lloyd. *Taran Wanderer.* Dell, 1980.

Baum, L. Frank. *The Wizard of Oz.*

Blish, James. *Star Trek.* Bantam, 1975.

Cleary, Beverly. *Henry Huggins.* Morrow, 1983.

———. *Ramona Quimby, Age Eight.* Dell, 1982.

Lewis, C. S. *Chronicles of Narnia.* Macmillan, 1986.

Lindgren, Astrid. *Pippi Longstocking.*

McCloskey, Robert. *Homer Price.* Penguin, 1976.

Tolkien, J.R.R. *The Hobbit.* Houghton Mifflin, 1984.

Growing Up

Blume, Judy. *Are You There, God? It's Me, Margaret.* Bradbury, 1970.

Brancato, Robin. *Come Alive at 505.* Knopf, 1980.

Carris, Joan D. *The Revolt of Ten-X.* Harcourt Brace Jovanovich, 1980.

Danziger, Paula. *There's a Bat in Bunk Five.* Dell, 1986.

Holland, Isabelle. *Heads You Win, Tails I Lose.* Harper and Row, 1973.

Guessing Books

Avallone, Michael. *Five-Minute Mysteries: Cases from Files of Ed Noon.* Scholastic, 1978.

Gelman, Rita. *Favorite Riddles, Knock-Knocks and Nonsense.* Scholastic, 1980.

Goldsweig, Beryl. *Artemus Flint: Detective.* Scholastic, 1975.

Juster, Norton. *The Phantom Tollbooth.* Random House, 1961.

Laycock, George. *Mysteries, Monsters, and Untold Secrets.* Doubleday, 1978.

McWhirter, Norris, and Ross McWhirter. *Guiness Book of Young Recordbreakers.* Sterling, 1978.

Packard, Edward. *Survival at Sea.* Bantam, 1982. (Also see other titles in the Choose Your Own Adventure series)

Piggin, Julia R. *Mini-Mysteries.* Scholastic, 1974.

Ripley's Believe It or Not, no. 30. Pocket Books, 1982.

Rockowitz, Murray, and Irwin Weiss. *The Arrow Book of Crossword Puzzles and Word Games.* Scholastic, 1980.

Sobol, Donald J. *Encyclopedia Brown, Boy Detective.* Bantam, 1978.

———. *Two-Minute Mysteries.* Scholastic, 1986.

Zim, Herbert S. *Codes and Secret Writing.* Morrow, 1948.

Identity

Distad, Audree. *The Dream Runner.* Harper and Row, 1977.

Klein, Norma. *Love Is One of the Choices.* Dial Books, 1978.

Parents

Arundel, Honor. *Love Is a Blanket Word.* Scholastic, 1976.

Babbitt, Natalie. *The Eyes of the Amaryllis.* Farrar, Straus and Giroux, 1977.

Blume, Judy. *Then Again, Maybe I Won't.* Dell, 1986.

Colman, Hila. *Sometimes I Don't Love My Mother.* Scholastic, 1979.

Cormier, Robert. *Eight Plus One: Stories.* Pantheon, 1980.

Danziger, Paula. *Can You Sue Your Parents for Malpractice?* Dell, 1986.

Dixon, Paige. *Skipper.* Atheneum, 1979.

Frantz, Evelyn. *A Bonnet for Virginia.* Brethren Press, 1978.

Girion, Barbara. *A Tangle of Roots.* Putnam, 1985.

Hentoff, Nat. *This School Is Driving Me Crazy.* Dell, 1986.

Hinton, S. E. *Tex.* Dell, 1986.

Kerr, M. E. *Dinky Hocker Shoots Smack.* Harper and Row, 1972.

Klein, Norma. *Mom, the Wolfman, and Me.* Pantheon, 1982.

Peck, Robert N. *A Day No Pigs Would Die.* Dell, 1986.

Rockwood, Joyce. *Enoch's Place.* Holt, Rinehart and Winston, 1980.

Samuels, Gertrude. *Adam's Daughter.* New American Library, 1979.

Zindel, Bonnie, and Paul Zindel. *A Star for the Latecomer.* Harper and Row, 1980.

Peers

Blume, Judy. *Blubber.* Dell, 1986.

———. *Freckle Juice.* Dell, 1986.

Brancato, Robin. *Something Left to Lose.* Knopf, 1976.

Conford, Ellen. *Anything for a Friend.* Archway, 1981.

Greene, Constance. *Beat the Turtle Drum.* Dell, 1986.

Myers, Walter Dean. *The Young Landlords.* Viking, 1979.

Pascal, Francine. *The Hand-Me-Down Kid.* Viking, 1980.

Rockwell, Thomas. *How to Eat Fried Worms.* Dell, 1975.

Siblings

Blume, Judy. *Superfudge.* Dell, 1986.

———. *Tales of a Fourth Grade Nothing.* Dell, 1986.

Conford, Ellen. *The Luck of Pokey Bloom.* Archway, 1983.

Peck, Richard. *Father Figure.* New American Library, 1979.

Margaret Atwell, California State University–San Bernardino

Sing-Along Books

Abisch, Roz, and Boche Kaplan. *Sweet Betsy from Pike.* Dutton, 1970.

Adams, Adrienne, illus. *Bring a Torch, Jeannette, Isabella.* Scribner, 1963.

Adams, Pam, illus. *There Was an Old Lady Who Swallowed a Fly.* Child's Play/Playspaces, 1973.

———. *This Old Man.* Child's Play/Playspaces, n.d.

Aliki. *Go Tell Aunt Rhody.* Macmillan, 1986.

———. *Hush Little Baby.* Prentice-Hall, 1968.

Bangs, Edward. *Yankee Doodle.* Scholastic, 1980.

Brand, Oscar. *When I First Came to This Land.* Putnam, 1974.

Broomfield, Robert, illus. *The Twelve Days of Christmas: A Picture Book.* McGraw-Hill, 1965.

Bryan, Ashley. *I'm Going to Sing: Black American Spirituals,* vol. 2. Atheneum/Macmillan, 1982.

Chase, Richard. *Billy Boy.* Golden Gate, 1966.

Child, Lydia M. *Over the River and through the Wood.* Scholastic, 1975.

Conover, Chris. *Six Little Ducks.* Crowell, 1976.

Crane, Walter. *The Baby's Opera.* Windmill Books, 1981.

de Paola, Tomie. *The Friendly Beasts: An Old English Christmas Carol.* Putnam, 1981.

de Regniers, Beatrice Schenk. *Catch a Little Fox.* Houghton Mifflin, 1970.

Emberley, Barbara. *Simon's Song.* Prentice-Hall, 1969.

Emberley, Barbara, and Ed Emberley. *One Wide River to Cross.* Scholastic, 1970.

Emberley, Ed. *London Bridge Is Falling Down.* Little, Brown, 1967.

Freschet, Berniece. *The Ants Go Marching.* Scribner, 1973.

Galdone, Paul, illus. *The Star Spangled Banner.* Crowell, 1966. (Words by Francis Scott Key)

Gauch, Patricia L. *On to Widecombe Fair.* Putnam, 1978.

Ginsburg, Mirra. *The Sun's Asleep behind the Hill.* Greenwillow, 1982.

Goudge, Eileen. *I Saw Three Ships.* Coward, McCann and Geoghegan, 1969.

Graboff, Abner. *Old MacDonald Had a Farm.* Scholastic, 1970.

Hart, Jane, ed. *Singing Bee! A Collection of Favorite Children's Songs.* Lothrop, Lee and Shepard, 1982.

Hazen, Barbara. *Frere Jacques.* Lippincott, 1973.

Hurd, Thacher. *Mama Don't Allow.* Harper and Row, 1985.

Ipcar, Dahlov. *The Cat Came Back.* Knopf, 1971.

Jeffers, Susan. *All the Pretty Horses.* Scholastic, 1985.

Johnson, James W., and J. R. Johnson. *Lift Every Voice and Sing.* Hawthorn, 1970.

Karasz, Ilonka. *The Twelve Days of Christmas.* Harper and Row, 1949.

Keats, Ezra Jack, illus. *Over in the Meadow.* Scholastic Books, 1985. (Words by Olive A. Wadsworth)

———. *The Little Drummer Boy.* Macmillan, 1972. (Words and music by K. Davis, H. Onorati, and H. Simeone)

Kellogg, Steven. *There Was an Old Woman.* Four Winds/Scholastic, 1980.

Kennedy, Jimmy. *The Teddy Bears' Picnic.* Green Tiger Press, 1983.

Kent, Jack. *Jack Kent's Twelve Days of Christmas.* Parents Magazine Press, 1973.

Langstaff, John. *Hot Cross Buns and Other Old Street Cries.* Atheneum, 1978.

Langstaff, John, ed. *Oh, A-Hunting We Will Go.* Atheneum/Macmillan, 1974.

Langstaff, John, et al. *The Swapping Boy.* Harcourt Brace Jovanovich, 1960.

Langstaff, John, and David Gentleman. *The Golden Vanity.* Harcourt Brace Jovanovich, 1972.

Langstaff, John, and Joe Krush. *Ol' Dan Tucker.* Harcourt Brace Jovanovich, 1963.

Langstaff, John, and Feodor Rojankovsky. *Frog Went A-Courtin'.* Harcourt Brace Jovanovich, 1955.

———. *Over in the Meadow.* Harcourt Brace Jovanovich, 1973.

Mills, Alan, and Rose Bonne. *I Know an Old Lady.* Rand McNally, 1961.

Nic Leodhas, Sorche. *Always Room for One More.* Holt, Rinehart and Winston, 1965.

———. *Kellyburn Braes.* Holt, Rinehart and Winston, 1968.

Paterson, A. B., illus. *Waltzing Matilda.* Holt, Rinehart and Winston, 1972.

Price, Christine. *Widdecombe Fair.* Warne, 1968.

Quackenbush, Robert. *Clementine.* Lippincott, 1974.

———. *Go Tell Aunt Rhody.* Lippincott, 1973.

———. *The Man on the Flying Trapeze: The Circus Life of Emmett Kelly Sr. Told with Pictures and Song!* Lippincott, 1975.

———. *Old MacDonald Had a Farm.* Lippincott, 1972.

———. *Pop! Goes the Weasel and Yankee Doodle: New York in 1776 and Today, with Songs and Pictures.* Lippincott, 1976.

———. *She'll be Comin' 'Round the Mountain.* Lippincott, 1973.

———. *Skip to My Lou.* Harper and Row, 1975.

———. *There'll Be a Hot Time in the Old Town Tonight.* Lippincott, 1974.

Rounds, Glenn, illus. *Casey Jones: The Story of a Brave Engineer.* Golden Gate/Childrens Press, 1968.

———. *The Strawberry Roan.* Golden Gate/Childrens Press, 1970.

———. *Sweet Betsy from Pike.* Golden Gate/Childrens Press, 1973.

Rourke, Constance. *Davy Crockett.* Harcourt Brace Jovanovich, 1955.

Sawyer, Ruth. *Joy to the World.* Little, Brown, 1966.

Seeger, Pete, and Charles Seeger. *The Foolish Frog.* Macmillan, 1973.

Shackburg, Richard. *Yankee Doodle.* Prentice-Hall, 1965.

Spier, Peter. *The Erie Canal.* Doubleday, 1970.

———. *The Fox Went Out on a Chilly Night.* Doubleday, 1961.

———. *London Bridge Is Falling Down.* Doubleday, 1985.

———. *The Star-Spangled Banner.* Doubleday, 1986.

Watson, Clyde. *Father Fox's Feast of Songs.* Philomel/Putnam, 1983.

———. *Fisherman Lullabies.* World, 1968.

Westcott, Nadine Bernard. *I Know an Old Lady Who Swallowed a Fly.* Atlantic Monthly/Little, Brown, 1980.

Yulya. *Bears Are Sleeping.* Scribner, 1967.

Zemach, Harve. *Mommy, Buy Me a China Doll.* Farrar, Straus and Giroux, 1975.

Zemach, Margot, illus. *Hush Little Baby.* Dutton, 1975.

Zuromskis, Diane, illus. *The Farmer in the Dell.* Little, Brown, 1978.

Yetta M. Goodman, University of Arizona, Tucson, and Ann Marek, Department of Human Resources, Sparks, Nevada

Children's Magazines

Archimedes. Address: Foundation for Education, Science and Technology, 211 Skinner Street, Box 1758, Pretoria, South Africa.

Blue Jeans. Address: D. C. Thompson and Company Ltd., Albert Square, Dundee DD1 9QJ, Scotland.

Boy's Life. Age range: 8–18. Boys, especially those involved in scouting. Address: Boy Scouts of America, 1325 Walnut Hill Lane, Irving, TX 75038-3096.

Canada. Address: Scholastic-TAB Publications Ltd., 123 Newkirk Road, Richmond Hill, Ontario, Canada L4C 3G5.

Chickadee. Age range: 4–8. The environment. Address: The Young Naturalist Foundation, Box 11314, Des Moines, IA 50347.

Child Life. Age range: 8–11. Health, safety, and nutrition. Address: P.O. Box 10681, Des Moines, IA 50381.

Children's Digest. Age range: 9–12. Health, safety, and nutrition. Address: P.O. Box 10683, Des Moines, IA 50381.

Children's Playmate. Age range: 5–8. Health, safety, and nutrition. Address: P.O. Box 10242, Des Moines, IA 50381.

Children's World. Address: Children's Book Trust, Nehru House, New Delhi 110002, India.

Cobblestone: The History Magazine for Young People. Age range: 8–14. American history. Address: 20 Grove Street, Peterborough, NH 03458.

Coulicou. Age range: 4–8. French children's magazine. Address: 300 rue Arran, St. Lambert, Quebec, Canada J4R 1K5.

Cricket: The Magazine for Children. Age range: 6–12. Literary magazine for young people. Address: Box 2672, Boulder, CO 80321.

Current Events, Read, and *Know Your World.* Current events. Address: Subscription Department, *Weekly Reader,* Secondary Periodicals, P.O. Box 16686, Columbus, OH 43216.

Dewan Perintis. Address: National Language and Literacy Agency of Malaysia, Cawangan Sarawak — Dewan Bahasa dan Pustaka Ma Aysia, Box 1390, Kuching, Sarawak, Malaysia (4-page English summary).

The Egg. Address: The Puffin Club, Penguin Books Ltd., Bath Road, Harmondsworth, Middlesex, Great Britain, UB7 ODA.

The Electric Company. Age range: 6–10. General interest reading. Address: P.O. Box 2896, Boulder, CO 80322.

Enter. Age Range: 10–16. News magazine about computers. Address: P.O. Box 2896, Boulder, CO 80322.

Family Computing. Age range: Entire family. Families who own or are about to own their first computer. Address: Neodata Services, P.O. Box 2511, Boulder, CO 80322.

Hibou. Age range: 4–8. French children's magazine. Address: 300 rue Arran, St. Lambert, Quebec, Canada J4R 1K5.

Highlights for Children. Age range: 2–12. General interest. Address: P.O. Box 269, Columbus, OH 43272-0002.

Humpty Dumpty's Magazine. Age range: 4–6. Health, safety, and nutrition. Address: P.O. Box 10225, Des Moines, IA 50381.

Jabberwocky. Address: P.O. Box 48–036, Auckland 7, New Zealand.

Jack and Jill. Age range: 7–10. Health, safety, nutrition. Address: P.O. Box 10222, Des Moines, IA 50381.

Mathitiki Estia. Address: Ministry of Education Committee, Nicosia School Committee, Nicosia, Cyprus (5 pages in English).

Mountain Standard Time. Age range: 8–13. By-kids, for-kids magazine. Address: 10144 89 Street, Edmonton, Alberta, Canada T5H 1P7.

Muppet Magazine. Age range: 7–13. Contemporary humor magazine. Address: 300 Madison Avenue, New York, NY 10017.

National Geographic World. Age range: 8–13. Nonfiction

of general interest. Address: Box 2330, Washington, DC 20013.

Odyssey. Age range: 8–12. Children with an interest in astronomy and space science. Address: Kalmbach Publishing Co., 1027 N. Seventh St., Milwaukee, WI 53233.

Orbit. Address: Private Bag R. W. 18X, Lusaka, Zambia.

Peanut Butter. Age range: 5–7. Nature, news, and activities. Address: 730 Broadway, New York, NY 10003.

Penny Power. Age range: 8–14. Consumer education. Address: P.O. Box 2859, Boulder, CO 80321.

Pennywhistle Press. Age range: 4–12. General interest. Weekly feature available through purchase of subscribing newspaper. Syndication information: Box 500-P, Washington, DC 20044.

Puffin Post. Address: The Puffin Club, Penguin Books Ltd., Bath Road, Harmondsworth, Middlesex, Great Britain UB7 ODA.

Ranger Rick. Age range: 6–12. Nature study, Ranger Rick's Nature Club Members. Address: Ranger Rick's Nature Magazine, The National Wildlife Federation, 1412 16th Street NW, Washington, DC 20036.

Scienceland. Age range: 5–8. Nurtures scientific thinking. Address: 501 Fifth Avenue, Suite 2102, New York, NY 10017–6165.

Seedling Series Short Story. Age range: 10–12. Short stories from all over the world. Address: P.O. Box 405, Great Neck, NY 11022.

Sesame Street. Age range: 2–6. Preschool prereading. Address: P.O. Box 2896, Boulder, CO 80322.

Stickers and Stuff Magazine (formerly *Stickers!).* Age range: 6–14. Sticker enthusiasts. Address: Ira Friedman Inc., 10 Columbus Circle, Suite 1300, New York, NY 10019.

Stone Soup. Age range: 6–13. Literary magazine. Address: P.O. Box 83, Santa Cruz, CA 95063.

3-2-1 Contact. Age range: 8–14. Science. Address: Box 2896, Boulder, CO 80322.

Turtle Magazine for Preschool Kids. Age range: 2–5. Preschool health, safety, and nutrition. Address: P.O. Box 10222, Des Moines, IA 50381.

Young Citizen. A civics and social education magazine. Address: Institute of Public Administration, 59, Landsdowne Road, Dublin 4, Ireland.

Young Miss. Age range: 11–17. Lifestyle magazine for teenagers. Address: 80 Newbridge Road, Bergenfield, NJ 07621.

Your Big Backyard. Age range: 3–5. Nature. Address: The National Wildlife Federation, 1412 16th Street, NW, Washington, DC 20036.

Yuva Bharati. Voice of youth. Address: Vivekananda Rock Memorial Committee, 36 Singarachari Street, Triplicane, Madras 600005, India.

Educational Press Association of America; Nancy Wiseman Seminoff, Winona State University, Minnesota

---

Publishers of Children's Writing

Young and Unpublished Authors

Lacuna, Lacuna Press, Box 10957, St. Louis, MO 63135. Editor: Beth Ivie.

3-2-1 Contact, Children's Television Workshop, One Lincoln Plaza, New York, NY 10023. Editor: Jonathan Rosenbloom.

Piedmont Literary Review, Piedmont Literary Society, Box 3656, Danville, VA 24541. Editor: David Craig.

Jump River Review, Jump River Press, Inc., P.O. Box 1151, Medina, OH 44256. Editor: Mark Bruner.

The Denver Quarterly, University of Denver, Denver, CO 80208. Editor: David Milofsky.

Publications for Children and Teens

American Girl, 830 Third Ave., New York, NY 10022.

Child Life, The Benjamin Franklin Literary and Medical Society Inc., P.O. Box 567 B, Indianapolis, IN 46206.

Cricket: The Magazine for Children, Open Court Publishing Co., P.O. Box 300, Peru, IL 61354.

Current Events, Read, and *Know Your World,* 245 Long Hill Rd., Middletown, CT 06457.

Highlights for Children, 803 Church St., Honesdale, PA 18431. Editor: Kent L. Brown, Jr.

Humpty Dumpty's Magazine, The Benjamin Franklin Literary and Medical Society, Inc., P.O. Box 567, Indianapolis, IN 46206. Editor: Beth Wood Thomas.

Jack and Jill, The Benjamin Franklin Literary and Medical Society, Inc., P.O. Box 567, Indianapolis, IN 46206.

Seventeen, Triangle Communications, 850 Third Ave., New York, NY 10022. Editor-in-Chief: Midge Turk Richardson.

Stone Soup, P.O. Box 83, Santa Cruz, CA 95063. Editors: Gerry Mandel and William Rubel.

Teen, Peterson Publishing Co., 8490 Sunset Blvd., Hollywood, CA 90069. Editor: Roxanne Camron.

Young Miss, Gruner and Jahr USA Publishing, 685 Third Ave., New York, NY 10017. Editor-in-Chief: Nancy Comer.

Mainly Poetry

Prairie Schooner, 201 Andrews Hall, University of Nebraska, Lincoln, NE 68588. Editor: Hugh Luke.

Prism International, E459 1866 Main Mall, University of British Columbia, Vancouver, British Columbia, Canada V6T IW5. Editor-in-Chief: Michael Pacey.

Pteranodon, Lieb/Schott Publications, P.O. Box 229,

Bourbonnais, IL 60914. Editors: Patricia Lieb and Carol Schott.

The Pub, Ansuda Publications, P.O. Box 158, Harris, IA 51345. Editor: Daniel R. Betz.

Published Poet Newsletter, Quill Penn Publishing Co.,

Box 1663, Indianapolis, IN 46206. Editor: Daniel L. Morris.

Susan Jamieson and Elaine Prairie

List of Teaching Activities in This Book

Author

Dorothy J. Watson is Professor of Education at the University of Missouri–Columbia, where she teaches graduate and undergraduate courses in reading education. For many years she was a classroom teacher and language arts supervisor in the public schools, and she has been involved in inservice teacher education programs around the world. Watson is the 1987 recipient of the International Reading Association's Teacher Educator of the Year Award, director of NCTE's Commission on Reading, and past president of the Center for Expansion of Language and Thinking. She is an active member of local and national teacher support groups and sponsor of the Mid-Missouri Student Reading Association. A commitment to a point of view about how children learn, especially how they learn language, has led her to work with teachers who are applying child-centered, whole language activities within the framework of a process curriculum of the language arts. From work with children and teachers have sprung research endeavors, curriculum development, writings, and presentations that relate to a transactional mode of literacy learning. Watson is coauthor, with Yetta Goodman and Carolyn Burke, of *Reading Miscue Inventory: Alternative Procedures* and coeditor, with P. David Allen, of *Findings of Research in Miscue Analysis: Classroom Implications.*